The Control of
Biblical Meaning

The Control of Biblical Meaning

Canon as Semiotic Mechanism

GEORGE AICHELE

TRINITY PRESS INTERNATIONAL
Harrisburg, Pennsylvania

Trinity Press International, P.O. Box 1321, Harrisburg, PA 17105
Trinity Press International is a division of the Morehouse Group.

Library of Congress Cataloging-in-Publication Data

Aichele, George.
    The control of biblical meaning : canon as semiotic mechanism / George Aichele.
        p. cm.
    Includes bibliographical references and indexes.
    ISBN 1-56338-333-0 (alk. paper)
    Bible – Canonical criticism. 2. Semiotics – Religious aspects – Christianity.
    I. Title.

BS521.8 .A53 2001
220.1′2 – dc21

                                                                    00-062853

Printed in the United States of America

01   02   03   04   05   06   10   9   8   7   6   5   4   3   2   1

For Connie,
Sara, Dan, and Paden

"But you, Daniel, shut up the words, and seal the book,
until the time of the end."

—Daniel 12:4, RSV

"These words are trustworthy and true...."
Blessed is he who keeps the words of the prophecy of this book.

—Revelation 22:6–7, RSV

CONTENTS

Acknowledgments   xi

Introduction   1
    Semiotics and Canon / 1
    Two Options / 4
    What This Book Is, and What It Isn't / 10

Part 1
THE CONTROL OF DENOTATION

1. A Semiotics of Canon   15
    Text, Intertext, Ideology / 15
    Canon and Meaning / 20
    Scripture and Canon / 24
    The Two Canons / 30
    Codex and Commentary / 35

2. The Technology of Text   38
    Oral vs. Written Text / 38
    Anxiety about Writing / 40
    Codex and Canon / 45
    The Printed Text / 50
    The Digital Bible / 55

3. Ideologies of Translation   61
    The Problem of Translation / 61
    Translation and Ideology / 63
    What Can Be Translated? / 67
    What Can't Be Translated? / 75
    Translating Canon / 80

4. The Imperial Bible   84
    The Canon as a Classic / 84
    The Eternal Empire / 87
    The Historical Empire / 91
    Fragmentary Empires / 96
    Postmodernism and the Canon / 100

Part 2
WILD CONNOTATIONS

5. **Babble On**   107
    A Zigzag Reading / 107
    No Perfect Language / 111
    God's Tongue / 117
    Spirit and Flesh / 122
    The End of Language / 126

6. **The Bleeding Page**   130
    The Text as a Symbol / 130
    Representamen / 134
    Object / 138
    Interpretant / 143
    Reading Circumcision / 146

7. **The Humanoids**   151
    Invasion of the Humanoids / 151
    The Son of Man in the Bible / 154
    Jesus' Story of the Son of Man / 159
    The Sons and the Son / 164
    Ideology and the Son of Man / 168

8. **David Reconfigured**   173
    David in the New Testament / 173
    David the Ancestor / 176
    David the Psalm(ist) / 180
    David the Warrior / 185
    Resignifying David / 190

9. **Signifying Jesus**   194
    Resistance to Canonical Control / 194
    The Name of the Name / 200
    The Sign of Jonah / 209

Conclusion: The Future of the Christian Canon   218
    The End of the Canon / 218
    Postmodern Semiotics / 223
    Further News from Nowhere / 226

Glossary   233

Bibliography   237

Index of Scripture and Related Texts   247

Index of Names   257

ACKNOWLEDGMENTS

I am grateful for many helpful suggestions and thoughtful comments from my friends in the Bible and Culture Collective, especially Elizabeth Castelli, Laura Donaldson, Tamara Eskenazi, Robert Fowler, David Jobling, Danna Nolan Fewell, Gary Phillips, and Ronald Schleifer. In addition, Jane Schaberg, Scott Stephens, Richard Walsh, and Janelle Lutzke read and offered helpful comments on various drafts of this book. I owe special debts to Erin Runions, Tina Pippin, Fred Burnett, Roland Boer, and Peter Miscall, whose generous advice has helped me many times. Whatever faults appear in this book do so in spite of the assistance of these generous friends.

Adrian College provided me with a year's sabbatical (1999–2000) during which much of this book was written. Portions of chapter 1, "A Semiotics of Canon," were presented in the inaugural meeting of the Bible and Cultural Theory Seminar in Melbourne, Australia, 2 July 1998. A much earlier version of that chapter also appeared as "Toward a Semiotics of Canon," in *Australasian Pentecostal Studies* 1, no. 2 (1998) 73–92. Portions of chapter 3, "Ideologies of Translation," appeared in much different form in two articles, "Translation, Narrative, and Theology," in *Explorations* (summer 1991) 61–80; and "Two Theories of Translation, with Examples from the Gospel of Mark," in *Journal for the Study of the New Testament* 47 (1992) 95–116. An earlier version of parts of chapter 6, "The Bleeding Page," appeared in Tina Pippin and George Aichele, "The Cut That Confuses," in *Culture, Entertainment, and the Bible,* ed. George Aichele (Sheffield: Sheffield Academic Press, 2000). An even earlier version was presented by Professor Pippin and myself in the Ideological Criticism Section of the Society of Biblical Literature in 1998. I am deeply grateful to Tina Pippin for her collaboration on that article and for her kind permission to include some of that material here. Portions of chapter 7, "The Humanoids," appear in "The Son of Man and the Sons of Men," in the forthcoming *festschrift* for Daniel Patte, *Reading Communities Reading Scripture,* ed. Gary Phillips and Nicole Wilkinson (Harrisburg: Trinity Press International, 2001). Portions of chapter 9, "Signifying Jesus," were presented in the Reading, Theory, and the Bible Section of the Society of Biblical Literature in 2000.

INTRODUCTION

Semiotics and Canon

In the final chapter of my book *Sign, Text, Scripture*, I began to explore implications of semiotic theory for understanding the concept of canon. That chapter included a brief "case study" of the intertextual appropriation of the Jewish scriptures in Mark 14:48–49 ("You come out with swords and clubs to arrest me as if I were a highwayman?...But let the scriptures be fulfilled" [trans. Richmond Lattimore]) and related texts. In this book, I explore further a series of semiotic problems associated with the canon(s) of the Bible. The questions and problems that I consider in the following chapters are grounded in the framework within which I wrote *Sign, Text, Scripture*, and they likewise push beyond the modernist semiotic theory derived from C. S. Peirce and Ferdinand de Saussure into adjacent areas of study, including poststructuralism, ideological criticism, cultural criticism, and media studies. My approach draws heavily on the work of Roland Barthes, Julia Kristeva, Umberto Eco, Jean-François Lyotard, and numerous others. However, these scholars have not written extensively about canon, and thus the present study will apply this semiotic method to questions that have not previously been addressed by it.

The word "canon," when applied to collections of texts, means "list" or "catalog." However, although "canon" may be used to signify any selection or arrangement of texts, a definition as broad as that would include such things as a publisher's backlist, the contents of a bookstore window, any bibliography, or a library card catalog. Such a broad definition of "canon" may be useful or even necessary for some types of analysis, but it obscures important distinctions between the writing, editing, copying, and interpretation of a text. It is true that these distinctions are, in practice, often very unclear, but in order to trace the relations between these activities of textual production, the distinctions must be maintained in theory. In addition, a broad definition would not distinguish, among other things, between the authoritative texts of some community, a scholarly database of historical documents, and a private collection of favorite texts. According to such a definition, many texts would then belong to more than one canon.

For my purposes in this book, I define the word "canon" rather narrowly, as follows:

1. a canon is a list or catalog of books that is believed to be indispensable by some group of people (I am not interested here in personal or private canons);

2. the canon is understood by this group of people to be an unchanging and complete repository of truths and values (hence the close association of the Christian canon with the "rule of faith");

3. more specifically in relation to semiotics, a canon establishes an intertextual network that provides a reading context through which any of its component texts can be understood correctly (in the eyes of this same community).

The community's desire for a canon is desire for a text that conveys truly an essential, authoritative message and that controls the interpretation of that message. All three of these criteria must be met for a group of writings to qualify as a "canon," as the term is used in this book. These three criteria add up, in the minds of those who accept the collected texts as a canon, to something like divine inspiration or divine authorship: for these people, the canon is the "word of God," however that phrase might be understood. An important consequence of these three criteria is that the canon "spiritualizes" the component texts, emphasizing the unity, univocality, and universality of the message that they transmit.

A canon is a machine, a semiotic mechanism—a machine made, not of wheels and levers, but of signifiers and signifieds, denotations and connotations. Canon limits: this is the basic function of the canon machine, as one ancient formula puts it, "neither to add nor to take away." Canon limits the number of accepted texts and also the range of acceptable interpretations. Each of the three criteria noted above indicates a desire on the part of the believing community—that is, the community that believes that the collected texts form a canon—a desire for identity, for power, and for meaning.

However, no canon (including the Bible) ever succeeds completely in satisfying these desires. The mechanism breaks down. In the following, I explore some of the ways that the biblical canon tries and fails to control the meaning of its component texts. Yet even though the canon cannot be totally effective, it exerts a tremendous amount of control. In particular, the New Testament powerfully rewrites and spiritualizes not only its own texts but those of the Old Testament as well. The Christian canon exists in order to make this rewriting possible. Indeed, a Jewish canon, in this sense of the word, is unthinkable except, as John Barton suggests, as the Jewish refusal of Christian appropriation of the scriptures (see further chapter 1).

Given the narrowness of my definition, some readers may wonder if the word "canon" denotes any actual object at all.[1] However, I would argue that this is in fact what the word means to many people, not only to many Christians and Jews but even to secular humanists who defend the "Great Books" as a canon, and for whom the theological phrase "word of God" might be translated into something like "Eternal Truth." The "Great Books" are venerated by those who believe that they express truths and values essential to Western civilization. As far as I can tell, all references to a canon as writings that possess authority over reading use a definition very much like the one above.

I am not interested in denominational variations concerning which books are or are not included in the Bible. In addition, I reject the claim that there is a "final form" of the canon. There has never been a final form of the Bible. Instead there are many different "bibles" that have been accepted as canonical in various Jewish or Christian communities. In order to avoid unnecessary complications, I limit my focus to the canon of the Protestant Christian Bible, except as noted. Nevertheless, I suspect that the semiotic phenomena that I will be examining here can be found in any Christian Bible. Furthermore, although my focus is on the biblical canon, I think that the principles and problems involved in this analysis would be much the same for any set of "canonical" texts, whether they be the writings of other religions or secular literary canons.

In order to avoid unnecessary translation difficulties, I limit my discussion to the Greek (Septuagint, New Testament) and English (Revised Standard Version) texts of the Bible. I restrict my discussion of the Old Testament to the Greek and English versions because that allows me to compare their language to the Greek and English versions of the New Testament. My interest is in how the New Testament "rewrites" the Old Testament, and the authors of the New Testament books apparently drew upon Greek translations of the Jewish scriptures (the Septuagint or LXX), not the Hebrew texts.[2] I choose the RSV translation because I regard it as a "literal" translation of the ancient manuscripts (see further chapter 3). Every translation betrays and transforms its source text, but a literal translation is more likely to record problems and defects that appear in the source text. Such problems and defects hinder the clear transmission of the canonical message, and thus they are of particular interest here. This matter is complicated by the fact that the RSV Old Testament is a translation of the Hebrew Masoretic text, not a retranslation of the Greek Septuagint translation of the Hebrew. I generally stay with the RSV for the English phrasing, but on a few occasions I translate words or short phrases from the LXX.

Any text,[3] from the simplest body gesture or verbal utterance to sophisti-

---

1. For a good summary of ambiguities in scholarly use of "canon," see Barton, *Holy Writings, Sacred Text*, chap. 1.
2. Aland and Aland, *Text*, 52.
3. Natural phenomena regarded by some humans as "texts," such as constellations of stars,

cated interactive computer systems, depends upon a subtle complex of social, cultural, and other factors that contribute to its production. Included in the other factors are basic physical structures of the material world that make it possible for humans to speak and hear, for paper and ink to be manufactured, and for computer chips to function. I understand semiotics not only as study of the structured and coded content of messages but also as examination of the material substances and mechanisms in which the messages are grounded and through which the messages are transmitted. With Régis Debray, I want to pursue these "material traces of meaning," and like Barthes, I seek a semiology that pursues the *deconstruction* of linguistics— that is, that uncovers the limits of language.[4] I pursue a semiotics that takes its starting point in the physical aspects of the medium. Most directly this material trace appears in the *hulē*[5] or sheer physical stuff of the signifier, but it also eventually includes the entire technological substratum that makes possible the use of matter to signify a message.

The meaning of a text determines its identity, and a completely meaningless text would not even be recognizable as "text." How then does the semiotic mechanism of canon "produce" the texts of which it is composed? Could texts be "liberated" from the canon, and if they could, what would this liberation do to them, or to the canon? A canon is more than the texts that make it up. How does canon, as the rejection of the physical limitations of the signifier in the name of an absolute signified, run up against the resistance of the signifier? How does the biblical canon signify, and what does it signify about its constituent texts? What does their canonical status imply about texts that are included in the Bible, as well as texts that are excluded from it? Canon stands in a peculiar relationship to ideology. How does a cultural-ideological complex come together in the form of a canon? How does a canon, which is a product of ideology and of culture, itself also produce ideology and culture? These are some of the questions that I explore in this book.

Two Options

Many writers on the subject of canon focus primarily on the history or the theology of the Christian canon. These studies express a clearly apologetic point of view even though sometimes the writer claims to adopt an "objective" point of view.[6] According to these scholars, books were accepted into the biblical canon because they are in fact God's word and the divine

---

patterns of tea leaves, or the spoor of wild animals, should also be included. For definitions of the words "text" and "ideology," see chapter 1.

4. Debray, *Media Manifestos*, 7; Barthes, *Barthes Reader*, 469.
5. I borrow this term from Husserl, *Ideas*; and Kristeva, *Revolution*.
6. I applaud the candor of Beckwith, *Old Testament Canon*, 6, in this regard.

presence within these writings is self-evident.[7] Canonicity is God's mark of approval of the text, and it appears as a quality within the texts themselves, or in their relation to each other, that makes them deserving of inclusion in the canon. Faith enables believers to recognize this textual attribute of canonicity. Canon can only be discussed sensibly within a community of faith, and to the outsider or nonbeliever claims of canonical authority will always be unjustifiable. Only those who believe in the canon can properly understand it.

Even some scholars whose theological views are not conservative hold an apologetic point of view regarding the Christian canon. For example, Robert Funk claims that "the great events of history precipitate song and poem, drive man to speech, prompt language commensurate with...the plenitude of paradigmatic events."[8] James Dunn returns again and again to a consistent core assertion that unites the otherwise quite diverse New Testament texts: "This conviction...would appear to be the irreducible minimum without which 'Christianity' loses any distinctive definition and becomes an empty pot into which men pour whatever meaning they choose." This core belief establishes limits of what is "acceptable" and "unacceptable" to Christian faith.[9] James Sanders speaks of the Bible's "nature as canon," an inherent hermeneutic of the "full canon," and a fair hermeneutic that establishes a "permissible range" of readings.[10] Views such as these suggest that canonicity is a quality that is inherent in the canonical texts, and they imply that this quality is absent from noncanonical texts such as "Q" (the hypothetical common source of the gospels of Matthew and Luke),[11] the noncanonical gospel of Thomas, and the Old Testament apocryphal writings.

Consider the position described by the philosopher R. M. Hare in the "University Debate."[12] Hare tells a story about a student who believes that her teacher wants to kill her; no argument or evidence can persuade this student otherwise. The student in Hare's parable sees something in the teacher that no one else does, and therefore the other people think that she is insane. This mindset is analogous to what Hare calls the believer's "blik." The blik is a kind of belief, and everything that the teacher does, considered in the light of this blik, reinforces this belief. No evidence can decisively refute it. The decision to fear the teacher (or not to fear him) makes a real difference to the student. Likewise, there may be no objective certainty that a text is

---

7. See Fernhout, *Canonical Texts;* and Ingraffia, *Postmodern Theory.*

8. Funk, *Parables and Presence,* 6.

9. Dunn, *Unity and Diversity,* 376, 265. See also Moule, *Birth,* 177.

10. Sanders, *Canon and Community,* 19, 47, 60–62. Fowler, "Postmodern Biblical Criticism," does not take this position, but he comes close when he approves of the principle "let the hermeneutic develop from the Bible itself" (25 n. 37). Sanders also uses similar language (*Canon and Community,* 76).

11. Dunn, *Unity and Diversity,* 306.

12. Flew and MacIntyre, *New Essays,* 103–5.

or is not canonical, but the text really must be either canonical or not, and
the decision on this matter is an important one. Faith helps the believer to
"see" the canonicity of the biblical texts.

The studies that maintain the canonicity of the Bible simply assert that
the canonical writings possess some inherent quality that makes them different from other texts. These studies do not identify clearly what this quality
is. The Bible is the canon because God has made it so. For this reason, the
Bible possesses a semiotic integrity, and the mechanism of canon transmits
a unified and coherent message, which is the "word of God." The identification of this message is the task of "biblical theology," which is associated
with the related claim that the Greek and especially Hebrew languages as
used in the biblical texts are somehow extraordinary, a special variety of the
language that appears nowhere else. James Barr has done much to demolish
this claim.

Biblical theology is similar to "canonical criticism," which holds that the
biblical texts can only be properly understood from the point of view of
those who believe them to be "scriptures," as opposed to ordinary writings.
Canonical criticism maintains, as does biblical theology, that the authority
and integrity of the canon are central to the meaning of the Bible.[13] This
tautology inevitably short-circuits any questioning from those who do not
accept the canon's authority, as Philip Davies notes:

> [T]he real danger of this kind of approach is not that it is unhistorical
> but that . . . it becomes a means of privileging a confessional-theological
> interpretation, on the grounds that literature produced by "communi-
> ties of faith" is legitimately addressed to them—and, implicitly, that
> those outside such communities are guilty of reading "against" the
> "message" of the text. I prefer to see theological reading as a legitimate
> option *among others,* and based not on a claim about the objective
> character of its contents but on the decision of the Church (or syna-
> gogue, though this is really a Christian problem) to adopt this literature
> as a canon.[14]

Barr, Davies, Barton, and Harry Gamble offer an alternative to the biblical theology approach to the canon of the scriptures. More skeptical in
orientation, they regard the biblical canon as the historical product of the
ideological, intertextual activities of human beings. No inherent quality
marks any text as canonical. In other words, "the word of God" is a characteristic, not of the texts themselves, but at most of the human understanding
of those texts. Canon functions much like many other cultural, economic,
and political mechanisms—that is, it is a system of power, of inclusion and

13. See Barr, *Holy Scripture,* esp. chaps. 4–5 and app. 2, for fully developed criticisms of
this view. For Barr's critique of biblical theology, see *Semantics.* In other respects, "biblical
theology" and "canonical criticism" are different. See Davies, *Scribes and Schools,* 49.

14. Davies, *In Search of 'Ancient Israel,'* 19 n. 4, his emphasis.

exclusion, in this case applied to texts. The student of canon does not need to be a subscriber to the faith in question any more than the student of Marxism needs to be a Marxist or the botanist needs to be a tree.

The position in this latter case is closer to the one expressed by the philosopher Anthony Flew in the same "University Debate" mentioned above.[15] Flew's story is as follows: two men argue whether the arrangement of vegetation in a forest clearing is a tended garden or simply a natural phenomenon. One believes it is a garden, and the other does not. They are unable to agree upon any empirical test to determine whether or not there is a gardener. As in Hare's story, there is no common framework of truth in which the argument can proceed. Flew concludes from this that the believer's claim is nonsensical because it requires an unnecessary proliferation of hypotheses. Similarly, no empirical criterion to determine whether a text is or is not canonical will ever be acceptable to both believers and nonbelievers. The claim that there is a mysterious quality in the canonical text itself, perceivable only by believers, means that only believers can discuss matters of canon. From the nonbelievers' point of view, this claim adds nothing to the discussion of the text and is best put to the side.

However, the opposition between these approaches to the canon is not as simple as I have just suggested. The scholars do not divide quite so neatly into believers and skeptics. On the believers' side, Dunn and Funk are skeptical in their treatment of the canon, and on the skeptics' side, Gamble hints at the idea that the biblical canon was inevitable. He identifies the necessary condition of the canonical texts' authority as their "capacity for continuing interpretation." Gamble also identifies the emergent "great church," the communities that eventually became the mainstream of Christianity and adopted the Christian canon, as "more conventional" than the gnostic Christians.[16] This apparent lack of consistency indicates that the ideological dimensions of the question of canon run wider and deeper than might otherwise appear.

Unlike the alleged garden in Flew's parable, which may be the product of (mis)perception, canons certainly do exist. No one disputes whether collections of texts are in fact regarded as authoritative by some people. In other words, at stake is not their existence as collections but whether these collections derive their authority (and authority is all that a canon is) from something that is actually there in the texts themselves or in the collection as a whole. Is the authority of the canon something inserted into the texts by God, or is it something added to the texts, most likely by their readers— the same readers who claim that the texts are authoritative? In this regard, the skeptical approach is more useful for my project, although even that approach does not fully raise the semiotic questions that I want to explore.

---

15. Flew and MacIntyre, *New Essays*, 96–99.
16. Gamble, *New Testament Canon*, 62, 74.

The questions that the skeptics raise are primarily historical in orientation. The history of the biblical canons, both Jewish and Christian, is important and complicated, and not a little obscure. Gamble claims that the canon of the Bible tends to conceal its own history.[17] Some historical matters are relevant to the semiotic questions, but I am not primarily interested in historical questions surrounding the canon, such as what the intentions of the original canonizers were or when exactly the Christian or Jewish canons were "closed." I am interested in canonical process, not as a historical series of developments, but as a semiotic and ideological mechanism.

Instead, I regard history itself as a semiotic construct, a story produced in the present. Itself a semiotic mechanism, history is deeply ideological. As someone's story about "how things were," history, like any story, communicates a message. History is the story that we create in order to make sense out of relics from a largely mysterious past. We cannot uncover or discover any history outside of the stories that we create, which is not to say that history is imaginary. Rather, whatever physical relics (texts, artifacts, bodily remains, or other material traces) or mental memories (our own or those of others) that we think have come to us from the past cannot speak for themselves.[18] They speak only through the stories that we choose to tell about them, and the truth of any narrative that we create to explain these relics or memories cannot be settled apart from human interpretation.

No intermediate position is possible between biblical theology and historical skepticism. The difference between these two views of canon is determined largely by theological interests. It is in either case a matter of faith—that is, of ideology. The two views are in effect two opposed theologies or ideologies of canon. The difference between them is clearly laid out in Charles Altieri's discussion of the importance of secular literary canons. Unlike Davies, quoted above, Altieri disapproves of "reading *against* a text," as advocated by W. J. T. Mitchell or Geoffrey Hartman—namely, the skeptical reading of "critical historicism."[19] Instead Altieri argues in favor of "reading *through* the work." In the latter case,

> [b]y submitting ourselves to its provisional authority as an integrated work, we can hope to construct the best possible case for the text as a window on possible values in experience. This...keeps authority in the imaginative processes of a dialogue with great minds, rather than placing it in some contemporary interpretive practice.[20]

---

17. Ibid., 75.
18. See Jameson, *Postmodernism*, 18.
19. Altieri, "An Idea and Ideal," 57, his emphases. Altieri defines "critical historicism" with a quote from Terry Eagleton: "Its task is to show the text as it cannot know itself, to manifest those conditions of its making...about which it is necessarily silent" (Ibid., 59 n. 1, quoting *Criticism and Ideology: A Study in Marxist Literary Theory*, 43).
20. Altieri, "An Idea and Ideal," 57.

Altieri applies something like the biblical theology position to secular literature. He even describes this sort of reading as an act of "faith," which stands in necessary contrast to the hermeneutics of suspicion. Although Altieri is not discussing theology or religion as such, his use of this term in a philosophical discussion of secular literary canons—a discussion which, for Altieri, seeks to justify the importance of canons—is very suggestive. Altieri does not state, as biblical theology would, that the canon is natural or inevitable or implicit within the canonical texts themselves, and in fact he even suggests that multiple canons do and should operate in the choices and identities of persons and communities. Nevertheless, he also contends that "[t]he crucial enabling step is to insist on reading authors as I think most of them intended to be read"—that is, with "a willingness to preserve demanding comparative standards that lead us to elicit the *work's basic force.*"[21]

Thus biblical theology recognizes the canonical text as containing its own authority within it, which is possible because each canonical text exhibits certain qualities, preeminent of which is its "capacity to interpret its own features."[22] The question of canon takes the form of the question of the source and location of meaning. For biblical theology, and indeed for most modern reading theories, a text's meaning lies somehow within the text, as an intrinsic quality of the text itself, put there perhaps by the text's author, and in the case of a biblical text, put there by an author inspired by God. The canonical text overflows with a surplus of meaning,[23] an abundance of significance that allows it to speak to all times and peoples. In other words, the canon is a form of the "classic" (see further chapter 4).

In contrast, postmodern semiotics holds that the meaning of any text lies, not in the text as such, but rather in the intertextual operations of reading. Meaning is what readers produce using the semiotic machines at their disposal. A canonical text "survives" as a meaningful book, not because of something that is "in" the text itself, but because of the exercise of institutional power. The canonical list of biblical texts achieves acceptance as authoritative, not because it is inherently authoritative, but because through the vicissitudes of the "history" (see above) that these texts tell, their human readers achieve positions of power and influence over others. According to this view, every text, canonical or otherwise, is better characterized not by a surplus but rather by the absence of meaning, an absence that must be forcibly filled from beyond the text.[24]

The history or meaning of any text is dependent on some understanding of that text as it is presently known—that is, how the surviving manuscripts are understood today. Therefore, the question of the history or the theology of the biblical canon is dependent on the intertwined questions of semiotics

---

21. Ibid., 38, 57, 53, emphasis added.
22. Ibid., 56, 53.
23. Ricoeur, *Interpretation Theory,* 45.
24. See Derrida, *Of Grammatology,* 15.

and ideology, not vice versa. We cannot identify the moment or the process by which the canon comes into existence unless we already know what the canon is. It is the canon that exists here and now that drives the search for its origin. Once again, rather than an appeal to final form, this is simply a description of hermeneutical limitation.

What This Book Is, and What It Isn't

This book explores some of the ways that the Christian canon controls the meaning of the various texts that are included in it. This semiotic control operates at various different "levels" of the Bible, and its success is always mixed at best. The book opens with four chapters (part 1) that explore further the concept of canon in relation to

1. semiotic theory and ideology,
2. textual media and the technologies of language,
3. the possibility and implications of translation,
4. the justification of the canon as a "classic."

These chapters explore questions that relate to the entire Bible, the corpus considered as a whole. It is necessary to distinguish the canon machine as an entirety from the texts that are its parts. The biblical canon is intertextual, but it is also metatextual. These chapters also serve as defense and elaboration of the three-part definition of canon offered above. I use these chapters to explore and clarify my own ideological presuppositions and to establish a conceptual frame through which specific texts are then read in the next five chapters (part 2). In the conclusion, I return again to some more general concerns, with special attention to postmodernism and electronic culture, in order to ask about the future of the canon.

Each chapter in the second part of this book offers specific readings of biblical and nonbiblical texts, displaying some of the ways that the biblical canon controls the meaning of its texts. Each chapter features a New Testament text that reinterprets the Jewish scriptures or other, noncanonical texts. These detailed readings uncover instabilities between the two or more texts, intertextual tensions in which the colonizing appropriation of the Old Testament by the New becomes explicit. These instabilities or tensions include, in various combinations, one or more of the following elements in New Testament texts:

1. Explicit (marked) references in texts such as Mark 14:48–49 that openly cite "the scriptures" or related terms (such as "the law and the prophets" or what is "written"), whether the denoted text can be identified or not.[25]

---

25. See Aichele, *Sign, Text, Scripture*, chap. 4.

2. Implicit (unmarked) references that quote a text from the Jewish scriptures more or less verbatim but without specifically announcing that they are doing so, for example, the use of "son of man" language from the book of Daniel and some references to David (see further chapters 7 and 8).

3. Rewriting of the Jewish scriptures that includes summaries or discussions of scriptural texts These might be combined with specific references of either type 1 or 2 above, but they also involve a more extensive transformation of the text. They include, but are not limited to, "typological" interpretations—for example, the relation between the stories of Babel and of Pentecost, or Paul's treatment of "circumcision" (see further chapters 5 and 6).

These types of intertextual relation are not clearly distinct from one another, and there are many cases in which two or more elements are present together. There are also many other cases of biblical intertextuality in which intracanonical or intercanonical tension does not appear.

Numerous other books discuss "inner-biblical exegesis" or the "echoes" of the Jewish scriptures in the New Testament.[26] What I explore in this book is the control of a text's meaning that is made possible by the intertextual tensions established within the bounds of a canon, especially when those tensions involve the double canonical collection of the Christian Bible. How does the tension between texts and between canons restrict the play of semiosis? How does it serve as apologetic or polemic—in other words, as a way to justify one ideology, one reading, at the expense of others?

Texts cannot speak by or for themselves. Only the living reader can read the text—that is, only the reader can use the text as a lens through which something else is interpreted, whether it be an event, a person, or another text. This concept is fundamental to the understanding of intertextuality. On its own, the New Testament does not interpret or read the Old Testament. Instead, I read the New Testament as though it were reading the Old Testament, or I read some other writer's text as though she were reading the New Testament read the Old Testament, and so forth. None of these readings are accurate receptions of some meaning already there in the texts. There is no neutral position, no ideology-free criticism, no nontheological study of the Bible. And that, of course, includes this book.

The biblical canon is a powerful intertextual, ideological mechanism. To contest this mechanism in any way, whether by advocating some other canon or by rejecting the authority of any canon (if that is possible), also requires an ideological move. As I have become more aware of Christianity's claim to ownership of the biblical texts, I have wanted to dispute that

---

26. For example, Fishbane, *Biblical Interpretation* and "Inner Biblical Exegesis"; Hays, *Echoes of Scripture*; and Marcus, *Way of the Lord*. Other texts referenced in this book also include this sort of discussion.

claim, to "steal" the texts and allow them to sink or float on their own in the secular cultural currents of our times, just like any noncanonical text does. I continue to regard myself as a theologian, albeit a postecclesiastical theologian.[27]

In this book, I am not interested in the extent or content of the canon as that is usually conceived in biblical theology, except as those matters also relate to the semiotic question. Insofar as biblical theology or canonical criticism, like Altieri's argument, implies that a single coherent message is transmitted in the Bible, or that the emergence of the biblical canon is inevitable, I reject these views. Thus I tend to agree with Barr and disagree with Brian Ingraffia. However, I disagree with the claims of both Barr and Ingraffia (made for quite different reasons) that the biblical texts have meaning "in" them.

The biblical canon is a very powerful force in the present world, and it functions in a primarily negative or reactionary way—that is, the canon *prevents* readers from freely reading the texts of the Bible. Part of the semiotic function of canon is to "reveal" the included texts to the reader in certain ways, but this revelation occurs because the canon also functions to conceal the texts from the reader—that is, it limits rather severely the possible readings of the texts. This is "the control of biblical meaning."

---

27. Altizer, foreword, xiii; see also Aichele, "Post-Ecclesiastical Theology."

PART ONE

The Control of Denotation

Chapter 1

A SEMIOTICS OF CANON

Text, Intertext, Ideology

A canon is an authoritative collection or list of writings accepted by some community of readers. The canon identifies the accepted texts and fixes the written form of those texts. Canon controls and maintains the understanding and transmission of the selected texts, and indirectly all texts (because the canon is authoritative), within that community. The controls in a discourse system make communication possible. Canon is just one form of control, one type of semiotic mechanism. Canon is not essential to communication, but it can be very effective. Canonical status is not something that is intrinsic to any text. No writing can by itself demonstrate its own authority or even its own truthfulness. If I write in this book the sentence "Every word in this book is the authoritative word of God," that does not increase in any way the value of this book. If this book is not the word of God, then that sentence is also not the word of God.

Although the word "text" often stands in a special relationship to writing, I use this word to refer to the materiality of any sign, written or otherwise. In other words, "text" here denotes the material aspect of the signifier, the physical stuff (*hulē*) or medium of the sign. "The Text ... practices the infinite deferral of the signified ...; its field is that of the signifier."[1] What I call the "text" is what Julia Kristeva calls the "genotext"—that is, "language's underlying foundation": "[A] *genotext* will include semiotic processes but also the advent of the symbolic."[2] The material base of language (Kristeva's "semiotic") is formed into meaningful communication (Kristeva's "symbolic") by means of conventional codes. The codes permit and channel the conjunction of signifier and signified, and in this conjunction the sign is forged. Apart from the codes, the text is merely an inert, meaningless surface. Indeed, the *hulē* of the signifier cannot be perceived directly; instead, it is "hyperphenomenal."[3] In other words, the materiality of the text can only be inferred as that which makes possible the transmission of a message,

---

1. Barthes, "From Work to Text," 76.
2. Kristeva, *Revolution,* 87, 86, her emphasis.
3. Debray, *Media Manifestos,* 51–52. See also Barthes, *S/Z;* and Aichele, *Limits,* chap. 1.

or perhaps that which hinders in some way the transmission. The hyletic matter of text can only be encountered through the signifier's *resistance* to meaning.[4]

Upon being chosen by the reader, the material stuff of the text becomes significant, a "phenotext"—that is, "language that serves to communicate." What Kristeva calls the "phenotext," Roland Barthes calls the "work."[5] According to Barthes, the "work" is a self-identical entity that may be found embodied in various physical (geno)texts. For example, a particular story in different copies or editions or translations into other languages or even other media remains "the same story." Further, the work (phenotext) is "readerly"—that is, the reader encounters it as always already meaningful. Insofar as the text resists the attribution of meaning, it is "writerly." For Barthes, the work is defined by society's recognition of an author and thus of an authority. The work is meaningful and complete; it is an ideological object of consumption. There is no meaning in the physical aspect of the signifier (the text); instead, meaning (the work) is always negotiated between the reader and the text, intertextually. The reader may play on or play with the text, but it cannot be consumed until it is transformed into a work. Canonizing a text is one way to turn it into a work.[6]

Theoretically, the material signifier (genotext) is distinct from the signified meaning or intellectual content (phenotext) of the message that is encoded in the sign. However, in practice, the signifier and the signified are just one thing, the sign. Nevertheless, the text is both more and less than any meaning ascribed to it, and it carries in the materiality of its signifiers the potential to negate any meaning that the reader may choose. Therefore there is always tension between the text and any canonical collection of which it is a part. This tension is a major focus of this book.

The concept of a biblical canon and the claims made on its behalf by believers do not describe actual states of affairs. Instead, they are symptoms of desire—that is, desire for a complete and unambiguous message, a desire that can never be fulfilled by any physical text. Reading is always an exercise of desire and of power—that is, of interest. There is no neutral reading; all reading is ideologically motivated. You never read without some interest in the text, some desire for meaning. This is true whether you are reading for personal pleasure, because someone or something else is forcing you to read, or for any other reason (even when you read because you're bored!). Your desire may not be a desire to read as such—you may be reading because you "have to"—but reading nevertheless becomes one way to achieve some desire. Reading gives you power, and if it didn't, you would not read. The canon is a semiotic mechanism that attempts to satisfy the reader's desire for

4. See further Aichele, *Jesus Framed*, chaps. 6–7; and Jameson, *Postmodernism*, 27, 67.
5. Kristeva, *Revolution*, 87; Barthes, *Pleasure*, 66–67, also "From Work to Text."
6. Barton, *Holy Writings, Sacred Text*, 152.

power by controlling the meaning of the text. However, all actual canons, including the Bible, inevitably fail to satisfy this desire for meaning. Canonical control fails because of "unlimited semiosis," in other words, because signifying systems always exceed any possible level of control. In this book, I explore both that desire and its failures, as reflected in the tensions between text and canon.

This postmodern understanding of reading as desire is said (by its critics) to imply that "you can read any texts that you want," that "you can read the text in any way that you want," or that "reality is subjective." It is true that you *can* read any text that you want (as long as you can find a copy), that you *can* read that text in any way that you are capable of imagining (and all reading requires imagination), and finally that you *do* always and only perceive reality from your own point of view. However, none of these statements offers terribly exciting news. More important is whether (or how) you *will* do any of these things. Often overlooked (by the critics) is the associated postmodern claim that "what you want" is not entirely up to you. Both biological nature and social environment program you to want some things and not others and to perceive only certain objects and only in certain ways. Belief is a product of the social and cultural contexts in which you live, just as desire is also produced in those contexts. You are the product of power, even as you produce power. No one has demonstrated this more carefully, and indeed more powerfully, than Michel Foucault, in all of his writings.

You are the product of ideology, which is a form of power. Ideology controls the texts that you select, the ways that you read them, and the reality that you perceive. There can be no correct, neutral, or comprehensive reading of any text, including the Bible. However, although ideology is not entirely unconscious, it is not entirely voluntary either. You cannot choose your ideology, and you are always trapped by it. You are never free from ideology. You achieve some degree of critical awareness of your ideology insofar as you become aware of other ideologies offering other options to you—other choices, other readings, other truths than your own. You can even change ideologies, but that also does not happen entirely under your control. One fairly extreme type of change in ideology is conversion from one religion to another. The person who converts probably does so with some degree of awareness that an important change is happening to her. This awareness may take the form of anxiety, fear, or other emotional pain. A moment may even occur when a deliberate, apparently rational decision is made, when arguments are entertained and conclusions are reached. However, the conversion process also involves crucial factors that the person cannot control and may not even be aware of.

Because it is a semiotic phenomenon, canon is ideological. All communication requires control, and ideology provides this control. Canon is an explicit form of ideology, part of the overall attempt to construct a meaningful human world. The semiotic mechanism of the biblical canon creates order, lines of power, markers of identity. Like all ideologies, the canon does not *reflect* some external, objective reality more or less well, but rather it *creates* reality, or better, it provides a filter or lens through which individuals and communities perceive reality.[7] Ideologies arise from the fact that humans are finite, fragile beings whose knowledge of anything is at best partial and limited. We have no ideology-free knowledge of anything, and even the ideal of objective scientific or historical knowledge is an ideological product. There is no escape from ideology.

As a result, every encounter with a text is driven by ideology. The hyletic text is itself an opaque surface over which ideology plays as it will—that is, according to human desire. The desire for meaning encounters the materiality of the text only as an obstacle, and never as reinforcement. This materiality only appears as incoherence, never as meaning. Meaning arises when two or more texts are brought together in the understanding of a reader. This is called "intertextuality." According to Kristeva, intertextuality is the "*intersection of textual surfaces* rather than a *point* (a fixed meaning)." Intertextuality is the "transposition of one (or more) system(s) of signs into another."[8]

As it applies to the understanding of texts, ideology takes the form of intertextuality. In other words, in relation to the transmission of messages, ideology takes the form of an intertextual context that clarifies the message's meaning. Ideology neither creates intertextuality nor is created by it, for they are two sides of one coin. No doubt for other purposes, "ideology" and "intertextuality" must be kept distinct. However, any ideology can be specified as an intertextual structure or nexus, provided that we recall that not all texts are *written* texts.[9] The reader's ideology consists of an intertextual network of texts, a network that constantly shifts, grows, and diminishes as the reader both reads new texts and forgets old ones. Hence a second or third reading of a text is not the same as the first one. The mechanism of canon attempts to stabilize the ideological network, to make it permanent.

Human consciousness and experience are always existentially and conceptually prior to the meaningless stuff that constitutes the material aspect of the signifier. Nevertheless, without that material stuff there is no text, and there can be no intertext. Every text is understood in the light of a great many texts that the reader has already encountered. These other texts are also reinterpreted in light of the new text. This is an important dimension of intertextuality—that is, intertextuality is not something extra added to the juxtaposed texts, but rather it is something that emerges between the texts, in the way that they are juxtaposed. The individual reader stands at the

---

7. See Sanders, *Canon and Community*, 25–26.

8. Kristeva, *Desire in Language*, 65, her emphasis; and *Revolution*, 59–60. For more on text and intertext, see Aichele, *Jesus Framed*, chap. 7; and *Sign, Text, Scripture*, chaps. 1 and 3.

9. See further chapter 2. The "reader" includes anyone who receives and tries to understand a text, whether written or otherwise.

junctures of an indefinite network of texts; the individual *is* that network. The reader is in this light no more than a knot at which many texts intersect one another.[10] Intertextuality is thus not something that readers create, but it is something that creates readers.

The texts in the intertextual mechanism resonate, interfere with, or otherwise contact one another in various and complex ways, and ideology is this intertextual weaving of texts. Normally the reader's ideology is unconscious, or at best semiconscious. Nevertheless, the intertextual network deeply influences the reading that the reader brings to any text. No meaningful reading (or writing) is possible without some intertextual context. The intertext enables the reader to

> recognize the text as a text, that is, a signifying object as opposed to a bunch of meaningless stuff; determine the limits of the text, where it begins and ends, and whether or how it denotes extratextual reality (the metagenres of history and fiction);

> identify the cultural and linguistic codes in terms of which the text should be read—that is, the correct genre, as well as any "microcontextual variations"[11] within that genre; and establish the correct meaning of the text through the use of those codes.

Intertextuality is always ideological, and canon is a very explicit, aggressive sort of intertextuality. Not all intertexts are canons. However, all canons are controlled and restricted intertexts, which means they are definitive, exclusive, and authoritative. The semiotic mechanism of canon intensifies the ideological process and makes the appropriate intertextuality explicit. The ideology manifested through the canon appears, not in the individual texts themselves, but rather in the ways in which the canonized texts are juxtaposed with one another (and with noncanonical texts) and held together in the interpretive practice of the believing community.

The establishment of a canon is the attempt by some group of people to clarify the texts' meaning and to realize narrative completeness through a metatextual and intertextual commentary; in other words, to create a text that can *explain itself*. The entire collection of writings restricts the reading of any one of the texts. The canon obscures and replaces the physical text itself (both texts that are included in the canon and texts that are excluded) with something else—a signified, or at least a signifying potential, that far surpasses any of the included texts. The biblical canon serves to unify and "translate" the language of the various biblical texts.[12]

---

10. See also Aichele and Phillips, *Semeia* 69/70, introduction.
11. Rabkin, *Fantastic*, 36.
12. See Gamble, *New Testament Canon*, 14, 75. See further chapter 3; and Aichele, *Sign, Text, Scripture*, 127 ff.

Canon is a form of the Peircean interpretant, and in fact it attempts to be what C. S. Peirce called the "final interpretant"—the ultimate meaning of the text.[13] It serves as a metalanguage, which is a language that explains the meaning of another language. Canon performs what Roman Jakobson called the metalingual function, which is to identify the proper codes for understanding the text. The canon is not code itself, but it guides the selection of reading codes. As a metalanguage, the biblical canon legitimizes certain interpretations of the Bible and delegitimizes others; it controls the way in which the Bible is read. In this sense, canon is "mythic" or mythographic, although the biblical canon contains much more than stories properly categorized as myths.[14]

Canon freezes the text, fixing its physical form and its relation to other texts, both canonical and noncanonical.[15] However, that which was frozen cannot become too frigid, or else it will die. The canon must continue to speak to the community that claims it, and therefore its meaning must retain some flexibility, even when it is believed to be Absolute Truth. It is the recognition of the Absolute Truth contained within the canon that gives editors and translators license to "correct" the component texts. No actual text, whether ancient manuscript or modern edition, presents the perfect, definitive version of the canonized book (the work), and revised and corrected editions and translations are always possible. Indeed, canonization makes these revisions inevitable.

Because of its ideological function, a canon also plays important social, economic, and political roles. The canon defines (in part) the believing community's identity, and the community claims ownership of the canonized texts. Canon is in effect an ancient form of copyright, or rather copyright in the modern world has replaced one important function of canon: protecting the texts from the distorted readings of "outsiders." The desire for canon is the desire to own the canonized texts, to have power over them. Canon identifies the listed texts as valuable, better than other, noncanonical texts. Canon also limits the individual reader's power over and possession of the text. As an "insider," the reader is not free to read the text in any way that she wants; she is bound to the canonical intertext. In this way, the canonized texts also "own" the reader.

Canon and Meaning

The canon establishes a strong distinction between what is within the canon and what is not. The desire for canon is the desire to control the meaning of a set of texts, from within that same set of texts, in order to estab-

---

13. Peirce, *Essential Peirce*, xxxvi–xxxvii.
14. See Barr, *Holy Scripture*, 169. See also Jakobson, *Language and Literature*, 69.
15. See Ehrman, *Orthodox Corruption*, 28.

lish clearly a single message of Absolute Truth. In other words, the canon must provide its own intracanonical commentary. If the canonical collection does not completely explain itself, then something else must explain it, some extracanonical commentary. If commentary is required, then the canonical collection cannot be authoritative apart from the commentary. This designated commentary, which must then also be authoritative, is thus an essential ingredient of the canon. However, this commentary is extracanonical, and it cannot be both canonical and extracanonical at once. Therefore, the canon must explain itself.[16] The canon machine must be complete and self-sufficient, and it must provide its own implicit, intertextual commentary.

Despite this, the biblical canon actually stands in an awkward and ambivalent relation to extracanonical commentaries. The canon requires external reinforcements because it fails to explain itself sufficiently. The extracanonical commentaries supplement the canon's control over its meaning. They rescue the canon, keeping it "alive" and authoritative by acknowledging its validity and its relevance to the contemporary world. Indeed, the commentaries themselves play an active part in the construction of the canon's authority. Without these commentaries, the canon dies.[17] If the books are no longer perceived to be relevant to their readers, the readers who believe them to be Absolutely True, the canon may become a venerated relic, like much of the Old Testament is already in many Christian churches, but it will no longer be read. The commentaries are essential to the canon itself, as canon, even though they are not themselves canonical.

A canon can be defined by its exclusion of that which it is not, namely, noncanonical texts.[18] The truth of a noncanonical text is thought to be inherently different from the truth of a canonical text, even if both texts are understood to state the same message. The meaning of a canonical text is indisputable, and therefore it is different from that of a noncanonical one. The noncanonical text may be true, but it is not True. It does not share in the authorization that defines the canonical message. Thus even noncanonical writings derive their truth value or meaning from the canonical message.

Noncanonical texts fall across a range of possibilities, of different ways to be noncanonical. At one extreme stand texts that are rejected from the canonical list because they are regarded as heretical or blasphemous, that is, unacceptable in some way to the believing community. They are not merely excluded from the canon, but they are also *forbidden* to the community. Regarded as dangerous and evil, these texts threaten the identity of the community. At the other extreme stand texts to which the believing community is indifferent. The community may know of these texts, but they do not read

---

16. See Gamble, *New Testament Canon*, 76.

17. Other supplementary systems, such as Protestant belief in biblical infallibility or Catholic belief in the apostolic succession, also "help" the canon to control the texts.

18. Barton, *Holy Writings, Sacred Text*, 27, 157–58.

them, not because the texts are forbidden, but because the people are not interested in them. Between these extremes appears a wide variety of other texts that may be acceptable and even valuable to the community (such as the commentaries noted above) but are finally regarded as nonauthoritative. These writings are neither forbidden nor regarded as dangerous or evil.

The canon produces a textual frame that functions in two related ways.[19] First, through the canon-frame the believing community identifies certain texts as essential to its own identity. Canon defines the identity of the group of people by drawing a line around a group of texts that is in some way associated with the people's beliefs and values. In the case of the Bible, this is apparent in criteria offered for the inclusion of books: for example, that the canonical writings must be "apostolic" and "orthodox." The believing community then identifies itself in relation to the canonized texts. James Barr argues that this identity-formation role can be overstated because canons do not create communities, but rather communities create canons.[20] Nevertheless, once the canon has been established, a community is not free to change it, at least not without struggle and transformation of the community itself.

Canonical catalogs are always conservative, even reactionary, and never innovative. The formation of the various Christian and Jewish canons occurs in contexts of communal self-definition, or redefinition. Once the canon has been established, correct identification of the canon is one of the necessary conditions for membership in the community. The canon draws an unambiguous line around the group, determining through its acceptance or rejection who is in and who is out of the group. For the community that selects a canon, all understanding and interpretation must be referred to this act of choice.

Second, interpretation is not merely something to be applied upon or added to the canonical text. Understanding begins with the choice of a text and its placement in the larger canonical grouping. The canon frames the textual content within a multitextual context; it is a metatext. Upon being chosen, that is, constituted as a canonical text, the text's words refer to a world that is our world, for we have chosen it. The selection of texts intends a world, or better, we intend the world through the selected texts. Therefore canon is about reality: it is ontological. Our understanding of space and time, the forms of human existence, is governed by this selection of canonical texts. By constituting the canon as our world, we also constitute the reader as ourselves. The question of canon is therefore also a question of value, an ethical question. In choosing some texts and rejecting others, we create meaning. The framed texts establish a world, most often in the form of a story, and they locate the believing community in that world. The canon frames the act of discovering or receiving or creating a meaningful world.

---

19. See also Aichele, *Limits,* 18 ff.
20. Barr, *Holy Scripture,* 41–43.

The reader is not likely to choose a meaning consciously. Ideology rarely works that way. What we choose is usually a story. Human beings cannot live without a story of some sort—that is, without a myth, without a world. Yet there is no simple identity between any story and its meaning. We do not all find the same meaning in the "same" story. These differences reflect ideological differences between readers, for no two readers (even more so, no two communities) are likely to share exactly the same intertextual network. These differences may be small or large. In extreme cases it might even be argued that the readers are not reading the same story, even though they are reading the same physical text. This is part of the reason why canons are desired, and part of the reason why they fail.

A canon creates reality, a shared world. Meaning is a correlate of ontology and of ethics. This is as true of secular literary canons as it is of religious ones. Within this framework, "belief" appears in the canonizing act that selects some texts and not others. James Sanders maintains that repetition as well as selection determines canon. However, not everything that is repeated, even from one generation to the next, is canonical. As Sanders also notes, the canonical texts must be paradigmatic for the community.[21] Canon is an operation of belief, and of ideology. A canon is like a story—indeed, a canon is a story of stories, or metastory. To tell a story is to choose some matters and to reject others; hence every story is a "canon" in a very broad sense of the word. Aristotle claimed that every story requires a beginning, a middle, and an end.[22] Any story can only tell some things, and never every thing; otherwise it ceases to be this story rather than some other one. What is not told is just as crucial to the story's identity and meaning as what is told. In other words, all stories are artificial, or fictional.

However, canon is also unlike story. Every story is inherently incomplete, dotted with "spots of indeterminacy" that must be "concretized" by the reader, often unconsciously, always intertextually, in order for the story to have any meaning at all.[23] No story can specify in advance the codes in terms of which it should be read, and thus there is always the possibility that different readers will apply different codes in order to decipher the "same" story—that is, the same physical text. Thus we disagree about the meanings of stories. No story can conclusively explain itself because every story is referentially incomplete. The story's reference is always at least somewhat indirect or interrupted. No story can interpret itself, and no story is read entirely by itself. In order for the story's meaning to be understood, it must be supplemented from "outside" of the story. This supplementation is provided by the reader's interpretation. Because no two readers share exactly the same

21. Sanders, *Canon and Community*, 22, 33, 36, 69–70.
22. Aristotle *Poetics* 30.1450b26–34.
23. Ingarden, *Literary Work*, 249. See also Aichele, *Limits*, chap. 3.

intertext, the meaning of the story is inevitably a matter of disagreement among its readers.

If the story is relatively unimportant—that is, outside of the canon—this disagreement does not bother us at all: "You have your opinion and I have mine." It is like a difference of taste. But if the story is an important one, one that defines who we are and that answers basic questions, then our disagreement is very troubling. We believe, not in texts themselves, but in particular ways of reading texts. If my way of reading an important text is challenged by other readers, then my belief is threatened. Canon identifies which texts are important or authoritative, and it also provides a hermeneutical context in which the important texts can be read correctly.[24] From the standpoint of the believing community, canon provides the only proper context in which the texts may be read. Canon specifies the proper codes in terms of which the text should be read, and thus it identifies a range of acceptable interpretations. The desire for canon is the desire for a text that interprets itself.

Once again, I emphasize that this is the ideal of canon, the desire that produces canon. No text or group of texts can interpret itself. Different readers and believing communities do in fact read the "same" canonized texts in very different ways. The biblical canon is unable to satisfy the reader's desire for understanding of the texts and also unable to prevent readers from bringing to the texts a wide variety of presuppositions and assumptions— that is, ideological intertexts—not authorized by the canon. However, the canon does have very powerful effects on how its component texts are read. We would read the gospel of Mark differently if it had never been included in the New Testament, and we would read the gospel of Thomas differently if it had been included![25] In effect the New Testament canon "quotes" the entire story of Mark, making it part of a much larger story, and thus it reduces or even eliminates the referential ambiguity that characterizes that text. The semiotic mechanism of canon provides in advance the intertext in terms of which the believing community agrees on the meaning of the important texts. The canon completes the inherent incompleteness of the story. The canon arises from the desire to end the ceaseless demand for a meaningful written text by completing the uncompletable story.

Scripture and Canon

The concept of canon is related to but also distinct from the older and vaguer concept of "the scriptures." Even though the words "scriptures" and "writings" are for the most part synonymous, a distinction must still be made between the scriptures and any other writings. The connotation

---

24. See Smith, "Sacred Persistence," 49–51. See also Faur, *Golden Doves*, 109.
25. See Barr, *Holy Scripture*, 44–45.

of "scripture" may range all the way from "writing," meaning any written text, to "canon," in the narrow sense presented in the introduction and used throughout this book. The scriptures are texts that are authoritative but not necessarily exclusive. The precanonical scriptures complement or conflict with one another in fluid and indefinite ways. Like the canon, the scriptures produce an intertextual effect on reading, but unlike the canon, they do not necessarily have a clearly defined limit. As John Barton says, the scriptures are perceived as holy texts, but a collection of scriptures need not be closed.[26] The complete extent of "the scriptures" is not necessarily defined for those who cite them. Early Christians or Jews could agree that some writings were scripture without agreeing about others. Hence New Testament references to Old Testament texts as "scriptures," or patristic references to either Old or New Testament texts as "scriptures," do not by themselves imply the existence of a canon.

Once the scriptures are transformed into the canon, they become the ideological metatext of the Bible, which is understood as a unified whole that transmits a single message with a single meaning. As a result, when the writings included in the biblical canon refer to each other as scripture, in effect they also refer back to themselves. This self-referentiality creates a semiotic feedback loop in which the text's meaning is restricted and controlled. The semiotic function of "the scriptures" (or related phrases) appears in the intertextual tension between two texts, where it enables the first text, the scripture, to signify in the message of the second text, which becomes in effect a commentary on the scripture and controls its meaning. The second text colonizes and appropriates the first one. In biblical texts that cite the scriptures, whether explicitly or implicitly, intertextual tension between the two Christian testaments, or between any text and the canon, comes to light.

Despite these nuances, it is not easy to distinguish between the meaning of "scripture" and the meaning of "canon." By the time the Christian and Jewish canons had been closed, and perhaps even prior to that point, any significant difference of meaning between the word "canon" and the word "scripture" had disappeared. "Canon" either replaced "scripture," or else the meaning of "scripture" changed and became synonymous with "canon."

The Bible does not describe itself as a canon, even though it does refer to the scriptures. Texts such as the following do not unambiguously assert the canonicity of the entire biblical collection:

> Deuteronomy 4:2—" 'You shall not add to the word which I command you, nor take from it; that you may keep the commandments of the LORD your God which I command you.' "

> 2 Timothy 3:16–17—"All scripture is inspired by God and profitable for teaching, for reproof, for correction, and for training in righteous-

---

26. Barton, *Oracles of God*, 28, 157.

ness, that the man of God may be complete, equipped for every good work."

Revelation 22:18–19—"I warn every one who hears the words of the prophecy of this book: if any one adds to them, God will add to him the plagues described in this book, and if any one takes away from the words of the book of this prophecy, God will take away his share in the tree of life and in the holy city, which are described in this book."

The word "canon" (Greek *kanōn*) does appear a few times in the Bible,[27] but always with the connotation of "rule" or "standard." Barton argues that there was no Christian or Jewish canon in the first few centuries of the common era. Instead, "[i]f the word 'canon' is to be used at all, then it should probably be in the sense in which the term was sometimes used in the early Church, to denote a 'norm' or regulative standard rather than a closed body of texts."[28] The use of the word as a technical term to describe an accepted and exclusive list of authoritative writings for Jews or Christians does not appear until the third century C.E., in the writings of Origen.[29] According to Barr, this technical use of " 'canon' in the sense of 'canon of scripture...' " appears *not* to derive from the sense 'rule, standard,' " but rather this use of the word "derives from the familiar Greek sense, as used of a table of figures or the like"—such as a list of texts.[30] Nevertheless, even in Origen's time, neither the Jewish nor the Christian canons in their present forms had been closed. Only the concept of canon, or the desire for a canon, had appeared.

The question of canon arises in the form of disputes over which writings are, or which believing community possesses, the genuine scriptures, authoritative writings containing the true message. The closing of the canon makes the scriptures comprehensive and exclusive. The canon is then clearly defined for all who recognize its authority. This definition separates the texts in the "canon of scripture" from all other texts, including commentaries and traditions of interpretation with which the canonized texts may have formerly been intermingled.

Canon fixes the text, identifying its proper wording and its importance in the collection of books. There are no partial or "fluid" canons, although prior to the canonizing of the texts, the list of scriptures as well as the contents of individual texts themselves may be fluid. The canonical collection is necessarily all-or-nothing. This does not rule out what Barr calls a "stepped canon."[31] Some texts may be central (such as the Torah in the Jewish scriptures), and other texts more marginal (such as the Writings). In these cases,

27. LXX Micah 7:4; 2 Corinthians 10:13, 15, 16; and Galatians 6:16. In the Apocrypha: Judith 13:6 and 4 Maccabees 7:21.
28. Barton, *Oracles of God*, 63.
29. Graham, *Beyond the Written Word*, 193 n. 13.
30. Barr, *Holy Scripture*, 49 n. 1, emphasis added.
31. Ibid., 41.

the canon is definitive about which texts are central and which ones are marginal; for example, in the way in which the books are sequenced in a list of titles or which books may be used, or in what ways, in worship. Changes in canonical status are not permitted.

It is not clear just what sort of historical event constitutes closure of a canon. Many biblical scholars still think that the Jewish canon was completed and closed before the Christian one. According to this theory, the Jewish Bible was established in connection with rabbinical discussions at the end of the first century of the common era, after the destruction of the temple in Jerusalem. However, although it is likely that the destruction of the temple began something that eventuated in the Jewish canon, it is doubtful that that something would have ended *as a canon* if Christianity had not developed into a primarily gentile religion with its own canon of scripture. It seems unlikely that the Jewish canon of Law, Prophets, and Writings was closed before the closing of the Christian canon of Old and New Testaments. Indeed, I suspect that the "original" and first canon is the Christian Bible. There were indeed earlier collections of books, and some of them, such as collections of alleged authentic writings by classical writers, may even have been called "canons."[32] However, it is only with the appearance of the Christian canon that the narrow sense of "canon" used in this book comes to refer to an actual collection of books.

It is not clear when the canon was closed in any Jewish or Christian community, but that may not have been until the fourth century c.e. or later. All of the early lists of New Testament books identified by Bruce Metzger are from the fourth century, except for Origen's list (quoted in the fourth century by Eusebius) and perhaps (but doubtfully) the Muratorian Canon.[33] Even among these lists there is considerable disagreement, suggesting that they do not evidence a closed canon so much as an ongoing struggle.

The fourth century was also the time in which emerging "catholic" Christianity became the state religion of the Roman Empire. The emperor Constantine pressured the churches to standardize their various versions of the scriptures, and if this standardization is not already a canonization, it is at least a further step in that direction. The Christian religion moved from the social periphery to the center, and its leaders and institutions became powerful. Heretical and heterodox individuals, groups, and tendencies were suppressed, and the ideology of a church that is united, universal, and rooted in apostolic tradition became dominant. One ideological function of the emergent Christian canon was to secure internal homogeneity (rejection of heresy), and another was to guarantee external legitimacy (presenting the Church as the true Israel, the heir to the divine covenant).

The effect of Constantine and his successors on the Christian canon was

---

32. Davies, *Scribes and Schools,* 25 ff.
33. Metzger, *Canon of the New Testament,* 305–15.

much the same as that of the Persian Empire and its policies on the post-exilic "canonization" of the Torah. The Persian rulers gave support to the exiles returning from Babylon to Judah, according to Ferdinand Deist: "It was in an effort to curb the influence of various sectarian groups that had formed during the power struggle... and with a view to ratifying the outcome of the struggle that a canon came into existence."[34] Deist uses the term "canon" throughout his discussion of this phenomenon, but even if the "canon of Torah" was established during the Persian period, the rest of the Jewish canon remained undetermined, and an incomplete canon is not, strictly speaking, a canon.[35]

The list of writings recognized as "scripture" in Judaism is defined differently than it is in Christianity, although it is identical in extent (but not in order) to the Protestant Christian Old Testament. The concept of canon is itself a fundamentally Christian one, and it is doubtful that Jews understand the concept of canon in the same way that Christians do.[36] The difference between Christian and Jewish views of canon corresponds roughly to what Kurt Aland and Barbara Aland call the difference between the "Greek" and the "oriental" views of writing:

> Greeks and orientals view the written word differently. For orientals the very letter had a sanctity of its own. The Hebrew text of the Old Testament, like the text of the Quran, is alike in all manuscripts (except for unintentional errors). For Greeks it was the message contained that was sacred.[37]

This distinction between "Greeks" and "orientals" seems to reflect the "biblical theology" position discussed in the introduction to this book, and in particular the differentiation between "Hebrew" and "Greek" thought in relation to language. It is now rather clear that in the first few centuries of the common era, no firm line can be drawn between Jewish and Hellenistic cultures. Nevertheless, the Alands' distinction between two different views of writing is an important one because it describes opposing positions concerning the relation between ideology and language.

For the so-called oriental view of writing, reality is language, and it cannot be separated from language—and vice versa. Barr claims that "for Judaism as it has developed, the Torah is not primarily a report of or witness to salvific events... [but] it is the divinely given *text*, essential for ritual wor-

---

34. Deist, "Canonical Literature," 72. Berquist presents a more detailed argument along these lines ("Postcolonialism and Imperial Motives"), and Davies presents a similar argument in regard to the Hasmoneans (*Scribes and Schools*, 180 ff.). See also Coote and Coote, *Power, Politics*, chap. 11.
35. Barton, *Oracles of God*, 28.
36. Ibid., 63.
37. Aland and Aland, *Text*, 286.

ship and for the establishment of legal norms."[38] Jonathan Brumberg-Kraus argues that

> [w]hile the collections of "Old Testament" and "written Torah" might more or less consist of the same contents—they clearly do not function in the same way vis à vis their applications in "New Testament" or the "oral Torah...." [I]n Judaism the locus of God's revelation is in the text alone. Scripture itself is the revelation. Among early Christians (and among later ones, I suspect, too), the revelation is something extratextual, the events in the life, death, and resurrection of Jesus Christ, for which "scripture" is primarily a testimony, an affidavit that it happened.[39]

Not all Jews adopt the "oriental" view of the biblical texts. For my purposes, however, the important thing is not that this view is oriental or Jewish, but rather that for this understanding of language, ideology cannot be separated from the intertextual network that produces it. Furthermore, the network has no center and no clear boundaries. Books, sentences, phrases, words, and even the shapes of specific letters in the text are meaningful, not because they have meaning *in* them, but because meaning only appears *between* them. Semiosis is unlimited. Meaning is always intertextual, and therefore also fluid and polyvalent. As Jacques Derrida says, "There is nothing outside of the text," or in other words, everything is potential text.[40] I am neither oriental nor Jewish, but this understanding of the intertextual construction and control of meaning is for all practical purposes the semiotic theory adopted in this book.

In contrast, for the so-called Greek view of writing, ideology is distinct from the texts through which it passes. Instead, meaning is contained in the text, like whiskey in a bottle. The universe consists of a set of extratextual objects to which language points, univocally, although with greater or lesser reliability. Language is at best an image of extratextual reality, and the signified reality is more important than the texts that signify it. In other words, the conceptual message (the ideological work) that texts contain is more important than the physical stuff of the texts themselves. Derrida describes this view of language and reality as "logocentrism," or the metaphysics of presence. For logocentrism, "reading and writing, the production or interpretation of signs, the text in general as fabric of signs ... [is] preceded by a truth, or a meaning already constituted by and within the element of the

---

38. Barr, *Holy Scripture*, 100, his emphasis.
39. Brumberg-Kraus, "Re: Canon." Similar views are expressed by Dan ("Midrash and the Dawn of Kabbalah," 128), Kermode ("Plain Sense," 184–85), and Ehrman (*Orthodox Corruption*, 282 n. 22).
40. Derrida, *Of Grammatology*, 158.

logos." Writing "comes from afar, it is external or alien: to the living, which is the right-here of the inside."[41]

This Greek, or logocentric, view of text is essential to mainstream Christianity and to its canon, and it will play a large part in the readings of biblical texts in part 2 of this book. Logocentrism emphasizes the extra-textual "revelation" that is transmitted through the semiotic mechanism. For Christianity, this revelation consists of the pre-Easter message conveyed by the Old Testament texts, especially as it is clarified in the post-Easter message of the New Testament texts.[42] The theological necessity that the scriptures contain a message to be correctly understood requires that Christians disregard the materiality of the text. The physical texts of the Old and New Testaments are nothing more than components of the signifying mechanism through which the authoritative revelation is transmitted. The material texts themselves are ultimately unimportant to Christians, and they are valued only because they contain precious contents, like a bottle of expensive whiskey, or a living body inhabited by a soul. The logocentric view of text generates the desire for reliable reception of that authoritative message that results in the Christian understanding of the canon. One purpose of this book is to explore further the relation between logocentrism and the Christian understanding of canon.

The Two Canons

Strictly speaking, Christianity does not have one canon divided into two testaments (as many scholars assume),[43] but rather it maintains two distinct canons. The Old and New Testaments of the Christian Bible present the dilemma of a double canon, a problem that has deeply influenced the development of Christian theology and that Christians have never adequately faced. In effect any given believing community can honor only one canon, and no group can ascribe absolute authority to two distinct canons. Canons are by definition totalizing and exclusive. One canon must dominate and subsume the other. According to Christian belief, the four canonical gospels must refer to one true story,[44] despite their evident and substantial differences both of meaning and of text. Likewise, both the Old and the New Testaments must connote the same thing, and the new must be the proper

---

41. Ibid., 14; *Dissemination*, 104. See also Detweiler, "Sacred Text," 225–28.

42. Robinson, *Problem of History*, 25.

43. Beckwith speaks of two canons (*Old Testament Canon*, 9), but because of his theological views (for example, 408), he does not acknowledge the problem that this presents. Beckwith does note that the conventional dating of the closing of the Jewish canon, at Jamnia in 90 C.E., presents difficulties for Christian acceptance of the Old Testament as canonical (4–5), but he argues that the Jewish canon was closed in the second century B.C.E.

44. The inclusion of multiple gospels in the New Testament does not encourage diversity but rather *subjects* diversity under its emphasis on a greater unity. See Gamble, *New Testament Canon*, 24–35, 88.

translation of the old. I will argue in chapter 3 that a logocentric theory of translation is necessary to this understanding of the Bible.

Both the New Testament and the Old Testament writings are appropriated for Christian reading by their canonization. However, the Christian Old Testament is not the same collection of books as the Jewish Tanakh.

> A canon may define the whole, and the same parts may figure in different canons. For Christian commentators the Psalms belong to a whole different from the whole to which they belong for Jewish commentators; they may agree that there are messianic psalms, but the plain sense of such psalms must be different for each, since the whole text for the Christian shows the fulfillment of the messianic promises.[45]

The Christian double canon transforms the Jewish scriptures into the first Christian canon, the Old Testament. The scriptures are rewritten, not physically but logocentrically.

This case is analogous to that of Pierre Menard, the fictional hero of a story by Jorge Luis Borges. Menard, a twentieth-century Frenchman, decides to write a book that will "coincide—word for word and line for line" with the novel *Don Quixote* by the seventeenth-century Spanish author Miguel de Cervantes. It will be, not a translation or a paraphrase or an "updating" of the story, but an *exactly identical* story: "To be, in some way, Cervantes and to arrive at *Don Quixote* seemed to him less arduous—and consequently less interesting—than to continue being Pierre Menard and to arrive at *Don Quixote* through the experiences of Pierre Menard."[46] In a letter to the story's narrator, Menard says, "My solitary game is governed by two polar laws. The first permits me to attempt variants of a formal and psychological nature; the second obliges me to sacrifice them to the 'original' text and irrefutably to rationalize this annihilation."[47] Menard does not complete his task, and the reader is told that all that he produced was two chapters and part of a third. Nevertheless, the nameless narrator confesses, "I often imagine that he finished it and that I am reading *Don Quixote*—the entire work—as if Menard had conceived it."[48] The narrator then compares Menard's text to Cervantes's:

> the fragmentary *Don Quixote* of Menard is more subtle than that of Cervantes. The latter indulges in a rather coarse opposition between tales of knighthood and the meager, provincial reality of his country; Menard chooses as "reality" the land of Carmen during the century of

---

45. Kermode, "Plain Sense," 181–82. See also Barnstone, *Poetics of Translation,* 163; and Wilken, *Myth,* 15–16. Dunn, *Unity and Diversity,* chap. 5, presents numerous examples.
46. Borges, "Pierre Menard," 49.
47. Ibid., 51.
48. Ibid., 50.

Lepanto and Lope.... The text of Cervantes and that of Menard are verbally identical, but the second is almost infinitely richer.[49]

Borges satirizes a whole complex of literary assumptions in this story: the value of authorial intention and the social context in which the text is written, the importance of the "original" text in interpretation, and the function of influence and imitation in literary history. Nevertheless, what Menard does to Cervantes's book is in effect what Christian appropriation of the Jewish scriptures has done to them. The Jewish scriptures are the writings of people for whom the messiah has not yet come, for whom the messiah is at best a vague figure. The Old Testament consists of Christian writings—not writings by Christians but writings for Christians—in which the messiah of the New Testament has been prophetically announced and a meaning-filled context for his life is provided. In order to transform the Jewish scriptures into the Old Testament, a rewriting of the texts had to occur—not the act of a Pierre Menard but something every bit as absurd and grandiose. Likewise, the New Testament consists of Christian writings, regardless of who their historical authors or original audiences might have been. Differences of narrative and belief between the various texts have been smoothed over and resolved into a greater truth. In each case, this canonizing rewriting is not a physical act that transforms or replaces the material *hulē* of the signifier, but it does change the signifier anyway because it changes the signification.

Therefore the Christian New Testament is not merely another canon—it never could be, for it is fundamentally incomplete without the Old Testament—but it is also, and primarily, a metacanon. Already in the second century C.E., before there was any canon, the Christian heretic Marcion understood the problem of a double canon. Marcion rejected the Jewish scriptures (which at that point were still fairly fluid, except for the Torah) and proposed instead his own collection of Pauline letters and a version of the gospel of Luke, from which "Jewish" material had been removed. Marcion's challenge to his fellow Christians made canon thinkable, specifically in the form of his rejection of the double canon. The need for a canon began to be expressed by early Christians, perhaps in part as a defensive reaction against Marcion's single-canon collection of texts. What Celsus called the "great church" rejected Marcion's rejection of the Jewish scriptures, and they claimed both an Old Testament and a New Testament for themselves. It was this double claim that led eventually (so Barton suggests)[50] to the Jewish formation of a canon.

Walter Bauer claims that Marcion was "the first systematic collector of the Pauline heritage," and Albert Sundberg even holds that Marcion's col-

---

49. Ibid., 51–52.
50. Barton, *Oracles of God*, 63.

lection was the first Christian canon.[51] Bart Ehrman agrees: "Marcion was evidently the first to insist on a closed canon."[52] In contrast, Harry Gamble denies that Christianity developed the New Testament as a reaction to Marcion's collection, as does Barton.[53] Whether or not Marcion's collection of texts was truly a canon depends on how strictly "canon" is defined. Other early collections of epistles and of gospels were apparently also in process of forming, but it is not clear that they were taken as either authoritative or closed. In any case, Marcion added impetus to the Christian canonizing process.

Marcion also insisted on just one gospel, not several. Gamble suggests that in the second century c.e. this may have been "common practice."[54] Nevertheless, it distinguishes Marcion's collection from the eventual canonical collection of four gospels. Also appearing in the second century, Tatian's *Diatesseron* recognized the problem of multiple gospels, but it used a different strategy to "solve" the problem. Tatian's harmony of the gospels was also eventually rejected by the "great church." Other scribes were also physically "correcting" and effectively harmonizing precanonical gospel texts.[55]

It is doubtful that either Marcion or Tatian subscribed to the "oriental," or intertextual, view described above. However, their opponents surely subscribed to something like the "Greek" view, for in terms of the semiotics of logocentrism, there is no ideological difficulty in the concept of a single gospel message presented in multiple gospel texts or in the concept of a single word of God presented in two different canons. For the emerging mainstream of the Christian Church, the "harmony" between the canons, like that between the gospels, need not be displayed in the physical texts themselves because it existed already in the understanding of the faithful reader.

If there had been no New Testament, there would have been neither the Christian Old Testament nor the canonical Jewish Bible, not in the form of canons. Barton has shown that "the prophets" was still a very fluid collection of texts during the first century c.e. and that it included some of what were later to be separated out as "the writings": "My thesis is that there was no canon at all in this sense [a closed collection of scripture], for either Jews or Christians, until well into the Christian era."[56] Barton suggests that Judaism probably would not have established a canon except for the need to resist the reinterpretation and appropriation of Jewish scriptures into the Christian canon.[57] The New Testament appropriation of the Jewish scrip-

51. Bauer, *Orthodoxy and Heresy,* 221; Sundberg, *Old Testament,* 122.
52. Ehrman, *Orthodox Corruption,* 186.
53. Gamble, *New Testament Canon,* 60; Barton, *Holy Writings, Sacred Text,* 36 ff.
54. Gamble, *New Testament Canon,* 27.
55. See Ehrman, *Orthodox Corruption;* and Petersen, *Gospel Traditions.*
56. Barton, *Oracles of God,* 57.
57. Ibid., 63. See also Barton, *Holy Writings, Sacred Text,* 19, 122–23. Although Resnick, "The Codex," does not actually say as much, his overall argument is congenial to this view.

tures turns them into something else, namely, the Christian Old Testament. This happens at different levels of the biblical texts, from the macro level of a single physical volume binding together two testaments into one unified object, to the micro level of numerous references, both intratestmental and intertestamental, to other texts within the intertextual network.

The paradox of the double Christian canon presents a fundamental theological difficulty that has been a major factor in the history of Christian thought from its beginnings to the present.[58] The theological problem of two Christian canons is textually manifested in the Bible itself. It appears in the instability of the New Testament texts' relations to the Old Testament writings—that is, an unresolvable tension between the texts involved. It also appears in similar instabilities within each of the canons, instabilities that would be mere inconsistencies in a noncanonical collection of texts. These tensions, and the resistance to canonical appropriation that they reflect, become points at which the reader's ideology is put to the test.

Canon is a form of intertextuality, but canon raises intertextuality to a high degree. The mechanism of canon makes understanding of its included texts possible, by providing an authoritative intertext, and it produces a "correct" reading for each text. (Once again, this is the ideal of canon.) This semiotic function appears also in the relation between the two Christian canons. The New Testament metacanon explains and absorbs the other canon—for example, by "fulfilling" its prophecies or by properly decoding its "parables."[59] However, the relation between the two Christian canons is not a tranquil one. The "echoes" of scripture between the canons are not peaceful reverberations or natural metamorphoses of some prior intrinsic meaning. Instead they are monstrous distortions, skewed rewritings of the other text.

Another of Borges's writings is relevant here. In the essay "Kafka and His Precursors," Borges maintains that Franz Kafka's stories and novels in effect create the works of his precursors: "[A]fter frequenting [Kafka's] pages a bit, I came to think that I could recognize his voice, or his practices, in texts from diverse literatures and periods." These "precursors" include texts by Zeno, Han Yu, Kierkegaard, Browning, Bloy, and Dunsany. Borges claims that "not all of [these texts] resemble each other. . . . In each of these texts we find Kafka's idiosyncrasy to a greater or lesser degree, but if Kafka had never written a line, we would not perceive this quality; in other words, it would not exist."[60] Although Kafka did not write the texts of the precursors, his texts cause the reader to read these precursors in a significantly different way.[61] Although they may continue to be important in their own right, the

---

58. See Bauer, *Orthodoxy and Heresy,* chap. 9, for discussion of how early Christians grappled with this problem.

59. Robinson, *Problem of History,* 48.

60. Borges, "Kafka," 199, 201.

61. This is reminiscent of T. S. Eliot's essay "Tradition and the Individual Talent," and indeed

precursors' works are changed by their relation to Kafka's works, a relation that is established retroactively from the reading of Kafka's writings. Borges does not assert any conscious intention to do this on Kafka's part, and indeed it seems quite possible that such a relation could exist between two or more works even if the respective authors were entirely unaware of each other. In other words, historical "influence," as that is usually understood, is not a crucial factor in intertextuality.

The Old Testament did not exist until the New Testament transformed the Jewish scriptures into Christian scriptures. The New Testament creates the Old Testament as that which is to be fulfilled, much as Kafka creates his precursors. However, Kafka's writings are not a canon, nor are the writings of all of his precursors. These writings may appear in one or another secular literary canon, but that is another matter. What is irony and paradox in relation to a single writer's oeuvre is ideological appropriation in a canon such as the Bible.

Codex and Commentary

The concept of scripture distinguishes between those texts that deserve commentary and all others. This is an important ideological function of the concept of scripture. In Jewish tradition, commentary (or "oral Torah") cannot also be scripture (or "written Torah"), much less canon.[62] No text can be both commentary and scripture. If a text is read as scripture, it does not function as a commentary, and to read that text as a commentary is to disregard its scriptural status. Conversely, to comment upon a text is to read that text as scripture.[63]

Nevertheless, texts within the Jewish scriptures do in fact comment on other texts within those scriptures, and this creates the "paradox" of inner-biblical exegesis, scripture that is also commentary.

> [T]he entire corpus of Scripture remains open to these invasive procedures and strategic reworkings up to the close of the canon in the early rabbinic period, and so the received text is completely compacted of teachings and their subversion, of rules and their extension, of topoi and their revision. Within ancient Israel, as long as the textual corpus remained open, Revelation and Tradition were thickly interwoven and interdependent, and the received Hebrew Bible is itself, therefore, the product of an interpretative tradition.

Borges includes a footnote to Eliot. See also Fishbane, "Inner Biblical Exegesis," 34. Funk, *Jesus as Precursor*, uses Borges's essay to support readings of Jesus' parables.

62. Faur, *Golden Doves*, 16, 133.

63. Benjamin argues in a parallel manner that translations transform texts into "originals" (*Illuminations*, 81). See further chapter 3.

With the closing of the corpus of Scripture, however, and the establishment of a fixed canon deemed prior in time and authority to
rabbinic exegesis, there was a tendency to forget the exegetical dimensions of Scripture and to see Scripture solely as the source and
foundation of later interpretation.[64]

The New Testament adds a second layer of inner-biblical exegesis and thus
raises the paradox to a higher degree. In addition, the texts of both the Jewish scriptures and the New Testament were written and copied and recopied
in ancient intertextual milieus in which they echoed yet other texts, including each other. Every text is in some way a commentary on other texts, for
no text is ever read or written in an intertextual vacuum. As Borges's essay suggests, intertextuality extends far beyond the influence of one text on
another text's author.

José Faur notes that the rabbinic categories of "oral" and "written" are
legal fictions, not empirical descriptions. A written commentary is nevertheless "oral."[65] One way of signifying the distinction between "oral Torah"
and "written Torah" in early Judaism was through the difference between
the physical formats of codex and scroll. The Torah and the rest of the Jewish
scriptures, the "written Torah," were all written on scrolls. Jewish communities continued to use the scroll format for their scriptures (especially texts
reserved for liturgical use) for hundreds of years after the codex was introduced. The codex format was apparently thought of as an intermediate stage
between speech and writing, not a finished written book. It was considered
suitable for rough drafts, or notes. When the Mishnaic traditions, the "oral
Torah," were first written down, codex "notebooks" were used for the transcription: "[t]he employment of the note-book was the most suitable way of
indicating that [the rabbis] were writing Oral Law for private, or unofficial
use, and not for publication."[66] In other words, the codex format signified
"nonscriptural" to the rabbis.

The early Christians wrote both the Old and the New Testaments in the
codex format. When the New Testament writings refer to the "scriptures,"
using that word (Greek *graphē*) or other terminology such as "the law and
the prophets" or "Moses" (for the Torah) or "David" (for the Psalms) or
"it is written," they often cite the Jewish scriptures—that is, the Septuagint.
These books create the Old Testament as the scriptures that deserve their
own commentary. However, in so doing the New Testament would seem to
have ruled against itself as a collection of scriptures. Thus if the New Testament in codex format comments on the Old Testament—if it is Christian
"oral Torah"—then it cannot be authoritative scripture in its own right.

---

64. Fishbane, "Inner Biblical Exegesis," 36. See also 25, 28.
65. Faur, *Golden Doves*, 103.
66. Saul Lieberman, quoted in Resnick, "The Codex," 11 n. 51. See also Barton, *Holy
Writings, Sacred Text*, 85–89, 95.

However, the Christian Old Testament was also written on codices. Barr disputes the idea that the New Testament is a commentary on the Old Testament and claims that the reverse description would be more accurate:

> The business of the New Testament is not primarily to tell what the Old really means, but to declare a new substance which for the Old was not there, although it was understood that it had prophesied its future coming. . . . It is more correct to say that the Old Testament was used to interpret the situations and events of the New.[67]

In other words, the Old Testament is a Borgesian precursor to the New Testament. This does not resolve the problem, however, since the Old Testament also cannot be both commentary and scripture. In either case, the situation is a contradictory one. Neither testament of the Christian Bible can be both a commentary on the other testament and scripture in its own right. The paradox of inner-biblical exegesis becomes a contradiction for Christians, who must have it both ways.

If the Christians thought of their writings as scriptures, then why did they abandon Jewish practice and write them on codices? Irven Resnick offers an intriguing suggestion:

> While the initial impulse to employ the codex in the primitive Christian community may have arisen from a sincere desire to avoid transgressing the law, an entirely different psychology would have been at work in the gentile Christian world. There it may have been especially in order to demonstrate that the community is no longer bound by the law that the codex was received as the vehicle for Christian sacred texts. What originally may have been an expression of submission to Jewish tradition in another setting became its opposite: an expression of disregard, if not contempt for, the Law. By the time the Church had become a largely gentile community—that is, by about the middle of the second century—Christianity had disavowed the use of the roll for biblical literature.[68]

The Christians changed their view of the codex as an appropriate medium for the scriptures. Perhaps the Christians also abandoned the Jewish distinction between scripture and commentary, and they reinscribed this distinction in the new concept of canon. I argue in chapter 2 that the codex as a material technology makes the practical realization of this concept possible. This in turn produces a situation that accounts for (but does not resolve) many of the intertextual tensions between the two Christian testaments.

---

67. Barr, *Holy Scripture*, 70.
68. Resnick, "The Codex," 12.

Chapter 2 _____

THE TECHNOLOGY OF TEXT

_____

Oral vs. Written Text

The semiotics of canon is not only concerned with questions of the control of meaning. Physical transformations of text coincide with and even produce, in various ways, the ideological features and problems described in chapter 1. The question of canon therefore also concerns the technology of the book: the production, maintenance, and distribution of the physical text. This is a frequently overlooked question in canon studies, where the canon is treated largely as a disembodied, conceptual entity. Only recently has the question of the material form of canonical texts, as an important dimension of the canon itself, begun to be addressed by biblical scholars.[1]

In a purely oral culture, canon is unnecessary. Indeed, a canon would be inconceivable in a culture in which writing is unknown. If there is anything like canon in preliterate oral culture, it must serve a somewhat different purpose, as well as being identified and understood in different ways. The spoken word is too mobile and slippery ever to be fixed in a canon. In an oral culture, there may be certain stories that "everyone knows." Some of the stories would have authoritative status, and they would define the community's identity. However, these stories would not form a self-explanatory whole. Furthermore, even when spoken words become "fixed" in the repetitious verbal formulas, rhyme or rhythm, and stereotypical images that characterize ancient epic poetry, still the concept of an unchanging text, distinct from the immediate and reciprocal presence of the face-to-face encounter, is foreign to an oral culture. The truth and authority of the spoken word are determined within the "live" situation of immediate encounter between present speaker and present audience—such as the "winged words" of the heroes of Greek mythology or the "word of the Lord" of Israelite prophets. Speech is a matter of face-to-face "presence." The question of authority is very real in oral culture, but the oral text is unavoidably fluid and fleeting.

_____

1. For example, Jaffee, "The Oral-Cultural Content" and "A Rabbinic Ontology"; and Gamble, *Books and Readers* and "The Codex." See also the important work of Ong, *Presence* and *Interfaces*.

In an oral culture, the medium is always the human body itself, especially the mouth, the ear, the face, the gesture. In a purely oral culture, language would seem quite natural, since spoken language and its gestural equivalents are largely coterminous with the adult human race. Orality/aurality requires only "natural tools," faculties built into the normal human body, and a "natural language" that children acquire more or less automatically from the larger human society about them. Language itself is artificial, but the desire to speak seems to be innate in humans. Adult humans of normal abilities are skilled in both body and verbal language. No special training or external tools are required.

Oral culture especially values individuals who have great skill with the spoken word: the trickster, con artist, or person of cunning such as Odysseus or Jacob. In oral culture, rhetoric develops into a noble field of study and a valuable skill. When purely oral culture comes to an end, the human body becomes less important, and the media of communication are partly separated from the body.[2] At the same time, in the post-oral world the rhetorically skilled orator is increasingly regarded as a politician, salesperson, or publicist, more and more to be mistrusted and even despised.

The written manuscript requires eyes and hands in addition to, and in some respects instead of, voices and ears. While the body remains necessary to read the words and to hold the pen, the written text has been separated from the human body in a way that "live" spoken words cannot be. This is both a drawback and a feature. The written text is dead and cannot speak for itself, but it can be copied and disseminated over a wide geographical area, and it can survive the limitations of human life and memory. Perhaps more important, for our purposes anyway, the written text demands technology in addition to that which is natural to most human beings.

Writing requires more than just the human body; it requires a surface to be written on and something to write with. This additional technology of the written text demands the additional skills of reading and writing. These skills are highly artificial in comparison to speaking and listening, and they provide their possessors with power that others do not have.[3] In the modern world, we take these skills for granted, but reading and writing are neither "natural" nor "normal." The skills of reading and writing make evident the artificiality of all language. No matter how transparent and effortless the skills of reading and writing may seem to those of us who have been using them for many years, there is nothing "automatic" about the learning of them. The lack of these skills remains an obstacle to many others.

Along with the written stage of mediation in communication comes a specialized class of technicians: the scribes. Scribal expertise is limited to a few, and literacy appears to the many as a mysterious and suspicious

---

2. Debray, *Media Manifestos*, 36.
3. Lévi-Strauss, *Tristes Tropiques*, 289–93.

but increasingly necessary activity. Even in this later phase of oral culture, sometimes called chirographic or manuscript culture, reading remains (like storytelling in the purely oral phase before it) a primarily collective and oral phenomenon, for the relatively few skilled readers usually read aloud to primarily illiterate groups. Reading in the ancient world was generally practiced as an "oral" phenomenon.[4]

Jacques Derrida has demonstrated the phenomenological priority of writing to speech. Writing makes evident the *différance* that is always already "present" in the spoken word.[5] This does not contradict the historical and cultural priority of the spoken word. Speech provides the historical-cultural context in which writing becomes possible. Writing never eliminates speech, and even in the contemporary world, the spoken word remains the basic form of human communication. Nevertheless writing does replace speech in certain important ways. Writing is a technology that is of greatest value in the absence of the writer. The demand for writing comes from the increasing number of situations in which face-to-face encounter with the originating voice is not possible. You do not usually write a letter or a book, a note or a shopping list, unless the anticipated recipient of the writing (even if it is yourself, as in the case of the note and the list) is not present, either in space or in time. You do not usually copy a text, either for archival purposes or to pass on to someone else, unless it is to be read in your absence.

In the case of the Jewish scriptures, this situation of absence arose during periods of exile, when the Israelite community was decentered and spread out over a large territory. The loss of the promised land and of the temple in Jerusalem were great shocks to the cultural identity of the exiled people. Writing thus provided a valuable way to maintain communal ties and to sustain the stories and traditions over the distances involved. It is in relation to these circumstances of exile and diaspora that the Torah and later the Prophets and finally the Writings were assembled and eventually "closed."

Anxiety about Writing

When the oral word must be supplemented or even replaced entirely by the written word, some sort of external guarantee is required. However, the written text cannot guarantee its own truth or authority. As a result, oral cultures are suspicious of writing. Plato has his hero Socrates complain about the effects of the written word in the *Phaedrus*. Socrates maintains that only by returning the written text to its oral "parent" can the meaning be "rescued."[6] The most reliable text is the direct, unmediated spoken word.

---

4. Davies, *Scribes and Schools*, provides a valuable survey of ancient Near Eastern scribal practices. See also Lévi-Strauss, *Tristes Tropiques*, 290.

5. Derrida, *Speech*, esp. 129–60. See also *Of Grammatology*.

6. Plato *Phaedrus*, 97, sec. 276. Plato writes of his own mistrust of writing in the "Seventh Letter" (*Phaedrus*, 112 ff.).

Socrates' comments are peculiarly relevant to Hebrew writings, for the oldest known Hebrew texts of the Jewish scriptures have no vowels and thus are unspeakable and meaningless until they are vocalized, when the appropriate vowels are supplied. This vocalization inevitably involves interpretation and thus identification of the correct words. The Hebrew texts must be returned to a state of orality before they can mean anything. In contrast, in Greek texts, vowels are already present.

In a purely oral culture, only memory guarantees against textual instability. However, writing is mechanical and anonymous, and the written text is "dead." Writing removes the oral texts from living memory and leaves the reader with the task of understanding. Unlike an oral text, a written text cannot provide its own explanation, for the speaker/author is no longer present, and any written explanation would itself have to be explained, and so on. Socrates describes writing as a "conceit of wisdom" that will result in ignorance.[7]

Written texts also tend to proliferate uncontrollably. Once the text leaves its author's hands, the author no longer has any control over it, or any effect on how the reader will understand the text's meaning. The possibility is inherent in any writing that readers will come to many different and incompatible (mis)understandings of the written texts. The anxiety aroused by this possibility eventually results in the widespread modern belief that the author's intentions determine the meaning of the written text. Belief in the author's intention supports a reading strategy whereby the reader seeks to compensate for the absence of the author. It is a symptom of the increasing distance between writer and reader.

An ancient instance of anxiety about the insecurity of written texts appears in the story in 2 Kings 22. This story presents an account of writing at the very moment that it becomes "scripture"—that is, an authoritative work. A scroll is discovered during the repair of the temple in the time of King Josiah. Even though the scroll is initially announced to be "the book of the law" (22:8), the discovery must be ratified by the high priest and the king (22:11) and, finally, by God, speaking through the presumably oral pronouncement of the prophetess Huldah (22:15 ff.). Once ratified, the newly discovered book provokes Josiah's actions to reaffirm the covenant (23:3) and to eradicate idolatry, as told in the story's sequel.

Whether or not the story in 2 Kings 22 has any historical basis, it reflects considerable anxiety about both the dangers of and the necessity for written texts. The story's characters (and perhaps also its readers) are anxious to secure the newly found scroll against the dangers that inevitably accompany any written text, both profane and sacred ones. The concept of authoritative scripture arises under circumstances when writing becomes

---

7. Plato *Phaedrus*, 96–97, sec. 275. See also Jaffee, "A Rabbinic Ontology," 537; Derrida, *Dissemination*, 61 ff. On writing as falsehood, see Lévi-Strauss, *Tristes Tropiques*, 293.

indispensable. This story is narrated as happening in Jerusalem just prior to the Babylonian exile, and it closely associates the newly discovered scroll with exile: "Thus says the LORD, Behold, I will bring evil upon this place and upon its inhabitants, all the words of the book which the king of Judah has read" (2 Kings 22:16). If this "book of the law" is some form of the book of Deuteronomy, as many scholars have suggested, then the "evil" described in the book probably connotes the Babylonian exile (see Deuteronomy 4:25–31, etc.), understood as God's punishment of Judah for idolatry and breaking the covenant. God's anger against the people of Jerusalem has arisen "because our fathers have not obeyed the words of *this book,* to do according to *all that is written* concerning us" (2 Kings 22:13, emphasis added).

The anxiety Socrates felt about writing is also felt by the apostle Paul, who favors the writing of "the Spirit of the living God, not on tablets of stone but on tablets of human hearts" over against the "written code [that] kills" (2 Corinthians 3:3, 6), which is discussed further in chapter 6. Such anxiety appears in even more explicit form in the apocryphal story in 2 Esdras 14, in which Ezra rewrites the lost scrolls of the Torah. This story is set in the period following the return from the Babylonian exile, but it was probably written after the destruction of the second temple by the Romans. In either case, it concerns a time of crisis and severe threat to community identity. Ezra, who is explicitly compared to Moses (14:3–6), says to the "Most High,"

> For thy law has been burned, and so no one knows the things which have been done or will be done by thee. If then I have found favor before thee, send the Holy Spirit into me, and I will write everything that has happened in the world from the beginning, the things which were written in thy law, that men may be able to find the path, and that those who wish to live in the last days may live. (2 Esdras 14:21–22)

Divine inspiration is represented as a cup that Ezra drinks, after which "my heart poured forth understanding, and wisdom increased in my breast, for my *spirit retained its memory;* and *my mouth was opened,* and was no longer closed" (2 Esdras 14:40–41, emphasis added). Ezra dictates the lost texts to five men, who inscribe them "in characters which they did not know" (14:42). This miracle would seem to guarantee the accuracy of the texts' transcription. Once again the living oral word resuscitates dead written words, and God, through a faithful scribe, is able to guarantee the security of the scripture. Through Ezra, God becomes the Socratic "parent" who rescues the written text. This story also emphasizes the importance of apocryphal writings—such as 2 Esdras itself—as sources of divine revelation.

The technology of writing makes "the scriptures" both possible and desirable. The concept of authoritative texts arises from the need to alleviate anxiety about writing. However, neither prophetic ratification nor miraculous dictation can satisfy this desire. When the written text is regarded as authoritative scripture, the anxiety is only exacerbated. No matter how authoritative they are, the scriptures remain written texts—that is, inherently incomplete and unable to explain themselves.

Once the oral traditions are translated into written form, they provoke a theological (ideological) response, which culminates eventually in the intertextual formation of canon.[8] The desire for canon arises because the living oral texts have "died"—that is, because they have become scripture. The desire is to bring those dead written texts back to "life." The need for a canon arises from the incompleteness of the texts, which becomes evident when they are "translated" from living oral traditions into inert writings, when they are separated from their "parent." Canon is the attempt to repair in writing the damage done by writing, to reproduce in the new medium an effect similar to that of oral performance. The sacred text must be a complete book, and its authority must be evident.

The biblical canon also arises from the desire to control the free dissemination of those writings. Because it is hermeneutically incomplete, every written text invites and indeed demands rewriting. On one hand, rewriting sometimes takes the form of physical alteration of a copy by a scribe who is either careless or deliberately trying to "correct" what appears to be a defective original text. Deliberate rewriting would include the two different endings added to "complete" the gospel of Mark as well as the various additions to the gospel of John. Numerous other variants among the oldest biblical manuscripts provide additional evidence of physical rewriting of the scriptures, both deliberate and accidental. Some ancient scribes apparently felt no obligation to copy the text exactly. Kurt Aland and Barbara Aland claim that there were wide variations in the copying of Greek writings that were eventually accepted into the New Testament, from word-by-word copies to others that featured liberal substitution of synonyms, "correction" of "errors," and so forth, until at least the closing of the canon.[9]

In the Mediterranean culture of the early common era, literacy remained a specialized skill, and nonliteracy was the norm. Nevertheless, there was already sufficient demand for written texts that a rudimentary "publishing industry" was flourishing. According to Harry Gamble, one important means of publication in this preprinting era was to encourage others to make their own copies of desired texts. In addition, authors themselves sometimes produced multiple copies of their books, with inevitable variations in the texts.[10] Written texts were fluid, at least during the early stages of copying, and the modern concepts of a standard edition or an author's autograph are unthinkable in this context. Uncontrolled dissemination of written texts

8. See Funk, *Parables and Presence,* 164.
9. Aland and Aland, *Text,* 64.
10. Gamble, *Books and Readers,* 82 ff., 118–20, 134–37.

was not then regarded, as it would be today, as plagiarism or a violation of copyright, for these concepts did not yet exist. However, uncontrolled reproduction of texts created a need to secure important texts against the "corruptions" that are themselves likely because, as Socrates said, the written text is separated from its "parent," the spoken word. The winged word of living speech could not be corrupted, at least not in that way. Only the dead word of writing could be.

On the other hand, and far more commonly, rewriting of a text also takes the form of an accepted interpretation or explanation that determines "what the words really mean." This is ideology at work. The physical signifier itself is not altered by this nonphysical rewriting, but the conceptual signified is carefully controlled by it. This nonphysical or conceptual rewriting of the text may be even more potent than the physical kind because it is invisible. Because of it, readers are unable to understand the text in any other way. The established reading is taken to be "natural" or "obvious," and anyone who reads otherwise is thought to be either demented or wicked.

Both of these kinds of rewritings are inevitable and perhaps even desirable. Nevertheless, once the texts become scripture—that is, once they become authoritative—then physical rewriting of the text must be controlled or stopped. The authority of the text must be guaranteed. The canonizing of a text is an attempt to eliminate the frailty and the vulnerability of the written text. Ideally, the canon guards against uncontrolled physical rewriting of the text by freezing the list of authoritative texts and the physical wording of the texts involved. In reality, during the preprint period, copying errors inevitably continue to occur. Furthermore, even after the printing press effectively eliminates these errors, ideological support for translation of the Bible and especially the preference of many Christians for "free," nonliteral translations and paraphrases of the Bible raise serious questions about the stability of the text of the canon, which will be pursued further in chapter 3.

Canonization is also an important way that nonphysical rewriting of the text is directed and limited. The biblical canon presents itself as an intertextual network that is self-explanatory. The canon supposedly controls its own reading; it is its own ideological mechanism. However, control of biblical meaning by this intertextual network is only partly successful, and the canonical collection fails as a self-sufficient commentary on its component texts. The canonized texts are still writings, and as writings they are inevitably incomplete. The incompleteness of the written text demands an overt, extratextual commentary to further control and restrict the conceptual rewriting of the sacred books by its readers—that is, an exegesis or explication of what the text means. Jewish or Christian theology saves the canon's authority by reinforcing it with extracanonical commentary.

Anxiety about the dangers that accompany the written word appears in a tradition of commentaries that begins prior to the completion of the Jewish scriptures and does not end with the closing of the canon. Jewish tradition regards these commentaries as "oral Torah." Even though it is not scripture, the oral Torah is required to complete the written Torah.

> In the discipleship-communities of the Sages Oral Torah was a form of tradition that overcame anything written or spoken.... The completion of texts, their genuine mobilization as a communication of Torah, was deferred beyond the linguistic word itself to the embodiment of the text in the form of a human act.[11]

Perhaps because of its logocentric understanding of text, Christianity has nothing quite like oral Torah. Nevertheless, the early Christians also began to generate a body of commentaries on their scriptures that has not yet reached an end. These commentary traditions complement and continue the attempt to secure and complete the authoritative written texts. They are symptoms of the power and influence of the canon: "[I]t is a peculiar property of canons that they constitute not just a community, but also a class of experts, who manipulate canon to expound and administer."[12] However, insofar as the commentaries are themselves also written, they are subject to the same incompleteness as any other writing. Any written attempt to state what the text means will itself have to be explained by yet another commentary, and so on. The demand for commentary and for completeness that is provoked in the written text is endless.

Codex and Canon

The Christian double canon—both the New and the Old Testaments—emerges at the same time that the codex becomes a significant format of book construction. The shift from scroll to codex is an important shift in the technology of book production. The codex is the format of the modern printed book, which features separate pages bound together at one edge. It is distinct from the much older scroll format, in which a number of pages are attached edge to edge to form a long strip, which was usually rolled up around a stick fastened at one end. Though the codex format was not invented by Christians, Colin Roberts and T. C. Skeat have shown that the codex is nevertheless especially associated with emerging Christianity.

Although Jews and others were familiar with the codex, the scroll format for books remained in widespread use among non-Christians long after the codex had become the standard format for Christian texts. The codex was first used in the Mediterranean world for informal writings, but not finished texts. Taking notes on codex tablets was widespread practice, but the *publishing* of books in codex format was unusual. In contrast, almost all of the

---

11. Jaffee, "A Rabbinic Ontology," 542. See also ibid., 541; and Barton, *Holy Writings, Sacred Text*, 100–101, 125, 190 n. 18.
12. Halpern, "Fallacies Intentional and Canonical."

ancient Christian manuscripts now known are in codex form, including the very oldest ones, and Christian scrolls are extremely rare.

There appears to be a relationship between the codex format and the Christian canon, but the exact nature of that relationship remains a mystery. Straightforward causality in either direction is improbable. Given the considerable ideological diversity of the early Christian groups, it is odd that they should generally agree on a common physical format for their writings. Another mystery, which may also have canonical or at least scriptural implications, concerns the widespread use of *nomina sacra*—special abbreviations for certain names and terms, especially "Jesus," "lord," "God," and "christ"—in early Christian texts.[13] The coincidence of these developments is probably not accidental, although the relationship between them has also never been clarified.

The codex format was already in widespread use among Christians well before the canon was closed. Roberts and Skeat explicitly deny that the codex format had any effect on the development of the canon, although they do admit an effect of the codex on smaller collections of gospels or Pauline epistles.[14] Such smaller combinations of gospels or epistles, as well as volumes consisting of a single book, continued to be produced in codex form after the formation of larger collections. However, this is not evidence against the impact of the codex on the canon. Roberts and Skeat also assume that the Jewish canon was already in place prior to the development of the Christian one, as do many earlier scholars. Yet although the Torah was undoubtedly closed by the first century C.E., the remainder of the Jewish canon was not closed until much later.[15] As I argue in chapter 1, an incomplete canon is a self-contradiction, and therefore the canonical status of the Jewish Bible cannot be used as an argument against the influence of the codex on the Christian canon.

Gamble argues that codex collections of epistles provided the core from which the New Testament canon developed.[16] The codex does not require that multiple books be physically bound together, but it does make the binding together of those books more feasible. Indeed, a single volume of the Christian Bible would be unusable in a scroll and perhaps unthinkable in a world that knew only the scroll format of the book. Although "single volume" is by no means equivalent to "canon," the singleness of the Christian Bible codex is an important aspect of its significance as canon:

> [I]n some ways the codex probably assisted in the conception and formation of a canon of Christian scripture. This type of book provided

---

13. See Roberts and Skeat, *Birth of the Codex*, 57; and Roberts, *Manuscript, Society*, 26 ff. See also Hurtado, "Origin of the *Nomina Sacra.*"
14. Roberts and Skeat, *Birth of the Codex*, 62 ff.
15. Barton, *Oracles of God*, 57.
16. Gamble, *Books and Readers*, 58 ff.

the technical possibility of compassing a series of documents far more extensive than any single roll could contain, and by the end of the second century certain documents were being collectively transcribed on a single codex. Certainly the four Gospels were made available in this way, and so also were the epistles of Paul.... The idea of the exclusive authority of four Gospels, or indeed of a "fourfold Gospel," could find tangible expression only in a codex that contained these and no others, just as the idea that Paul had written to seven churches and no others (and so addressed the Church at large) gained concretion by transcribing the letters together in one codex. The form in turn probably helped to promote and to standardize such collections as well as the rationales behind them. Ultimately, when, in the fourth century, all the writings that the Church had come to value as scripture could be transcribed in a single large codex like Codex Sinaiticus or Codex Vaticanus, the codex gave forceful physical representation to the concept of a canon of scripture, connoting its unity, completeness and exclusivity.[17]

There are several plausible reasons for Christian adoption of the codex format for the scriptures. In each case, the codex itself signifies something about the texts collected in it; it is an intertext or ideology produced by the whole—that is, a canon. All of the following reasons may well have been at work.

1. Roberts and Skeat note that the codex was first used for very practical, mundane sorts of writing—for example, as notebooks used by students or by authors for rough drafts, the finished text of which would be written on a scroll.[18] For ancient readers and writers, the codex occupied a halfway position between speech and writing, and it was not regarded as a real book. Barton maintains that the "oral" status of the codex notebook appealed to Christians during the first two centuries.[19] Irven Resnick adopts a similar view.

2. The early Christian shift from scroll to codex may signify a shift from scripture to commentary. Martin Jaffee cites the claim in the Palestinian Talmud that oral Torah was written in "notebooks," probably codices. Resnick also notes evidence that oral rabbinic commentaries on the scriptures were transcribed in codex form. He claims that this Jewish practice, and not the Roman use of the codex, is the origin of the Christian practice.[20] Resnick suggests that Christians initially adopted the codex out of respect for the Jewish scriptures, which at that time were always written on scrolls.

17. Gamble, "The Codex."
18. Roberts and Skeat, *Birth of the Codex,* 19–23.
19. Barton, *Holy Writings, Sacred Text,* 68–88.
20. Jaffee, "A Rabbinic Ontology," 537; and "The Oral-Cultural Content," 51. Resnick, "The Codex," 3, 11–12.

3. Resnick also suggests that the codex later came to signify to Christians a rejection of the Jewish law. He argues that Christian adoption of the codex and Jewish refusal of the codex both resulted from mutual desire to distinguish their scriptures from one another.[21] If this is the case, then the codex was adopted for one set of ideological reasons, and kept for quite a different set of reasons.

4. The codex format permitted the packaging of a large quantity of text in a smaller, more easily handled configuration than is possible with the scroll. A single codex was more readily portable than a bundle of scrolls and thus better suited to a rapidly expanding religion. Christian adoption of the codex might also reflect continuing belief that the end of the world is coming soon and that there is no time to produce the more polished formal writing associated with the scroll.

5. The codex format made it easier to bind together multiple books in one cover, thus making it possible to publish four gospels or the letters of Paul side by side in one physical volume and eventually to publish two complete testaments side by side in one volume, signifying one message, one Truth.

The different technologies of codex and scroll entail different types of reading. In contrast to the scroll, the codex format makes it easy for the reader to flip back and forth between pages within a book and also between one book and another.[22] Both the scroll and the codex support a linear reading, but unlike the scroll, the codex also encourages that linearity to be interrupted or transformed into a nonsequential zigzag. The codex is a crude form of hypertext. The nonlinearity of the codex format makes explicit the intertextuality of reading. Roland Barthes calls this intertextual zigzag "tmesis" or "skipping," that is, "a seam or flaw resulting from a simple principle of functionality":

> a rhythm is established, casual, unconcerned with the *integrity* of the text; our very avidity for knowledge impels us to skim or skip certain passages . . . in order to get more quickly to the warmer parts of the anecdote (which are always its articulations: whatever furthers the solution of the riddle, the revelation of fate) . . . it does not occur at the level of the structure of languages but only at the moment of their consumption.[23]

However, nonlinear readings are not peculiarly Christian. Rabbinic midrash also encourages zigzag readings, and the Jews used codex notebooks to transcribe oral Torah "for unofficial use." The Talmud itself is another

---

21. Resnick, "The Codex," 7–10.
22. Kermode, "Plain Sense," 182–85.
23. Barthes, *Pleasure*, 10–11, his emphasis.

form of nonlinear text.[24] The textual juxtapositions that characterize the Talmud are nonlinear and hypertextual, but it is a different sort of hypertext than the Christian double canon in one codex. Perhaps the temporal coincidence of the writing down of the Talmudic traditions and the spread of early Christian biblical codices is not accidental. The Talmud may have provided an alternative nonlinearity to that of the Christian Bible.

The ideological dangers of the codex format are considerable. The nonlinear zigzag fails to respect the canonical sequence of texts: in effect, this type of reading allows Prophet to precede Torah, New Testament to precede Old Testament, the Revelation of John to precede the book of Genesis. The intertextuality of the zigzag reading does not necessarily conform to the ideological control of the canon. Thus the codex format carries within it the potential for disintegration of the canon. Despite these dangers, the codex also makes it technically possible to include both canons in one physical book, and in so doing to avoid confrontation with the dilemma of a double canon. The sort of nonlinear reading permitted by the codex format would appeal to anyone who wanted to see how one text might "fulfill" or otherwise connect to another text. The practical convenience of the codex for orthodox nonlinear readings such as these would provide a motivation for adopting that format.

As Gamble notes, the single codex of the Christian Bible connotes to many people that it is one single book and that consequently it transmits a single consistent message—that is, that the two testaments and all of the writings in them are in total accord. The canonical writings are holographic—that is, every book in the canon connotes the same message. In addition, the codex makes possible the physical representation within the canonical volume itself of a proper sequence of books, and this physical sequence is not unimportant. It is part of the message of the whole collection. For Christianity, the concept of a canon includes not only a comprehensive *list* of books but also a correct *order* in which that list is arranged. This sequencing is already somewhat in place prior to the adoption of the codex, most apparently in the early privileging of the Torah over the prophetic books, but the representation of this sequence must lie outside of the scriptures themselves until they are bound together in a single codex.

Until it was possible to actually bind all of the canonized texts together in a single codex, the canon could be no more than a list of titles of the books to be included, not the books themselves, with the exception of very short books that could be written together on a single scroll, such as the Minor Prophets. The entire Jewish scriptures on a single scroll would be

---

24. Jaffee refers to "scrolls or other sorts of written surfaces" on which the Mishnah was written ("A Rabbinic Ontology," 534; "The Oral-Cultural Content," 32). The oldest extant fragments from the Mishnah (from the seventh century) are on scrolls, although by the twelfth or thirteenth centuries the Talmud was also written on codices. See also Roberts and Skeat, *Birth of the Codex*, 59–60.

too large for any reader to manage, and the Christian Bible would be even worse. Gamble notes that only by the fourth century C.E.—the same period that a recognizable Christian canon first appears—had the technology of manufacturing codices developed enough to permit a single volume as large as the complete Christian Bible.[25]

Whether or not the codex format actually contributed to the ideology of the Christian double canon, as a technology it made that canon practically possible. The codex permitted the production of an actual physical object—a *single* volume—that is the Christian *double* canon. It made clear the differences of sequence between the Old Testament and the Jewish scriptures in a way that a bundle of scrolls could not. The sequencing of the canonical books was both practical and ideological, which is most apparent in the placement of the New Testament writings after the Old Testament writings. By enclosing all of the canonical books within a single binding, the codex signifies the overcoming or even the nonexistence of problems associated with the physical aspects of the written text, especially the loss of the immediate presence of the living speaker. The codex is itself a machine that makes possible the canon machine. It assembles the complete intertextual network in a format that can be easily used as such—that is, as a (meta)text that explains itself. The codex produces the ideological effect of the double canon even as it conceals that double canon in a single volume.

The Printed Text

The Bible was canonized because of the demands of chirographic culture, which is also known as manuscript or scribal culture. In this late phase of oral culture, written books and the attendant technology of writing and reading were known. Books were written and copied by hand, and therefore their production was labor-intensive by modern standards. Even in the scriptoria, piecework "assembly lines" where multiple copies were quickly produced by groups of scribes, each word of each text had to be copied by a human being. During this time, literacy rates and therefore the demand for books tended to be low. Books were relatively expensive. Reading and writing were regarded as valuable skills, but they were not thought to be universally necessary, any more than we think today that everyone should be able to operate a printing press or manage a computer network. In the ancient world, wealthy or powerful people were not necessarily literate, but they were able to hire scribes to read and write for them, much as a modern executive hires secretaries or computer network managers.

With the arrival of print culture, so called because of the central importance for it of texts produced on movable type printing presses, a new writing technology becomes available to produce and therefore to control

---

25. Gamble, *Books and Readers*, 67.

the text.[26] In print culture, the scribes are replaced by new elite groups of technicians. A complicated and expensive machine, the printing press requires expert operators. The press and its operators are considerably less accessible to the average person in the modern world of print culture than the scribe was in the ancient world of oral culture. The publishing industry that stands between writer and reader in print culture is likewise largely invisible to the reader. It is signified chiefly by the printed book itself, the physical object that by its very presence, among other things, reminds the reader of the writer's absence. The printed text is thus even further removed from the bodily, face-to-face encounter of live speech than is the manuscript. Print culture introduces a further level of technology, added on top of the technology of writing as well as that of speech, which continues to remain necessary.

Further stages of text production are also introduced into the sequence connecting and separating the writer and the reader. The movable type printing press brings with it the professional apparatus of the modern publishing industry: typesetters, press operators, publishers, editors, copyreaders, paper makers, and many more. Each new procedure of text transmission inevitably inserts further social and technological levels (mediations) between the sender and the receiver of the message.

In print culture, the text is no longer a hand-copied manuscript; instead, it is a printed copy run off the press by the hundreds or thousands. The printing press and the manufacture of paper (as opposed to papyrus or parchment, the main writing materials of chirographic culture) make possible the relatively quick, cheap reproduction of numerous exact copies of any printed book or other writing. Unlike the manuscript, which varies in significant detail from one copy to another, the text of each printed copy from a given press run is exactly identical to every other one, word by word and page by page, except for accidental defects in the paper or binding. The printed book is mass-produced and features interchangeable parts—that is, a given page in any copy is exactly the same as it is in any other copy. All printed books are "copies." When every copy of a book is physically the same, the physical aspects of the text become less evident and important.[27] The materiality of the signifier becomes less apparent. The author's "original" drafts become important to collectors and historians, but their interest in those drafts is very different from that of the reader. They value the text, not as a signifier, but as a signified.

The transformations involved in the shift from manuscript to print culture present a serious threat to the canon of scripture. The technology of

---

26. For an extensive survey of the changes associated with or produced by the movable type printing press, see Eisenstein, *Printing Press,* esp. vol. 1, chap. 2. See also Ong, *Presence;* and esp. *Interfaces,* chap. 1.

27. Eisenstein, *Printing Press,* 1:81–82.

printing, along with concurrent radical social transformations,[28] replaces important textual control functions of the canon. The ready availability of cheap printed copies discourages hand copying. Printing maintains the text against "scribal drift" and even encourages removal of scribal corruptions. Elizabeth Eisenstein notes that printing stimulates both the desire to produce vernacular translations of the Bible and also the desire for "corrected" Hebrew, Greek, and Latin editions.[29] Scholarly interest in the history of the text's transmission is promoted. The lively competition of the marketplace for books also encourages Bible publishers to produce error-free texts. However, the net effect of the printing press is to diminish the demand for a canon because the need to secure the physical limits of the individual book and of the canonical list as a whole has already been addressed by circumstances arising from the mechanical reproduction of the texts.

The beginnings of print culture in Europe are often associated with Johannes Gutenberg's printing press and Martin Luther's German translation of the Bible. Eisenstein notes that numerous Bibles, both in Latin and vernacular translations, were printed prior to Luther's version. Another important early use of the printing press was to print papal indulgences.[30] Nevertheless, the Protestant Reformation "reopened" the Christian canon, both by revising the Old Testament and by not revising the New Testament. More important than the specifically Protestant versions of the Bible is the fact that Protestants were apparently unable to completely close the canon again once they opened it. The ideology of the "priesthood of all believers" placed canonical power in the hands of an increasingly literate community with access to the Bible. The eventual emergence of new canons in groups such as the Christian Scientists and Latter-day Saints, and the amorphous expansion of the canon in liberal movements such as Unitarianism, are among the consequences of Protestant reopening of the canon.

Henceforth the security of the canon will always be in doubt. Regardless of the intentions of the Protestant reformers themselves, the "priesthood of all believers" opened the way to individual interpretation. It also implied that each believer should be a reader, and therefore it produced a demand for large numbers of printed texts. Reading became simultaneously an individual and a mass phenomenon. The widespread dissemination of printed texts encouraged the desire for universal literacy, eventually bringing an end to the reign of the scribal elite. The power once associated with the ability to read and write disappeared, or rather it shifted to another set of abilities.[31]

Reading itself changes with the change in technology. The actual tech-

---

28. These transformations include the industrial revolution, the end of feudalism, the rise of the middle class, the exploration of the New World, the rise of the modern university, and so forth. These all play important parts in the modern demise of the canon.

29. Eisenstein, *Printing Press*, 2:686 ff.

30. Ibid., 1:330, 303.

31. Widespread literacy by means of compulsory education is accompanied by other features

niques of reading do not change, for the alphabet remains unchanged and a printed codex is still a codex, but the reader's relation to the text changes. Print culture is private, individualized: the reader sits quietly, alone with a book. This is distinctly unlike the reading of texts, and especially of the scriptures, that characterized the earlier stage of the handwritten manuscript, not to mention the communally shared, traditional performances of purely oral culture. In the context of chirographic culture, reading was usually done out loud and in public places to groups of people. Reading was still an oral process. When everyone becomes a scribe, writing loses its mysterious power. Print culture requires and eventually creates a large reading audience to support it. Reading as a skill becomes available to nearly everyone, and the encounter with the text becomes a private matter, an experience that each person has all alone, even though millions of people have had that experience. Just as the publisher takes control over the book's editing, printing, and distribution, so the reader takes control over the book's meaning.

Print culture "desacralizes" the written text.[32] Reading and writing themselves become "easier" and more "natural," even as the process of publishing a text becomes more technically elaborate. This privatization of reading further weakens the hold of canon on the beliefs of the reader.[33] Private reading loosens the authority of the text, for that authority is less and less derived from some commonly accepted creed or commentary tradition and more and more dependent on the personal choice of the reader. In print culture, no one can successfully dictate how the text should be read. Both the content and the meaning of the canon become matters for the reader's personal beliefs, and readers increasingly feel free to pick and choose the "canon within the canon" that best pleases them.

The publishing industry becomes an alternative canonical force, for the technology of the printing press guarantees the stability of the printed text itself. In addition to the changes noted above, substantial economic changes are also associated with the transition to printing. The content and physical arrangement of the book fall more and more into the hands of the publishers, whose interests are likely to be in sales and profits more than clearly theological matters. The press itself requires capital investment and technical expertise, and its product can also be mass-produced, far beyond the levels of the most productive scriptoria. The printed text is intrinsically a mass phenomenon, and widespread literacy is required to generate demand for books, as well as systems of sales and distribution to supply that demand, on a scale much larger than the handwritten manuscript ever entailed. Print culture mass-produces not only books but also readers. This also reduces Christian control over the canonical texts.

---

of modern capitalism, including "extension of military service and the systematization of the proletariat" (Lévi-Strauss, *Tristes Tropiques*, 293).

32. Debray, *Media Manifestos*, 161.

33. See Jameson, *Postmodernism*, 389.

Both the technical ability to produce quickly and cheaply many copies of a book and the availability of that printed book to many people in exactly identical copies raise legal and economic questions of intellectual property. Economic incentives give publishers reason to guard against unlawful copying. Eisenstein details the close association between emerging capitalism and the early printing press. Concepts of intellectual property correspond to both the increasing commercialization of publishing and the increased privatization of reading.[34] The book has many potential owners, and with the rise of modern economic systems, not only the individual texts but also the right to make copies of the text can be owned. The author gets the responsibility for having written the book, and maybe some royalties from its sale. The reader buys a copy of the book to do with as she wishes, except that she may not make further copies to sell to others. The publisher (who may be the author, but increasingly is not) holds the copyright, which is the legal right to make and sell copies or otherwise dispose of the book. As a result, the dissemination of the text is more tightly controlled than it was previously.

The desire to guarantee the authority of the text continues to operate within reading communities, but in print culture this need is increasingly addressed by laws governing copyright and ethical codes that prohibit plagiarism. The development and wide acceptance of such rules further indicate that the concept of canon as a guarantee of authority and completeness has become unnecessary. The mechanism of the biblical canon initially appeared as a way to secure property of the Christian Church—that is, the Bible—against heretics, Jews, and other opponents of right belief. In print culture, the security that canon provides for the biblical texts begins to crumble because it is replaced by other types of security, other semiotic machines.

The churches still claim that they own the Bible. Nevertheless, even though Bibles are now freely given away, modern translations and editions of the Bible are also copyrighted, often by church organizations. The Bible has become another item to be bought and sold in a capitalist economy. In the modern world of print culture, the Bible must compete as one book among many others on the shelves of booksellers. For the most part, the Bible continues to be printed as a single codex, although modern editions often contain additional noncanonical matter (such as footnotes, chapter or page headings, or commentary articles) alongside the canonical texts. This blurs the canonical distinction between scripture and nonscripture. An extreme case of this is the Scholars Version of the Bible, in which one volume devoted to the gospels includes the noncanonical gospel of Thomas along with the four biblical gospels, copyrighted by a secular publisher.[35] This is another example of the "opening" of the canon made possible by print culture.

---

34. See Eisenstein, *Printing Press,* 1:120 n. 239
35. Funk et al., *Five Gospels.*

The Digital Bible

The personal computer and private telephone line, along with related electronic devices (especially radio, television, and electronic recording technologies), open up revolutionary possibilities for communication and publication that have not yet been fully explored. With the arrival of printed text, everyone became a scribe; so now with the advent of digital or electronic text, everyone can become a publisher. The writer no longer needs the large-scale investment of the publishing industry in order to make public her work, and anyone who can afford a personal computer and access to the World Wide Web can both prepare text and disseminate that text to a potentially global audience.

However, this electronic privatization of publishing is illusory. The World Wide Web can be accessed in complete privacy, like a printed book, but the individual's use of the World Wide Web (as a "surfer") can be detected and traced by others, and in this way it is public, almost "oral." The World Wide Web and most of the countless texts available on it are simultaneously available to many millions of people around the world. Attracting the attention of some portion of that online audience remains a problem, and it is into this niche that traditional print publishers have already begun to move, along with a new breed of "web publishers" providing sophisticated "search engines."

The electronic digitization of text requires the extension on a global scale of the economic and technological base that makes the electronic medium possible. Even the simplest computer requires a huge industrial and organizational support structure, both for its manufacture and for the software that runs on it. The manufacture and maintenance of computers have become so intricate that some of it can only be done by other computers. Computers also require electricity to power them and telephone lines (or their equivalent) to connect them together. The production of computers, telephones, and related equipment, as well as the formation of international communications systems connecting them together, requires massive economic and technological investment. The industrial and organizational base required for electronic culture is much more extensive than that of print culture.

Nevertheless, just as the publishing industry is relatively invisible to the average reader, so the computer and telecommunications industries are relatively invisible to the computer or telephone user. We only become aware of these infrastructures because of the intense competition between different manufacturers and service providers, or when the systems break down. What is most visible is the local computer and telephone equipment itself, which again adds further layers to the semiotic process. As in previous culture-media shifts, electronic culture democratizes one set of artificial skills (those of the scribe and the printer) even as it introduces yet another level of technological expertise, in this case, hardware and software design skills that

are reserved for yet another elite. Also required are highly trained experts
to build and service the complicated electronic machinery. Once again, the
new medium leads to a shift in the power to send and receive messages.

In other ways, the digital media revolution suggests a return to scribal,
manuscript culture.[36] E-mail is in some respects more "oral" than written. The World Wide Web site is in effect a digital scriptorium. The online
page becomes the electronic automated version of the manuscript reader's
recitation of the text in the scriptorium, where a room full of scribes simultaneously transform a single text (itself probably a copy) into numerous
handwritten copies. Now a Web page located at a single online site may
be downloaded to computers anywhere, and nearly instantaneously. The
transmission of text through individual copying once again becomes a way
of publishing, although the copies are now made automatically at high speed
and low cost. The digital nature of the text means that each copy is an exact
duplicate of the source text, unless it is modified by its recipient. There are
no inadvertent scribal errors.

The handwritten manuscripts of the biblical texts were frequently altered
by the scribes who copied them. Canon was an attempt to guard against
such alterations. Once a book was canonized, it was recognized as authoritative, and deliberate modification was not permitted. The printing of books
usurped the text-stabilizing function performed by the biblical canon, and
thus the printing press reduced the need for the canon. The technology of
the printing press effectively protected the printed text from large-scale, uncontrolled changes, whether they took the form of pirating, censorship, or
vandalism. The coincident development of legal and ethical strictures regarding copyright and plagiarism provided further secular security for the
printed texts.

In electronic culture, the threats to the canon posed by print culture grow
even stronger. Like the handwritten manuscript, electronic text can be easily
modified, but these modifications will generally be deliberate "corrections"
or "corruptions" of the text. The digitizing of text makes it possible for
nearly anyone to prepare, copy, or modify texts, skills that were formerly
the property of a relative few. Anyone with a computer can physically rewrite
the digital text in any way. With readily available software, you could go
through the entire Bible and replace the word "God" with the word "Dog,"
nearly effortlessly and in a matter of a few minutes. More complex and
theologically substantial revisions would not require much longer or greater
effort. No longer is "the canon within the canon" just an abstraction. Adding
books to or deleting them from the canon is as simple as copying or deleting
the appropriate files. Any reader can create her own canon and modify it
at any time, much like Thomas Jefferson's famous "cut and paste" Bible,
only much more easily. The distinction between commentary and scripture

---

36. See Ong, *Presence*, 91, 260.

is erased, once again threatening the stability of the texts in the biblical canon and representing a further loss of security for the canon as a whole.

The concept of intellectual property that is so important to print culture—laws of copyright, rules against plagiarism—is also seriously threatened by the new technology, and the modern understanding of intellectual property will have to be substantially transformed if the concept is to survive at all. Maintaining textual integrity in the face of electronic challenges may be a continuing role to be played by the canon. As the World Wide Web increasingly replaces traditional hard-copy sources for texts such as the Bible, something rather like "scribal drift" appears again. The concept of the "original text" loses all value. Altered copies of popular texts are as likely to proliferate online and via user downloads as are unaltered copies, unless some way is available to discriminate among them.

As long as "correct" copies of the digitized text are kept in secure archives, their integrity is safe. Questions such as which World Wide Web site actually has the "correct" texts, how secure the texts really are, and how readily available the texts are to the reading public will become important. This too will change the function of the canon, if not its contents. The canon of the Bible on the World Wide Web is not the same canon as that of the printed Bible, just as printed Bibles are not the same as manuscript Bibles, and just as the Jewish scriptures and the Old Testament are not the same.

Although it would be possible to place the entire Bible in a single digital text file, and thus maintain the appearance of the codex as a single physical volume, it is more practical to put each of the biblical books in its own digital file, much like the separate scrolls of antiquity. This of course means that the sequence of books in the canon may be radically altered. Except in cases where more than one book is written on a single scroll, the ancient scrolls have no inherent sequence, and the sequence must be defined by some external mechanism. Although Jews and Christians differ about the sequence, the codex enforces a sequence of books within a single volume, a sequence that becomes significant, if it was not already. The Torah precedes the Writings, and the Old Testament comes before the New Testament.

In contrast, if the file names in a directory of digitized canonical books correspond to the book names, then (in English) Exodus comes before Genesis, and Daniel comes before either of them! And 1 Chronicles precedes them all. Unless the respective files are kept in separate directories, Old Testament and New Testament books are thoroughly mixed up. The actual physical order in which the computer stores the files on the disk is determined by the computer, but the reader is not usually aware of that, nor is the sequence on the disk usually significant in the reader's access to the text. In the digital Bible, the sequence of books becomes arbitrary and essentially meaningless, for depending on the software and hardware used, multiple files may be accessed at once.

Although the smallest computers suitable for accessing text are no larger

than a medium-sized paperback book, they are capable of storing and re-
trieving substantial libraries. Skipping back and forth between computer files
is much easier and faster than it is with any codex. Searching for specific
text strings is a simple and thorough procedure. The computer overlooks
nothing. With the advent of sophisticated parsing software, traditional Bible
concordances and the ideological control that they exercised over text re-
trieval will soon be extinct. The user can create a complete, accurate, and
specialized index in seconds. Advanced research programs and World Wide
Web pages featuring multiple translations of the Bible, lexicons, and even
manuscript versions (both digitized text and manuscript page image) enable
nearly instant access to textual information that formerly required many
years of painstaking labor or difficult and expensive travel. Storage and
transportation of the text files are also much easier than for either the scroll
or the codex. The entire Christian Bible, in "plain" text files, uncompressed,
requires less than six megabytes for the Revised Standard Version, and it fits
easily on a few cheap floppy disks or a single small removable hard disk.

The medium may not be the message, but it does profoundly influence
the message. On a computer, the Bible becomes fluid, more like it was in
precanonical days. Neither the physical volume of the codex nor the technological intricacies of the printing press remain as obstacles to the free
alteration of the canon. The materiality of the signifier has disappeared into
glowing pixels on the monitor screen and invisible magnetic or optical variations in the storage medium. The physical texts and even the canon itself
seem to be dissolving. The digital Bible appears in multiple text files, which
can be easily added to, deleted, or modified to suit the reader's preference.
The individualism of the print culture reader's control over the text reaches
a new height. However, a totally individualized canon is no longer a canon.
Canon is necessarily a *community* product.[37] The decomposition and re-
composition of the canon made possible and perhaps inevitable in electronic
culture may lead, not to another canon, but instead to the disappearance
once and for all of any canon.

The reader of a printed book needs the book, working eyesight, proper
light, and the ability to use the book. The latter involves knowing how to
read, knowing the language in question, and understanding how books are
arranged: for example, how chapter and verse numbers function in Bibles.
Today this all seems quite minimal in the way of "operating requirements,"
and to many people in the modern world, these complications are taken for
granted and invisible. Although the printed book stands between the reader
and the writer, it seems to the modern reader that nothing at all stands
between the reader and the book. One can read a printed book without
any additional operating system or hardware. As a result of print culture,
reading has come to seem totally "natural" to us.

---

37. See Sanders, *Canon and Community*.

However, the reader of an electronic text needs all of the above, plus a computer, appropriate software, and possibly access to a network where the text is archived. The computer "reads" the file for the human reader, or in other words, we read the digital book with the aid of the computer. Just as the use of the codex makes apparent the sequence of the canon, so the use of digital text makes apparent the technology of reading. No human being can read digitized text straight from a magnetic or optical recording. Yet at the same time, the physical aspect of the text is less apparent than ever. The reader's interaction with the computer is different than it is with the printed book or the manuscript or the spoken word. The digital words appear on a glowing monitor screen, and the reader manipulates their movement on this screen by means of a keyboard or pointing device. A common interface metaphor for displaying digital text requires the reader to "scroll" through a series of "pages," which in turn are viewed through a "window" on the monitor "screen." This screen is the same one that both connects the user to and separates the user from the larger "world" of the network—also often represented as "pages"—or that displays static or moving images, perhaps simultaneous to its display of the text.

These interface metaphors may be just interim stopgap strategies, and one wonders how long the format of the hard-copy book will survive in competition with this new medium. Perhaps both the codex and the scroll will eventually be replaced by yet another format, not yet imagined but more appropriate to digital text. Perhaps the keyboard and the monitor screen will give way to more efficient or pleasing ways for human beings to interact with the computer. Perhaps text itself will be transformed once again into something nonalphabetic, whether sounds or graphic icons.

Lovers of printed books are horrified by these possibilities, just as Socrates and other ancient thinkers were horrified by written books. Modern bibliophiles argue that computers will never replace books, and that is true, just as written texts have never fully replaced the spoken word and print has not entirely replaced handwriting. Nevertheless, one of the great benefits of computers has been their ability to serve as the eyes, ears, voices, and hands of people who lack one or more of these organs. The natural organs of communication for human beings (eyes, ears, voice, hands) are no longer necessary, for the computer can represent the text to the recipient in various sensory forms.

Some contemporary "cyberpunk" authors and theorists depict a future world in which the human body itself will be dismissed as unnecessary "meat" and even abandoned altogether. If that should ever happen, human beings would exceed even the pure translatability of Pentecost.[38] Human-

---

38. See McCaffery, *Storming the Reality Studio.* The Pentecost story is discussed further in chapter 5, and a cyberpunk novel in which Pentecost figures explicitly is discussed in the conclusion of this book.

ity would then become pure digital "spirit," even as the sheer materiality of text would vanish entirely. The extreme of this view is well criticized by Katherine Hayles. Electronic culture may not have so extreme an effect, but it will make the biblical canon obsolete, at least in the form that it has been known so far.

With each new stage in the technology of text, the previous stage and its products are not abolished but transformed. Oral and handwritten texts are still produced today, and printed texts will continue to be used even after computer networks have become ubiquitous. However, the context in which texts in older media are produced and read has changed profoundly, and so their semiotic function also changes. Although spoken words and handwritten notes retain their daily usefulness, a live poetry performance (not a "reading"!) or the calligraphic skills of a professional scribe play significantly different roles in print culture than they did in oral culture. An analogy might be to the role of the local cobbler or blacksmith in a modern urban environment. We still need cobblers and smiths, but in quite different ways than they were once needed. In electronic culture, the biblical canon as a written codex will continue to exist, but its significance will be quite different. Likewise, the canon as a theological (ideological) mechanism will have to change or die. I will return to this matter in the conclusion of this book.

Chapter 3 _____

IDEOLOGIES OF TRANSLATION

The Problem of Translation

There is a close connection between Christian confidence in the reliability of translation and Christian willingness to resolve or overlook the dilemma of a double canon. Christians are able to ignore or dismiss the dilemma of the double canon in part because Christian adoption of the logocentric view of text permits confidence in the absolute translatability of the Bible. As I noted in chapter 1, the "Greek," or logocentric, view of language stresses the separability of thought and language, and it privileges the conceptual content (signified) of the message over against the physical medium (signifier) of the message. For logocentrism, the meaningful signified of the message is contained within the material text, like whiskey in a bottle. This meaning has been put into the written text by a writer, and it can be removed from the text by a reader. The meaning can also be moved to a different text by a translator. The textual signifier is simply a dispensable transmitting mechanism. In other words, Christians believe that the message contained within the Bible can be separated from the source text signifiers and attached to other, quite different, signifiers with no harmful effect on the signified content. This understanding of the relation between the Bible's message and its textual embodiment plays an important role in the Christian ideology of the canon.

The word "translation" comes from Latin roots meaning "a change of place." I write (some place, some time) and you read (another place, another time), and a kind of translation occurs. The translation of any utterance requires movement both in space and in time. However, that alone is not what is usually meant by translation. Roman Jakobson identifies three distinct types of translation: *intralingual* translation as the rewording or paraphrase of a text using the same language, *interlingual* translation as "translation proper" of a text from one language to another, and *intersemiotic* translation as "an interpretation of verbal signs by means of signs of nonverbal sign systems."[1]

_____

1. Jakobson, *Language and Literature*, 429.

Every translation requires a transfer of meaning and an exchange of signifiers that jeopardize the prospects of communication, for the process of translation may change the substance or the form of the message. A well-known traditional saying identifies the translator as a traitor, one who betrays the original text, rewriting it and turning it into something else. Translation inevitably replaces and therefore betrays the physical source text: "[T]here is in every act of translation—and specially where it succeeds—a touch of treason. Hoarded dreams, patents of life are being taken across the frontier."[2] The translator is a thief, one who steals the message from its former place and places it elsewhere.

The problem of translation concerns the relation of the translated text to its source text. The practical value of translation must always be relative to the needs and situation of the message's recipient. For those who are fluent in the language of the source text, there is no problem of translation. However, for those who are not so fluent, there may be no way to determine the fidelity of a translation. Indeed, it is not at all clear exactly what "fidelity" in translation would be, as I will show below.

Anyone who does not know the language of the source text must depend on translation as a mechanism for communication of the text's message. For this person, translation is a convenience that grows in direct proportion to the importance of the translated text. This reader gains little if any insight into the meaning of the source text through the translation, and instead the translation entirely replaces the source text, which remains unknown. For the reader who does not know the language of the source text, the "bad" translation is a betrayal, a deception or caricature, and the "good" translation is clear, authentic, and authoritative. However, without knowledge of the source text, the reader has no way to know which is which. The translation, whether good or bad, makes the foreign text into a recognizable work. It eliminates the babble/Babel of strangeness and replaces it perfectly with the familiar, the intelligible. As the philosopher Willard Van Orman Quine says, "For translation theory, banal messages are the breath of life."[3]

Written texts most profoundly present the problem of translation. The notion of fidelity to a source text must be quite different in a purely oral culture than it is in a print culture. Written texts raise the question of the translation between thought and speech to a higher degree, for spoken words may be translated into writing, and reading translates written words into speech or thought. The creation of alphabets and writing down of oral traditions make possible, and indeed necessary, the distinction between the linguistic medium (the signifier) and its significant content (the signified). Far more

---

2. Steiner, *After Babel,* 233. See also Derrida, "Des Tours de Babel," 199–200. The connection between translation, (mis)communication, and thievery is dramatized in the character Ermes Marana, in Calvino's novel, *If on a Winter's Night a Traveler.*

3. Quine, *Word and Object,* 69.

than speech, writing permits endless and multiple interpretations of the text, and it turns understanding of the message into misunderstanding. This is the point of Socrates' story of the myth of Theuth in the *Phaedrus:* writing is both powerful and dangerous because in it semiosis is out of control, unlimited. The possibility that translation from speech to writing will transform the words and their meanings beyond recognition threatens the philosopher's search for truth. Anxiety regarding translation is at least as old as the anxiety regarding writing described in chapter 2, and it is another form of the same thing.

Transcription is also translation, and surely this contributes to Socrates' anxiety. Translation from speech into writing requires the addition of a fourth type of translation to Jakobson's three, namely, "intermedial translation." Audio or video recordings of written or spoken text also qualify as intermedial translations, as do digitized (electronic) text. Intermedial translation is as much subject to the betrayal of both signifier and signified as is any other type of translation. It mixes all three of the other types of translation, for it remains within the "same" language but does not involve any rewording of the text, although it does involve a change (both gain and loss) of possible meaning. The crucial difference in intermedial translation appears in the change of physical medium, and since this change is itself nonverbal, intermedial translation is perhaps closest to what Jakobson calls intersemiotic translation. Any translation is a struggle with the material dimensions of language, and intermedial translation especially—because it concerns itself primarily with the physical medium—makes the reader more aware of the materiality of the text. Changing from one medium to another, perhaps even more than translation proper (within a single medium) from one language to another, is always a matter of violence, disruption, and distortion.

Translation and Ideology

People have been translating texts for many thousands of years, but without any assurance that the message sent is in fact the message received. The question of the possibility of translation is crucial for any understanding of language or of scripture. Conversely, questions of the nature, meaning, or authority of scripture are inseparable from the question of translation. Anxiety regarding intermedial translation has already been described. A similar anxiety concerns interlingual translation of the scriptures.

Interlingually translated texts may continue to be regarded as authoritative scriptures, or the process of translation from one language to another may be thought to change the texts so much that they lose their authority. Even when perfect translatability is affirmed, the fear lingers that it will fail. In contemporary global culture, interlingual translation is widely accepted and indeed indispensable in day-to-day life for many people, but readers still tend to regard a source text (whether holy scripture or secular writing) as superior to its translations. The text is believed to be more authoritative when presented in the language in which it was first written than it is in any translated version. This is especially true of scholars, who are usually expected to master the original languages of the texts that they study. Scholars suspect that translation of the text means transformation of the message, that something essential may have been lost or changed in the translation process. Scholars know that translators are thieves.

Two centuries or more after Socrates distinguished between the seminal spoken word that arises from the living dialectic of minds and the poisonous written word that kills the memory, Jewish scribes began to translate the Hebrew scriptures into Greek, producing what is traditionally known as the Septuagint (LXX), the first translation of the Jewish Bible. Contrary legends describe the production of the Septuagint as receiving either divine approval or disapproval. In one story, presented in the ancient "Letter of Aristeas," God favors the act of translation by granting miraculous unanimity to the multiple translations produced by the seventy (or seventy-two) translators. A similar story can also be found in Philo's *Life of Moses*. In the opposing account, God indicates disapproval of the Greek translation by sending unnatural darkness over the earth. The Talmudic tractate *Soferim* describes the evil of the Greek translation as comparable to that of Aaron's golden calf.

During the period that the Septuagint was being translated, alphabetic writing was becoming more and more influential upon the Hellenized Mediterranean world, although oral culture was still dominant and the vast majority of people were nonliterate. It was to this cultural transformation in the technology of text, the transcription or intermedial translation of the ancient traditions, and the attendant threat of loss of their meaning, that Judaism and Christianity—religions for which the written word is extremely important—responded with their different views of the translatability of scripture.[4]

In the oldest stratum of the Jewish scriptures, the story of the tower of Babel (Genesis 11:1–9) tells of an aboriginal loss of a single universal language, which may also be God's language, and of the confusion of all human tongues (see further chapter 5). The story suggests that God's disruption of human speech makes translation both necessary and impossible. The story explicitly asserts that "the language of all the earth" has been "confused"

---

4. Islam also has great concerns about translation of the scriptures. Muslims believe that Allah dictated his revelation through Muhammad in Arabic (in a story not unlike that of Ezra in 2 Esdras 14), and therefore the only true Koran is the Koran in Arabic. Arabic is the one divine language. The transcription of Muhammad's dictation is miraculously accurate, and so there is no fear of loss through intermedial translation. The product of a translation of the Koran into any other language is not holy scripture. For Islam, the problem of translation is eliminated, or rather it is absorbed into the larger hermeneutical problem—the question of the book's meaning.

by God, and it implicitly denies that any human language is the language of God. The multiplicity of human languages is a punishment (or perhaps a gift) from God. The one original language, shared by God and mythic humanity, has been shattered.

The story of Ezra reciting and thus rewriting the Jewish scriptures (2 Esdras 14) situates the production of the canonical texts in the spoken word. Nevertheless, the oldest copies of the Jewish scriptures are themselves unspeakable, for they contain no vowels and little in the way of word divisions or punctuation. These texts could not have been transcribed, except through an intermedial diminution. By themselves, the written Hebrew texts, or "written Torah," are nonsense and dependent upon vocalization for significance. They must be read aloud, spoken, in order to replace the deficient written text and become meaningful, and the "oral Torah," or traditional commentary on the text, is necessary to produce that intermedial translation.

Meaningful language (and theology) arises in relation to unspeakable difference. The written text must be "broken" by speaking it in order for it to become meaningful: "once 'heard' by the children of Israel and processed in their minds, the vocal text is in fact the oral Law."[5] An ignorant gentile can learn to vocalize the Hebrew texts of Torah, but the vocalization won't be right until it is guided by oral Torah. Unless the reader understands what the words mean, she cannot know what the words say. In contrast, the Greek texts of the Septuagint and the New Testament include vowels, and therefore these texts are more easily spoken aloud than unvocalized Hebrew texts could be. They do not explicitly require the supplementary text. All written texts are inherently polysemic, but the gulf between a written Hebrew text and its oral reading is more evident than it is for a vocalized Greek (or English) text.

For Judaism, only the "written" text or scripture can be authoritative. Even after the oral Torah is written down, as in the Talmud, it is still "oral." Nevertheless, Judaism holds the written Torah in creative tension with the oral Torah, and multiple and conflicting interpretations of the scriptures, such as those of the medieval Kabbalists, are tolerated. As early as the Deuteronomic materials, one finds a willingness to play freely with the "written" text in the confidence that the resulting "oral" interpretations are not only permitted but are required, no matter how tangential or contradictory they might be to one another: "[W]ithout vocalization the consonantal text has many [possible] senses, different combinations, and opposite readings."[6] Jewish interpretation of the biblical texts is open to the polysemy

---

5. Faur, *Golden Doves*, 136.
6. R. David ibn Abi Zimra, quoted in Faur, *Golden Doves*, 136. The essays in Hartman and Budick, *Midrash and Literature*, trace rabbinic midrash, considered both as an interpretative activity and as the compilation of the results of that activity, back to its roots in the Hebrew Bible, then through its development following the destruction of the second temple, with special focus on the Haggadah, to its relation to the medieval Kabbalah, and then on into the modern

of the canonical scriptures and to the intertextuality both among them and between them and noncanonical writings. Within rabbinic thought there is a potential for confidence in the face of the intertextual abyss, the possibility of what José Faur calls a "literal theology" and the recognition of what Jacques Derrida calls "the circumcision of the word."[7] The material written text is distinct from its "oral" reading, but the intermedial tension between oral Torah and written Torah serves to emphasize the text's materiality.

Jewish and Christian traditions both permit from very early dates the translation of the language and of the concepts of the Hebrew scriptures. Nevertheless, Jewish tradition reflects ambivalence about the status of the translated texts, as the conflicting legends about the translation of the Septuagint indicate. Hebrew is thought to be the holy language in some Jewish communities, and Jews are divided about the status of the scriptures in translation. Some Jews accept the Septuagint or other translations of the scriptures as "written Torah," authoritative scripture, but others hold that only the Hebrew text is "written."[8] In other words, they regard the translated text as at best a (nonscriptural) commentary on the original text. Interlingual translation is rejected, but intralingual translation is accepted. The fact that the translated texts are vocalized, at least in the case of the Septuagint, may have something to do with this ambivalence. In addition, the preferred status of the Septuagint, over against the Hebrew text, in the early Christian canon further complicates matters, for parts of the Septuagint may have been "corrupted" by Christian translators.

Jewish ambivalence regarding the translatability of the scriptures stands in contrast to Christian acceptance of translation. For Christians there can be no problem of translation.[9] The New Testament gospels represent, in Greek, sayings of Jesus that were supposedly originally spoken in Aramaic or Hebrew. However, there never was a Hebrew or an Aramaic source text of the New Testament gospels. The gospels are from their beginnings already "translated" into Greek, although traces of Aramaic or Hebrew may be found in them at points. Indeed, assuming that the sayings in the gospels were originally oral utterances by Jesus, a double translation has occurred, from speech to writing and also from Aramaic to Greek—that is, a double theft (intermedial and interlingual). On one hand, if translation without loss or alteration of meaning is not possible, then both the sayings themselves and their meanings have been hopelessly lost. The words have been irrecov-

---

period and the emergence of "literature." For contestation of some of these claims, see Green, "Romancing the Tome."

7. Faur, *Golden Doves,* 142; and Derrida, "Shibboleth," 346.

8. Faur, *Golden Doves,* 192; see also Dan, "Midrash and the Dawn of Kabbalah."

9. Conservative Catholics who believe that the Vulgate is inspired by God and superior to all other versions (including ancient Greek and Hebrew manuscripts), as well as Protestant fundamentalists who believe that the King James Version is so inspired, are exceptions to this. However, I doubt that either of these beliefs represents the "oriental" or intertextual view of text.

erably changed. On the other hand, if perfect, absolutely clear translation is possible, then there is no need for anxiety. The spoken words are long gone, but the meaning survives and lives on.

Christian acceptance of translation extends to the Old Testament as well. Evidently the writers of the New Testament texts accepted the Greek Old Testament as "written," for they quote the Old Testament "scriptures" from the Greek translation.[10] Not only do New Testament texts cite the Greek Old Testament as the authoritative "scriptures," but the oldest complete Christian Bible manuscripts include the Septuagint alongside the New Testament. The Old Testament was canonized by the Christians in Greek translation, not in Hebrew. The "Letter of Aristeas" was of special interest to early Christians, many of whom—prior to Jerome at least—believed that the Greek text of the Old Testament was superior to the Hebrew text.[11] The Christian Old Testament was *never* the "Hebrew scriptures"! Philip Davies notes the irony that despite this, contemporary Christian Old Testaments are usually translated from ancient Hebrew manuscripts, not Greek ones, in effect rewriting the Christian Bible.[12] In this way, modern Christian Bibles are double canons all the more!

The Christian Bible was further translated—or rather, translated again—from Greek into Latin, Coptic, and Syriac, beginning in the second century C.E., which suggests that the Greek texts in both testaments were by then regarded as authoritative scripture. Despite this, the New Testament texts may not have been regarded as "written." The wide range of textual variations among the oldest manuscripts of the New Testament writings suggests that at least some early Christian copyists did not regard these texts as "written." In addition, the New Testament texts may have been written to serve as "oral" commentary on the Jewish scriptures. The four distinct and not readily reconcilable gospels are not unlike multiple midrashim—that is, oral Torah. In any case, further translations of the "already translated" Bible indicate that early Christians believed that the nonphysical conceptual contents of the Bible could be passed on indefinitely, regardless of inevitable changes to the physical text. Perhaps Jewish concerns about translation of the scriptures were no longer relevant to the Christians, who were by that time mostly gentiles. The logocentric view of language had by then come to dominate Christianity.

What Can Be Translated?

Logocentrism is quite different from the Jewish distinction between oral and written Torah. Oral Torah is required to supplement and make mean-

---

10. Aland and Aland, *Text*, 52.
11. Sundberg, *Old Testament*, 172 ff.
12. Davies, *Scribes and Schools*, 184.

ingful the written Torah, but oral Torah does not identify a nonphysical meaning contained in and transmitted through the written Torah. Although oral Torah is commentary, it is not an intralingual or metalinguistic translation of "what the written Torah really means." For oral Torah, meaning is intertextual—that is, there is no separate realm of truth or reality outside of the play of texts. In contrast, logocentrism regards the physical text as merely the conveyor of nonphysical, extratextual meaning, and it mistrusts the frailty and vulnerability of writing.

Not all Jews accept the view that the physical text itself is necessary and that the signifier is just as important as, or even more important than, the many signifieds that may be ascribed to it. However, all Christians must accept the contrary logocentric emphasis on the importance of the signified for ideological (theological) reasons. An important interest of mine in this book is the ideological impact of the logocentric view on the Christian concept of canon and how this view controls the supposed contents of the textual container.

Christian affirmation of logocentrism is apparent in the theory of "dynamic equivalence" that dominates the study and practice of Christian Bible translation. The theory of dynamic equivalence holds that the ideological content of the text belongs to a realm that the physical material of the text may transmit but never fundamentally transform. It regards the physical text as a container, with the meaning (the transmitted message) enclosed inside it. This meaning can be removed from one container-text and replaced ("translated") in another container-text without serious damage to the meaning itself.

As in the traditional view of metaphor, for dynamic equivalence, the text is merely the "vehicle" that transports the meaning (or "tenor") from the writer to the reader. If you're sending a package from Cleveland to Chicago, it doesn't matter whether you send it by United Parcel or Federal Express or whether the delivery service uses a Mack truck or a Dodge. What really counts is, not the transport system, but the package that you're sending. A bad translation simply misses (or poorly conveys) that which a good translation never would miss (or would convey properly). If the package winds up in Cincinnati, or if it is damaged in transit, then you've been betrayed. However, that should not happen if the shipping company does a good job. You have good reason to expect that your package will arrive at the proper destination and in good condition. Likewise, a good translation is always possible for any text into any language.

Among the foremost advocates of dynamic equivalence, Eugene Nida and Charles Taber argue that a translated work should have on its readers the same effect that the source text has on its readers.[13] Nida and Taber assume

---

13. Barr suggests a similar view (*Semantics*, 265–66), although this is not entirely consistent with some of his other comments on language.

that the work's author wants to produce specific, identifiable effects in her audience, including a high degree of comprehension of a univocal message, which in turn may be received accurately by the receiver. Nida and Taber treat the biblical writings as though they are in general unambiguous and aim at a clear, practical result. They explicitly compare Bible translation to the translation of practical manuals for the aviation industry. For them, translation leads to the goal of correct understanding in "a matter of life and death": "we aim to make certain that [the average reader] is very unlikely to misunderstand [the translated text]."[14] For Christians, it seems, the Bible is a kind of "how to do it" manual for righteous living, or salvation.

Similarly, Quine imagines the case of a linguist seeking to understand a language previously unknown to the larger world.[15] Perhaps Quine's linguist is a missionary, one of Nida's Bible translators, or maybe an explorer or anthropologist seeking fame and fortune. The linguist must rely solely on native informants and their willingness to confirm by way of simple gestures the linguist's guesses as to what their sentences mean. Quine assumes that the natives are willing for the linguist to learn their language. In this scenario, both parties want the message to be successfully transmitted, and there is a corresponding complicity between the source text and its translation.

According to the theory of dynamic equivalence, translation is not at all concerned with the material text itself. The text merely conveys the meaning. Translation is solely concerned with the content of the message, not the container. Because this theory views the meaning contained in the text as something distinct from the physical text itself, dynamic equivalence implies the existence of a real extratextual world that can be known as such, apart from any story or other linguistic intertextual frame. The signified conceptual content can be understood on its own, without requiring physical textual embodiment. This extratextual reality serves as the standard by which all literary and philosophical questions must be judged, including the quality of a given translation. Also located in this real world are all the possible signified objects of any story, including God, human beings, and everything else that actually exists. Indeed, a principle value of translation, according to dynamic equivalence, is that it enables us to learn about these possible objects from a broader variety of sources than we otherwise could. Ambiguity in translation is an imperfection, which may be overcome to a considerable degree and which is tolerated only when it expresses the author's intention in the source text—for example, a deliberate pun—and hence is part of the identified meaning of that text.

Since the meaning contained in the text can be completely separated from the textual medium, according to the theory of dynamic equivalence, the translation of a translation (translation into a third language) does not

---

14. Nida and Taber, *Theory and Practice,* 1.
15. Quine, *Word and Object,* 28 ff.

present a serious problem, and an infinite series of translations is theoretically possible. Reverse translations (back into the original language) can also be used to check the correctness of the translation.[16] Translation of translation opens the way for translation of those parts of the Bible that are "already translated," including translations of the entire Greek Bible. Dynamic equivalence supports Christian emphasis on the signified message or propositional content, as distinct from the physical text that embodies it. Transmission and reception of this message—valid interpretation and appropriate practical response—are of greatest importance. Indeed, there is nothing of value in the text besides the message that it conveys.

Through dynamically equivalent translations of the Bible, Christianity seeks to possess the biblical contents in the form of what Roland Barthes calls a "work." A work is a self-identical, ownable thing, something that can be used and consumed—in this case, a canon. The numerous languages requiring Bible translations in global Christianity present no threat as long as the interpretation of the text is single and universally accepted. When the Spirit of God is on your side, you can freely transform the original text. You can be assured of the transferability of meaning, and word-by-word translation may even appear to be an obstruction to faith. Hence the confidence and boldness of Christian Bible translators:

> if by coincidence it is possible to convey the same content in the receptor language in a form which closely resembles that of the source, so much the better; we preserve the form when we can, but more often the form has to be transformed precisely in order to preserve the content.[17]

Standing opposed to linguistic logocentrism and the theory of dynamic equivalence is the theory of "literal translation." Letter-by-letter translation of any written text is impossible, and so the term "literal" is somewhat misleading. Even the most literal of translations inevitably changes the signifiers of the source text in many ways. However, if "literal translation" is used to describe a translated text whose signifiers correspond closely on a word-by-word basis to those of the source text, then the practice of literal translation is consistent with the theory of literal translation.

Literal translation foregrounds the role of ideology in every act of translation. Two translations of a given source text may both be literal ones in

---

16. "This was actually a very common practice by missionaries in their translation of the Bible into indigenous languages, often after creating a written form of the language into which the Bible was to be translated. Then reading and writing had to be taught to the natives so that they could read the translated Bible! But what they did was use the King James Version as the basis—this happened all through the Pacific islands and often in Australia. It is still widespread, with translators working from an English translation as the primary text" (Roland Boer, private communication, 3 May 2000). Steiner (*After Babel*) notes several famous cases of translation of a translation.

17. Nida and Taber, *Theory and Practice*, 105–6. Contrast Frege, *Translations*, 46 n; and Derrida, "Living On," 154.

that they both adhere closely to word-by-word correspondence to the source text and yet may differ greatly from each other in the messages that readers derive from them. As Quine notes, this is not only possible but likely because

> manuals for translating one language into another can be set up in divergent ways, all compatible with the totality of speech dispositions, yet incompatible with one another. In countless places they will diverge in giving, as their respective translations of a sentence of the one language, sentences of the other language which stand to each other in no plausible sort of *equivalence* however loose.[18]

If no differences of practical consequence demonstrate that one of the translations is more useful than the other one (see further below), then the only reason that a reader could give for choosing one translation over the other would be that she liked what it said better. In other words, the preferred translation would be the one that conforms to beliefs that the reader already has. This ideological dimension is concealed in the identification of equivalent meaning in dynamically equivalent translations. In fact, reverse translations often turn out quite different than the source texts, and even when they don't, this proves, not that the translation was accurate, but only that the same "manual" was used to produce both the translation and the reverse translation. Unambiguous confirmation of identity between the message received and the message sent is simply not possible.

Literal translation is not interested in the transmission of nonphysical content or meaning that is so highly valued by dynamic equivalence. It may appear that equivalence of meaning is still involved in literal translation, on the word-by-word level, but this assumes that individual words have meaning apart from their linguistic context. What counts as "meaning" will be discussed further below, but for now I note only that judgments of truth require both a logical subject and predicate—that is, a complete proposition.[19] Individual words are not usually complete propositions, and their meanings can vary widely from one linguistic context to another. As Quine says, equally valid translation manuals may produce meaningfully divergent sentences.

In other words, the literal translation of a text is not necessarily the clearest transmission of meaning. According to Walter Benjamin, the great modern advocate of literal translation, "no case for literalness can be based on a desire to retain the meaning."[20] Criteria such as "accuracy" or "fidelity" have little if any relevance to literal translation. For literal translation, fidelity can only be a matter of expression, not of content:

---

18. Quine, *Word and Object*, 27, emphasis added. See also Nida and Taber, *Theory and Practice*, 5.

19. Frege, *Translations*, 43 ff.

20. Benjamin, *Illuminations*, 78.

A literal rendering of the syntax completely demolishes the theory of reproduction of meaning and is a direct threat to comprehensibility. ... [T]ranslation must in large measure refrain from wanting to communicate something, from rendering the sense, and in this the original is important to it only insofar as it has already relieved the translator and his translation of the effort of assembling and expressing what is to be conveyed.[21]

Literal translation emphasizes instead the strangeness of the text, what George Steiner calls the "alternity" of its language.[22] The closer you get to a truly word-by-word translation, the more incoherent the translated text often becomes, and literal translations are sometimes quite incoherent. This is because literal translation stresses the materiality of text. The physical stuff of the text, itself meaningless, is nevertheless indispensable to the transfer of meaning-filled messages. Any text manifests indeterminacies and ambiguities that cannot be controlled or overcome by anyone, not even the sender of the message. These ambiguities and indeterminacies become evident when the material text fails to convey a satisfactory meaning. Literal translation reproduces the uncertainties of the source text's meaning, not the interpretations that would resolve them. The theory of literal translation is thus closed related to both the Jewish understanding of written Torah and the postmodern concepts of intertextuality and unlimited semiosis that were discussed in chapter 1.

Benjamin describes the "prototype or ideal" of translation as "the interlinear version of the Scriptures," in which parallel lines of text in two languages are juxtaposed on one page quite "literally" side by side, word by word. Not "word *for* word," the translation does not replace the source text. The value of literal translation lies, not in infallible transmission of a message, but rather in supplementation of the source text. The source text is incomplete, consisting only of "fragments of a greater language." This is its "translatability." According to Benjamin, the translation glues together fragments that "match one another in the smallest details, although they need not be like one another."[23] Instead of precisely transmitting the meaning of the source text, literal translation reveals a "pure" or "true" language lying between the texts:

It is the task of the translator to release in his own language that pure language which is under the spell of another, to liberate the language imprisoned in a work in his re-creation of that work. For the

---

21. Ibid., 78.
22. Steiner, *After Babel,* 473. Famous instances of literal translation include Hölderlin's translation of Sophocles and Buber and Rosenzweig's translation of the Jewish Bible.
23. Benjamin, *Illuminations,* 82, 71, 78.

sake of pure language he breaks through decayed barriers of his own language.[24]

Benjamin's quasi-mystical concept of the pure language suggests a Kabbalistic return to pre-Babelian unity. Benjamin claims that all translation aspires to this unified language, even though it is itself unspeakable, because it is the language of God.[25] In the tension between the source and translated texts, the space of the interlinear, something appears that may not be in the texts at all and that is in fact ineffable but that is somehow crucial to the questions of language, God, humanity, space, and time. For Benjamin, pure language inhabits that interlinear space, and it can only appear in translation. All language depends upon pure language, even though pure language can never truly appear in any impure, ordinary language. In case these comments appear overly bizarre or mystical, compare the words of Paul de Man, who goes to great lengths to deny the messianic implications of literal translation but who still says, "in Hölderlin['s extremely literal translation of Sophocles], translation *occurs*. . . . I feel it, that there is something there."[26]

This interlinear "something" is not disembodied or nonphysical meaning, like the conceptual, signified content that is prized by advocates of dynamic translation. For literal translation, there is nothing outside of the (inter)text. Instead, the interlinear tension between source and translated texts permits the signifiers once again to emerge in their meaningless materiality: "[the translator] must go back to the primal elements of language itself and penetrate to the point where work, image, and tone converge."[27] What appears in the interlinear juxtaposition of texts is language speaking only itself, self-referential language, what Barthes called the "rustle" of language. According to Benjamin, pure language is beyond meaning, without meaning—that is, it is physical, hyletic language.

Thus the mundane practicality of interlinear translation has its mystical aspect, and yet this mystical aspect is itself profoundly material. The pure language is both physical and yet also supernatural or magical. In effect, the translation re-creates the source text as "the original." The recovery of pure language in literal translation brings the source text back to life. Not unlike Jorge Luis Borges's notion of the textual "precursor," discussed in chapter 1, literal translation reveals or exposes the source text in previously

---

24. Ibid., 80.
25. Ibid., 79. The Kabbalists' readings of the scriptures included meditations on the shape of the Hebrew letters, on their numerical values, and on the significance of misspellings. Each reading was regarded as a fragment of the total meaning of the text—a total meaning that is far greater (and less coherent) than the surface or conventional meaning. The Kabbalists sought to find in the post-Babelian languages of humanity, and especially in the language of the Torah, echoes of the true language of God. See Faur, *Golden Doves;* and Scholem, *Kabbalah.*
26. de Man, *Resistance,* 104, his emphasis.
27. Rudolph Pannwitz, quoted in Benjamin, *Illuminations,* 81.

unknown ways, not with new meaning, but in greater linguistic depth. In the words of Benjamin, "[t]he life of the originals attains in [the translations] to its ever-renewed latest and most abundant flowering."[28] However, meaning is so loosely attached to translations that they should not themselves be translated. Once it has been translated, the source text can never be the same, even though it has not been physically altered at all.

According to Quine's scenario, translation occurs in an act of complicity—that is, the native peacefully welcomes the foreign linguist and assists him in his attempts at translation. In contrast, Steiner argues that the reason that languages multiply is to exclude the "others," anyone who is not already one of "us"—strangers, outsiders, barbarians, and perhaps even linguists—from understanding "our" messages. Human communities hide behind language, and any translation, no matter how much it may pretend to reveal, always conceals even more. Translation is never innocent, and it is sometimes quite violent. This is especially true in the case of writing because in writing the text is freed from any one determining context. Literal translation forces the reader back to the materiality of the source text, not in order to receive a message that is contained there, but rather to uncover the "primal elements" in which pure language rustles. In this way, literal translation stands diametrically opposed to the logocentric continuity of signified meaning that is of greatest importance to dynamic equivalence.

Like Barthes's categories of the writerly and the readerly text, to which they correspond rather closely, both literal translation and dynamic equivalence represent ideal and ultimately impossible goals. They are two extremes between which the practical task of any actual translation will be located, suspended in the force field that these extremes generate. The practical reality of translation lies along the spectrum defined by these contradictory positions. This too is an ideological spectrum, along which actual translations may be situated and rated as more or less literal or dynamic.

Neither dynamic equivalence nor literal translation is inherently "good" or "bad." However, each of these views or values of translation sets before itself a peculiar kind of perfection, an ideology of language and text. Because of this difference, the association of many Christian Bible translations with the theory of dynamic equivalence, and the general rejection of the theory of literal translation by Christian Bible translators,[29] has important consequences for the canon.

---

28. Benjamin, *Illuminations,* 72. See also ibid., 81.

29. Some Christians advocate what they call "literal" translation and oppose dynamic equivalence. However, they also favor certain Bible translations on the grounds that the chosen translations are more accurate or faithful to the "original" text. This remains a kind of dynamic equivalence view, even though that term is rejected. Regardless of their views, Christian translators have produced some fairly literal Bible translations, such as the RSV.

What Can't Be Translated?

Because it is itself meaningless, the physical aspect of the sign or hyletic signifier cannot be translated. The physical signifier can be copied, or in the case of differing alphabets, it can be transliterated with more or less precision, but unlike transcription, which does not replace the signifier with another one in the same medium but changes it fundamentally, transliteration is not translation. Transliteration concerns a change of alphabets, not a change of languages.[30] Conversely, there are numerous cases in which the "same" physical signifier means quite different things in different languages. For example, the German word *Gift* means the same as the word "poison" in English. The French word *pain* is pronounced rather like the English word "pan" and means the same as the word "bread" in English. The result is a nontranslatable "confusion of tongues." These interlingual homonyms are also not translations of any sort.

Disagreement regarding the possibility of translation focuses on the impact of translation on the meaning of the text, the signified content of the message. Dynamic equivalence asserts that, with proper care, the signified content can be separated from one physical signifier and correctly attached to a different one. The meaning will still be the same as it was before, and the act of translation will not change the message in any important way. Again, this is a form of logocentrism. In contrast, literal translation claims that transfer of meaning is not at all the task of the translator, and indeed, "[m]eaning is served far better ... by the unrestrained license of bad translators."[31] Here the alternative, intertextual view of language and meaning is supported.

Two distinct types of meaning are involved in this disagreement. Both play extremely important roles in part 2 of this book in the analysis of canonical relations involving specific biblical texts. One type of meaning is denotation; the other is connotation.

1. *Denotation* (also known as reference or logical extension) is the ability of a word or sentence to indicate some object, whether physical or conceptual, in the extratextual world. The denotation of a declarative sentence determines its logical value to be either true or false. Truth value is determined when the denotations of the words and phrases in the sentence point to some object or state of affairs in the real world. For example, the sentence "the messiah is the son of David" is true if the person designated as "messiah" falls under the concept represented by "the son of David."[32]

---

30. I do not want to minimize the changes that are involved in transliteration, especially in view of the current tendency on the Internet for the ASCII/Roman/English alphabet to submerge all others. My point here is only that this is not a matter of translation.

31. Benjamin, *Illuminations*, 78.

32. See Frege, *Translations*, 21–78, esp. 51.

2. *Connotation* (also known as sense or logical intention) is what a word signifies about its denoted object. Connotation connects the signifier to the denoted object. It is the intelligible content of a word—that is, its availability to function within well-formed linguistic structures. The connotation of a word is that word's intertextual relation to other words, the "mode of presentation" of the denoted object through language.[33]

Connotation and denotation are extremely important semiotic concepts, and they play a large role in the remainder of this book. Connotation is always intertextual, and therefore ideological, because it is established within limits defined by the cultural and linguistic context (Who is "David"? Is "son of David" to be taken in a strictly genealogical sense? What is "the messiah"?). People learn the connotations of words in cultural contexts, and this transmission inevitably reflects ideological differences. However, although connotation is purely linguistic and conceptual, it is not private or personal. The connotation of a word "may be the common property of many people, and so is not a part or a mode of the individual mind. For one can hardly deny that mankind has a common store of thoughts which is transmitted from one generation to another."[34]

One way to determine the connotation of a word is to identify objects that the word denotes. However, connotation is not simply determined by denotation, for otherwise nonsense words, metaphors, and other sorts of figurative and poetic language, in which words do not directly denote any real object, would never occur. It is quite possible for a sentence to connote something even though it denotes nothing. However, the truth value of such a sentence is limited to the realm of the fictional. "Darth Vader is the father of Luke Skywalker" is a true sentence, but it is true only within the secondary, fictional reality narrated in the *Star Wars* movies. Its truth is of a different metaphysical order from that of "George Lucas was the director of *Star Wars,*" which is true within the primary, nonfictional world of everyday reality.

Denotation may often be determined through practical consequences. However, two conditions limit the possibility of translating according to denotation. Both conditions reflect the logocentric judgment that extratextual reality is superior to the text itself.

1. The denoted object must actually exist. The text to be translated cannot be a fictional one, or a lie. Translation is always problematic in the case of fictions because fictional statements denote the extratextual world only ambiguously at best. The denotation or reference of fic-

---

33. Ibid., 57. Barthes defines connotation as a "second-order signifying system" (*Elements,* 91). See further Barthes, *Elements,* 89–94; and *Semiotic Challenge,* 173–78.
34. Frege, *Translations,* 59.

tional statements is "split," and the lack of an extratextual denoted object leaves only the connotation of the statement for its meaning.[35]

2. The meaning of the text must be more important than is the physical text itself. In other words, the physical words of the text cannot be important in their own right, as in many poetic texts where physical qualities of the words and their arrangement are crucial to the poem.

If the concern in translating is to transmit only the denotation of prag-matically true sentences, such as a scientific report or technical instructions, then dynamically equivalent translation is preferable. There should be no serious disagreement regarding the validity of such a translation. It does not matter if the sentences in the source and the translated texts have differing connotations, as long as they point to the one correct denoted object. Per-haps the clearest example of this is the "how to do it" book. As long as the translated text tells me how to do whatever "it" is correctly, it makes no difference if the translation takes great liberties with the source text.

As I noted above, satisfactory practical consequences are a measure of dynamic equivalence in translation, and the text itself is unimportant to advocates of dynamic equivalence. In fact, Nida and Taber maintain that the significance of the Bible or the contexts in which it might be read are analogous to that of a manual for aviation mechanics.[36] For the theory of dynamic equivalence, it is the denotation of the Bible's text that is holy, not the physical text itself. The Bible is a "how to do it" book, and thus dynamic equivalence is most appropriate to it. There are indeed a few bib-lical passages that contain specific practical directions, analogous to "Wear safety glasses when operating power tools" or "Pump the throttle before starting the motor." Nevertheless, the vast majority of passages in the Bible consist of abstract philosophical sayings, metaphorical poetry, and most of all, narratives. None of these passages has the identifiable denotation of a technical manual. In other words, no phenomenon in the extratextual world could serve as a basis for critical judgment between competing translations of these passages.

As an authoritative list of texts, the canon presents a message, divine Truth, and that message depends heavily on connotation. In a famous essay, Barthes argued that all advertising messages, despite their evident denotative differences, have only one connotative message, namely, "Buy this product!" This connotation is the "bottom line" of the advertisement, and all other meaning is subservient to it: "We must not suppose that the second mes-sage (of connotation) is "hidden" beneath the first (of denotation); quite the contrary: what we immediately perceive . . . is the advertising character of the

---

35. Jakobson, *Language and Literature*, 85. Examples of split reference will be given in part 2 of this book.

36. Nida and Taber, *Theory and Practice*, 1.

message, its second signified ... : the second message is not surreptitious."[37] Likewise, for the believing community, the canon of the Bible, throughout its length and breadth and despite its numerous denotative incoherencies, discrepancies, and contradictions, has only one connotative message, namely, "This is Absolute Truth. This is God speaking." All other messages in the biblical texts are understood in relation to this "second signified." It is therefore in relation to connotation that the Bible present serious difficulties for translation. The disagreement noted above regarding translation depends upon the problem of the translation of connotation. This is where the difference between dynamic equivalence and literal translation is crucial to the semiotics of canon.

Connotation presents problems for translation in several ways. Any word or sentence that denotes some object also connotes something about that object. Proper names may seem to be an exception to this, since a name usually simply denotes the one who bears it. However, proper names cannot be translated, only transliterated. According to Benjamin, imperfect human language touches pure, divine language through the power to give names.[38] Nevertheless, most proper names do connote something about those who possess them, such as gender, family affiliation, ethnicity, or other features. At minimum, the name's connotation is restricted to its ability to denote an object, even if it does not actually denote any object. In that case, the proper name retains the minimal connotation of "the name of (X)." If it loses even that connotation, then the name is no longer recognized as a signifier. Likewise, different namelike phrases such as "son of David" and "son of God" may both denote the same character (see further chapters 8 and 9), even though these phrases also signify different sets of connotative conditions that must be fulfilled for either of them to appear in a true sentence. In the New Testament, both "son of David" and "son of God" are used to denote a single person, the character Jesus, but the two phrases have quite different connotations.

These difficulties associated with proper names influence the semiotics of narrative. According to Jean-François Lyotard, names serve as narrative "linchpins," connecting phrases and allowing different connotations to be attributed to the same denoted object. This connection is always contingent, and never certain, but the network of proper names establishes a narrative "reality." Barthes likewise argues that "[w]hat gives the illusion that [the story's character] is supplemented by a precious remainder (something like *individuality* ...) is the Proper Name."[39]

The relation between narrative and connotation has further consequences for translation. Every narrative is at least somewhat (but inescapably) fic-

37. Barthes, *Semiotic Challenge*, 176.
38. Benjamin, *Reflections*, 317–24.
39. Barthes, *S/Z*, 191, his emphases. See also Lyotard, *The Differend*, 40–46; and Frege, *Translations*, 47, 62.

tional, and reality, no matter how it is defined, is always more or less than any story. The meaning of a story is constituted by crucial decisions made by its reader. "Empty signs" (signs that do not denote) inevitably open up the possibility of "divergent infinite series" of connotations.[40] The hyletic text itself denotes nothing at these points, and the reader makes up the difference. The reader's desire for meaning cannot tolerate this lack of meaning, and the reading generates a series of connotative choices. The denotation of the story, no matter how empirical, historical, or realistic it is, always depends upon these connotative choices, which are not themselves "in" the story. Even in the most realistic stories, narratives that are most transparently denotative, connotation dominates over denotation. Every story is what Jakobson calls an "aesthetic message," in which the "poetic function" of language is dominant. Its denotation or truth value is split between the more or less apparent denotation of some extratextual reality and the more or less explicit denotation of its own status as a message.[41]

It is possible to understand the connotation of a sentence without knowing whether or not that sentence is true. However, if the connotation is unknown, or if the words in the source text have idiosyncratic or multiple or contrary possible connotations, then semiosis will be uncontrolled. Earlier I used as an example the sentence "The messiah is the son of David." If I don't know who David is or what a messiah is, then I cannot be certain whether or not the sentence is true. If I suspect that "son" is being used metaphorically, then I may not know what the sentence means. When the denoted object does not exist, or its existence is uncertain, then identification of connotation becomes crucial. If the signs are empty, then connotation threatens to run wild. In sentences that do not denote anything, such as fictional statements, or sentences whose denotation is indeterminate or unverifiable, such as poetical utterances, the signifier or physical body of the text interferes with complete translation. In such cases, a more literal translation respects the opacity of the signifier and does not fill in the empty signs.

Connotation connects the denoted object to the text itself, but for this reason connotation also separates the material signifier from any possible denotation—that is, from a truth value. In other words, connotation may either interfere with denotation, or it may support denotation. On one hand, if the biblical texts are poetic or fictional, with uncertain or multiple connotations, then literal translation will best retain the connotative ambiguity of the material text. On the other hand, if the most important thing about the biblical texts is their denotation, their meaningful relation to reality, then the Christian logocentric view of the text and its meaning may be justified.

---

40. Frege, *Translations*, 32–33.
41. Jakobson, *Language and Literature*, 62–94. See further chapter 5.

Translating Canon

If the meaningful message that is to be separated from the physical stuff of
the Bible's texts cannot be identified, then there is no Bible to be translated.
Or rather, each translation of the Bible produces a different Bible. Each
translated Bible is a different "tangent," a deviation from the source text
"thereupon pursuing its own course."[42] That literal translation is an ideological maneuver is perhaps made most clear in Benjamin's reference to "the
interlinear version of the *Scriptures*" (emphasis added). Literal translation
of the Bible uncovers a bunch of writings, perhaps even a collection of scriptures, but in any case, multiple texts that have no integrity, no consistency.
They are just so many fragments of language. Literal translation identifies
many Bibles, a shimmering opalescence of pure language that is always able
to mean more (or less) than anyone could ever think. None of these Bibles
is the same as any other Bible. None of them is the one Bible, the true Bible.

This multiplicity of Bibles is not able to explain itself, or to speak authoritatively with a single voice. It cannot be universal, the same message in
every language and in every age. Nor is it apostolic (see further chapter 4).
In the last analysis, it is not the canon. This is why some translators of the
New Testament, like translators of practical manuals or scientific reports,
reject literal translation in favor of dynamic equivalence.

The logocentric view that has come to dominate Christianity in the form
of dynamic equivalence holds that translation separates the proper meaning
of a statement from the sign to which it had been attached, the material linguistic body, whether temporary sound or permanent recording. This view
further holds that translation connects this meaning to a different sign of the
same or another type. The text's connotation clearly denotes an actual object, and the goal of the translation is to keep this denoted object always the
same. Dynamic equivalence requires that the biblical narratives be nonfictional, and this is what Nida and Taber's Bible translators, like all Christians,
believe that they are. According to Christian belief, there can only be one
Bible, independent of any particular language, just as there is in the creed
only one holy, apostolic, catholic Church.

Therefore the Christian double canon is defined in relation to logocentrism in translation. If dynamic equivalence is impossible, then Christianity in its present form is impossible. In order to accept the New Testament
as authoritative canon and not merely oral Torah, Christians have to deny
that Hebrew is the holy language, and they have to affirm the possibility
of perfect translation—that is, dynamic equivalence. Christians believe that
there is no holy language, or rather that every human language is or can be
a holy language, as the story of Pentecost implies (see further chapter 5). If
Christians believed that the Bible contains the specific holy words of God,

---

42. Benjamin, *Illuminations,* 80. See also ibid., 82.

they would be far more reluctant to translate it. Christianity becomes the logocentric religion par excellence, and the "letter" of the biblical texts is ignored in favor of their "spirit" (see further chapter 6). In choosing the logocentric view of language, Christianity makes a fundamental theological move—an ideological move—which redefines the nature of the scriptures.

The theological consequences of Christian belief in the dynamically equivalent translatability of the scriptures are immense.[43] The purpose of language is understood to serve as a clear and useful channel by which straightforward and accurate communication of messages is possible, and translation furthers that purpose. The ideal content of the message can be readily and completely separated from the physical aspects of the texts in which that message is contained. The material body of the source text is merely one among many possible embodiments of the connoted meaning, and that body is itself unimportant, to be cast aside and replaced as needed.

The possibility of separating the material signifier from the signified meaning also permits a theoretical distinction between translation (which transfers meaning) and exegetical interpretation (which uncovers meaning), and it supports the view that a theologically neutral or perfect translation is possible, although perhaps only with the help of God. Christian Bible translators who advocate this view feel free to modify (or "clarify") the source text's connotation in translated texts that they believe denote equally well its extratextual object. These translators rearrange the language of the translated text, sometimes quite substantially, in order to retain what they think is the proper meaning of the source text.

Christianity regards translation as a miracle, as in the "Letter of Aristeas" or the story of Pentecost. God guarantees that the meaning of the Bible remains secure and unharmed, forever. Perhaps this ideological move is unavoidable, given the early history of the Christian movement and especially the texts that eventually became the Christian scriptures—that is, given the Christian need to treat those texts as canonical. The consequent disregard of the physical text of the Bible plays a substantial part in disregard of the dilemma of a double canon. The scriptures are understood to connote a uniform, universal, authoritative, and perfectly translatable message. Evident textual inconsistencies and contradictory connotations can be ignored or overcome through hermeneutical maneuvers, for the Old and the New Testaments are believed to denote the same object.[44] The double canon is then not a problem but merely two different ways to denote one coherent

---

43. These consequences are explored further in Aichele, *Sign, Text, Scripture*, especially chap. 1. See also the essays in Bailey and Pippin, *Semeia* 76, esp. Robert P. Carroll, "Cultural Encroachment and Bible Translation: Observations on Elements of Violence, Race, and Class in the Production of Bibles in Translation" (39–53).

44. Bauer quotes Irenaeus as follows: "In this way the elder, the disciple of the apostles, discoursed about both Testaments and showed that both derive from one and the same God" (*Orthodoxy and Heresy*, 199).

extratextual reality. Similarly, the four canonical gospels must denote one true extratextual story, despite their evident differences both of connotation and of the written signifier. The violence done by this "translation" to the physical texts is of no consequence because the inner, spiritual meaning, the practical content of the message, is all that counts.

In order to accept the texts in both testaments as canonical, Christianity has to adopt a logocentric understanding of translation and language, and hence of scripture. To choose otherwise would require a very different sort of Christian faith. To opt now for literal translation would require abandonment of the Christian faith. One textual alternative to this dilemma would be to follow the lead of Marcion, who eliminated the Old Testament. Many Christians have in fact done something like this, by relegating the Old Testament to second-class status.[45] Likewise, many Christians have followed Tatian's lead and transformed the multiple and textually inconsistent gospels into "the Gospel," a single, clear message, usually featuring the gospel of John, or selections from Paul, into which bits and pieces from other New Testament writings are fitted as needed. Unlike Marcion and Tatian, these Christians do this, not in writing, but in the ideology that informs their understanding of the Bible. They identify a "canon within the canon," and they thereby implicitly confess that the biblical canon as a whole has failed to satisfy their desire for a self-explanatory, authoritative message.

In order to maintain the double canon, Christianity must remain committed to a logocentric translation ideology such as that of dynamic equivalence. Christians focus on the sacred content of the words and not on the words themselves. They sacrifice the physical text of the Bible in order to redeem its meaning: "the very renunciation of the pleasure of the text, understood as story and about bodies, is itself a turning from corporeal pleasure to spiritual contemplation."[46] Such a sacrifice in the Christian understanding of language and of narrative may equal or even exceed the dilemma of the double canon in its impact on Christian thought and action.

As a consequence of this understanding, Christianity has been unable to tolerate hermeneutical diversity. From the apostle Paul's early distinction between the spirit and the letter of the law, on through the separation from and growing polemic with Judaism and the suppression of heresies, Christianity has come to favor totalizing, univocal interpretations of the biblical texts and aggressive opposition to any who would differ from the established

---

45. In the second century, "[t]he reckless speed with which, from the very beginning, the doctrine and ideology of Marcion spread can only be explained if it had found the ground already prepared. Apparently a great number of the baptized, especially in the East, inclined toward this view of Christianity and joined Marcion without hesitation as soon as he appeared, finding in him the classic embodiment of their own belief. What had dwelt in their inner consciousness in a more or less undefined form until then, acquired through Marcion the definite form that satisfied head and heart. No one can call that a falling away from orthodoxy to heresy" (Bauer, *Orthodoxy and Heresy*, 194).

46. Boyarin, " 'This We Know,' " 481.

dogma. Faur relates this tendency to Christian acceptance of translation and the consequent denial that Hebrew is the holy language. Even in the ancient allegorical understanding of the scriptures, Christian interpretation drives toward univocity, and diversity is dealt with through schism and exclusion. This continues to be true long after allegory has been surpassed by scientific, historical, and other post-Enlightenment methods of interpretation.

Christian sacrifice of the physical text of the scriptures has had important repercussions for Christian attitudes towards Jews, Muslims, and those of other religions and belief systems, including atheists, for according to the Christian ideology of the canon, the Bible must be brimming with clear, coherent meaning. How could any willing reader fail to understand the message of the Bible? These views of canon, and of translation, have played their part in the long sorry history of Christian anti-Semitism as well as other forms of religious arrogance and intolerance. In freeing the meaning of the canonical texts from their physical embodiments and allowing the unlimited translation of the scriptures, Christianity set itself on that course of intolerance and even fanaticism from which it has not yet freed itself.

Chapter 4

THE IMPERIAL BIBLE

The Canon as a Classic

One of the primary criteria for the Christian canon at the time that it was developed, and this remains true for alleged secular canons today, is that the included texts must have universal or "catholic" status.[1] Regardless of the specificities of their production, the various canonical texts may not be addressed exclusively to limited or parochial interests or communities, but instead they must express truths that are important to all readers. The canon must be valid throughout time and space.

The criterion of universality is reflected in ancient arguments that the emerging New Testament must include exactly four gospels and Pauline letters addressed to only seven churches.[2] There are also seven "catholic letters" in the New Testament, and the book of Revelation likewise opens with letters addressed to seven churches. To ancient peoples, numbers such as four and seven symbolize totality and completeness; they connote God. Hence even though the gospels disagreed among themselves, their fourfold quality suggested a larger wholeness, and Paul's letters, although they were addressed to seven specific churches, could speak to every church.

Whether these arguments actually motivated the historical selection of texts to be included in the New Testament, or whether they are after-the-fact rationalizations, makes no difference in the present context. Like all understandings of what a canon is, the criterion of universality must be understood as an ideal for the canon, an aspect of its ideological function, and not necessarily the actual reality. The criterion of universality played an important role in the initial conceptualization of the Christian double canon, and it continues to do so for those who still believe in the Bible's authority.

The catholic or universal value of the Christian canon is in jeopardy in the modern world. The canon of the Bible was threatened by the emergence of print culture during the Renaissance, and it is put into even greater danger by the electronic culture that blossoms in the contemporary world. The

---

1. Gamble, *New Testament Canon,* 69.
2. Ibid., 76–77.

technology of printing itself and the socially sanctioned values that discourage plagiarism and copyright violation substantially reduce the need for the security provided by the canon. The implications of digital publishing and the World Wide Web are not yet fully understood, but they promise at the very least a radical reevaluation of the canon. These material transformations of text provide alternative ways to guarantee that the authoritative writing remains unchanged.

Coincident with the impact of print technology, the rise of modern Western secularism presents a serious threat to the authority of the canon's message, and the global culture that dawns with and through the spread of electronic technology further challenges the significance of the Bible. The Bible's status as the "word of God" is undermined and overthrown in the light of emerging scientific and humanistic ideas and revolutionary social and political developments. Critical understanding of the scriptures and especially of the history of canon formation leads to disregard for the canon as a totality. The Bible and its component texts must compete, without privilege, in a world that is increasingly aware of a great many different texts, associated with numerous cultures, lifestyles, philosophies, moral and political systems, and religions.

In other words, the Bible has difficulty functioning as a canon in the contemporary world. Indeed, its day may well be over. In the Christian churches, the Bible still *seems* to be the canon, but its authority is increasingly disputed and rejected even there. Multiple and violently conflicting interpretations divide believing communities, and others who do not belong to such communities read the Bible as though it were ordinary secular literature. Likewise, the secular academic world is convulsed with disagreements over whether a canon of "Great Books" must be studied. If canonized books continue to have any authority at all, it is less and less canonical authority, strictly speaking, and more and more something else. A canon of scriptures may be no longer conceivable to present-day human beings, except in the way that cannibalism, parchment, or the Pony Express is conceivable.

The canon criterion of universality survives in the contemporary understanding of the "classic," and one way to try to salvage the importance of the biblical canon has been to redescribe it as a classic. One scholar who redescribes the Bible in this way is the theologian David Tracy. Tracy calls for a "revisionist theology" that will confront the "crisis of meaning" in the contemporary post-Christian world by means of "analogical imagination."[3] This theology will reenvision the traditions of Christianity that are embodied in various classic works, especially the canonical scriptures and in particular the gospels, which contain the Christian community's "dangerous memory" of Jesus.[4] Along similar lines, Harry Gamble describes the Bible's

---

3. Tracy, *Blessed Rage*, 3–4.
4. Tracy, *Analogical Imagination*, 235.

demand for continuing reinterpretation as the "necessary condition" for the authority that has been ascribed to it.[5] Tracy claims that like all classics, the biblical texts require continual reinterpretation because no adequate form can be found for them. They are provocative and excessive. Nevertheless, the Bible is encountered by its readers as containing a norm, a truth that challenges the reader and that places interpretation at risk.[6]

According to Tracy, the human world today is characterized by the collapse of modern existentialist humanism. This breakdown entails the suspicion of the integrity of the conscious self, of any metaphysical closure, teleology, or history, and also the loss of denotation and its replacement by the "power of the negative." Reality itself is up for grabs. Echoing Kafka, Tracy says that "the center is not in contact any longer; the center, one hears, has become horizon."[7] This uncanny situation requires the presence of negativity in the form of analogical imagination, so that as the theologian seeks to reenvision the classics of her tradition, the ambiguity of both the classic work and the contemporary situation will not be overlooked. The theologian must engage in ongoing and endless conversation with people of other traditions, and also with classic works. She can have no expectation of ultimate and decisive truth, but she can be confident that criteria of relative, de facto adequacy will permit meaning to emerge:

> In the uncanny sense of a reassurance in the unknown depth of the self and the unknowable depth of history and nature alike, we begin to recognize in all the classics some always-already affirmation in and through their very negations. We recognize that uncanny affirmation only because we finally sense some reality, vague yet important, which we cannot name but which is, we sense, not of our own making. We recognize that reality when we recognize the disclosive and transformative power in every classic of our post-modern situation.[8]

Robert Funk also argues a position not unlike Tracy's.[9] According to Funk, the texts of the New Testament provide "authentic access" to the originating "ground" of the Christian tradition. There is something hidden within these ancient texts, closely associated with the intentions of their human authors, and this something is reinterpreted over and over again in various times and situations. The canonical texts crystallize the living oral tradition and thereby threaten to obscure their own originating impulse. Nevertheless, the plurality of the texts (for example, the four gospels, the

---

5. Gamble, *New Testament Canon*, 74.

6. Tracy, *Analogical Imagination*, 115; *Plurality*, 13–15, 68.

7. Tracy, *Analogical Imagination*, 355. See also ibid., 349; and *Blessed Rage*, 105 ff.

8. Tracy, *Analogical Imagination*, 363–64.

9. See especially Funk, *Parables and Presence*, 152. For similar treatments of the biblical canon as a classic, see Stendahl, "Bible as Classic"; Schneidau, *Sacred Discontent;* and Schüssler-Fiorenza, *Searching*, 9–11.

two testaments) and their particularity keep open the possibility of a re-occurrence of the original, oral word-event in a way that will inevitably transform the tradition once again.[10]

The Eternal Empire

Frank Kermode notes that the question of the literary classic is a question of authority. Kermode claims that the concept of the classic arose during the second century C.E. This was the very period during which Christian groups began to consider the desirability of a canon, perhaps in response to Marcion's heretical collection of authoritative texts. The idea of a classic "is a received opinion as to the structure of the past and its relation to the present. It is a question of how the works of the past may retain identity in change, of the mode in which the ancient presents itself to the modern."[11] To call a text a classic is to understand it as simultaneously past and present. The question of the classic thus requires an understanding of history and temporality. In this respect, the question of the classic is closely related to the question of canon.

Kermode delineates two distinct views of the literary classic. The first view of the classic text, which also provides a first definition of universality, is what Kermode calls the imperial (or imperialistic) theory. The imperial classic is particularly associated with chirographic, or manuscript, culture, the culture that produced the canon of the Bible. This view of the classic is the one adopted by T. S. Eliot, and in it the Roman poet Virgil plays an important role.[12] According to Eliot, what makes Virgil's poetry a classic work is that it provides a criterion for all of European civilization. Virgil

> acquires the centrality of the unique classic; he is at the centre of European civilization, in a position which no other poet can share or usurp. The Roman Empire and the Latin language were not any empire and any language, but an empire and a language with a unique destiny in relation to ourselves; and the poet in whom that Empire and that language came to consciousness and expression is a poet of unique destiny.[13]

The Roman Empire is the parent of modern Europe and hence of Western civilization, and Virgil is for Eliot the definitive Latin poet; therefore Virgil is the unique criterion of all Western culture.

---

10. Funk, *Parables and Presence*, 9, 169, 174, 185–86.
11. Kermode, *The Classic*, 16; see also 15.
12. Ibid., 23 ff. Kermode's book *The Classic* consists of the 1973 T. S. Eliot Memorial Lectures, given at the University of Kent. Kermode's lectures are themselves an extended reflection on Eliot's 1944 lecture to the Virgil Society, "What Is a Classic?" (in Eliot, *On Poetry*).
13. Eliot, *On Poetry*, 70–71.

Virgil's poetry is a classic work because it is the mature expression of a mature civilization, and maturity is the chief characteristic of the classic, according to Eliot. Eliot admits that maturity is almost impossible to define, but he claims that maturity can be recognized by those who are mature, and "if we are mature we either recognize maturity immediately, or come to know it on more intimate acquaintance."[14] In other words, mature people recognize the maturity of others. This circularity is highly suspect, as every child wishing to dispute adult judgment knows. However, Eliot specifies another sense of the word "maturity" somewhat more clearly. "Maturity" may mean ripeness or coming-of-age, acceptance of the responsibilities of adulthood, fulfillment of a purpose. Eliot describes the maturity of the classic work as characterized by order, stability, equilibrium, harmony, and complexity of structure. In addition, maturity means the end of innocence and childhood, the culmination of a period of preparation and growth.

Eliot maintains that classical maturity is inevitably followed by cultural decline, senility, and death. After its classical phase, a civilization can only go downhill; it has reached its pinnacle and is incapable of producing further great works. The classic "realizes the genius of the language," and because it perfects the language, it also exhausts the language of its own time "so that [the language] must, after yielding a diminishing crop, finally be left in fallow for some generations."[15]

Kermode, modifying Eliot, claims that the human cycle of generation—for cultures as well as for individuals—is crucial to the creation of new meanings for the literary work. Meaning is not unchanging, but rather it constantly either grows or dies. The classic is a kind of cultural peak, beyond which lies only degeneration and ultimately death. Some historical eras are more creative than others, although even times of decline contribute to the overall cycle. Even within Eliot's framework, the low points of cultural immaturity or senescence are essential to the classical high point. Nevertheless, the imperial classic does have, as Eliot says, an afterlife and a destiny—that is, the classic becomes universal, both in space and time.

The classic work is an absolute, a text that speaks to everyone, everywhere. This concept of catholicity or universality also appears to be central to Tracy's effort to identify the biblical canon as the Christian classic. According to Eliot, the classic is itself the culmination of a long historical progression, the movement toward a "common style" and a "community of taste," with a literature characterized by structural complexity and distinguished by subtlety and refinement.[16] The classic work is critical of the past and confident of the present, and it contains the whole power and greatness of a people, all at once. The English language, according to Eliot, is not

---

14. Ibid., 54.
15. Ibid., 65, 66.
16. Ibid., 57.

suitable for a classic. There is too much variety of style in English literature, and the sensibility is too provincial, too far removed from the imperial metropolis. One wonders if Eliot was not hoping that his own poetry and plays might change all that.

Kermode notes that a myth of empire underlies this view of the classic. The myth claims that the empire is eternal. This myth commences with the Roman emperor Constantine—who has some historical connection with the canonization of the Christian Bible—and it is passed on to the Holy Roman Empire through the famous Donation of Constantine. The imperial classic is a product of this myth. The emphasis on Rome in this theory unites religion and culture, a union that greatly appealed to the extremely conservative Anglo-Catholic Eliot. In addition, the emphasis on Virgil unites pagan and Christian, according to a well-known tradition in which Dante (another of Eliot's heroes) plays a part.

In the Middle Ages, it was believed that the empire, like the Church, existed both in time and outside of it, changing its "disposition" but not its essence.[17] The empire had been "translated" to a new place and time, as Kermode notes, and as Eliot also recognizes in his essay on Dante. Although this cultural translation is distinct from the linguistic translation that was discussed in chapter 3, it is worth recalling once again Christian acceptance of logocentric translatability and the importance of that belief to the Christian double canon. The Bible can be translated with confidence, according to advocates of dynamic equivalence, because its basic message is clear, universal, and timeless. The Bible is a classic of this eternal empire.

What supports belief in the translation of eternal empire from one temporal disposition to another is the method of allegory, which Kermode takes in a very broad sense. Developed initially by Greek Platonist and Stoic philosophers in order to allow them to continue to find credible truths in their own "classics," such as the works of Homer, allegory was seized upon by early Jews and Christians as a way to read the Bible. It is an interpretive tool that has continued to be used, in one way or another, down to the present. Allegory "holds that the classic has meanings contemporary with us which, quite possibly, an informed contemporary [of the writer] could not have discovered."[18] Unlike modern hermeneutical theory, allegory treats the classic as indifferent to the author's intention. As Tracy says, "Classics, whether texts, symbols, events, persons, or rituals, command attention.... [W]e become persons capable of recognizing the otherness of the classic. To understand these texts at all is inevitably to understand them differently from how their original authors or their first audiences understood them."[19]

Allegory maintains that the obvious connotation of a text may not govern

---

17. Kermode, *The Classic*, 32. See also Wilken, *Myth*, 23, 68–70.
18. Kermode, *The Classic*, 75.
19. Tracy, *Plurality*, 15–16.

its true meaning. The ancient Stoic philosophers first described the gap between the signifier and its signified that constantly threatens the possibility of communication, and they developed allegory as an attempt to bridge the gap.[20] In order to truly understand the text, the reader must probe beneath the surface or "literal" meaning, which may indeed be obscure, incredible, inconsistent, or of little value, to deeper levels of connoted meaning, through which the text finally denotes a single eternal truth. There is a fundamental unity underlying the allegorical message of the text as a whole, a single truth or denotation in the text that does not change throughout time and space—that is, an Absolute Signified. The text denotes a divine, eternal truth, and in a sacred text such as the Bible, that truth is God, and God's word. The various levels of meaning associated with allegory serve as mediations between the single unchanging, universal truth that the text finally denotes and the particularities of its readers' local contexts.

The allegorical method played an important role in Christian readings of the Bible from the earliest days of Christianity through the Middle Ages, and varieties of it are still found today in popular forms of Christianity. Although its metaphysical implications would be objectionable to "biblical theology," the allegorists agree with biblical theology that the biblical canon represents a single coherent message throughout. Eliot's understanding of the "mature" language of the classic also suggests the claim of biblical theology that the Hebrew and Greek languages used in the biblical texts are special. If the Bible is a classic, then its language must be more perfect than it was at any other time.

Allegory is an ancient form of logocentrism, separating the contained meaning (signified) from the textual container (signifier). In chapter 3, this way of thinking was identified with dynamic equivalence, which is committed to the absolute translatability of the biblical texts. This position also contributes to Christian resolution (or dismissal) of the problem of the double canon. The unity of meaning that allegory seeks in the text is evident in the typological reading, for which a character in one story (such as Adam or David) is seen to prefigure in various ways a character in another story (such as the messiah or more specifically Jesus). When typological figuration crosses over between the two biblical testaments, the overall unity of the Bible becomes clearer and the doubleness of the canon disappears.

At deeper levels of allegorical truth, the fundamental unity of the moral message of the Bible (such as the human condition as determined by original sin, or God's justice and mercy) or of its philosophical significance (such as the salvation of the nations or the meaning of history) is revealed to be manifest in every part of each of the books. According to allegory, the Bible is holographic.

---

20. Jakobson, *Language and Literature,* 413–15.

The Historical Empire

With the Renaissance comes the introduction of modern scientific, philolog-ical, and historical methodologies, all of which contribute to the demise of allegory. For the most part, this modern world correlates closely with print culture, to which it is closely related (see further chapter 2). During the Ren-aissance and the following centuries, the reborn philosophies and sciences split the cosmos radically into two distinct realities: the Cartesian subject (mind, thought) and the object (extended space-time, the "thing itself"), be-tween which any reunion is impossible, or so at least says Immanuel Kant. It becomes necessary to discover the truth appropriate to each of these real-ities. On one hand, there is a predominantly subjective reality—that is, the sphere of literature, art, and at least some aspects of philosophy and religion. On the other hand, there is a reality from which all traces of the subject have been (subjectively) eliminated—that is, the objective sphere of the sciences, technology, and history.

Accompanying this new schizoid world is a second major theory of the classic, according to Kermode, which brings with it a second understanding of universality: the "modern classic."[21] The modern classic belongs espe-cially to print culture, the culture in which the canon begins to lose its usefulness. The modern classic rejects the myth of eternal empire, and in-stead it regards the classic as a historical product, to be approached in terms of the culture(s) that initially generate, and then modify, maintain, or destroy it. Truth is defined as denotation of the empirical, historical world, as op-posed to the unchanging, ideal truth of the imperial classic. History replaces or even "translates" eternity as the locus of truth and reality, and the classic identifies the spirit of "historicized" empire.[22]

The allegorical method of text interpretation is replaced by the modern hermeneutics especially associated with Friedrich Schleiermacher and Wil-helm Dilthey, for whom the intention of the author is an important key to understanding the meaning of the text. The growing importance of the silent, individual reader in print culture is accompanied by the emergence of the romantic ideology of the solitary author who writes in order to express her deepest thoughts and feelings.[23] According to Kermode, modern art and literature are distinguished from their ancient predecessors by the "roman-tic image" or symbol—the concrete truth that the artist uncovers through her suffering and isolation. This is not the symbol as understood in classical allegory, for no analogy or explication is involved. Instead, "[t]he situation

---

21. Kermode, *The Classic,* 114.
22. Ibid., 67.
23. "I . . . use 'Romantic' in a restricted sense, as applicable to the literature of one epoch, beginning in the late years of the eighteenth century and not yet finished, and as referring to the high valuation placed during this period upon the image-making powers of the mind at the expense of its rational powers, and to the substitution of organicist for mechanistic modes of thinking about works of art" (Kermode, *Romantic Image,* 43).

is something like this: In each poem there is something (an individual intu-ition—or a concept) which can never be expressed in other terms. It is like the square root of two or like pi, which cannot be expressed by rational numbers, but only as their *limit*."[24]

The detailed and extreme individuality of romantic literature (especially the novel) creates the illusion of intimate contact between reader and writer. Accordingly, the romantic modern hermeneutics identifies the author's inten-tion with the one true meaning of the text.[25] This is a secular extension of Luther's identification of the "plain meaning" of the scriptures with the ac-tion of the Holy Spirit, the Bible's "author," upon the faithful reader. As does the Holy Spirit, the human author's intention dictates how the text should be understood. According to this ideology, the writer (whether di-vine or human) "owns" the text in a way that the reader cannot, and the reader is obliged to respect that ownership. The text has been produced by its writer, and if it contains any truth at all, it must be the writer's truth. The gap between signifier and signified can no longer be repaired by an al-legory of eternal truth, and instead the desire of the reader is to bridge the historical gap between herself and the intention of the writer in producing the text.

The meaning of the text is not limited to its denotation, which in the case of fictional texts is often nonexistent, but it also includes the connotation that the text originally had. Modern hermeneutics understands this to be the meaning that the writer intended to express. The physical text of the work is merely the lens or window through which the writer's intended meaning is revealed to the reader, and the successful reading results in a "fusing of horizons" between reader and writer. Thus this modern reading "requires the reader to use his learning in order to approximate to a reading of the classic possible to an informed contemporary of the author's."[26] In other words, critical understanding seeks a dynamically equivalent translation of the text.

Romantic hermeneutics, along with the rest of the modern world, cannot be understood apart from print culture (see further chapter 2). The excesses and imbalances of the romantic sensibility are encouraged and even pro-duced by the transformation from oral to print culture. The emergence of print culture requires a translation of culture, but this is not at all the *trans-latio imperii* that was described by Eliot. As Kermode says, "the classic of the modern *imperium* cannot be . . . a repository of certain, unchanging truths. Truth in art . . . will have the hesitancy, the instability, of the attitude

---

24. W. K. Wimsatt, his emphasis, quoted in Kermode, *Romantic Image*, 159. See also Kermode, *The Classic*, 109.

25. Kermode, "Plain Sense," presents an excellent discussion of problems associated with this and related concepts.

26. Kermode, *The Classic*, 75. See also Gadamer, *Truth and Method*.

struck by the New World, provincial and unstable itself, towards the corrupt maturity of the metropolis [Rome]."[27]

Unlike ancient oral culture, which produced the imperial classic, modern print culture brings with it sensitivity to the relativity and temporality of language. The modern classic lives in time, beginning at a definable point in the life of its writer and surviving the challenges of history until it reaches the present reader. If it is a classic, the Bible must be such a work. However, as its religious authority declines—and as literacy spreads, due to print culture— there is a growing tendency to regard the Bible as at best a compendium of stirring narratives, moral and philosophical insights, and beautiful poetry. The texts' meanings are understood to be human ideas, and like all human ideas they may well be mistaken. According to the modern viewpoint, the Bible still contains truths, and it may even denote historical events, but it is the task of critical scholarship to identify the objective circumstances of the biblical texts' production, the points of origin that are crucial to determining their meaning.

Critical understanding of the classic text encourages the search for a point of origin, which is understood to determine finally the meaning and value of the text. It is once again its author's intention. This point of origin is what Jacques Derrida calls the *archē*. The desire to ground historical meaning in an *archē* is also very much a product of logocentrism.[28] It is within this modernist historical frame that scholars such as Tracy and Funk consider the Bible to be a "classic." Although in some respects Tracy's theology suggests the eternal, allegorical empire of the imperial classic, nevertheless in his confidence in the possibility of meaning and his hope that humanity may find a home, Tracy turns finally to something like Kermode's modern, historically grounded understanding of the classic. Tracy's postmodern theology is compromised because of this.

This modern historical and hermeneutical framework has long played a significant role in the ideological self-understanding of Christianity. Bart Ehrman notes that an early point of contention between the "proto-orthodox" Church and its gnostic opponents was whether the scriptures should be interpreted "literally" ("grammatical, lexical, and historical exegesis") or allegorically.[29] Although numerous Christian theologians have drawn upon allegorical readings of the Bible, such readings have always been regarded with some suspicion. Despite the close association of modern historical interpretation with print culture and especially with romantic thought, orthodox Christianity from its beginnings has tended to regard itself as a "historical" religion, for which its roots in the past, the *archē* located in Jesus and the apostles, have been in some way definitive. Perhaps

---

27. Kermode, *The Classic*, 113.
28. Derrida, *Of Grammatology*, 60.
29. Ehrman, *Orthodox Corruption*, 20–21, 123. See also Moule, *Birth*, 163.

the earliest statement of this Christian belief appears in the New Testament itself, where it emerges as a central theme of the Acts of the Apostles.[30]

It seems anachronistic that ancient Christian or Jewish texts should be "modern" or even "romantic." However, Erich Auerbach detects romantic eccentricity in several biblical narratives. The imperial classical *epistémè* of ancient Greece and Rome and the neoclassicism that imitates it during the Enlightenment demand of literature very clear and distinct genres of tragedy and comedy. In contrast, the modern classic as found in romantic art and literature freely mixes the two genres. Auerbach argues that much of the Bible not only does not fit the imperial classic's opposition of genres, but instead it mixes the tragic and the comic in ways that are more characteristic of print culture and the modern classic. For example, during the passion narratives in the gospels, the humble fisherman and disciple Peter denies having any association with Jesus and thereby betrays him at the very moment that Jesus, the son of God, is condemned by the priests.[31] This places a traditionally comic character (the lower-class working man) in a traditionally tragic context (the suffering of the aristocratic hero).

Furthermore, the criteria for biblical canonicity themselves imply a historical *archē*. In addition to catholicity, the other criteria used to define the Christian canon were apostolicity, orthodoxy, and traditional usage.[32] These criteria for the canon come together in the ancient but still widespread ideology of "the apostolic age," which is the belief that there was a time of beginnings, a time when the Christian Church was pure and unified and true to the teachings of its founder, Jesus, and when these teachings were transmitted without distortion by his apostles. Belief in the apostolic age plays a significant role in the emergence and self-justification of the "early Catholic" or "proto-orthodox" communities that eventually become the mainstream of Christianity, what the pagan critic Celsus called the "great church." This belief both justifies and is supported by the Christian canon.

According to the ideology of the apostolic age, the New Testament texts themselves are canonized because they are the direct or indirect products of reliable apostolic memory of the words and deeds of Jesus, and the Old Testament texts are canonized because they are the "scriptures" of Jesus and the apostles. The letter to the Ephesians describes the Church as "the household of God, built upon the foundation of the *apostles* and *prophets,* Christ Jesus himself being the cornerstone" (Ephesians 2:19–20, emphasis added). In the second century, Papias of Hierapolis says that the written texts that eventually become Christian scriptures are inferior to the oral traditions passed on by "living and surviving" eyewitnesses to the words and deeds of

---

30. Wilken, *Myth*, 31–37. See also Barton, *Holy Writings, Sacred Text,* 82–83.
31. Auerbach, *Mimesis*, 40 ff.
32. Gamble, *New Testament Canon*, 67–72. Gamble explicitly rules out inspiration as a criterion. Contrast Detweiler, "Sacred Text," 218–23.

Jesus and his disciples.[33] For early Christians, there are two possible sources of authority, "the divine scriptures [or the Law and the Prophets] and the Lord"[34]—that is, the Jewish scriptures and the words of Jesus. First Timothy 5:18 states that "the scripture says, 'You shall not muzzle an ox when it is treading out the grain,' and, 'The laborer deserves his wages,'" quoting Deuteronomy 25:4 alongside words of Jesus (Luke 10:7; compare Matthew 10:10), hence treating both of these quotations as "scripture."

The "apostolic age" lasts until the apostolic origins of the Christian movement have faded into a remote past and divine revelation has ceased after the deaths of the last eyewitnesses to Jesus' life. It is only then that Christian orthodoxy, the original, "virginal" Christian faith, is challenged and threatened by the errors and falsehoods of the various heretics. The heretical views arise as deviations from or distortions of the original, correct belief of the apostles. It is then that texts associated by tradition with the apostles become important to the church and are eventually canonized in the New Testament.

This ideology of a theologically pure apostolic age, through which Christians even today are connected historically to the original, true revelation of Jesus, is also implied by the modern notion of the Bible as the Christian classic. It appears in the ideology of an *archē* of pure Christian faith that is transmitted essentially unchanged by means of the biblical canon. There may be an eternal "essence" or message at the core of Christianity, but that essence can only be encountered through the medium of history. Modern readers demythologize ancient texts such as the Bible and sort through and discard concepts that are now known to be mistaken (such as belief in demons or miracles) so that they can still learn from and value those truths that have withstood the test of time (enduring truths of the human condition). In this way of thinking, historical exegesis is nothing less than a secularized version of the eternal, imperial classic.[35] The eternal message has been made known through (and concealed within) a sequence of historical embodiments.

However, the historically embodied truths of the modern classic are not "eternal" in the same way that ancient allegory conceived the truth of the eternal, imperial classic. Modern truths are not beyond history; instead, they have survived in the specific, contingent histories of human beings. This historical understanding of truth differs from Kermode's concrete, romantic image only in emphasis. Like truth, the image is not a point of access or bridge between history and eternity, but rather it is a moment in which the eternal is found embedded in time, incarnate:

---

33. So says Eusebius in his fourth-century book *Ecclesiastical History* (3.39.4).
34. Hegesippus, quoted in Bauer, *Orthodoxy and Heresy*, 214.
35. See Kermode, *The Classic*, 137.

For what was thought of as beyond time, as the angels...or the *imperium* were beyond time, inhabiting a fictive perpetuity, is now beyond time in a more human sense; it is here, frankly vernacular, and inhabiting the world where alone, we might say with Wordsworth, we find our happiness—our felicitous readings—or not at all.[36]

Readers of the Bible frequently search, at least tacitly, for a "canon within the canon." This too is an *archē*. In order to "save" the biblical texts in the modern secularized context, and to distinguish between those denotations that can be allowed to be fallible and those that cannot, certain key texts or "material principles" are identified by theologians and biblical scholars.[37] This reestablishes a kind of historical empire, for these principles then serve as criteria for a reading of the entire canon. They become a reading lens or filter that emphasizes the denominational or other ideological commitments of the reader. These selected texts, or the principles by which they are selected, serve to explain or to explain away all other selections. Any other principles or texts that could also be selected to interpret the biblical texts, and with just as much reason, are dismissed. Much of the labor of modern critical study of the Bible centers upon the identification, elaboration, and contestation of such criteria for reading. Eliot's choice of Virgil's Rome as the empire that produced European civilization (that is, his own civilization) suggests a similar approach, and it is in this context that Tracy's arguments concerning the Bible as a classic should also be situated.

Fragmentary Empires

In each of the configurations delineated by Kermode, the classic is closely associated with empire. The classic work always conveys power. It stands opposed to the vulgar, the parochial, and the barbaric as that which alone has universal value. The biblical canon—whether the Jewish scriptures or the Christian Bible—is also both the product and the producer of imperial ideology (see further chapter 1): "The canonical text is not a unified whole; it is not a body of literature at all. Instead, it is an assemblage held together only by the imperialist power that first created it."[38] The Constantinian adoption of Christianity stands closely correlated to the establishment of the Christian canon and the triumph of the "great church," the eternal empire of orthodox Christian faith. Similarly, the Renaissance initiates the global expansion of European civilization and colonialism, and the ideology of the

36. Ibid., 140.
37. Gamble, *New Testament Canon*, 86.
38. Berquist, "Postcolonialism and Imperial Motives," 28. See also ibid., 24. Compare Lévi-Strauss: "Writing may not have sufficed to consolidate human knowledge, but it may well have been indispensable to the establishment of an enduring dominion" (*Tristes Tropiques*, 293).

historical, modern classic supports European belief in the antiquity and the originality of European Christian culture.

These two historical and political moments correspond to Kermode's two definitions of the classic. From the eternal point of view, these definitions are two temporal dispositions of one truth, and from the historical point of view, one imperial myth is "translated" into another. Whether empire is understood as eternal and allegorical or as contingent and historical has important consequences for how the Bible is read as a classic, but in either case the reading remains in an imperialistic mode. In addition, for either reading, the Bible remains deeply logocentric in its distinction between the text and its message. Both the eternal empire and the historical empire are readily "translatable," through dynamic equivalence, even though the metaphysical implications will be different in each case.

As modern critical scholarship comes into full bloom in the nineteenth century, it subjects itself to critical scrutiny. The subjective contribution to the construction of meaning is recognized. The resulting self-critical perspective understands meaning and truth themselves to be historical products of power and desire. However, when historical understanding of the classic becomes self-critical, then not only does the critical concept of the classic change, but the classic work itself also changes to conform to the new idea. This results in works of literature and of criticism that question themselves and further results in a collapse of the distinction between literature and criticism.

The romantic hermeneutics of modernism discovers within itself its own "other." Allegory is reinvented as "horizontal rather than vertical"—that is, fluid and amorphous intertextuality, a network of texts that is flat and decentered, not hierarchical.[39] Like the canon, the classic is always intertextual and ideological. According to this surpassed modernism, or postmodernism, one reason that the classic work is able to endure from one generation to the next is because its meaning is complex and finally indeterminate or "open," inviting plural readings. No single eternal truth underlies the text.

From this critical perspective, each text is understood to signify a plurality of possible meanings, only some of which any one reader could possibly discover. This plurality of meanings is highly contextual, and it varies with temporal, cultural, and individual ideological differences. The text is understood to be "intrinsically plural," and the number of its potential meanings actually increases over time.[40] The writer becomes merely the first among many different readers, and even at that the writer's reading of the text is no more valuable than that of any other reader. The writer is no longer the proper owner of the text's meaning. Indeed, the text has no proper meaning, and from the standpoint of its reader, the author is "dead."[41]

---

39. Jameson, *Postmodernism*, 168. See also Deleuze and Guattari, *A Thousand Plateaus*.

40. Kermode, *The Classic*, 129. See also ibid., 107–14, 121.

41. Barthes, *Roland Barthes*, 142–48; and *Rustle*, 49–55. See also Kermode, *The Classic*, 137. See further chapter 2.

Kermode's view on this matter is similar to the views of Tracy, Funk, and Gamble, noted above. The work continues to offer different meanings to different readers and to different ages, and thus to "stay alive" through its continued contemporaneity. The classic work is, in effect, the text that survives because it continues to be read. That is an important reason, but it is not the only reason. The classic also survives because in one way or another it represents a system *of* power and a system that is *in* power. The classic text survives because it is not destroyed or abandoned. The task of the postmodern historian is not so much to pinpoint the text's moment of origin, the *archē*, but rather to trace the "trajectory" of the text's reception and transformations through its various embodiments.

In the twentieth century, this historical self-critique is applied to the Christian ideology of the apostolic age. The status of Christianity as a "historical religion" is itself seen to be the product of ideology. Belief in an original point of Christian revelation and in the priority of the orthodoxy of the "great church" is thoroughly criticized by scholars such as Walter Bauer.[42] In contrast to the story of an apostolic age of pure Christian faithfulness, the surviving evidence suggests that the early Christian movement was manifold and quite diverse from its beginning and for several hundred years, at least until the Constantinian triumph of the "great church" and the canonization of the Bible, both during the fourth century. Early Christian groups ranged from Jewish Christians (more or less Hellenized) to Marcionites, Montanists, and a wide variety of gnostics and other syncretizers, as well as the "great church" of "early Catholicism."[43] According to Bauer, the reciprocal concepts of "orthodoxy" and "heresy" emerged as ideological weapons used by these widely varying Christian groups in order to combat one another.

In other words, "orthodoxy" and "heresy" are relative terms, definable only from a particular ideological point of view. From some other point of view, the denotation of these words would change or even reverse. Neither the theological views that triumphed in the fourth century nor any of the views that did not triumph are the true or proper form of Christian faith, at least not in any sense that could be justified historically. "The apostolic age is a creation of the Christian imagination"; it is a "myth of Christian beginnings."[44] Christianity did not actually begin in that way. Eusebius, the fourth-century historian of Christianity, was also one of the foremost advocates of the victorious position and a major contributor to this myth. In fact,

---

42. See also Wilken, *Myth*. Dunn (*Unity and Diversity*, 4) notes that this sort of criticism is found already in the nineteenth century, especially in the work of F. C. Baur. Ehrman surveys the criticisms of Bauer's study and concludes that "despite the clear shortcomings of his study, Bauer's intuitions were right *in nuce*: if anything, Christianity was even less tidy and more diversified than he realized, and contrary to his opinion, we do not need to wait for the second century to begin painting this picture" (*Orthodox Corruption*, 8).

43. Moule sketches an even earlier range of possibilities (*Birth*, 153–54).

44. Wilken, *Myth*, 158. See also Mack, *Myth of Innocence*.

nearly all of the evidence for the ancient struggle between Christian groups has survived in texts produced by the eventual victors, who thus get to call themselves the "orthodox." Hence Ehrman refers to their predecessors as "proto-orthodox."

Orthodox Christian writers created the illusion of the apostolic age, and they, by and large, also defined the canon of the Bible. Their followers copied most of the manuscripts of the Bible that have survived. Ehrman demonstrates that unacceptable textual material was removed from copies of the scriptures or altered through the "corrections" of orthodox Christian copyists. Nevertheless, inconsistent scribal practices permitted many textual "errors" to survive, and the extant early New Testament manuscripts are riddled with textual material that appears to be the product of significantly different Christian movements.[45]

The victorious orthodox views also appear in retrospect as a compromise between the extremes of the various heresies. For example, the Chalcedonian christological formula regarding two natures in one person assumes a middle position between adoptionism and monophysitism, while rejecting both of those views as extremes. Compromise would also account for the paradoxical and even contradictory qualities of orthodox trinitarian dogma. This suggests that the orthodoxy that eventually triumphed is itself derivative from heresy and not the other way around, contrary to the ideology of the apostolic age. As far as I can tell, neither Bauer nor those influenced by him go quite this far, although Ehrman comes close.[46] The chronological priority of "heresy" is implied by the wide popularity of nonorthodox views, especially in the Eastern churches, and also by the relatively "late" appearance of "early Catholicism" in the New Testament texts. Both adoptionism and varieties of gnosticism appear earlier in the texts.

If there is no recognized authority—no institutionally sanctioned position—then "orthodoxy" and "heresy" have little meaning. Christian diversity continues to the present day, but ever since the fourth century C.E., heresy has been defined as beliefs that are rejected by authoritative agencies of established churches. Only a church with some base of institutionalized power can define "right belief." In the fourth century, one group gained the favor of the Roman emperor, and the others did not. With that favor came the power to eliminate their opponents. The Christians who eventually "won" were most numerous and vociferous in the vicinity of the imperial capitol. Bauer also notes that the "orthodox" of Rome appear to have been better organized than their various opponents, and the great church had "the form which was the most uniform and best suited for mass consumption."[47] One of the central characteristics of early Catholic New Testament

45. Ehrman, *Orthodox Corruption,* 277. See also Dunn, *Unity and Diversity;* Robinson and Koester, *Trajectories;* and Petersen, *Gospel Traditions.*

46. Ehrman, *Orthodox Corruption,* 278.

47. Bauer, *Orthodoxy and Heresy,* 221; see also Coote and Coote, *Power, Politics,* 11. The

texts such as the Pastoral letters and 2 Peter is their strong emphasis on church organization.

When the political status of Christianity changed under Constantine and his successors, the "orthodox" Christians were both geographically positioned and institutionally organized to use this change to their advantage. Other Christian groups were less willing or able to adjust to the new situation—and perhaps also less theologically pragmatic—and thus they became the "heretics." The triumph of "orthodoxy" is a political triumph; it is the *human construction* of "right belief" as "apostolic faith."[48] The double canon of the Christian Bible is an outstanding product of this contest, and of the victory of the "orthodox." The Bible becomes a canon at the same time—and for the same reasons—that the empire becomes Christian.

Postmodernism and the Canon

The foregoing analysis anticipates a postmodern understanding of canon. Jean-François Lyotard makes it clear that postmodernism is not simply another historical era, but rather an element *within* modernism:

> The postmodern would be that which, *in the modern,* puts forward the unpresentable in presentation itself; that which denies itself the solace of good forms, the consensus of a taste which would make it possible to share collectively the nostalgia for the unattainable; that which searches for new presentations, not in order to enjoy them but in order to impart a stronger sense of the unpresentable.[49]

The postmodern appears in the deconstruction of the modern. The postmodern condition fits neither Eliot's notion of cultural or linguistic maturity, nor the modern concept of a continuous, linear historical sequence. Language no longer denotes extratextual truth, but instead language is an exercise of power—not the ancient, magical *poiēsis* of oral culture, but a measure of the limits of individual or mass consciousness. History is understood to be a fragmentary, subjective, and profoundly ideological fiction that is created in response to present interests.

Postmodernism belongs to an age of both the death of God and the death of man.[50] The postmodern age is often viewed as a time of decline, particu-

---

Marcionites were also well organized, "[b]ut Marcion himself, the most dangerous of all, to a large measure paralyzed his own cause insofar as he excised with his own hand the source of natural increase for his community by his inexorable rejection of procreation" (Bauer, *Orthodoxy and Heresy,* 221).

48. Dunn, *Unity and Diversity,* 1, 377. See also Kermode, *The Classic,* 28–32, on the role of Constantine in relation to the concepts of empire and the classic.

49. Lyotard, *Postmodern Condition,* 81, emphasis added. Not all postmodern theorists agree with Lyotard's views, and it is a point of serious disagreement between Lyotard and Jameson. In any case, "postmodern" does not simply mean "current" or "contemporary."

50. See Foucault, *Order of Things,* 387.

larly by those, like Eliot, who bemoan the loss of traditional sensibilities and values, the rejection of established privileges, and the shattering of canons. If the present age is a postmodern one, it is also a post-Constantinian age, and all of the formerly recognized authorities of imperial Christianity are at least put in question, and often simply rejected or forgotten altogether. From this point of view, the Western world appears to be slipping away from the great high points of Renaissance civilization, and our creative and humanizing powers are devalued in the name of organizational and technological efficiency. Genuine human community seems likely to be swallowed up by gigantic, complex, and segmentized social structures. These structures threaten to do away entirely with the significance of the individual and therefore with traditional human values.

However, the postmodern does not automatically equal whatever is contemporary, nor does the postmodern necessarily come after the modern. Postmodernism is not a *telos*, a culmination, but simply the most distinctive mark of the culture that is emerging at this time. Lyotard says that neither the traditional narratives of Western civilization (the classics of eternal empire) nor the modern "grand narratives" (the classics of historical empire) can serve the needs (or meet the desires) of postmodern human beings. Postmodernism is "incredulity toward metanarratives" such as these. As Fredric Jameson says, "We are left with that pure and random play of signifiers that we call postmodernism, which no longer produces monumental works of the modernist type but ceaselessly reshuffles the fragments of preexistent texts, the building blocks of older cultural and social production, in some new and heightened bricolage."[51]

This "new and heightened bricolage" plays with the universal metanarratives, breaking them up and rearranging the pieces. The result is an intertextual "paralogy" of "micronarratives," a fluid multiplicity of stories that serves to destabilize the metanarratives and to reveal what they have excluded, "producing not the known, but the unknown."[52] According to Lyotard, this postmodern discourse is the only option that contemporary human beings have to avoid the terrorism of a totalized system. In contrast to both the imperial and the modern classical metanarratives, postmodern micronarratives are local and particular. They are not universal, but instead they are partial stories, in the sense both of "incomplete" or "fragmentary" and also "biased." Postmodern discourse consists of a many-sided conversation that generates a fluid, noncentered network of narratives, an unbounded intertext in which meaning is constantly shifting and reconfiguring itself, never fixed or stable.[53]

---

51. Jameson, *Postmodernism*, 96. See also Lyotard, *Postmodern Condition*, xxiv.
52. Lyotard, *Postmodern Condition*, 60. See also Kermode, *Genesis of Secrecy;* "Plain Sense"; and *The Classic*, 135–41.
53. Deleuze and Guattari, *A Thousand Plateaus*, 9.

The mythic story of an apostolic age of purely orthodox Christian faithfulness sounds rather like another metanarrative, or part of one. In contrast, Bauer's description of the early Christian movement sounds like a paralogy of little narratives. Many diverse groups each claim to transmit the pure apostolic faith while they struggle to fend off the deviant views of their opponents, whom they consider to be heretics. The concept of the postmodern resonates with circumstances under which no canon or classic would have yet been possible. In postmodernism as in early Christianity, there is a "pure and random play" of texts (gospels, acts, epistles, apocalypses, psalms, prophecies, wisdom texts, and other writings), about which there is no consensus, no community of taste.[54] Even when theologically distinct early Christian groups use the same texts (such as letters or gospels, or portions of the Jewish scriptures), they read them in remarkably different, incompatible ways, "ceaselessly reshuffling" them, to use Jameson's words, and even physically rewriting them, as Ehrman demonstrates. This does not describe a situation of established "orthodoxy," much less "catholicity" or "apostolicity."

However, postmodernism also differs from the situation of early Christianity in important ways. Postmodernists generally regard plurality of texts and of readings as a *good thing*. Plurality is something to be valued and encouraged, not only in one's own group but also in the "others," those who do not see things our way. For postmodernism, there is no one "right belief," and terms such as "orthodoxy" and "heresy" are not merely relative but lack any possible meaning in a postmodern context.

Furthermore, the early Christian paralogy of multiple beliefs and scriptures does not deconstruct the metanarrative of the apostolic age, but rather it is absorbed and concealed by that metanarrative. The establishment of the Christian canon in the fourth century is a consequence of the triumph of the orthodox "great church." Thereafter the canon is used by victorious Christian communities to ensure careful intertextual control of the meaning of the scriptures and to guard against the sort of pluralistic free play that characterizes postmodern intertextuality. The biblical canon was created by the victorious orthodox Christians in order to terminate the heretical (pre-orthodox, but also postmodern) plurality and paralogy of texts and readings, not to stimulate it.

Tracy develops his understanding of the Bible as a classic in relation to "our post-modern situation," and in some respects he is correct. From one point of view, postmodern plurality and fragmentation cry out for the stability and authority of the classic. Nevertheless, the "post-modern situation" that Tracy describes is at best a tame variety of "the postmodern condition." Following Paul Ricoeur, Tracy insists that the metaphoric fictionality of the biblical texts is grounded in and returns the reader to an extratextual

---

54. See Ehrman, *Orthodox Corruption*, 22–25.

reality. Tracy claims that belief arises from an encounter with a limit, in which wholeness is revealed. The "power of the whole" revealed as other, as mystery, creates the religious classic, according to Tracy, and this in turn makes possible what he calls the analogical imagination. Tracy describes "the uncanny whirlpool of the chaos of pure equivocity" as

> a chaos whose own uncanny *fascinans et tremendum* power must one day discover that its own radicality and liberating power is ultimately empowered by, because rooted in, the same reality as its analogical counterparts: the always-already, not-yet event of the yes disclosed in the grace of Jesus Christ.[55]

Here Tracy's views are not at all postmodern. For postmodernism, there is no root, no *archē*. Here too postmodernists probably differ from early Christians.

At the beginning of this chapter, I stated that redescription of the Bible as a "classic" is an attempt to salvage the authority of the Christian canon in a world that apparently no longer needs canons. Postmodern criticism makes continued acceptance of either an imperial or a modern classic problematic. The postmodern concept of unlimited semiosis unsettles the clear denotation of texts and the finality of any signified, and it deconstructs the logocentrism that plays an important role in both the imperial and the modern classic. The limits and the identity of the text are put in question. The task (and perhaps the impossibility) of translation resurfaces, and the two Christian canons can no longer be assumed to convey the same message, or any message at all. "Reality," "truth," and "history" are understood to be constructs, the productions of particular perspectives that depend in part at least on the interests of the observer. The observer herself is seen to be an ideological product, a juncture in an intertextual network. In a postmodern world, the canon machine grinds to a halt.

Human beings today may no longer be able to conceive the classic with the seriousness of Eliot or Tracy or Kermode. In other words, the classic, like the canon, may no longer be able to function in the contemporary Western world.[56] Even to speak of "today" or "the Western world" signals a misleading sense of singularity, a metaphysical wholeness that corresponds to nothing. Whose present age? Whose Western world? The word "classic" is already in danger of losing any specificity that may remain to it in our world, used as it is now for Coca-Cola and Wendy's hamburgers, certain types of rock music, and any car over twenty-five years old, among other things. That discussion of the classic can be conjoined at all with discussion of the postmodern suggests that the world has become a very dif-

---

55. Tracy, *Analogical Imagination*, 421. See also ibid., 163 ff.; and "Metaphor and Religion," 97–99.
56. See also Detweiler, "Sacred Text," 225.

ferent place. The conditions of human existence have changed. This change is comparable to other great transformations of human existence, such as the Constantinian triumph of Christianity, or the Renaissance, in which fundamental structures of human life and thought were challenged and forever altered. I will return to these matters once more in the conclusion of this book.

PART TWO

Wild Connotations

Chapter 5

BABBLE ON

Human nature, essentially changeable, unstable as the dust, can endure no restraint; if it binds itself it soon begins to tear madly at its bonds, until it rends everything asunder, the wall, the bonds and its very self....

If it had been possible to build the Tower of Babel without ascending it, the work would have been permitted....

We are digging the pit of Babel.

— Franz Kafka, *Parables and Paradoxes*

The [Hebrew] text says: God proclaimed his name loudly, the name which he himself has chosen and which is thus his. Already one can see that the conflict is a war between two proper names and the one that will carry the day is the one that either imposes its law or in any case prevents the other from imposing its own. God says: Babel.

— Jacques Derrida, *The Ear of the Other*

A Zigzag Reading

The story of the tower of Babel (Genesis 11:1–9) is often read as a myth narrating the loss of a language that humanity once shared with God. The Babel story serves as a crucial ideological hinge in the larger canonical sequence of stories, for according to the story itself, all human language must be on "this side" of Babel, "after Babel." No translation could transcend such a cultural gap. In this way the biblical text makes its own denotation (truth value) problematical, for no stories from pre-Babelian times (Genesis 1–10) could possibly survive this catastrophe. The story of Babel implies that the preceding chapters in the book of Genesis are fabrications—either lies or fictions. In addition, if one reads the sequence of stories in Genesis 1–11 as part of a continuous chronology, then it is not at all clear that the human tongue that is "confused" at Babel speaks initially the language of Eden. Multiple human languages (LXX: *glōssa*, "tongue")[1] are already mentioned

---

1. As I explained in the introduction, I use the Septuagint (LXX), not the Hebrew text of the Jewish scriptures, because that is the text referenced in the Greek New Testament.

in the preceding chapter in Genesis, in the genealogy of the descendants of Noah, at 10:5, 20, and 31.

If it is read under canonical control, the stories in Genesis 1–11 are arranged in a linear, causal sequence, in which each new story builds upon the previous one—that is, the stories themselves pile up into a narrative tower. Despite the paradoxes noted above, the stories are read as though they were a coherent linear history. The reader scrolls through the continuous narrative sequence without skipping or stopping. So read, the Babel story describes the creation of "natural" human languages as the result of a "fall" from a single, divine language. It tells of a monumental linguistic crash.[2] This story is the final one of a series of "falls" that begins with the famous Fall, the original sin of Adam and Eve in Genesis 2–3. On this canonical reading, the calling of Abram (Genesis 12:1), which follows the Babel story after one of the frequent genealogies, is the first in the next group of stories. The stories of Abra(ha)m continue the linear sequence and begin the story of the response to this cumulative disaster that will occupy the remainder of the Bible.

However, this collection of stories resists the reader's desire for clear answers—that is, for an authoritative canon. An alternative reading pattern may also be used to comprehend this material—a pattern that rejects canonical control. The alternative reading pattern regards each of the stories in Genesis 2–11 as rehearsing a single basic configuration common to them all, a nonlinear, noncausal array that represents only one fundamental human action and one fundamental divine response, retold with various characters, details, and settings. For this reading, the stories in Genesis 2–11 provide a collection of narrative variations on the single theme of the loss of Paradise, resulting from unavoidable conflict between human beings and God. At Babel, it is the language of Paradise that is lost. Humanity's estrangement from God reappears in each act of human rebellion and divine rejection, and Babel is the final catastrophe only in the sense that it happens to be the last one in line.

Indeed, apart from the reference to Shinar (Genesis 11:2), which appears also in Genesis 10:10 along with a reference to Babel, the Babel story might just as well directly follow the first creation story, Genesis 1:1–2:4a, as an alternative to the Eden story. Unless the desire for a name is itself a pun on the name "Shem,"[3] there is no reference to Shem or to Nimrod (from Genesis 10), or to any other named human being or community, in the Babel story itself until the very end, at which point the community no longer exists ("its name was called Babel," Genesis 11:9). The opening of the Babel story itself seems to invite a nonlinear approach: "Now the *whole earth* had one

---

2. See also the discussion of Neal Stephenson's novel *Snow Crash* in the conclusion of this book.

3. See Spina, "Babel."

language (LXX: *cheilos hen kai phōnē mia,* "one lip and one voice") and few words" (Genesis 11:1, emphasis added). This strongly implies that the events of Genesis 10 have not preceded this story, despite the sequence of chapters. The "sons of men" (LXX: *hoi huioi tōn anthrōpōn*) at 11:5 may also represent the entire human race, not just some group of human beings.

The assembly of these stories could be a result of redaction of different sources. Even if it is, the problem for the reader remains. Already something like canon appears to be at work within just these few chapters of the Bible, pressing toward a reading of the collected stories according to the linear pattern. However, it is also apparent in just these few chapters that this canon is already unable to compel such a reading. The reader is confronted with the problem of whether to read the stories in their linear sequence, or whether a nonlinear reading is permitted, or perhaps even required. Unfortunately, it is easy to slip almost unconsciously back and forth from one of these patterns to the other one, even though differences between the theological implications of the two contrary readings are considerable.

This question of reading is a theological and hermeneutical question, or in other words, it is an ideological question. I choose to read the stories, not in a linear sequence, but in a nonlinear, zigzag fashion. This alternative reading is valuable for my purposes, as it throws into relief the control exercised by the canonical reading. As I suggested in chapter 2, the zigzag style of reading, flipping back and forth in the text, is made convenient and easy by the physical format of the codex, in contrast to the scroll. The zigzag reading rejects the linear teleology of the sequence of narratives. I choose a nonlinear reading not only for these reasons but also because I am reading the story of Babel, an Old Testament story, in conjunction with the story of Pentecost from the New Testament, and that will require me to skip back and forth, to break up the text.[4] Thereby I give the story of Babel an intertextual context that is not that of the Jewish scriptures, although my reading is hardly an orthodox Christian one, either. Nevertheless, my choice of reading remains an ideological one, as is every reading choice, and it both reflects and resists the ideology of the Christian canon.

"Babel" is Hebrew for Babylon, but I do not call the inhabitants of Babel "Babylonians," for that would suggest historical denotation. The questions that the story of Babel raises are not questions of history. Genesis 10 notwithstanding, I understand the initial language of the Babelians to be what Umberto Eco calls an "Edenic" language (see further below). Prior to the events at Babel everyone speaks one language, the mythic true language of God in the Garden of Eden (Genesis 2–3). The Babelians' language gives them godlike power. The language of Eden is a divine tongue of creative power, the same words used by God to create everything in Genesis 1. For this language, nothing stands between the desire to do something and the do-

---

4. Barthes, *Pleasure*, 10–11.

ing of it: "Behold, they are one people, and they have all one language; and this is only the beginning of what they will do; and nothing that they propose to do will now be impossible for them" (Genesis 11:6; compare 3:22).

After the Babel events, this one language has been "confused" (Hebrew *bâlal*, Greek *sunecheen*) by God; the tongue has been twisted and tied up. The one perfect language with its "few words" (11:1) is replaced by many imperfect languages, and communication becomes difficult and maybe even impossible:

> After the Fall, which, in making language mediate, laid the foundation for its multiplicity, it could be only a step to linguistic confusion. Since men had injured the purity of name, the turning away from that contemplation of things in which their language passes into man needed only to be completed in order to deprive men of the common foundation of an already shaken language-mind. *Signs* must become confused where things are entangled. The enslavement of language in prattle is joined by the enslavement of things in folly almost as its inevitable consequence. In this turning away from things, which was enslavement, the plan for the tower of Babel came into being, and the linguistic confusion with it.[5]

In contrast, after the Pentecost events (Acts 2:1–42), all obstacles to communication have been swept away. At Pentecost, the many human tongues become transparent to the divine Spirit, and their differences are swept away before the Spirit's fiery breath:

> And they were all filled with the Holy Spirit and began to speak in other tongues, as the Spirit gave them utterance. Now there were dwelling in Jerusalem Jews, devout men from every nation under heaven. And at this sound the multitude came together, and they were bewildered, because each one heard them speaking in his own language. (Acts 2:4–6)

The many human languages of "every nation under heaven" are not, however, replaced by a single Spirit-language, and so the Pentecost events do not simply reverse the Babel events. In fact, Acts 2 does not cite Genesis 11, and there is no explicit link between the biblical stories of Babel and Pentecost. There is some common vocabulary among the texts of these stories in the Septuagint, the Greek translation of the Jewish scriptures, and the Greek New Testament—words such as *glōssa* (tongue) and *phōnē* (voice)—but given the similar themes of the two stories, this is not surprising.

However, there is a substantial intertextual echo between the stories. In Genesis 11:7, 9, the text plays between the words *sugcheō* ("let us confuse their language," "the Lord confused the language") and *sugchusis* ("its name

---

5. Benjamin, *Reflections*, 328–29, his emphasis.

was called Babel [Confusion]"). The latter two occurrences of this play in the LXX represent the Hebrew text's play on *bâlal* ("confusion" in Hebrew) and *bab-ilu* ("gate of god" in Akkadian). A similar wordplay is also suggested in the appearance of *sugcheō* ("they were bewildered [confused]") and *ekcheō* ("I will pour out [suffuse] my Spirit") in Acts 2:6, 17–18. At Babel, God "confuses" the people's tongues and causes them to babble in "confusion," whereas at Pentecost the people are "confused" at the many languages being spoken and understood while the Spirit is "suffused" upon them. This intertextual echo emphasizes that in the connection between these two stories different views of language are in tension with one another. These two views of language have already been described in part 1 of this book, and they will be further explored below. Each of these views has important semiotic and theological consequences that are, unfortunately, largely ignored by the biblical stories' readers.

No Perfect Language

Before these views can be explored, however, a digression is necessary. As I noted above, the story of Babel implies a divine predecessor to the confused human tongues. It posits a single language that was spoken by human beings before the Babel events, a language that has been lost or corrupted after Babel.[6] This is apparently the language spoken by Adam and Eve in the Garden of Eden, a language of innocence, given by God to the human beings. The language of Eden is perhaps even the language of God, the divine, perfect language. Genesis 2–3 tells the reader that God speaks the same tongue that the humans do, and so does the serpent.

The search for this Edenic language has played a significant role in Western theories of language from ancient times to the present, and it has even contributed to the rise of modern linguistics and philosophy of language.[7] The Edenic language was presumed to be a language of perfect clarity, a "pure conceptual notation"—that is, a language so transparent and unambiguous that confused or deceptive statements in it would be impossible. In this respect, the language of Eden sounds rather like the language of Pentecost: " 'Are not all these who are speaking Galileans? And how is it that we hear, each of us in his own native language?' " (Acts 2:7–8).

Eco explores how such an "Edenic" language would work. However, his focus is not on the text of Genesis 2–3 as such. Eco's reference to the Garden of Eden story provides little more than a springboard from which he can launch his study of a specific instance in which "aesthetic language" inevitably generates contradictory messages. According to Roman Jakobson, aesthetic messages are dominated by the "poetic function," which is one

---

6. Eco, *Search*, 7–9.
7. For extended discussions of this history, see Steiner, *After Babel;* and Eco, *Search*.

of the six functions[8] performed by language, and in which "[s]imilarity superimposed on contiguity imparts . . . its thoroughgoing symbolic, multiplex, polysemantic essence." The poetic function contributes to the unlimited semiosis of the text. "The poetic function projects the principle of equivalence from the axis of selection into the axis of combination," with the result that physical aspects of the signifier are emphasized and the denotation of the message is confused.[9] Indeed, the poetic function is particularly fertile in connotation and feeble in denotation: "[t]his function, by promoting the palpability of signs, deepens the fundamental dichotomy of signs and objects."[10]

Aesthetic messages arise from formal alterations in the language of the message that produce additional signifying "levels" of the message. In short, these messages are richly metaphorical and intensely connotative. What they signify most directly is, not some object in the extratextual world, but rather another message. However, these messages are unlike traditional allegory or otherwise coded messages that denote on a more esoteric level some extratextual truth. Instead, the second message or further level of the aesthetic message points "back" to the physical stuff of the message itself, the concrete aspect of the signifiers. The text is self-referential. As Eco says,

> to create an aesthetic message, there must also be alterations in the form in which it is expressed, and these alterations must be significant enough to require the addressee of the message, although aware of a change in the *content-form,* to refer back to the message itself as a physical entity.[11]

In other words, an aesthetic message contains some ambiguity or confusion of meaning. The message acts like any other message about extratextual reality, but it also makes the recipient aware of the physical medium of the message's text itself. As Jakobson says, the reference is split (see further chapter 3). All aesthetic messages are fictional—that is, their denotation of reality is disrupted in this way and is therefore at least somewhat problematic. "The text of fiction conserves the representational orientation of the words, but the secondary symbolic system formed by these words (the narrative) possesses the autonomous, non-instrumental character of the poetic text."[12]

Eco's hypothetical Edenic language purports to be a language that Adam and Eve could have used in the garden. Some of the possible messages that

---

8. Jakobson, *Language and Literature*, 85. The other language functions are the referential, emotive, conative, phatic, and metalingual. See further Aichele, *Sign, Text, Scripture,* chap. 1.
9. Jakobson, *Language and Literature*, 71.
10. Ibid., 69–70.
11. Eco, *Role*, 90, his emphasis.
12. Ducrot and Todorov, *Encyclopedic Dictionary,* 259.

are conveyed in this imaginary language are not at all aesthetic or ambiguous: "if two [signifier] sequences are joined to each other, their [signified] cultural units are thus brought into reciprocal predication."[13] This is the way that every language works. However, in any language even relatively frank, unambiguous messages are vulnerable to the potential within the intertextual repertoire of that language to produce aesthetic messages using the same signifiers. The connotation of any message is always dependent on its intertextual context, and a message that is unambiguous in one context could at any time be included as part of an aesthetic message in which its connection to any context is disrupted. Any language that can produce ambiguous messages—and every human language can—is flawed in such a way that doubts are raised about the meaning of *every* message, even the clearest ones, stated in that language. The pure, perfect language of God, given to human beings in the Garden of Eden, should not be so flawed. If it is flawed, that implies certain theologically troublesome things about God's limitations.

The disruption of linguistic order by aesthetic messages is, as Eco notes, a matter of narrative and ideology, not linguistic structure. In the case of Genesis 2–3, it is a matter of theology. Although the poetic function highlights the hyletic substance of the message's text, it does so by means of the message's form, and especially by means of its "content form" (as distinct from its "expression form").[14] The content form is the meaning or connotation of the words, the mental understanding of the message by its recipient.

Eco lays out the hypothetical Edenic language around two series of binary oppositions. The first pair of oppositions features a finite list of simple ideas or mental signifieds that derive from possible experiences within the narrative world of the biblical story: "Yes vs. No," "Good vs. Bad," "Beautiful vs. Ugly," and so forth. These pairs of oppositions establish the content form of any message in the Edenic language.[15] Eco identifies six pairs of signifieds; additional ones could no doubt be added, but they would not significantly change his argument. Each term in each of the opposed pairs is defined simply as the logical complement of the other term. Thus all the possible colors are named either "Red" or "Blue." Every color is either red or blue, and no color is both red and blue. This is much simpler than in any actual language, but the fundamental structure remains the same. No matter how many words are created for different colors, there will always be another unnamed color in between any two named ones.

The second pair of oppositions features the sounds or physical signifiers used to connote these contents. These oppositions establish the expression

---

13. Eco, *Role*, 93.

14. This distinction comes from Louis Hjelmslev. See Eco, *Search*, 20–24. In addition to the content form and expression form, there is a content substance (the denoted objects) and an expression substance (the *hulē* of the signifier).

15. Eco, *Role*, 92. See also Eco, *Search*, 20–23.

form—that is, the rules according to which the signifiers may be used. Eco's imaginary Edenic language requires only two simple signifiers, one vowel, "A," and one consonant, "B," arranged according to a simple "combinatory rule" that permits an "infinite series of syntactically correct sequences."[16] Eco's choice of these signifiers recalls a remark of Ferdinand de Saussure's: "It is precisely because the terms *a* and *b* as such are radically incapable of reaching the level of consciousness—one is always conscious of only the *a/b* difference—that each term is free to change according to laws that are unrelated to its signifying function."[17] Perhaps there is also an echo here of Jesus' prayer to "Abba" in another biblical garden (Mark 14:36). An additional consequence of this expression form that Eco also does not mention is that this language, if spoken, would sound like a kind of stuttering or babbling. The Edenic tongue is glossolalic. In Eco's imaginary language the Hebrew and the Greek texts of Genesis 11:1 are correct, and the pre-Babelian language—the language of Eden—is not primarily a language of the tongue but of the lip.[18]

The expression form and the content form are correlated in the system of signs (signifier → signified) that forms the Edenic language. For every formal difference of content (signified), there is a corresponding formal difference of expression (signifier). This double string of oppositions establishes a further series of metonymic "connotative chains" through which the language-user can move easily and usually unconsciously from one sign to another related sign. The relation between the signs appears both at the level of the signifier and at the level of the signified. For example, in Eco's imaginary Edenic language, one moves from "good" to "beautiful" by moving from "ABBA" (the word for "good") to "ABBBBA" (the word for "beautiful"), but this move is also possible because good things are often thought to be beautiful, and vice versa. This opens the further possibility of using a signifier to connote a signified other than its normal one, but from the same connotative chain— that is, as a metaphor.[19] Anything described as "ABA" ("edible") may come also to signify "good" ("ABBA"), and so forth. Through these connotations and their metaphoric consequences, the formal chains link the signs together into intertextual mental and perceptual configurations. Ideology arises from this "natural" usage of the language.

However, along with this linguistic power comes danger. Similarity can henceforth be superimposed on contiguity, and aesthetic language has appeared. The connotations open up the "limitless possibilities of semiosis," which is both the power of signs to refer endlessly to other signs and the

---

16. Eco, *Role*, 93.

17. Saussure, *Course*, 118.

18. See Eco, *Search*, 303–4. Compare the language of the "Falabalas" in Stephenson, *Snow Crash*.

19. Eco, *Role*, 94.

inability of any signifier to refer definitively or absolutely to any signified.[20] Every signified is also a signifier, and vice versa, and there is no last or final signified. In part 1, this understanding of language was described as diametrically opposed to the logocentric view that dominates Christian thought about the canon.

Eco notes that a contradiction results from this double series of oppositions when they are placed in the Eden narrative of Genesis 2–3. Two of the signs seem arbitrary and out of place in the sequences that Eco establishes. These are the words "serpent" ("ABBBA") and "apple" ("BAAAB"), which are crucial signs of disruption in the Garden of Eden story. The opposition between serpent and apple is of a different order than the other oppositions: "This is the only antithesis which denotes objects rather than qualities of objects or responses to them. . . . [T]hese two cultural units are incorporated in the code only after a factual judgment issued by God about the nontouchable status of the apple."[21]

All of the other content oppositions refer to generic characteristics that might apply to many different objects, in various combinations. The opposition between the specific objects, serpent and fruit, derives from God's command (" 'of the tree of the knowledge of good and evil you shall not eat, for in the day that you eat of it you shall die,' " Genesis 2:17) and the serpent's response when the woman invokes this command (" 'You will not die. . . . [Y]ou will be like God, knowing good and evil,' " Genesis 3:4–5). God's command (eat → punishment) and the serpent's rejection of that command (eat → reward) require the narrative complementarity of the serpent and the fruit. This is Eco's initial supposition.

The irregularity of the serpent and apple signs disrupts the connotative chains and introduces a semantic imbalance into the Edenic language system. God has "committed a grave error."[22] The story requires that if the apple ("BAAAB") is forbidden and thus bad ("BAAB"), then the serpent ("ABBBA"), which is its binary opposite, must be good ("ABBA"). Presumably the serpent, as a "creature that the LORD God had made" (Genesis 3:1), must in any case be good (1:25). This generates a contradiction, for in the Eden story, after the serpent speaks to her, "the woman saw that the tree was *good* for food, and that it was a *delight* to the eyes, and that the tree was to be desired to make one wise" (Genesis 3:6, emphasis added). The forbidden, hence bad, fruit is nonetheless edible, good, and beautiful. The Edenic language is thus inherently ambiguous because it permits and even requires this contradiction. Indeed, as the presumed creator of this language, God is responsible for confusing "the presumed natural order of things."[23] The connotative chain has been broken.

---

20. Ibid., 98.
21. Ibid., 92.
22. Ibid., 95.
23. Ibid.

God's error results in the creation by Adam and Eve of a metaphor that conceals the linguistic contradiction without eliminating it. They must distort their language, or in other words, they must re-create it. They have no alternative. The system of the language itself invites and even demands this distortion. By attempting to repair the broken connotative chains, Adam and Eve create a metaphor that tampers irreversibly with the linguistic system itself. Through this metaphor the language becomes self-referential or aesthetic. Through the play of metaphors, the message undermines the oppositions that are essential to its own significance. Therefore, although Eco does not use the term in this essay, the Eden story deconstructs itself.

Adam and Eve's metaphor provokes a "language passion" in them that corresponds to their desire for the forbidden fruit.[24] This language passion takes the form of self-referential play with the physical stuff of language itself (the "expression substance"), which they have become aware of thanks to the poetic function in operation. At first, Adam and Eve experience the materiality of language as magical, and then as arbitrary. By playing with the language, the humans violate and transform it, and that is how they come to understand how the linguistic system works. This in turn leads to the possibility of destroying the system and then to even greater linguistic (and cultural) creativity—that is, to the reversal of the divine prohibition. In their ability to play with language, the human beings have already become like God (Genesis 3:22).

Eco concludes that it is in the very nature of language to generate distortion of or disobedience to a message because language permits, and in fact encourages, the construction of metaphors—that is, the slippage of denotation into connotation. Even the perfect Edenic language must be flawed and ultimately opaque, not transparent at all.[25] God's Word, the fiat through which God creates men and women and everything else ("the fish of the sea, and . . . the birds of the air, and . . . the cattle, and . . . all the earth, and . . . every creeping thing that creeps upon the earth," Genesis 1:26), is also God's Law, understood as verbal command (" 'You may freely eat of every tree of the garden; but of the tree of the knowledge of good and evil you shall not eat, for in the day that you eat of it you shall die,' " Genesis 2:16–17). Nevertheless, God's Word/Law brings with it *of necessity* its own inevitable misunderstanding and transgression. The original sin is linguistic. What is the case for the primeval language of Eden, which is itself broken and confused in the Babel events (according to the canon), will also be the case for any language.

Thus it is not true that the Babel story designates the moment in the Bible when semiosis is liberated from any original signifier or terminal sig-

---

24. Ibid., 97. See also Eco, *Search*, 21.
25. Eco, *Role*, 90 ff.

nified and flows freely. Unlimited semiosis is already flowing in Eden.[26] The nonlinear, zigzag reading allows Babel even to *precede* Eden, or at the very least, to be a different version of the same story. One could press still further than this and argue, following or at least inspired by Eco's analysis, that just as humankind has been created in the "likeness" or "image" of God, so also the linguistic corruption that taints the entire human world already in the Garden of Eden must itself arise in the divine realm and infect God's own language. Even the perfect language demands the play of metaphor and connotation.

The physical system of the language itself invites and even demands its own confusion. The disorder of the signifiers is inherent in the signifying material itself. In addition, no entirely coherent system of connotative chains could be maintained in any possible story, language, or linguistic world. All language is confused, and no tongue is not confused. Nothing was lost at Babel, after all; instead, a fundamental necessity of language was realized there. There was no crime at Babel, nor did God punish anyone. The story of Eden implies that even God is constrained by the inherent imperfections of language.[27] God either deliberately creates the linguistic flaw or is unable to prevent its occurrence.

Eco hints at and toys with an even more radical analysis of the Eden story, a kind of treatment that he abjures in his later writings. This more radical treatment of the story of Eden would regard the interpretive choices (signifieds) that confront the reader of the story, not as coming from within the text of Genesis itself (where they were created by an author-god), but rather as coming from the interplay between textual signifiers and the reader's desire. This is the position that I am arguing in this book. In other words, it is the reader, finally, who inevitably plays with language and eats forbidden fruit with Adam and Eve. The story itself is the serpent, inviting readers to playful reading, and the readers have broken the prohibition ("don't read this sentence") before they even know what it is. The physical text, the sensuous "tongue" of the story, scatters the readers in confusion. The desire for a complete, self-explanatory text—that is, desire for a canon—is defeated from the very start. It is frustrated by the flaw in language itself.

God's Tongue

The Edenic language of the Babelians may not be the same as any known form of Hebrew, but perhaps it is some pure Hebrew of which actual Hebrew is a degenerate version. Over the centuries this has been a widespread

---

26. Ibid., 95, 98.

27. This opens the prospect of a linguistic approach to classical problems associated with the divine nature, such as the problem of evil, or the contradiction between divine eternal omniscience and genuine human freedom. I will not explore that opening here. Eco's analysis of Genesis 2–3 also contrasts remarkably to that in Romans 5.

view. The story of Babel implies that no present human tongue is the pure or true language of God and that the pure divine language is at best broken and hidden within our impure, faulty human tongues. Eco suggests, following Walter Benjamin, that the one pure language prior to Babel comprehended all human languages or, in other words, that every actual human language contains a fragment of that lost language.[28] Julia Kristeva takes a similar view: "This theme of a *universal language* (*langue*) and multiple languages (*langues*) that manifest it but also occult it and muddle its purity . . . is magnificently represented by the mythical sequence of the tower of Babel."[29]

In their Edenic language the people of Babel say, " 'Come, let us build ourselves a city, and a tower with its top in the heavens, and let us make a name for ourselves, lest we be scattered abroad upon the face of the whole earth' " (Genesis 11:4). This concord between the Babelians appears to be what spurs God's jealousy. However, this suggestion of utopian harmony raises the question of whether the destruction of Babel was a liberation or a failure for humanity. Two possibilities are produced by the two contrary reading patterns noted at the beginning of this chapter. They reflect two alternative interpretations of the Babelians' "fall":

1. either the Babel events result from the cruel tyranny of humans over other humans (humans are the bad guys, justly punished by God),

2. or the events result from humanity's righteous rebellion against divine tyranny (God is the bad guy, unjustly oppressing humans).

In either case, the humans lose. Many commentators on this story assume that there must be something sinful or wrong about the Babelian desire. Given the events of recent times, it is hard to believe that such unity of purpose could be achieved apart from a totalitarian society.[30] Therefore, this reading treats the story as though it were realistic and history-like. Nevertheless, the widespread assumption that God made the correct decision at Babel reveals significant ideological commitments on the part of the reader. Among other things, it justifies God's action—that is, God acts in this way only in order to counter the tyrannical ambitions of the Babelians. The linear, canonical reading of the Babel story, which is aligned with (1), regards their defeat as the defeat of sinners and the righteous victory of God. The canonical context of the story, at the end of the mythic sequence of Genesis 1–11, makes such an assumption difficult to avoid.

The alternative zigzag reading, which is aligned with (2), disagrees. This reading suggests that it is precisely the free consent of multiple human be-

---

28. Benjamin, *Illuminations*, 69 ff.; and Eco, *Search*, 345. See also Barnstone, *Poetics of Translation*, 239–48.

29. Kristeva, *Language*, 99, her emphasis.

30. Stephenson's novel also assumes that the precollapse Sumerians/Babelians had a rigidly totalitarian society featuring a glossolalic language (*Snow Crash*, 201–34). See also Hayles, *Posthuman*, 273–77. See further the conclusion of this book.

ings to labor together in their own collective interest that most threatens the ultimate tyrant, God. Perhaps the purity of the language of Paradise allows or even encourages genuine social harmony. This understanding of the story of Babel requires a nonrealistic reading: it treats the story as utopian fantasy, not history. Utopian fantasies hold out the dream of a freely harmonious human society. For example, William Morris's novel *News from Nowhere* describes a peaceful communalistic society to which "every one [contributes] according to his ability" (Acts 11:29) and in which goods are "distributed . . . to all, as any had need" (2:45). As a long-time member of a labor union, I am well aware of both the naïveté and the real potential of collective action. Although the limited successes and the glaring failures of attempts at voluntary collective action in the real world justify skepticism regarding such an interpretation, rabbinic commentary on Genesis 11 holds that God did not destroy the Babelians (as he did the inhabitants of Sodom) because of their love for one another.[31]

In any case, the vertical tower, symbol of unity, is abandoned by the Babelians. God scatters the people in horizontal, anarchic dispersion. The story never says that the tower was destroyed, merely that the Babelians "left off building the city." In the terms of Gilles Deleuze and Félix Guattari, a hierarchical, "arborescent" structure gives way to a nonstriated, "rhizomatic" one. The "signifying regime" of Babel—the desire for a name—disintegrates, and humanity enters a new "postsignifying regime."[32] Semiosis is no longer bound up in the totalizing Absolute Signifier—although exactly what the tower signifies is never clear—but now it can and must flow freely. Ironically, the Babelian desire not to be scattered (" 'lest we be scattered abroad upon the face of the whole earth,' " Genesis 11:4) results in their being scattered: " 'Come, let us go down, and there confuse their language, that they may not understand one another's speech.' So the LORD scattered them abroad from there over the face of all the earth, and they left off building the city" (11:7–8).

The confusion (or pouring together) of tongues (LXX: *sugcheōmen . . . tēn glōssan,* 11:7) coincides with the spreading out of people. As Fred Burnett notes, the confusion of tongues resulting from the Babel events destroys the harmony between these people by eliminating the signifying difference essential to meaningful communication: "The building project failed because each word had no opposite. The word 'brick' would have been no different from the word 'mortar.' "[33] The words are fused together (con-fused), and the signifying differences between them disappear. To use Eco's example, every word and every sentence has become a segment of an endless "BABABABABA." The Babelians have become barbarians.

---

31. ʾAbot de-R. Natan [vs. 1] 12.26b.

32. Deleuze and Guattari, *A Thousand Plateaus,* 117–23. See also Spina, "Babel." The relation between names, narrative, and translatability is discussed further in chapter 3.

33. Fred Burnett, private communication, 14 December 1995.

The Babel story does not say that the elimination of linguistic difference at Babel leads to the genesis of different languages. Instead, according to Genesis 10, the various human languages emerge during the repopulation of the earth after the Flood, where they are apparently not a punishment from God. In contrast, Genesis 11 suggests that the languages of Babel's survivors are vestiges and fragments of lost harmony, the linguistic remains of a lost Paradise. After Babel, language is "confused"—it zigs and zags. The confusion of tongues is accompanied by the separation and disuniting of the people. In the post-Babel world, language keeps people apart just as much as it brings them together, and maybe even more so. The outcome of the Babel events suggests that the function of language from now on is to *prevent* clear communication—not to reveal a message but to conceal one. George Steiner describes this linguistic obscurity as the fundamental "alternity" of language:

> [T]he proliferation of mutually incomprehensible tongues stems from an absolutely fundamental impulse in language itself. . . . The potentials of fiction, of counterfactuality, of undecidable futurity profoundly characterize both the origins and the nature of speech. . . . [D]ifferent tongues give to the mechanism of "alternity" a dynamic, transferable enactment. They realize needs of privacy and territoriality vital to our identity.[34]

Something has gone seriously out of control at Babel: the story narrates a great catastrophe of human civilization, a culture crash of the highest magnitude. The Babel story unveils a paradox: it begins with an apparently utopian vision of human community, but its seemingly dystopian conclusion describes what any human language must always be. As Benjamin hints ("signs must become confused where things are entangled"), language after Babel is an inescapably physical thing, an obstacle or barricade to communication. Eco traces a similar view of language to Epicurus's "Letter to Herodotus": "men's natures according to their different nationalities had their own peculiar feelings and received their peculiar impressions, and so each in their own way emitted air formed into shape by each of these feelings and impressions, according to the differences made in the different nations."[35] According to Epicurus, language comes from the body. Words are shaped air—that is, physical, not spiritual, and local, not universal. Eco notes that Lucretius adopts a similar view, and elsewhere Eco also associates this view with Vico.[36] Language is the signifying tower itself, made of brick and mortar, or as Franz Kafka says, it is a wall: "[T]he Great Wall alone

---

34. Steiner, *After Babel*, 473.
35. Epicurus in Oates, *Stoic*, 13. See also Eco, *Search*, 88; and Assmann, "Curse and Blessing," 87.
36. Eco, *Semiotics*, 107–8.

would provide for the first time in the history of mankind a secure foundation for a new Tower of Babel. First the wall, therefore, and then the tower."[37]

In contrast, at Pentecost the one Spirit does not speak a single divine language, but rather it speaks multiple human tongues simultaneously. No return to singularity of language is required because language itself has become dispensable. Initial language differences are swept away before the "sound . . . from heaven" (Acts 2:2) and the outpouring (*ekcheō*) of the Spirit of God. Once again, something is out of control. However, this is not another culture crash but rather precisely the opposite. The apostle-speakers at Pentecost find themselves speaking "other tongues" (*heterais glōssais*, 2:4) that they had not known before: " 'How is it that we hear, each of us in his own native language?' " (2:8). Once you've got the Spirit ("tongues as of fire," 2:3), the physical, Babelian particularities of language become superfluous, even irrelevant. Pentecost erases Steiner's linguistic "alternity." The localized, post-Babelian tongues are swept up in the universal message. Pentecost is to logocentric semiotics and "dynamic equivalence" in translation as Babel is to unlimited semiosis and "literal translation" (see further chapter 3).

Michel Serres argues that each medium of communication (whether oral, written, printed, or electronic) generates its own "noise," which derives from the sheer materiality of the signifier. This noise or static both makes it possible for the signifying system to function at all and also obscures the meaning of any message. At Pentecost, despite the sound from heaven, there is no noise, no static, or better yet, even the noise speaks clearly:

> The noise is made message before the word is made flesh. . . . It is a question of knowing whether a network without constraints of crossroads, interchanges, intersections with parasites can be constructed. Where a given element can have a relation to another element without the constraints of mediation. This is the model of Pentecost.[38]

After Pentecost, language no longer stands between people. As Serres notes, communication has become immediate, unmediated. Language is no longer a hindrance because the physical, Babelian language has been completely and permanently replaced by clear spiritual connection between all the peoples of the earth. That connection is the universal transmission of the Christian message. At Pentecost, communication becomes independent of the materiality of language, and language becomes, not merely logocentric, but *logos* pure and simple, untrammeled by any signifier.

At Pentecost, language as a physical "tongue" has been replaced by "tongues as of fire" (Acts 2:3), and the message has become entirely indepen-

---

37. Kafka, *Parables and Paradoxes*, 25.
38. Serres, *The Parasite*, 41, 44–45.

dent of the physical medium. The noise or static that Serres associates with language has ceased. The wall of Babel vanishes. The story of Pentecost suggests that physical, Babelian language is no longer around to interfere with transmission of the message. The physical stuff of language is consumed by its inner "spirit." Pentecost is therefore not about translation but about never needing translation again. The material flesh of language dissolves away, and the one spiritual truth shines forth.

Spirit and Flesh

For the Babelians, language is a physical thing, a confused tongue. The language of Babel is incarnate language, inscribed in the flesh of a textual body. The Babelian is the one whose tongue is confused, the one for whom every word may be a betrayal or a trap. The physical aspect of the Babelian tongue makes possible the telling of untruths—lies and fictions—the positing of otherness, or what Steiner calls "alternity." Indeed, alternity is already present in the "language passion" of Adam and Eve. At the same time and for the same reason, the Babelian is the one for whom language is a secret code, an insider's language to be shared only with "my own people," those who are like myself. Language after Babel is nomadic, tribal language; because of its materiality, it cannot be universal. The pre-Babelian grand narratives (" 'let us make a name for ourselves,' " Genesis 11:4) are no longer possible, and instead the Babelians favor local differences, a buzzing "paralogy" of micronarratives. This is why the story of Babel is a postmodern one.[39]

Between Babel and Pentecost lies the time of writing, the time of scripture. Language after Babel is a language of scripture—that is, the language of a written text. As Eco says, "[A]nother result of the confusion of Babel was the multiplication of letters." Humanity loses the primeval "spirit of sensual speech," the "natural" language of Adam, according to Böhme, when it is "transferred . . . into a crudely external form."[40] The "external form" of post-Babelian language appears in writing, whether chirographic, printed, or digital. Writing is quintessentially confused language. As Socrates says, writing is the cause of great loss: "Those who acquire [writing] will cease to exercise their memory and become forgetful. . . . [The written text] is quite incapable of defending or helping itself."[41] Like the Babelians themselves, the written text is disseminated without control. Perhaps writing is itself the "confusion" of tongues at Babel, and the story of Babel is about the invention of writing. Among other things, the tower of Babel is a scriptorium!

---

39. See Lyotard, *Postmodern Condition,* 60–61.

40. Eco, *Search,* 32, 183. Lévi-Strauss notes the coincidence of the invention of writing and urban, imperial civilization, in which masses of people are exploited and enslaved (*Tristes Tropiques,* 292).

41. Plato *Phaedrus* 96–97, sec. 275.

Perhaps the language of Babel becomes confused because it has been written and therefore translated. Writing is a language of the "flesh," as the apostle Paul puts it (see further chapter 6). The Babelians agree, although perhaps for different reasons. The story of Babel concludes with the very situation that makes scriptures desirable in the first place. Babel is a story of diaspora (LXX: *diespeiren*, Genesis 11:8), and the Babelian view of language is the view of the refugee or exile, the outsider. Within the diasporic world after Babel, the values and beliefs of the Babelians are endangered. Writing allows the Babelians to bridge the growing distances between them and to transmit the messages in which their beliefs and values are encoded. Paradoxically, the physical aspect of writing frees the language of Babel from the limits of space and time. As it transfers the message from speech, writing translates the message into a different medium (an intermedial translation), but it also enables the message's translation over great distances and periods of time.

The language of Babel is material language, and the materiality of the signifier cannot be translated. Nevertheless, the Babel events are themselves a translation, a global translation of people ("from there the LORD scattered them abroad over the face of all the earth," Genesis 11:9) that destroys their Eden-like harmony. The Babelians abandon their upward, arborescent tower-building, and instead they scatter outward, rhizomatically, horizontally. "Needs of privacy and territoriality" lead to the flight of all humanity from Babel. Once again an alternative reading is invited, a nonlinear zigzag: "[t]hus the Biblical myth is reversed, the confusion of tongues is no longer a punishment, the subject gains access to bliss by the cohabitation of languages *working side by side:* the text of pleasure is a sanctioned Babel."[42]

"[L]anguages working side by side" suggests Lyotard's postmodern paralogy of micronarratives. It also suggests Benjamin's model of "literal" translation as interlinear. As Benjamin claims, translation is the "arcade" through the "wall" of language.[43] Translation breaks through Kafka's Great Wall of Babel:

> When translation aspires not to identical reproduction but to a differing re-creation, ... then diverse linguistic cultures enrich each other and the world. Then Babel's fall is a signal of grace, and a writer of immense complexity and expressive resonance like Kafka reveals his immaculate power in many tongues.[44]

However, there are always dangers in translation, dangers of betrayal and deception, of the loss or transformation of meaning (see further chapter 3).

---

42. Barthes, *Pleasure*, 3–4, his emphasis. See also Deleuze and Guattari, *A Thousand Plateaus*.
43. Benjamin, *Illuminations*, 79.
44. Barnstone, *Poetics of Translation*, 237.

The desire for a canon arises in association with the politics of exile and persecution, and with the need to secure the text in an insecure world. The desire for canon is desire to return to the tower, and to the garden, to establish authority. It is also the desire for Pentecost. Like the story of Babel, the story of Pentecost begins with a scene of unity: "When the day of Pentecost had come, they were all together in one place" (Acts 2:1). The Pentecostian[45] desire for meaning corresponds to the Babelian desire for a name, and the "other tongues" of Acts 2:4 echo the confused tongues of Genesis 11. Nevertheless, Pentecost is not a second Babel, nor is the sequence of events in the Babel story simply reversed in the story of Pentecost. At Pentecost, the supernatural Spirit does not replace other media of communication (speech or writing) with a new alternative. Indeed, the Holy Spirit is not a medium at all; instead, it is the end of human need for any medium. The Spirit brings the possibility of language "without the constraints of mediation."[46]

The Spirit eliminates any influence of the physical medium on communication. Serres contrasts the Spirit at Pentecost to Hermes, the Greek god of messages and hence of translation. Hermes is the intermediary, the "neck" through which communication passes: "[t]he noise, the wind of the Paraclete, overturns and transforms this system, replacing it with another, a new one."[47] Another medium would simply replace one neck with another. The Holy Spirit eliminates the system that requires a neck. The story of Pentecost is not about translation, but rather it is about the disappearance of the physical aspect of language. The remainder of Acts 2 provides two distinct and contradictory sequels to the arrival of the Spirit.

Robert Wilken notes the crucial role of the Pentecost story in the creation of a "myth of Christian beginnings," a story of an idealized apostolic age.[48] Once again, a linear, canonical reading is required. The Pentecostian tongues are not confused, babbling, glossolalic. There is nothing physical about them. Although the Pentecostians "praise God," we are not told what language(s) they use. For the Christian, logocentric view of language, it does not matter. Responding to the desire for meaning (Acts 2:12)—in effect, the desire for canon—the long speech of Peter and the apostles (2:14–43) brings the fiery tongues under control. Nothing like Peter's speech happens in the story of Babel. Under Peter's direction, the story of Pentecost becomes a story of empire and totalization. Peter's account grounds a grand narrative. At this point, the story of Pentecost becomes a modern one, the beginnings of a story of historical empire (see further chapter 4).

Peter's understanding of Pentecost is expressed in the language of what Deleuze and Guattari call paranoia—that is, a totalizing, hierarchical dis-

45. "Pentecostal" here could be misconstrued. Pentecostian is to Pentecostal as Babelian is to Babylonian.
46. Serres, *The Parasite*, 45.
47. Ibid., 42.
48. Wilken, *Myth*, 33–37.

course. The horizontal, Babelian flow of people and language is redirected and becomes once again vertical. The Pentecostian orientation is turned toward global unity, a universal metanarrative, and a totalitarian singularity of denotation: " 'This Jesus God raised up, and of that we all are witnesses' " (2:32). As witnesses, the apostles maintain control over the situation.[49] At Pentecost, Peter builds a new tower, but it is not a physical one, despite his own nickname (*petros*, "rock"). "No one, not Peter, not the narrator, can summarize what happened, 'what it means,' without claiming knowledge of all the languages in the world. The implicit claim of Peter's speech is that all the speeches made earlier in Acts 2, in all the different languages, were identical to it."[50] Taming the Spirit, Peter reintroduces translation, and dynamic equivalence at that. Once again, the apostles become the "neck," the narrow channel through which the message must pass (Acts 2:37–43).

However, after his speech, or perhaps in spite of it, neither Peter nor any of the apostles appears in the scene of communal unity and sharing with which Acts 2 closes:

> And all who believed were together and had all things in common; and they sold their possessions and goods and distributed them to all, as any had need. And day by day, attending the temple together and breaking bread in their homes, they partook of food with glad and generous hearts, praising God and having favor with all the people. And the Lord added to their number day by day those who were being saved. (Acts 2:44–47)

There are no longer any obstacles or walls, no tongues separating these people. In this little story appears a harmony that never existed: a community that transcends language, but also a community in which the Spirit has *not* come under apostolic control, Peter's claims notwithstanding (2:32, 37, 42). The situation is well described by Serres: "Let us now imagine that any speaker speaks in his own language and every hearer understands in his own, whatever the language and whatever the location. In that case, the relations can be considered many-many and the network that describes them is decentered."[51]

As it follows after Peter's speech in Acts 2, the appearance of this community of radical sharing appears to be consequent or concomitant to the great new influx of "those who received his word" (2:41), which Peter's speech produces. But this decentered community of sharing could not derive from Peter's totalizing speech. Instead it seems to come from a radical, "many-many" side of the Pentecost events themselves.[52] The linear, canonical reading is again subverted by a noncanonical, zigzag reading.

---

49. See ibid., 37–41. See also Deleuze and Guattari, *Anti-Oedipus*.
50. David Jobling, private communication, 4 June 1996.
51. Serres, *The Parasite*, 42.
52. See Wilken, *Myth*, 36.

It was noted earlier in this chapter that the ambiguities of the Babel story leave room for the reader to read the pre-Babel community as either totalitarian or harmonious. In the linear reading of that story, God rightfully punishes human domination over other human beings, but in the nonlinear one, God becomes jealous of how *good* people are to each other, and God becomes the unjust dominator. In either case, God is the Babelians' enemy. In the two distinct "sequels" to the Pentecost events described above, something like these two alternatives appears again, and again the alternatives result, respectively, from a linear and a nonlinear reading:

1. The universalism of Peter's speech (God is the good guy, bringing salvation to the world)

2. The simple communalism of the early Christians (humans are the good guys, taking care of each other)

In neither of these readings is God the opponent of the Pentecostians; instead, God has become their ally. The two sequels may represent two different conclusions to the Pentecost story, or they may merely speak two different "tongues" that narrate the same story, one single story, " 'each [one] in his own native language' " (Acts 2:8).

In either case, at Pentecost, translation is supported or rather eliminated by the Spirit, and unlike at Babel, the divine presence poses no threat. Instead of confused tongues and literal translation, the perfect dynamic equivalence of Spirit-translation enables everyone to receive clearly the very same message. For the same reason, after the Pentecost events writing can be no longer a physical obstruction to meaning because writing, the flesh of the text, has become unimportant. Peter's speech freely transforms the source texts in his citations from "the prophet Joel" and "David" (Psalm 16). In fact, Peter makes no reference at all to the "scriptures" (*hē graphē);* Joel and David are themselves present at Pentecost in the Spirit, speaking through Peter.

Pentecost authorizes and indeed demands violence to the written text in the name of the logocentric understanding of the inner meaning of the text. Transmission and reception of the apostolic message—valid interpretation and appropriate response—reinforce the Christian ideology of the biblical stories' coherence, universality, and truth. Christians have to affirm the possibility of perfect translation—that is, the possibility of Pentecost. In other words, Christians must reject (with Paul) the flesh of language, the physical linguistic wall or tower of Babel. Christianity chooses Pentecostian spirit over Babelian flesh. Thus the meaning of "scripture" itself has changed.

The End of Language

By itself, the story of either Babel or of Pentecost means something quite different than it does in tandem with the other. Each story by itself narrates a human movement from speech to gibberish, an incoherence that results from an encounter with God. Each story opens itself to two contrary readings, one linear and one nonlinear. The canonical reading enforces a linear sequence, in each of the stories. Put together in the Christian double canon, the two stories are not mirror images of each other, but instead they complement one another, creating between them a new, greater whole. Pentecost ends what Babel begins. Pentecost re-creates Babel as an initial narrative structure that is entirely compatible to its own concluding structure. The New Testament story of Pentecost rewrites the Old Testament story of Babel, transforming it into a story that leads to something else, something that will culminate eventually at Pentecost. Through the canonical juxtaposition, Pentecost rewrites Babel as a story of loss, a loss that is undone at Pentecost. In this way the story of Pentecost "translates" the story of Babel.

What defines the present human world is (in part) the relation and the tension between these two stories. The Babelians are recognizable, ordinary human beings after they are driven from the city. In contrast, the Pentecostians are not human; instead, they appear to be more highly evolved beings. The story of Pentecost is a science-fiction story about a future metamorphosis of the human race. Acts 2:5–6 tells us that among "devout men from every nation under heaven," "each one heard [the Pentecostians] speaking in his own language." Pentecost is a time of many human tongues. However, upon the arrival of the Spirit, the unison of fiery tongues replaces the cacophony of fleshy tongues. For the Pentecostians, the Spirit functions like the universal translator used in *Star Trek* or the more amusing "Babel fish" from Douglas Adam's science-fiction parody *The Hitchhiker's Guide to the Galaxy*. The physical medium of language is no longer necessary for the Pentecostians, or it has become completely transparent, for they live in a realm of pure signifieds, without signifiers. What tongue could Peter possibly use to address the Pentecost crowd (Acts 2:14 ff.)? Surely Peter speaks in (and with) no tongue at all. Thanks to the spiritual tongues of fire, Peter and the Pentecostians have become telepathic.

The canonical, complementary relation between Babel and Pentecost entails that human beings live now in the time that stretches from the mythic past of Babel to the fabulous future of Pentecost. The time between Babel and Pentecost is the time of writing and of translation—that is, the time of ambiguity and lost meaning. Between these two stories lies all the space and the time of confused human tongues. It is the linear space and time of the real world, a space and time that is still happening, still under way.

Contemporary human beings live after Babel, for their tongues are confused. The Babel events have already happened in the mythic past, but the Pentecost events have not yet happened. If Pentecost had already occurred, human beings would not still be here in this world, living in this way, doing these things. Human tongues would not still be confused. (Or could there have been a second Babel after Pentecost, a great zigzag? Surely not in the

Christian canon!) The world could not go on as though nothing has changed after Pentecost. Apparently the only people who have realized this are those Christians who are called "Pentecostals."

In the Pentecost story, the reader again has the choice between a linear reading, stringing the stories in Acts 2 in narrative succession, or a zigzag reading that skims and skips, treating the two sequels to the arrival of the Spirit as incompatible alternatives. Most readers tend to read the two sequels as one linear story. Perhaps this is because Christian readers want to agree with Peter, as opposed to the "others" who mock the speakers in Spirit-filled tongues, saying, " 'They are filled with new wine' " (Acts 2:13). Serres's suggestion of nonlinear, rhizomatic possibilities in a "decentered" network of "many-many" relations is contradicted both by Peter's totalizing speech and by the univocity of the Pentecost story's sequel in the remainder of the book of Acts. The story of utopian communalism is swallowed up in the ongoing, linear, canonical reading.

In this way, the canonical linearity of Babel-Pentecost conflicts with the canonical linearity of Genesis-Revelation. The linear complementarity between Babel and Pentecost deconstructs itself, and an adjustment must be made. The believing reader must overlook the impossibility that Pentecost has already occurred.

Perhaps the story of Pentecost narrates a mythic return to the language of God, the pure language of the Garden of Eden, long since lost or fragmented. This would involve a fantastical unwinding of history back to its beginnings. Some readers suggest such an understanding. Both before Babel and after Pentecost, writing and translation are unnecessary. Steiner holds that "[t]he tongue of Eden was like a flawless glass; a light of total understanding streamed through it. Thus Babel was a second Fall," and Benjamin implies that Edenic language was unmediated.[53] Even if Pentecost involves a multiplicity of human tongues, as the story itself says, then it still results in the utopian communalism of Acts 2:44–47. This little story also suggests a return to Eden-like harmony such as that with which the Babel story begins. One is reminded again of fantasies such as Morris's *News from Nowhere*—except that in Morris's vision of a future world, as in Karl Marx's, there is no longer any need for religion. After Pentecost, churches will be as unnecessary as they were in Eden.

However, Pentecost does not simply restore the language of Paradise. The language of Eden was supposedly a language of total clarity, but Eco's analysis seriously challenges that idea. Even if the Holy Spirit speaks through human tongues with perfect dynamic equivalence, as the Pentecost story suggests (2:4–11), Eco's analysis shows that the tongues themselves will still be flawed. The message will inevitably be distorted. In contrast, if Pentecost involves telepathy, as Peter's speech implies, the consequence is flawless

---

53. Steiner, *After Babel*, 59; Benjamin, *Reflections*, 328.

transmission of a universal, totalizing message. Eco's conclusions about an Edenic language imply that the Spirit-languages of Pentecost must be something other than human language, no longer bound to the laws of semiotics, and the speakers themselves must be superhuman beings. In that case, the message has been severed from the physical medium, and language in its present forms exists no longer.

After Pentecost, the canon of scriptures will no longer be needed. Nevertheless, the story of Pentecost contributes to the fusing together of the Christian double canon. It serves as a reading lens through which the Jewish scriptures are refocused to become the Old Testament canon, while the apostolic preaching becomes the New Testament canon.[54] Pentecost makes Babel necessary. The canonical status of the Pentecost story gives the Babel story its own canonical status, displacing the alternative zigzag reading possibilities with a unified, linear sequence.

For the Christian community, Babel also rewrites Pentecost, and that rewriting also happens in the ideologically controlled context of the Bible. Babel always arises in and returns to a science-fiction dream or fantasy of Pentecost: the desire to be liberated from the flesh of language. Disparities of language and meaning are overcome through logocentric readings of the texts (" 'we hear, each of us in his own native language,' " Acts 2:8), and the physical text itself is disregarded. The effects of Babel will appear no more on the day of Pentecost. Like the Spirit at Pentecost, the Christian Bible as a canon claims possession of and transforms the Babelian scriptures, absorbing their fleshy, hyletic tongues and replacing them with fiery ones announcing a single truth.

54. See also Boyarin, *A Radical Jew*, esp. chap. 1; and Kermode, "Plain Sense," 185.

Chapter 6

THE BLEEDING PAGE

Progress in reading is preceded by an act that traverses the material solidity of the book to allow you access to its incorporeal substance. ...The margin of the pages is jagged, revealing its fibrous texture; a fine shaving—also known as "curl"—is detached from it, as pretty to see as a wave's foam on the beach.
> —Italo Calvino, *If on a Winter's Night a Traveler*

The law is an invention of the book, invention of a book with the authority of law.
> —Edmond Jabès, "The Key"

This word to be circumcised, this word of someone's to be circumcised, this word to be circumcised for someone, this word is an *open* word. Like a wound, you will say. No, first of all like a door: open to the stranger, to the other, to the guest, to whomever.
> —Jacques Derrida, "Shibboleth"

The Text as a Symbol

According to C. S. Peirce, there are three types of signs: icons, indexes, and symbols. The icon, the simplest type of sign, resembles in some way the object that it signifies. For example, a road sign indicates with a wavy arrow that there are curves in the road ahead, and a photograph resembles the photographed object. The second type of sign is the index, which stands in a more or less natural connection to its signified object. For example, smoke is an effect produced when something is burning, and coughing can be a symptom of illness. In both icon and index, the relationship between the signifier (road sign, smoke) and its signified (road curves, fire) is either direct and unmediated or mediated only by correlations that are largely independent of human culture or creativity (such as processes of combustion or infection). There is little or no need for some further semiotic link to join together the signifier and the signified.

However, most linguistic signs are neither icons nor indexes. There are a few exceptions to this—for example, onomatopoetic words such as "wham"

130

and "crash" are highly iconic, and pronouns such as "I" and "this" function as indexes, as do proper names. Nevertheless, most words belong to Peirce's third category of signs, the symbol.[1] In the symbol, the sign's relation to its meaning is purely arbitrary and artificial. The connections between symbols and their extralinguistic objects must be learned in ways that are dependent upon human culture and therefore profoundly ideological. Unlike icons and indexes, signs that are symbols and their meanings can only be learned intertextually, in the play of language.

According to Peirce, the linguistic symbol is composed of three elements, all of which are necessary to its meaning. The "representamen" is the physical signifier itself, such as a spoken or written word. The "object" is what is signified by the word, the conceptual representation that accompanies the word whenever it is used, regardless of whether that concept corresponds to an actual or ideal entity. Both icons and indexes also involve these two elements. The "interpretant" is the intertextual link that connects the purely artificial word, the symbol's representamen, to its object. The interpretant, learned when the meaning of the symbol-word is learned, is the understanding that arises when the word is encountered and that guides the receiver of the word toward its proper object. As its name implies, the interpretant interprets the relation between the signifying representamen and signified object. To continue with terms introduced in chapter 3 of this book, the interpretant of a word is its connotation, and the actual or ideal object to which the word points is its denotation.

Both connotation and denotation are important aspects of the meaning of linguistic signs, but as Roland Barthes and others have noted, the denotation (object) of a word usually depends on its connotation (interpretant). The representamens of icons and indexes stand in more direct relations to their objects, and thus they require little in the way of connotation. However, without adequate understanding of its connotation, the receiver of the symbol will not be able to identify the denoted object. In that case, the truth value of any statement in which the symbol appears would remain unknown. Denotation thus involves a narrowing down of connotative possibilities, a closing off of meaning. In this way, denotation is the end of meaning. As Barthes says,

> the raw material of denotation, with its dictionary and its syntax, is a system like any other; there is no reason to make this system the privileged one, to make it the locus and the norm of a primary, original meaning, the scale for all associated meanings.... [D]enotation is not the truth of discourse:... [denotation is] a particular, special-

---

1. Not all symbols are words: for example, the dollar sign, military insignia. Note that Peirce's understanding of the symbol is quite different from that of theologians such as Paul Tillich.

ized substance used by the other [connotative] codes to smooth their articulation.[2]

There is a further complication to Peirce's theory of the symbol. According to Peirce, the three components of the symbol are themselves interchangeable. Every interpretant (connotation) may itself serve as the representamen (signifier) of yet another object (denotation), and so on, without limit. In other words, every signifier is also a signified, and vice versa. There is no stopping or starting point for signification, no Final Signified and no First Signifier. On a mundane level, every word is defined by using other words, and there is no end to definition. The connotation of a word generally appears in the intertextual relation between other words, which themselves have further connotations, and so on.

On a more sublime level, the clear binary distinction between signifier and signified, so important to semiotics, is deconstructed. Everything signifies, and therefore everything is a text.[3] Connotation is the site of what Umberto Eco and others call (following Peirce) unlimited semiosis. Because semiosis is unlimited, proper denotation, the "one right meaning" or truth value of any phrase, should never occur. Denotation does occur, to be sure, but only as a result of the ideological closing off of free semiotic play, the shutting down of "wild connotations."[4] Denotation occurs because finite human beings cannot be satisfied with the infinite deferral of meaning that is opened up by unlimited semiosis.

Because connotation is the intertextual operation that connects a sign to its denoted object, connotation is crucial to the meaning of the symbol. However, precisely because it is intertextual, connotation can be slippery and subjective, varying wildly from one context to another. The message's receiver desires the closure of meaning, determined truth. The function of the biblical canon is to satisfy this desire, to ensure the denotation of the canonical texts, and therefore to prevent unlimited semiosis from occurring. Connotation is what canon seeks to control, for if the connotations of a text are controlled, then the denotations will also be controlled. In other words, the canon attempts to supply the definitive interpretant for its component texts.

This discussion has so far been principally concerned with particular signs—that is, individual words. However, it applies equally well to larger linguistic units, such as sentences and even entire stories. Indeed, according to Gottlob Frege, the semiotic aspect of denotation belongs in particular to sentences, where it takes the form of truth value. Only sentences can convey complete thoughts and can thereby be judged to be true or false.[5] However,

---

2. Barthes, *S/Z*, 7, 128.
3. Derrida, *Of Grammatology*, 158.
4. de Man, *Allegories*, 208.
5. Frege, *Translations*, 31, 62–63. Frege does not use the terms denotation and connotation

in order for the sentence to denote, connotation must be at work. Barthes goes further than this, and he argues that every narrative takes the form of a great sentence: "To narrate...is to raise the question as if it were a subject which one delays predicating; and when the predicate (truth) arrives, the sentence, the narrative, are over, the world is adjectivized (after we had feared it would not be)."[6] Therefore narratives also connote and denote. Stories are meaningful, and some stories are even "realistic"—that is, they appear to denote the everyday, primary world. Stories can also be true or false, just like sentences. Sentences and narratives made up of many sentences may then also be treated in the same way that words are, as Peircean symbols, and their meanings will also take the interrelated forms of denotation and connotation.

In the preceding chapter of this book, I examine the biblical stories of Babel (Genesis 11) and Pentecost (Acts 2) as though these two stories stand in what Peirce might call an indexical relation, a kind of linear complementarity. Their relation is not a purely indexical one because some measure of interpretation is required to get from one story to the other one, and in the case of those two stories this minimal interpretant is evidenced by the quotations from Franz Kafka's parables at the beginning of that chapter. No story can be purely iconic or indexical. Nevertheless, within the intertextual frame of the Christian double canon, these two stories point to each other, and this relationship itself presents some measure of the difference between the Christian Old Testament and the Jewish scriptures.

In this chapter, I look at three narrative texts in which themes of circumcision and writing are brought together in the triadic relation of the Peircean symbol. In other words, each of the three texts is either the representamen, the interpretant, or the object of one of the others. Here appears yet another form of canonical intertextuality because two of these texts come from the New and Old Testaments, respectively. The third text is a noncanonical one, once again from Kafka. Although this text-interpretant links together the two canonical texts, it is also intrusive and disturbing, and it introduces a further, and important, complication to canonical signification.

Kafka's story serves as a commentary on the scriptures, a narrative interpretant that links representamen to object. As I have already noted, the desire for canon is the desire for a text that interprets itself. Canon seeks to explain itself. However, the inevitable failure of the canon to satisfy this desire leads to extracanonical commentary—that is, the attempt of church or synagogue to save the canon's control of biblical meaning. Commentary is noncanonical supplementation that further signifies the canonical status

---

but rather "reference" (*Bedeutung*) and "sense" (*Sinn*) (ibid., ix–x). Later editions of the English translation of Frege's book translate *Bedeutung* as "meaning." I stay with the older translation in this case because I regard both denotation and connotation as forms of meaning.

6. Barthes, *S/Z*, 76.

of the biblical text. Paradoxically, then, commentary itself becomes "canon-ical." Because semiosis is unlimited, commentary becomes scripture, and scripture becomes commentary.

Representamen

In his first letter to the church in Corinth, the apostle Paul argues that those who are already circumcised should not reverse the process, and those who are not yet circumcised should not become circumcised (1 Corinthians 7:18): "For neither circumcision counts for anything nor uncircumcision, but keep-ing the commandments of God" (7:19). Because it belongs to the "flesh," circumcision is indifferent to salvation. However, in his letter to the Galatian Christians, Paul uses much stronger language:

> Now I, Paul, say to you that if you receive circumcision (*peritemnēsthe*), Christ will be of no advantage to you. I testify again to every man who receives circumcision that he is bound to keep the whole law. You are severed from Christ, you who would be justified by the law; you have fallen away from grace. (Galatians 5:2–4)

If you cut off your foreskin, then you cut off Christ. The foreskin is an icon of the flesh; indeed, it *is* the flesh.[7] But at the same time, the foreskin is also a Peircean symbol, and like all symbols it requires interpretation, as does any law.

Paul frequently conjoins circumcision and the law. Circumcision "binds" one to the law. The flesh is not mentioned in Galatians 5:2–4, but the spirit, which Paul often sets over against the flesh, appears in the very next verse: "For through the Spirit, by faith, we wait for the hope of righteousness. For in Christ Jesus neither circumcision nor uncircumcision is of any avail, but faith working through love" (Galatians 5:5–6). The cutting of human flesh prescribed by the law of God is superseded for Paul by the spirit, by faith, and by love.

However, Paul still has some use for cutting, for after a few verses of exhortation to his readers to remain loyal to him, he concludes this passage in Galatians, "I wish those who unsettle you would mutilate (*apokopsontai*, castrate) themselves!" (5:12). A similar opposition between mutilation and circumcision (as well as spirit and flesh) appears in Philippians 3:2–3: "Look out for the dogs, look out for the evil-workers, look out for those who mu-tilate the flesh (*tēn katatomēn*). For we are the true circumcision (*peritomē*), who worship God in spirit, and glory in Christ Jesus, and put no confidence in the flesh." These two Greek words, *apokoptō* and *katatomē,* are both translated in the Revised Standard Version as "mutilate," even though they denote different types of cutting (chopping off vs. carving). Nevertheless,

---

7. See Boyarin, *A Radical Jew,* 77.

from a standpoint of the flesh, there is little difference in connotation. From Paul's point of view, the bodily mutilation involved in circumcision or castration is fitting for those who stand on the side of flesh and the law, and in opposition to himself and the Holy Spirit. For those who follow Paul's teaching, no circumcision is necessary. For those who do not, circumcision does not cut deeply enough!

There is no talk of writing in these Pauline passages. However, writing and circumcision are explicitly juxtaposed in Romans 2:25–29:

> Circumcision indeed is of value if you obey the law; but if you break the law, your circumcision becomes uncircumcision. So, if a man who is uncircumcised keeps the precepts of the law, will not his uncircumcision be regarded as circumcision? Then those who are physically uncircumcised but keep the law will condemn you who have the written code (*grammatos*) and circumcision (*peritomēs*) but break the law. For he is not a real Jew who is one outwardly, nor is true circumcision something external and physical. He is a Jew who is one inwardly, and real circumcision is a matter of the heart, spiritual and not literal.

In this text, Paul seems to agree with the words of Jesus in the gospel of Thomas, saying 53: "If [circumcision] were beneficial, their father would beget them already circumcised from their mother. Rather, the true circumcision in spirit has become completely profitable." For Paul, "real circumcision" is inward and spiritual in contrast to the outward, literal "written code." The written code is for Paul a law of "flesh" or body, in contrast to the hermeneutical freedom and power provided by the Spirit of God.

Paul's famous opposition between the letter of the written code and the Spirit of God in 2 Corinthians 3:1–6 contains no mention of circumcision, but it does pursue a related thought:

> Are we beginning to commend ourselves again? Or do we need, as some do, letters (*epistolōn*) of recommendation to you, or from you? You yourselves are our letter of recommendation, written on your [or our] hearts, to be known and read by all men; and you show that you are a letter from Christ delivered by us, written not with ink but with the Spirit of the living God, not on tablets of stone but on tablets of human (*sarkinais*, "fleshy") hearts. Such is the confidence that we have through Christ toward God. Not that we are competent of ourselves to claim anything as coming from us; our competence is from God, who has made us competent to be ministers of a new covenant, not in a written code (*grammatos*) but in the Spirit; for the written code (*gramma*) kills, but the Spirit gives life.

Paul's language in this passage echoes Jeremiah 31:31–33 and Ezekiel 31:18 and 36:26, but it also strikingly resembles Socrates' attack upon writing in the *Phaedrus*. The physical writing, on "tablets of stone" or "with ink," stands opposed to the "Spirit of the living God" who writes intimately, on human hearts.[8]

A similar theme appears in Romans 7:6: "But now we are discharged from the law, dead to that which held us captive, so that we serve not under the old written code (*grammatos*) but in the new life of the Spirit." As Richard Hays says, "Where Scripture remains only an inscribed text, it becomes *gramma*, indicting the readers with aching consciousness of their distance from what the text promises or alienating them with speech that seems incomprehensibly remote."[9]

The heart on which Paul's "letter of recommendation" is written is not actual living tissue, but rather it is a metaphor for the inner, spiritual person. Paul's vivid metaphor contrasts sharply with the "literal" inscription of the flesh, the writing of the law that is circumcision. Instead, this spiritual writing is the "true circumcision" that Paul associates with his gospel for the gentiles, the spiritual "new covenant" of which he is a minister. Hays suggests that for Paul, "in the new covenant incarnation eclipses inscription"—that is, incarnation of "the message of Jesus Christ" in the "fleshy" Christian community. As a result, "[i]n this eschatological community of the new covenant... *texts* will no longer be needful. Scripture will have become a 'self-consuming artifact'; the power of the word will have subsumed itself into the life of the community, embodied itself without remainder."[10] Despite the alleged fleshiness of this community, this sounds more like the telepathic paradise ("without remainder") described in chapter 5, the community of the utopian Spirit-languages of Pentecost.

Hays claims that Paul's rhetoric is not dichotomous but rather dialectical,[11] but in Paul's theology, the Holy Spirit and the grace or promise of God stand opposed to both circumcision and faith in the law/flesh, just as they do to the physical expression/substance of writing. According to Elizabeth Castelli, this does indeed establish a dichotomy:

> [T]his language identifies the fundamental values of wholeness and unity with Paul's own privileged position vis-à-vis the gospel, the early Christian communities he founded and supervises, and Christ himself.... To stand for anything other than what the apostle stands for is to articulate for oneself a place of difference... to stand in opposition, therefore, to the gospel, the community, and Christ.[12]

---

8. Compare Socrates: "another kind of communication [than writing]... written on the soul of the hearer together with understanding" (Plato *Phaedrus* 98, sec. 276). See further chapter 2. See also Ong, *Interfaces*, 237; and Aichele, *Sign, Text, Scripture*, chap. 1.

9. Hays, *Echoes of Scripture*, 168.

10. Ibid., 129, his emphasis.

11. Ibid., 150, 176.

12. Castelli, *Imitating Paul*, 87.

For Paul, circumcision of the flesh and the materiality of writing are aligned with one another in mutual, dichotomous opposition to the Holy Spirit and the grace of God. Perhaps at some deep level (the "place of difference") circumcision is even identical to writing.

Paul's rejection of the necessity or desirability of circumcision and his rejection of the "written code" are two correlated aspects of Paul's larger project of "spiritualizing" the body as it appears in the Jewish scriptures. Daniel Boyarin argues that "[s]ince for [Paul], these physical entities and connections have been fulfilled/annulled by their spiritual referents, 'according to the flesh' becomes a hermeneutical term referring to the literal, the *flesh of language* as well."[13] Boyarin stresses that the question is one of *reading*—that is, whether the physical text of the scriptures is to be read "according to the flesh" (that is, the local truths of the body) or "according to the Spirit."

Paul is the great psychoanalyst, seeking to liberate his readers from their bondage to desire, to replace id with ego. Like Freud, Paul interprets an Oedipal dream. It is the dream of circumcision as a not-so-mystic, un-erasable writing pad. In other words, the foreskin is a fetish, an uncanny sign (symbol) of something unsaid and perhaps even unsayable. The bloody circumcised foreskin is also an iconic metaphor for the written, physical page of scripture, a curl or "scroll" of the text that saves. It is the fleshy page of scripture, the material aspect of the signifier. According to Paul, this written code cannot save. The foreskin is Christ, whose blood redeems, but only if he is not "cut off" from you—that is, only if he is "written on your hearts." If Christ is cut off, then *graphē* becomes *gramma,* and Christ becomes the "remainder," the inert curl of the page.

Perhaps this explains how Paul can write his rejection of the written code. In this he is once again like Plato. In fact, not only are these words attacking the written code themselves written, but assuming that Paul wrote these words (or had them written by a scribe) on parchment, they were actually inscribed on dead animal tissue, flesh, quite unlike the "letter from Christ delivered by us," written by the Spirit on living human hearts. This self-referential irony or "aesthetic language" in Paul's message brings what Roman Jakobson called the "poetic function" of language to the fore (see further chapters 3 and 5). The denotation of Paul's words bends back on their connotation in a semiotic feedback loop.

The only way that Paul can dare to write words such as these without destroying his own message is if he believes—and he probably does—that the physical text itself, the literal, written code, is nothing more than a vehicle or channel for spiritual meaning, a parchment or foreskin that may be discarded ("we are the true circumcision") after it has served its purpose.

---

13. Boyarin, *A Radical Jew,* 77, emphasis added. See also Boyarin's continuing discussion of this relation (ibid., 77–81).

This logocentrism or spiritualizing of the scripture is an important means by which the New Testament colonizes the Old Testament. In other words, even though the Christian canon is still a long way from formation in Paul's day—indeed it has not even been conceived as yet—what Paul does here raises the question of canon. It may be no coincidence that Paul's devotee Marcion developed the first Christian canon—albeit a heretical one.

For Paul, reading according to the Spirit is reading in freedom (2 Corinthians 3:17). However, although his own reading is highly innovative, Paul's "hermeneutical freedom" is not a releasing of wild connotations but rather a careful restraining of them, in which the Spirit controls denotation through a *pesher* supporting Paul's authority *(exousia)*.[14] For Paul, the "abstract" and "dead" *gramma* of the "written code" is not the same as the "living and speaking presence" of the *graphē* of "scripture." Paul trusts the Spirit to restrict the possibilities for meaning, not to open them up: "Scripture becomes—in Paul's reading—a metaphor, a vast trope that signifies and illuminates the gospel of Jesus Christ."[15] The "gospel" here is the tenor, the univocal, logocentric contents conveyed by the textual vehicle of scripture. What is important then is not the physical text, but what Paul's reading can make it say.

Object

The textual representamen is composed of Paul's words conjoining the law, flesh, circumcision, and writing. To this written signifier corresponds a Peircean object, which in this case is another text—namely, the Old Testament, or as Paul calls these writings, "the scriptures." In Paul's letters, the scriptures themselves invite the reader to understand circumcision not only according to the flesh but also according to the spirit. This invitation appears already within the Jewish scriptures themselves in the metaphoric rewriting of circumcision (of the lips in Exodus 6:12 or of the heart in Jeremiah 4:4), and also, and much more so, in the colonizing reappropriations of Jewish circumcision in the New Testament. In addition to Paul's letters, circumcision is mentioned numerous times in the Acts of the Apostles, but relatively rarely elsewhere in the New Testament.[16]

---

14. Marks, "Pauline Typology," 81 ff. Hays, *Echoes of Scripture,* contests Marks on certain points but agrees regarding Paul's hermeneutical freedom. Paul's practice in this regard is similar to Peter's sermon at Pentecost (see further chapter 5). Both Hays and Marks give examples of hermeneutical liberties taken by Paul. Marks notes the importance in Luke-Acts of the "domesticated view" that Paul interprets the scriptures in an apologetic or expository way, rather than a revisionary one ("Pauline Typology," 75–76). This view has the effect of downplaying the hermeneutical liberties that Paul takes with the scriptures.

15. Hays, *Echoes of Scripture,* 149. See also ibid., 130–31.

16. Luke 1:59; 2:21; John 7:22–23; Acts 7:8, 51; 10:45; 11:2–3; 15:1, 5; 16:3; 21:21; Romans 2:25–3:1; 3:30; 4:9–12; 15:8; 1 Corinthians 7:18–19; Galatians 2:3, 7–9, 12; 5:2–

In his letter to the Galatians, Paul mentions Abraham (Galatians 3:6 ff.) and Abraham's "offspring" (*sperma*, 3:16). According to Paul's "allegory" (4:24), one of Abraham's sons is "born according to the flesh" (4:23), the son of a slave. The other one is "the son of the free woman through promise," or as Paul later states, "according to the Spirit" (4:29). Once again, the law/flesh enslaves, and the spirit brings freedom. In Romans 4:9–13, Paul similarly distinguishes between Abraham's circumcision according to the law and the promise that he received through faith:

> [Abraham] received circumcision as a *sign or seal of the righteousness which he had by faith* while he was still uncircumcised. The purpose was to make him the father of all who believe without being circumcised and who thus have righteousness reckoned to them, and likewise the father of the circumcised who are not merely circumcised but also follow the example of the faith which our father Abraham had before he was circumcised. The promise to Abraham and his descendants, that they should inherit the world, did not come through the law but through the righteousness of faith. (Romans 4:11–13, emphasis added)

The story of Abram/Abraham's circumcision in Genesis 17 introduces the theme of circumcision in the Torah. God makes a covenant with Abraham:

> "Behold, my covenant is with you, and you shall be the father of a multitude of nations. No longer shall your name be Abram, but your name shall be Abraham. . . . This is my covenant, which you shall keep, between me and you and your descendants after you: Every male among you shall be circumcised. You shall be circumcised in the flesh of your foreskins, and it shall be a *sign* of the covenant between me and you." (Genesis 17:4–5, 10–11, emphasis added)

José Faur notes that "the rabbis conceived of circumcision as a 'sign,' in the sense of the 'credentials' of God."[17] Paul's comments are consistent with this but also distinguish between circumcision and the promise of God. To use another of Paul's phrases, circumcision is a "letter of recommendation" (2 Corinthians 3:2), God's mark that ratifies a preexisting faith.

Paul's distinction in 2 Corinthians 3 between writing on the flesh and by the Spirit does lead into his discussion of Moses' veil (3:7–4:6), yet another fleshy page, a veil "over the mind" that conceals "the glory of the Lord" (3:15, 18). However, Paul's circumcision comments do not include discussion of another object-narrative of his circumcision texts, which appears in a more remarkable circumcision passage involving Moses. The fact that Paul does not explicitly mention this story that appears in Exodus 4 is not entirely

---

3, 6, 11; 6:12–13, 15; Ephesians 2:11; Philippians 3:3, 5; Colossians 2:11, 13; 3:11; 4:11; Titus 1:10.

17. Faur, *Golden Doves*, 200 n. 18.

surprising, for the relation that I am considering here is that of the Peircean symbol, not the icon or index. The connection is therefore an artificial one, established through the judgment of a reader.

In Exodus 4, God tries to get Moses ready to go back to the people of Israel in Egypt, but Moses resists God at every turn. There is talk of Israel as the firstborn son of God and also of the firstborn sons of the Egyptians (4:22–23). Finally Moses takes leave of his father-in-law, Jethro, and goes on his way, returning to Egypt with his wife, Zipporah, and his son or sons.[18] Moses is instructed to go to Pharaoh and threaten him with the death of the Egyptians' sons. In the wilderness, Moses encounters Aaron, who has come out to meet him on the holy mountain. Moses and Aaron return together to Egypt, where they preach and perform miracles and are believed and followed by the Israelites.

The story in Exodus 4:24–26 interrupts what looks like an otherwise continuous story. It appears to be a dreamlike intrusion into the sequence. This story reverberates with God's threat to kill the Egyptians' firstborn sons because it occurs immediately after that threat, and before the reunion of Moses with Aaron. The verbal ambiguities of this "intractable narrative"[19] and of its relation to its larger context—the birth of the son of Moses, the chosen people as the sons of Israel, the sons of the Egyptians—are reminiscent of Barthes's well-known discussion of the ambiguities in a similarly mysterious and violent story, the wrestling match between Jacob and the angel in Genesis 32.[20] The reader cannot keep track of all these sons, and the pronouns outrace their antecedents.

Zipporah's story appears in the Revised Standard Version as follows:

> At a lodging place on the way the LORD met him and sought to kill him. Then Zipporah took a flint and cut off (LXX: *perietemen*) her son's foreskin, and touched Moses' feet with it, and said, "Surely you are a bridegroom of blood to me!" So he let him alone. Then it was that she said, "You are a bridegroom of blood," because of the circumcision (LXX: *peritomēs*).

A strikingly different translation of this same passage is offered by Michael Fishbane:

> And on the way, at a resting spot, YHWH encountered him and sought to kill him. Then Zipporah took a flint and cut off the foreskin of her son and touched his penis, saying: "You are now a bridegroom of

---

18. The LXX text of Exodus 4:20 is "sons." Only one son is mentioned in the preceding (2:22) and following (4:25) stories.
19. Burns, "Zipporah."
20. Barthes, *Semiotic Challenge*, 246–60.

blood with YHWH." So he released him, and she said: "You are a bridegroom of blood through the circumcision."[21]

It is not clear whose life is threatened by God, nor does either translation resolve this matter. Like the deity in the story of Jacob wrestling, God is behaving like a monster or wild beast. It is uncertain whom God is trying to kill and why God wants him dead.

Furthermore, just as God's attack seems irrational, so does God's appeasement. Uncertain denotation is here produced by an insufficiency of the signifier. Nevertheless, Zipporah has understood what the book's reader cannot. Somehow she alone knows just what to do. These gaps in the narrative must be filled in by the reader, and Zipporah is a very good reader. It is as though she has already read the larger story in which she appears to be a minor character. It seems that she already knows the canon—at least the canon of Torah. Once again the text loops back on itself and presents an aesthetic message. Zipporah's story both invites and staves off the threat of semiotic chaos.

Zipporah carves the body of her son, releasing the curl of his foreskin to touch it to the genitals ("feet") of her husband, according to the RSV. Or perhaps she touch Moses with her *knife*. Otto Eissfeldt suggests this latter reading,[22] and Fishbane's translation leaves the matter uncertain. Are there two separate cuts here—two circumcisions? These ambiguous words might mean merely (as Fishbane's translation also allows) that she touched Gershom's penis while circumcising him. In any case, Zipporah must be not only a good reader but a good writer as well—that is, handy with the knife—for whatever it is that she does, it works! The reader of Exodus 4 has a tougher time of it. Enigmatically, the text says, "He let him go." Does God let someone go, or does Moses let Gershom go? Again, the signifiers are inconclusive. The reader has no difficulty understanding possible connotations of this sentence, but still the denotation is confused.

The strangely erotic (and possibly incestuous) suggestion of the bloody foreskin (or knife!) touched to Moses' (or maybe the son's) "feet" and the sleazy horror-movie overtones of the "bridegroom of blood" hint at a monstrous, albeit salvific, crime. Boyarin notes that "erotic implications were to be most fully developed in the midrashic and (later) mystical readings of the rite of circumcision. In those readings, the performance of that rite was understood as a necessary condition for divine-human erotic encounter—for seeing God." In Jewish tradition, circumcision enables the male Israelite "to take the position of the female" in the faith-relation to God—that is, to become a "Daughter of Zion."[23] Instead of the female becoming male, as in the gospel of Thomas, saying 114, the male must become female.

21. Fishbane, *Text and Texture*, 70.
22. Eissfeldt, *Old Testament*, 192.
23. Boyarin, "This We Know," 485, 496.

The monstrous "bridegroom of blood" may be Moses, Gershom, or God. The two translations cited above reveal remarkably different readings of Zipporah's words in Exodus 4:25: are "you" a bridegroom of blood to *me* (that is, Zipporah) or to *YHWH?* Fishbane bases his translation on the cryptic letters *ly* in the Hebrew text.[24] Furthermore, although the final sentence in the RSV text ("Then it was that she said, 'You are a bridegroom of blood,' because of the circumcision," 4:26) seems to be an explanation, it is unclear what need there is to explain anything. This statement looks like a later commentary, attempting to explain an otherwise intrusive and apparently irrelevant story. However, Fishbane makes a strong case that the story belongs with Exodus 1–4.[25] Fishbane's translation renders the sentence more coherently, and the New Revised Standard Version similarly moves the text in this direction ("It was then she said, 'A bridegroom of blood by circumcision' "). The Septuagint offers no help in clarifying any of this, for instead of Zipporah's intriguing "bridegroom of blood" language, the much tamer statement "I stop the blood of the circumcision of my child!" (*Estē to haima tēs peritomēs tou paidiou mou*) appears twice.

As Boyarin puts it, the foreskin is an ugly blemish that must be removed. In the story of Zipporah, the foreskin is both more and less than a metaphor; it is narrative incarnate. It is simply the simple flesh of story, which the reader discards once she has understood its meaning—or so Paul suggests—and Zipporah is its scribe. Yet in Exodus 4, the foreskin is also the site of profound ambiguity, an occasion for wild connotations. Zipporah's story presents another kind of aesthetic message, different than Paul's, and yet also one in which denotation again loops back on connotation.

Zipporah writes the canonical text of the circumcised penis, the fleshy text of scripture that Paul rewrites according to the spirit.[26] As in Paul's letters, circumcision in Exodus 4 is both symbol and icon. Zipporah's knife divides as it unites—the flesh of the son, the son and the father, Israelites and Egyptians, and eventually Jews and Christians. However, like the story's anonymous narrator, Zipporah has no need of these oppositions—there is no circumcision for *her* in this story—even though she "writes" them. Zipporah blurs the oppositions in the very act of establishing them. She is Friedrich Nietzsche's immoralist, Jean-François Lyotard's differend, Michel Serres's parasite. In other words, Zipporah rescues the moral order and the possibility of meaning from a position "outside" of the system of meaning. In a similar fashion, Exodus 4:24–26 affirms the law even though it is itself beyond the law, or as Kafka says, "before the law."[27]

---

24. Fishbane, *Text and Texture,* 70 n.
25. Ibid., 70 ff.
26. I owe this thought to Roland Boer, private conversation, 2 July 1998.
27. Kafka, *Parables and Paradoxes,* 60–79. This little story also appears in Kafka, *The Trial,* 267–76.

Interpretant

Paul's letters never refer explicitly to Zipporah's story. Some connotative interpretant is required in order to link the text-representamen provided by Paul's letters to the text-object of Exodus 4:24–26. Because it will be necessarily a commentary, and because no text in the Christian double canon explicitly links the texts of Paul and Zipporah, this connotative association comes from outside of the biblical canon. This third story will unite writing and circumcision in a way that completes the connection between the other two, although it will jeopardize the logocentric unity of the biblical message. It will test canonical closure and open up (again) the possibility of unlimited semiosis.

Kafka's story "In the Penal Colony" offers such a connection. According to Walter Benjamin, in Kafka's writings, "modern man lives in his body; the body slips away from him, is hostile toward him. It may happen that a man wakes up one day and finds himself transformed into vermin. Exile—his exile—has gained control over him."[28] In this particular story, an officer of a distant penal colony explains the design and demonstrates the operation of a peculiar machine to an explorer who happens to be visiting the island colony. The machine, designed by the colony's former commandant himself—who was a man of "perfect organization," so the reader is told[29]—consists of three parts: the Bed, the Designer, and the Harrow. The condemned man is initially laid face down on the Bed. The Designer consists of a mechanism of cogs that operates the Harrow according to a preset pattern or program, not unlike a player piano or mechanical loom. The Harrow is a glass plate that slides back and forth on a steel ribbon. It operates like the print head of an electric typewriter or computer printer. The Harrow supports a number of movable needles that are made to vibrate in such a way, once the machine is turned on, that they inscribe the sentence of the condemned man on to the page of his naked flesh, etching it with "acid fluid" and also rinsing away the blood.[30]

The sentence inscribed by this dreadful machine is always a death sentence. The condemned man is letter by letter and word by word "sentenced" to death. The machine in the penal colony is a writing machine, a word processor. The words of the sentence etched on the body signify in all three of Peirce's ways in Kafka's story. They are not merely symbols, in the Peircean sense, of the abstract judgment of the law. As etchings on his skin, the physical words are also potent indices of the concrete suffering of the man. This writing is violent and cruel and ultimately lethal. Finally, the words are icons of the materiality of language. The man's skin becomes a "carbon copy" of the written sentence that has been programmed into the Designer:

---

28. Benjamin, *Illuminations*, 126.
29. Kafka, "Penal Colony," 193.
30. Ibid., 209.

[W]riting is only a transcription of the divine word, or even writing from the finger of God, but in any case it is a copy, a double of a spoken word that already exists without the writing, itself doubled on the two tables and their two faces as if to indicate its character as carbon copy, as repetition. Its function is to make God's word stable, durable, and obligatory, to be his Law.[31]

The body of the condemned man is slowly rotated on the Bed so that his skin is eventually entirely covered by the inscription of the sentence. With each rotation of the condemned man's body, the machine's needles cut deeper and deeper, and the man eventually bleeds to death. Only by *becoming* the text is the condemned man enabled to "read" his own sentence:

Enlightenment comes to the most dull-witted [the officer says]. It begins around the eyes.... Nothing more happens than that the man begins to *understand* the inscription, he purses his mouth as if he were listening. You have seen how hard it is to decipher the script with one's eyes; but our man deciphers it with his wounds.[32]

The violence of reading necessarily corresponds to the violence of writing. "Of course the script can't be a simple one," the officer calmly explains, "it's not supposed to kill a man straight off, but only after an interval of, on an average, twelve hours; the turning point is reckoned to come at the sixth hour."[33] The embellishments and flourishes of the alphabetic script provide for most of the actual writing. Indeed, writing is never anything but embellishment, the meaningless little marks that distinguish one letter from another. If you take away the embellishment, then only a meaningless line is left. Nevertheless, too many embellishments make the script illegible. Embellishment both provides and prevents the meaningless difference that enables writing to signify.

Kafka's story is about writing, but like both Paul's letters and Zipporah's story, it is also about reading, about understanding and misunderstanding. It too is self-referential and aesthetic, because once again, its denotation loops back upon its connotation. However, although narrative texts loop back on themselves through the poetic function of language, they also point beyond themselves to extratextual reality, whether actual or imagined, utilizing the referential function of language. The reference of the aesthetic message is split (see further chapter 3). Like all of Kafka's stories, "In the Penal Colony" is possessed by a dreamlike quality that cries out for interpretation, but that also resists the reader's attempts to understand it. Just as, at the end of the story, the explorer refuses to allow the soldier and the condemned man to

---

31. Kristeva, *Language,* 100.
32. Kafka, "Penal Colony," 204, emphasis added.
33. Ibid., 202.

accompany him as he flees the island of the penal colony, so this story never lets its reader get "onboard."

The reader's nonunderstanding appears within the story as well. Much as in Kafka's novel *The Trial,* the accused man is never told his sentence or allowed to contest it. There is no access to "the law," only submission or defiance. Neither the condemned man nor the soldier who guards him ever understands what the officer and the explorer are talking about. They are silly, slapstick figures—"like a submissive dog"[34]—nightmarish comic relief in Kafka's dream world. The explorer finds that the judicial procedures of the officer, like the script in which the sentence is written and the working of the machine itself, are incomprehensible. In addition, when the explorer tries to read the text of the machine's plans, all he sees is "a labyrinth of lines crossing and re-crossing each other, which covered the paper so thickly that it was difficult to discern the blank spaces between them," not unlike an overabundance of embellishments or the shredded flesh of an executed convict.[35] Once again, semiotic difference disappears as the blank spaces that are essential to this difference disappear. As Benjamin says, "In Kafka the written law is contained in books, but these are secret; by basing itself on them the prehistoric world exerts its rule all the more ruthlessly."[36]

The explorer learns that the officer and his writing machine have fallen on hard times. The new commandant, who is not as wise as the former one, who invented the machine, does not understand the importance of the machine and refuses to encourage its use. Consequently the performance of the machine is no longer up to its former levels of perfection—it now makes disturbing noises—and the officer fears that executions will soon be stopped altogether. The next death sentence may be for the machine itself. The officer begs the explorer to lend his support to the cause of the machine, but the explorer refuses, revolted by the entire gruesome process. In desperation, the officer releases the condemned man, readjusts the settings on the Designer, climbs into the Bed himself, and inscribes on his own body his own sentence: "BE JUST."[37]

In response to the officer's commands, the machine obeys perfectly, in absolute, uncanny silence. It is as though it knows its master's desires and welcomes him to its embrace. However, as the process continues, the machine begins to fall apart. The cogs pop out of the Designer, and the needles of the Harrow begin to jab randomly at the body of the officer. The officer dies quickly and without the execution of his "sentence." He also does not achieve understanding. The writing machine jams and leaves the page of the dead man's body smeared and illegible—another incomprehensible text. His

---

34. Kafka, "Penal Colony," 191. These words are reminiscent of the final words of K., the hero of Kafka's novel *The Trial* (286).
35. Kafka, "Penal Colony," 202.
36. Benjamin, *Illuminations,* 115.
37. Kafka, "Penal Colony," 219.

body is left hanging, a grotesque crucifix impaled on the motionless Harrow, dangling over the pit into which the machine had previously discarded the dead bodies:

> [The officer's face] was as it had been in life; no sign was visible of the promised redemption; what the others had found in the machine the officer had not found; the lips were firmly pressed together, the eyes were open, with the same expression as in life, the look was calm and convinced, through the forehead went the point of the great iron spike.[38]

"In the Penal Colony" is a story about the incarnation of justice, and about its failure. As a story about death and judgment, it is also an eschatological story. Eventually the explorer flees the island of the penal colony, but only after he has visited the grave of the former commandant and seen the inscription on it (written "in very small letters"): "[T]he Commandant will rise again and lead his adherents from this house to recover the colony. Have faith and wait!"[39] The messianic commandant will restore his machine to its former excellence, and all will be well. Nevertheless, this epitaph is described as "ridiculous," and the former commandant's few remaining followers appear to be "poor, humble creatures." Another of Benjamin's comments seems pertinent:

> Kafka's world, frequently of such playfulness and interlaced with angels, is the exact complement of his era which is preparing to do away with the inhabitants of this planet on a considerable scale. The experience which corresponds to that of Kafka, the private individual, will probably not become accessible to the masses until such time as they are being done away with.[40]

Reading Circumcision

In Peircean terms, circumcision is a symbol of the covenant between God and Abraham and his descendants, but it is also an icon for inscription, writing. Circumcision carves in and out and around these texts just as the texts themselves inscribe or circumscribe a relation between father and son, or between the Lord and "him," whoever he is in Exodus 4. As Jacques Derrida says, the word itself is circumcised. Derrida speaks of writing as though it were an act of cutting into a surface or plowing the ground. Writing is produced by the spur or point of the pen spearing the page—the page

---

38. Ibid., 225.
39. Ibid., 226.
40. Benjamin, *Illuminations*, 143.

which is itself a tissue or text, a fleshy veil. To circumcise is also to inscribe; it is an "incision of Nothing."[41]

Circumcision is an unrepeatable event, and as such it runs counter to the effect of the poetic function, which is also the principle of "canonical process," namely, the repetition of the text.[42] The Derridean spur is also the spoor, the trace or remainder.[43] It is the text as a body to be read, but also a body to be eliminated by the reader, and a body that has already been eliminated by the writer. The meaningful logocentric reading both contains and overlooks the meaningless writing, the worthless script. Connotation and denotation both emerge from and conceal the violence of inscription. Kafka's story suggests and even invites both the desire for meaning and the violence that that desire provokes. It signifies its own exclusions, its remainder.

Paul's letters do not make the connection between writing and circumcision or mutilation explicit and central in the way that "In the Penal Colony" does. Kafka's story not only resists Paul's constrained hermeneutics of the spirit, but Kafka's world is diametrically opposed to Paul's. It is a world of the flesh. Nevertheless, as Jorge Luis Borges says, Kafka creates his precursors, and one of these precursors, although not so noted by Borges, is the New Testament letters of Paul. Kafka is a "strong misreader" of Paul—in this respect not unlike Marcion—just as Paul himself strongly misreads the Jewish scriptures, according to Herbert Marks.[44]

Paul says that circumcision binds one to the law, just as the prisoner is bound to the Bed of Kafka's machine. One must be bound in order to be cut, and vice versa. Circumcision is a sentence of judgment written on the flesh, and to that statement, Zipporah also can agree. The officer in the penal colony, that faithful servant of the law, mutilates himself and carves his own flesh. The iconic circumscription of his body is also its symbolic circumcision, demanded by the colony's law. It is the revelation of radiant justice.[45] However, it is also futile and doomed, and the officer is condemned by his own attachment to the law.

When Paul's letters are regarded as Kafka's precursors, albeit precursors by way of opposition, Paul's connection between circumcision and writing, and between flesh and the physical text, come into focus. Furthermore, if Paul's letters may be read as precursors to Kafka's story, then the Jewish scriptures may also be read as precursors to both Paul and Kafka. Indeed, another Kafka precursor, also unnoted by Borges, is the story of Zipporah's

---

41. Derrida, "Shibboleth," 345. See also Derrida, *Spurs*, 39.
42. Jakobson, *Language and Literature*, 86; and Sanders, *Canon and Community*, 22. See also the quote from Kristeva above, regarding the "character [of writing] as carbon copy, as repetition" (*Language*, 100).
43. Derrida, *Spurs*, 41, 161 n. 21.
44. Marks, "Pauline Typology," 88. See also Hays, *Echoes of Scripture*, 182.
45. Kafka, "Penal Colony," 209.

circumcising of her son. Moses' son's body is inscribed with the law; he is condemned and "sentenced," not unlike the officer in Kafka's story, even though Gershom himself is perhaps rather more like the original condemned man of that story, the "submissive dog," than the officer who eventually "sentences" himself. Both Gershom and the condemned man remain silent bodies, passive objects of violence, nearly abandoned by the narrative.

In the context provided by Exodus 4:24–26, Paul's association of the foreskin with Christ and the connections that Paul makes between circumcision and castration are rich in connotation. "In the Penal Colony" offers a third story, "a third term, which is not, however, a synthesizing term but an eccentric, extraordinary term."[46] This third story makes apparent some connotations and conceals others. This is what any commentary, any text-interpretant, does. In this way, I trace a reverse trajectory, in which later texts explain earlier ones.

I am concerned, not with the intentions of writers here, but rather with the ideology of readers. Just as the authors of the stories of Abraham and Moses in the Torah did not intend Paul's rewriting of those stories, so neither Paul nor the writers of Torah intended Kafka's rewriting, and none of them intended my rewriting. Kafka's story becomes a connotative interpretant linking Paul's letters to Zipporah's story. Regardless of anyone's intention, Kafka's story connects the representamen that is Paul's letters to the object that is the Jewish scriptures, or in terms of my interest, the Christian Old Testament. By way of Kafka's text, Paul's letters denote Zipporah's story. I take Kafka's story as an intertext, a node of transition—it is my own circumcision of meaning. It allows a connection to be made, in a way that it would perhaps not otherwise be made.

There is nothing objective or impartial about this reading. I choose Kafka's text as an interpretant for the biblical texts of Exodus and Paul, and not some other text. I decide to connect Paul to Zipporah by way of that gruesome machine. Reasons can be given for these choices, but as in the child's game of "Why?" behind every reason there is another reason. My reasons ultimately come down to my interests, my desires, my act of will. There is nothing natural or automatic about the ideological operation of any interpretant. The connection between writing and circumcision is not there "in" these texts. Rather, it emerges from the tension *between* the texts, a tension that is highlighted by my zigzag reading, indeed, because it is *created* by this reading. This trajectory is not grounded in necessity, and surely there are other connotations to Paul's texts. This is not a canonical, orthodox reading of the scriptures: Kafka's commentary on Paul and the Jewish scriptures is heterodox at best.

Other possible text-interpretants would undoubtedly leave the reader more securely within the canonical boundaries. These other readings are

---

46. Barthes, *Pleasure*, 55.

in fact quite easy to find (for example, the vast majority of commentaries on the texts of Paul or of Exodus), but such readings are just as artificial and arbitrary as the reading by way of Kafka's story that I have presented here. Whether you attempt to secure the boundaries of the canon or whether you seek to break them open, in either case ideology is involved. Insofar as some other readings of Paul or of Exodus 4 claim to be free of ideology, historically objective, or authorized by the texts themselves, then they are either dishonest or uncritical.

Hays takes Paul's own hermeneutical freedom as a warrant for similar freedom on the part of the Bible's readers, but he also recognizes that to do so is dangerous. Hays insists that certain constraints should remain in place—namely, the ones that Paul himself acknowledged: God's covenant faithfulness and "the death and resurrection of Jesus as the climactic manifestation of God's righteousness."[47] These constraints control the spiritual message of the Christian canon. I accept Hays's invitation to hermeneutical freedom, and I acknowledge his warning of danger, but my selection of Kafka's story as interpretant violates the constraints. The reading offered here does not recognize Paul's *exousia,* and it stands instead in "a place of difference."[48] Thanks to Kafka's "eccentric" text, my reading tears free from the Christian double canon. Peirce's triadic symbol opens up through the noncanonical interpretant—through the "wild connotations" that Kafka's story releases—once again the prospect of unlimited semiosis, a prospect that the biblical canon can never entirely foreclose.

I do not claim to have touched every point on this trajectory of texts. There are probably many other texts that belong just as well along the curve that I have traced, and there are probably other curves as well—that is, completely different, inconsistent, contradictory readings that my own circumcising reading has foreclosed. If Peirce is correct about the interchangeability of the components of the triadic symbol, there is nothing to keep a reader from starting, for example, with Exodus 4 as the text-representamen, instead of Paul's circumcision texts, or with Kafka's story.[49] As Boyarin says, it is a question of reading. Each of these options would result in a different reading of the scriptures, and a different arrangement of texts, from the one presented here. Each would reflect a different ideology. No reading would be any "better" or "worse" than this one. That is how intertextuality works. The meaning of a text does not lie in the text itself but in the juxtaposition of texts (representamen and object), which itself can be justified only in terms of some further arrangement of texts (interpretant).

The biblical canon seeks to control this arrangement, but it fails, in large part because of unlimited semiosis. The biblical texts of Exodus (and Gen-

---

47. Hays, *Echoes of Scripture,* 191.
48. Castelli, *Imitating Paul,* 87.
49. Earlier versions of this chapter started with Kafka's story.

esis) and especially Paul's letters invoke not only the circumcision of the body but also an inevitably ideological circumcision of narrative and of language itself. Circumcision once more becomes a metaphor, and the spirit again replaces the flesh. Nevertheless, these biblical connotations are still not enough. I choose Kafka's story as Paul's interpretant rather than some other one because it highlights the Bible's control over its own meaning *and* the failure of that control.

Kafka's commentary brings the reader back to the materiality of the text, the very materiality that the logocentric understanding of the Christian Bible seeks to erase—that is, the materiality that stands always in tension with the double canon. Régis Debray notes that "having too fully deciphered the world as a sign, we forget there is a world underneath, and that the letter itself has a body."[50] As Freud might have said, sometimes a penis is only a penis. The written diagram of the machine, the sentence written on the skin, the writing on the commandant's tombstone—in Kafka's story, writing is the circumcision of the body, the sentence of law that I must understand in my flesh although not necessarily in my mind. Through the lens provided by Kafka's story, the materiality of the biblical texts comes into view, albeit briefly.

---

50. Debray, *Media Manifestos*, 56.

Chapter 7 _____

THE HUMANOIDS

Ezekiel (chapter 1) has "visions of Elohim" in which he sees a humanoid in a wheeled chair, surrounded by other beings with the
"appearance of the forms of humans...," and in Daniel 7 Daniel sees
a figure (presumably humanoid, having a head, white hair, and being able to sit) and another human figure (called "the Humanoid...")
who comes in or with clouds.
— Philip Davies, *Whose Bible Is It Anyway?*

Invasion of the Humanoids

In the passage quoted above, Philip Davies translates various Aramaic and
Hebrew phrases in the books of Ezekiel and Daniel with the word "humanoid." In this passage, Davies is discussing "reference to the body of the
deity" in the Bible. However, later in the same book, Davies again uses the
term "humanoid" in a discussion of the phrase "son of man" in Daniel 7:13
("I saw in the night visions, / and behold, with the clouds of heaven / there
came one like a son of man, / and he came to the Ancient of Days / and was
presented before him"). In that discussion, Davies suggests the possibility
that the humanoid of Daniel 7:13 may denote a human being who symboli-
cally represents the people of Israel, described in 7:27 as the "people of the
holy ones of Elyon."[1] Davies argues that God (Elyon or Most High) dies in
Daniel 7, for "on either side of chapter 7 lie two dispensations, the 'before'
and 'after,' the rule of the old bearded and white-haired Elyon, and the rule
of the new humanoid being."[2] What remains after Elyon's death is a chaotic
world, ruled either by human beings or by a multitude of warring gods, but
in either case, a world in which the God of Israel is no longer present. It is
a world not unlike our present-day, (post)modern world.

Strictly speaking, human beings cannot be humanoid since "humanoid"
means "humanlike" and to be "like" something is not to be that thing. The

---

1. Davies, *Whose Bible*, 129. The RSV translates this phrase as "people of the saints of the
Most High."
2. Davies, *Whose Bible*, 130. See also ibid., 133.

151

word "humanoid" connotes something that is not human but that never-theless possesses important human characteristics. In that sense, this term is appropriate for the divine being described in Ezekiel and Daniel. Other sorts of beings can also be humanoid. The extraterrestrial aliens who appear at the end of the movie *Close Encounters of the Third Kind* are humanoid, as are most of the creatures that appear in the television series *The X-Files*. Even "E.T." is humanoid. If Ezekiel or Daniel, or some other text, speaks of a "humanoid" being, then this term connotes both humanity and nonhumanity at once.

Consequently, to use the term "humanoid" to describe a human being is to create strange linguistic effects, to distort the signification. It suggests that humans are humanlike, and therefore nonhuman. Davies's use of this term gives to the familiar phrase "son of man," which is so full of acquired canonical meaning, a noncanonical overtone, suggesting something out of a science-fiction story—perhaps an alien being or a monster. Humanoid characters indeed appear in many science-fiction stories, such as those noted above, as well as other stories not usually considered science fiction, such as Homer's *Odyssey*, Kafka's "The Metamorphosis," and Shakespeare's *A Midsummer Night's Dream*. Angels, mermaids, and elves are all humanoid, as are chimpanzees and some robots.

None of these characters is an ordinary human being, by any standard. Humanoids are often superhuman beings, and sometimes they are even supernatural ones. They generally have a physical form resembling (more or less) the human norm, but not always. According to the *Oxford English Dictionary*, that which is humanoid is "distinguished from anthropoid as being more human in *character*" (emphasis added). Thus the supercomputer HAL 9000 in the movie *2001* is humanoid, as are the TV heroes Flipper the dolphin and Lassie the dog.

Humanoid characters allow the stories in which they appear to raise profound questions about human nature and identity—that is, questions about what the important human characteristics are. In the humanoid being, the conventional, ideological boundaries between human and nonhuman—whether animal, machine, or god—disappear. Stories about humanoid beings frequently make it clear that no matter how nonhuman the humanoids appear, they still remain human in some significant way.

Often humanoid beings appear in science-fiction stories as the product of the deliberate, controlled evolution of human beings into something else. Sometimes the power of the human mind is enhanced through drugs or direct neural linkage with computer networks or telepathic union with other minds. Sometimes the human body is connected to or transformed into a machine, often by way of computerized prostheses. The body's physical components, powers, and longevity may be radically altered through genetic manipulation or interbreeding with other species. These changes are often accompanied by profound social and cultural transformations.

However, the humanoid is not merely something out of science fiction. It does not require computers, cloning, drugs, or alien sex to transform humanity, for human beings have been re-creating themselves over and over again for thousands of years already, beginning with simple tools, language, clothing, the use of fire, and agriculture. In this light, the "original sin" in the Garden of Eden begins humanity's self-transformation, or from another point of view, that transformation begins already prior to the evolutionary appearance of Homo sapiens.

The question of what makes one "human" has troubled philosophers and scientists for centuries, and it is unlikely ever to be settled. The boundaries between human and nonhuman being are produced by ideology, and it is human nature continually to question human nature and to remake human beings. The existentialists argued that there is no fixed human nature, and more recent postmodern thinkers agree. There is nothing natural about human beings: humanity is already and has always been humanoid. According to Michel Foucault, "As the archaeology of our thought easily shows, man is an invention of recent date. And one perhaps nearing its end."[3] Indeed, according to Katherine Hayles, "[W]e have always been posthuman."[4] Human beings are their own creators, the products of culture. We are ideologically fabricated, artificial beings, "cyborgs" in the sense that Donna Haraway uses that term. Indeed, the very concept of "nature," whether scientific or metaphysical, is a product of ideology, at least insofar as nature can be understood and manipulated by human beings. Nature is itself a human, ideological construct.

However, it may be in Davies's case that these fantastical overtones of the term "humanoid" are merely accidental. Perhaps it is instead the political uncorrectness of the traditional translation "son of man" that motivates Davies's use of the term. The ancient languages of the Bible are undoubtedly sexist in both the singular phrase "son of man" and its plural version, "sons of men." Attempts to translate these gender-exclusive phrases using gender-inclusive language inevitably produce bizarre effects.

For another example, Marvin Meyer translates saying 106 of the gospel of Thomas as follows: "When you make the two into one, you will become children of humankind, and when you say, 'Mountain, move from here!' it will move."[5] The inclusive language of Meyer's translation also results in words with an odd, almost unearthly ring to them, the sort of language that aliens might use if they were to meet far-future descendants of human beings: "Greetings, children of humankind!" Again the science-fictional overtones are evident. This is especially so when Meyer's choice of words is contrasted to the equally inclusive term "people" that the New Revised Standard Ver-

---

3. Foucault, *Order of Things,* 287.
4. Hayles, *Posthuman,* 291.
5. In Kloppenborg et al., *Q-Thomas Reader,* 152.

sion of the Bible uses to translate *tois huioi tōn anthrōpōn* in Mark 3:28: "Truly I tell you, people will be forgiven for their sins and whatever blasphemies they utter." The sons of men may be nothing but ordinary "people," but the use of terms such as "humanoid" or "children of humankind" to designate them suggests that they are stranger than that.

The desire to make the Bible "speak" in acceptable, nonoppressive language is probably a factor in these translations, but I think there is something more to the matter than that alone, at least in Davies's case. This something more appears differently in the ways that the two Christian canons treat the phrases "son of man" and "sons of men," even as these phrases join the two canons together. Despite the fact that the phrase in both its singular and plural forms is plainly gender-exclusive, I consider the plural phrase to connote human beings regardless of gender. I understand the connotation of the plural phrase to be "descendants of human beings," but I retain the more literal English translation because I want to examine the physical text of the Bible as well as the meanings associated with those texts. I realize that phrases such as "daughters of men," *thugateras tōn anthrōpōn,* in LXX Genesis 6:2 (compare Daniel 11:17) may count against my understanding, and I agree that the logocentric understanding of the message produced by the biblical canon tends to submerge women into "men." My understanding may finally be a privileged one for those like myself who are physiologically the sons of men.

The Son of Man in the Bible

"Son of man" in both its singular and plural forms means a variety of things in the Bible. The numerous texts in which this phrase appears, and the meanings attached to those texts, are points at which the tension between the two Christian canons is quite evident. As it has been in previous chapters of this book, once again the play of connotation and denotation is extremely important here. In the Greek Old Testament, both the singular phrase, *huios anthrōpou,* and the plural phrase, *hoi huioi tōn anthrōpōn,* are nearly always used with the connotation of "human being." For example,

> "Who are you that you are afraid of man who dies,
> of the son of man who is made like grass...?"
> > (Isaiah 51:12)

> The LORD is in his holy temple,
> the LORD's throne is in heaven;
> his eyes behold, his eyelids test, the children of men.
> > (Psalm 10:4 [11:4 RSV])

There is no apparent tension between the Christian canons regarding the plural phrase "sons of men," which is always used in both the Jewish and the Christian Bibles and related writings to connote human beings. The most numerous occurrence of the plural phrase is in the Psalms, although it also appears with this meaning in several other passages in the Septuagint. The book of Ecclesiastes uses a slightly different phrase, "sons of man" (*hoi huioi tou anthrōpou*), to connote "human beings." The plural phrase "sons of men" also appears with this connotation in what are known as the apocryphal writings, although these writings are not apocryphal in the LXX.[6] Theodotion's Greek translation of Daniel 2:38 also uses the plural phrase with this meaning, but the "Old Greek" version simply has *anthrōpōn*, "men."[7] In the Pseudepigrapha, the plural phrase with this connotation appears in 1 Enoch 69:6.

The singular phrase "son of man" also appears many times in the Greek Old Testament. Unlike the plural phrase, which appears in the Old Testament both with and without articles, the singular phrase is anarthous in the Old Testament. Perhaps the best-known instances of the phrase appear in Ezekiel, where it connotes "human being" and appears to function as a name or title for the prophet himself.[8] The singular phrase in Daniel 8:17, although situated in a supernatural context, also denotes the human being Daniel, and similarly in 1 Enoch 60:10, the singular phrase denotes the human narrator. The singular use of the phrase elsewhere in the Old Testament connotes a generic human being, "anyone."[9]

In contrast, the singular phrase *huios anthrōpou* may connote a supernatural being in the Old Testament only once, in Daniel 7:13:

> With the clouds of heaven
> there came one like a son of man,
> and he came to the Ancient of Days
> and was presented before him.

However, this verse narrates the moment of cosmic transition, identified by Davies, when God (Elyon, the Ancient of Days) relinquishes the traditional divine powers to a successor, the humanoid one, as the next verse indicates:

6. See LXX Psalms 4:3; 10:4; 11:2, 9; 13:2; 20:11; 30:20; 32:13; 35:8; 44:3; 48:3; 52:3; 56:5; 57:2; 61:10; 65:5; 88:48; 89:3; 106:8, 15, 21, 31; 113:24; 144:12; and 145:3, as well as Genesis 11:5; 1 Samuel 26:19; 1 Samuel 7:14; 1 Kings 8:39; Proverbs 8:4, 31; 2 Chronicles 6:30; Ezekiel 31:14; Jeremiah 39:19; Micah 5:6; and Joel 1:12. See also LXX Ecclesiastes 1:13; 2:3, 8; 3:10, 18, 19, 21; 8:11; 9:3, 12. For apocryphal texts, see LXX Wisdom of Solomon 9:6; Psalms of Solomon 9:4; Odes 8:82; 1 Esdras 4:37; Judith 8:12; Ecclesiasticus 36:23; and Daniel 3:82 (in the "song of the Three Young Men," 60).

7. "[I]n the case of Daniel, ... Theodotion's edition supplanted the Old Greek [of the LXX] at a very early date" (Greenspoon, "Theodotion").

8. See LXX Ezekiel 2:1, 3, 6, 8; 3:1, 3, 4, 10, 17, 25; 4:1, 16; 5:1; 6:2; 7:2; 8:5, 6, 8, 12, 15, 17; 11:2, 4, 15; 12:2, 3, 9, 18, 22, 27; 13:2, 17; 14:3, 13; 15:2; 16:2; 17:2; 18:2; 20:3, 4, 27; 21:2, 7, 11, 14, 17, 19, 24, 33; 22:2, 18, 24; 23:2, 36; 24:2, 16, 25; 25:2; 26:2; 27:2; 28:2, 12, 21; 29:2, 18; 30:2, 21; 31:2; 32:2, 18; 33:2, 7, 10, 24, 30; 34:2; 35:2; 36:1, 17; 37:3, 9, 11, 16; 38:2, 14; 39:1, 17; 40:4; 43:7, 10, 18; 44:5; 47:6.

9. See LXX Job 16:21; 25:6; 35:8; Psalm 8:5; 79:16, 18; 143:3; Isaiah 51:12; Jeremiah 2:6; 27:40; 28:43; 30:12, 28. Apocryphal texts are LXX Judith 8:16 and Ecclesiasticus 17:30.

> And to him was given dominion
>> and glory and kingdom,
> that all peoples, nations, and languages
>> should serve him;
> his dominion is an everlasting dominion,
>> which shall not pass away,
> and his kingdom one
>> that shall not be destroyed. (Daniel 7:14)

If Davies is correct, even in this case the connotation of the phrase is not supernatural but rather human.[10]

The singular "son of man" also appears in Theodotion's translation of Daniel 10:16 ("And behold, one in the likeness of the sons of men touched my lips; then I opened my mouth and spoke" [RSV]). In the wording of this verse, the "Old Greek" text has *cheiros anthrōpou* (hand of man) where Theodotion has *huios anthrōpou*, and the following sentences in the book of Daniel suggest that this phrase (in either translation) connotes a supernatural being. Apparently drawing upon Daniel's usage of the singular phrase (and interpreting its meaning as supernatural), 1 Enoch also uses the singular phrase numerous times to connote a heavenly being, although in light of Davies's discussion of Daniel 7:13, connotation of a human being cannot be ruled out here either.

This single instance of the phrase "son of man" in Daniel 7:13 is very important because it provides the precursor in terms of which several New Testament texts present the "son of man" as a supernatural figure. Daniel 7:13 becomes an intertextual junction through which the New Testament, in its description of Jesus, accesses and effectively rewrites the Old Testament "son of man" language. Through this intertextual connection, the New Testament canon is able to reinterpret and transform the connotation of the Old Testament phrases.

In the New Testament, in contrast to the Old Testament, the phrase is in the singular with only two exceptions, and it includes both definite articles with only three exceptions. In effect, the New Testament signifies "the son of the man," and this suggests a particular being, which contributes to the canonical denotation of Jesus as the only, exclusive son of man. In this, the New Testament phrases contrast sharply with the Old Testament appearances of the anarthous singular phrase. What was "a son of man" in the Old Testament—a generic human being, except perhaps in Ezekiel and Daniel—becomes "the son of man" in the New Testament.

Outside of the gospels and Acts, in the New Testament there are few "son of man" sayings, and all of them are either plural or anarthous. The plural "sons of men" in Ephesians 3:5 evidently connotes ordinary human

---

10. See also Vermes, "The Use," 328; and Moule, *Birth*, 63.

beings. The plural phrase appears only one other time in the New Testament, in Mark 3:28, and that exceptional instance will be discussed further below. Hebrews 2:6, quoting LXX Psalm 8:5 (8:4 RSV), suggests through its apposition of the singular phrase "son of man" with the word "man" that a generic human being is meant. As in Hebrews 2:6, Revelation 1:13 and 14:14 both omit the definite articles, but the language in these verses ("one like a son of man") is strongly reminiscent of Daniel 7:13 and 10:16. The sole appearance of the phrase in the Acts of the Apostles is at 7:55–56. Stephen sees the resurrected Jesus in an otherworldly context, suggesting a nonhuman, supernatural being, and he describes Jesus as the son of man (singular phrase, with articles). This statement continues the prevailing tendency in the gospels to treat the son of man, in the singular, as a heavenly, supernatural being.

However, in the gospels this tendency is complicated by the story (or stories) that Jesus tells about the son of man. This story is described in detail below. The phrase "son of man" appears frequently in the gospels, but only in Jesus' words. The gospels tell stories about Jesus, and in those stories, the character Jesus himself tells a story (or several stories) about the son of man. This generates multiple levels of denotation and of discourse within the narratives.[11] In order to figure out who Jesus is, and thus to figure out what any gospel is about, the reader must figure out what sort of being the son of man is and what his connection with Jesus is.

Readers often interpret Jesus himself as the son of man. Nevertheless, it cannot simply be assumed that Jesus is the son of man. Some of the things that Jesus says about the son of man come true for Jesus, but not all of them do. Furthermore, although these words could be used to speak about oneself,[12] that they would be repeatedly used in this way seems odd. What would audiences think about Hamlet if he repeatedly referred to himself as "the prince of Denmark"? Even if the "son of man" sayings in the gospels should not be understood as Jesus' own words but rather as comments provided by a narrator,[13] that claim also presumes that Jesus' "son of man" sayings all refer exclusively to him. The gospel texts do not require this presumption.

In the gospel of John, Jesus' "son of man" sayings consistently emphasize the nonhuman, supernatural qualities of the son of man.[14] The son of man has come from heaven and will return again to heaven. He comes with divine authority and delivers eternal life. One possible exception to this supernatural connotation is John 6:53 ("'Unless you eat the flesh of the Son of man and drink his blood, you have no life in you'"). However, that saying becomes baldly cannibalistic if it is not read in tandem with 6:54

---

11. See Calvino, "Levels of Reality," 101–21.
12. Vermes, "The Use," 320.
13. Fowler, *Let the Reader Understand*, 127–54.
14. John 1:51; 3:13, 14; 5:27; 6:27, 53, 62; 8:28; 9:35; 12:23, 34; 13:31.

(" 'he who eats my flesh and drinks my blood has eternal life, and I will raise him up at the last day' "), which turns the whole saying into a metaphorical message—namely, supernatural salvation.

A second possible exception is John 12:34, in which other people speak the phrase to Jesus in a question: " 'How can you say that the Son of man must be lifted up? Who is this Son of man?' " Here both the denotation and the connotation of the phrase are in question, but it is a question to which the rest of John's story gives an unequivocal answer. Jesus also explicitly identifies himself as the son of man in John 8:28 (" 'When you have lifted up the Son of man, then you will know that I am he' "). Because John's Jesus is clearly a supernatural being (John 1:1–18), this also suggests a supernatural identification of the son of man.

In the synoptic gospels, it is not clear whether Jesus is himself the son of man or whether he is talking about someone else in the sayings. Even though the fully articulated phrase "the son of (the) man" seems to denote a specific individual, it does not follow from that alone that the individual in question is Jesus. Unlike the gospel of John, in the synoptic gospels Jesus never says explicitly that he is the son of man.

Indeed, the similarities between the phrases in Mark 9:12 and 9:13 (see below) suggest that in this saying Jesus parallels the suffering of "Elijah" to that of the son of man. Jesus' phrases " 'they did to [Elijah] whatever they pleased' " and " '[the son of man] should suffer many things and be treated with contempt' " do not necessarily signify two separate events.[15] On the contrary, Jesus' repetition of the phrase "it is written (*gegraptai*)" for both the son of man and Elijah suggests that these figures are united in fulfilling the scriptures. That "Elijah" in this saying represents John the Baptist is suggested by Mark 6:14–29. The close relation between Jesus and John the Baptist has long been noted (see Mark 1:4–15), and Jesus' cry from the cross is also understood by the bystanders as an appeal to Elijah (15:34–35). In addition, Mark 8:27–28 specifically identifies Jesus himself as John the Baptist or Elijah, although the identification may be mistaken (see again 6:14). This statement introduces the crucial dialogue of 8:29–33, in which the son of man figures prominently. Does the "son of man" somehow unite Jesus, John the Baptist, and Elijah? The association between Elijah, John the Baptist, and the son of man is hardly unequivocal, but it does further confuse the identification of the son of man in Jesus' story.

Both intratextual and intercanonical signification appear in Mark 9:12–13. Nevertheless, it is not clear what scriptures have been fulfilled by the suffering of Elijah and the son of man. The passage alludes to Malachi 4:5–6, although that text does not mention the son of man. Isaiah 53:3 might

---

15. Readers frequently assume that this passage distinguishes between "Elijah" (who "comes first") and the son of man (for example, Marcus, *Way of the Lord*, 94–110; and Taylor, *Saint Mark*, 394–95). Mark's text itself does not authorize this reading, but the New Testament canon does.

be another possibility.[16] In any case, the association of the son of man with Elijah *is* written in the structure of this very passage in the gospel of Mark. The repeated word *gegraptai* serves as self-referential brackets in this text to conjoin "son of man" and "Elijah" (or John the Baptist). Mark's character, Jesus, here refers to the gospel of Mark as "written." In so doing, the text presents an "aesthetic message" (see further chapter 5).

Jesus' Story of the Son of Man

In the following, I lay out Jesus' story of the son of man as the gospel of Mark presents it, and then I note similarities and differences to the "son of man" stories presented by Matthew and Luke. (The "son of man" story presented by the gospel of John is summarized above.) The gospel of Mark's sequence of all of Jesus' explicit sayings about the son of man, in both direct and indirect speech, presents Mark's story of Jesus' story of the son of man, in fourteen "lexias,"[17] as follows:

1. "The Son of man has authority on earth to forgive sins." (2:10)

2. "The sabbath was made for man, not man for the sabbath; so the Son of man is lord even of the sabbath." (2:27–28)

3. "All sins will be forgiven the sons of men, and whatever blasphemies they utter." (3:28)

4. The Son of man must suffer many things, and be rejected by the elders and the chief priests and the scribes, and be killed, and after three days rise again. (8:31)

5. "Whoever is ashamed of me and of my words in this adulterous and sinful generation, of him will the Son of man also be ashamed, when he comes in the glory of his Father with the holy angels." (8:38)

6. [Jesus] charged them [Peter, James, and John] to tell no one what they had seen, until the Son of man should have risen from the dead. (9:9)

7. "Elijah does come first to restore all things; and how is it written of the Son of man, that he should suffer many things and be treated with contempt? But I tell you that Elijah has come, and they did to him whatever they pleased, as it is written of him." (9:12–13)

8. "The Son of man will be delivered into the hands of men, and they will kill him; and when he is killed, after three days he will rise." (9:31)

9. "Behold, we are going up to Jerusalem; and the Son of man will be delivered to the chief priests and the scribes, and they will condemn

---

16. However, see Moule, *Birth*, 81–83.

17. Barthes, *S/Z*, 13–14. Note also Barthes, *Semiotic Challenge*, 229: "The [Bible] verse is an excellent working unit of meaning.... For us, a verse is a lexia."

him to death, and deliver him to the Gentiles; and they will mock him, and spit upon him, and scourge him, and kill him; and after three days he will rise." (10:33–34)

10. "The Son of man also came not to be served but to serve, and to give his life as a ransom for many." (10:45)

11. "They will see the Son of man coming in clouds with great power and glory. And then he will send out the angels, and gather his elect from the four winds, from the ends of the earth to the ends of heaven." (13:26–27)

12. "The Son of man goes as it is written of him, but woe to that man by whom the Son of man is betrayed! It would have been better for that man if he had not been born." (14:21)

13. "It is enough; the hour has come; the Son of man is betrayed into the hands of sinners." (14:41)

14. "You will see the Son of man seated at the right hand of Power, and coming with the clouds of heaven." (14:62)

In assembling this story, I have done violence to each of the sayings by ripping it out of its narrative context in the gospel in order to place it next to the others in this sequence. I have included little if any connective or contextual material. The story would be different if more of that material were included. I have also chosen to omit Mark 12:6 and 13:32, which might be regarded either as "son of man" or as "son of God" sayings, or as neither. Ambiguities concerning the identity of the son and his relation to Jesus appear also in each of these cases.

Mark's story of Jesus' story of the son of man opens by describing a being with godlike powers, the power to forgive sins (lexia 1) and to rule over the sabbath (2). However, this supernatural quality is put in doubt already in lexia 2 by the associated claim that "the sabbath was made for man." This suggests that all human beings are "lord even of the sabbath." In lexia 3, the humanity of the sons of men is emphasized even more, for their sins and blasphemies will be forgiven. This human element is accentuated again by means of the son's suffering and death (4), although the reference also to resurrection may suggest that the son is more than human. The son who comes in apocalyptic glory (5) possesses supernatural characteristics— the power of judgment—but the previous two verses (Mark 8:36–37) speak only of the man (*anthrōpos*) who gives or loses his life. In this respect, lexia 5 echoes 2, for "man" and "son of man" appear to be in apposition. Lexia 6 again refers to resurrection, but lexia 7, almost immediately following it in Mark's text, describes human suffering, and it may also suggest that the son of man is Elijah (or John the Baptist).

The next two lexias (8 and 9) repeat the combination in lexia 4 of a suffering and dying son of man who will be raised from the dead. Lexia 10 describes a human son of man, a suffering servant who dies for others. Lexia 11 appears in the middle of Jesus' apocalyptic discourse and has a strong apocalyptic flavor, much like that of lexia 5. In contrast, the next two lexias (12 and 13), which come at crucial points in Mark's passion narrative, once again emphasize the son of man's suffering and weakness. In these two sayings, Jesus comes as close as he ever does in Mark's gospel to identifying himself as the son of man. Finally, lexia 14 returns to the theme of the son of man's apocalyptic return at the side of God.

Although significantly rewritten, the "son of man" phrase in Daniel 7:13 echoes in several of the lexias in Mark's story of the son of man (5, 11, 14, and perhaps also 1). In all of these sayings, the son of man has supernatural characteristics. However, there is a deep theological inconsistency in this story-within-a-story. Mark's Jesus' story of the son of man oscillates back and forth between two contrary themes. In the lexias just noted, the son of man is given marvelous, supernatural characteristics. He is godlike, powerful, glorious, and authoritative. In these cases, the phrase connotes an extraordinary, supernatural being.

In contrast, in other lexias, the son of man is described in terms connoting an uncanny but entirely human being. The son is weak, he suffers, and he dies at the hands of other human beings and for the sake of others. Heinz Eduard Tödt notes that "in this Gospel the designation Son of Man is used in a way which makes it obvious that Mark was intent on two aspects of it, namely on the one hand the transcendent coming Son of Man and on the other hand the suffering Son of Man." Tödt exempts Mark 2:10 and 2:28 from this judgment, and he claims that "Mark . . . no longer understood the use of the name Son of Man as a designation for Jesus acting on earth with full authority."[18]

In Mark's version of Jesus' story, the son of man is fantastically and paradoxically associated both with the supernatural realm and with ordinary human beings.[19] Several of the lexias connote a human being, others connote a supernatural being, and yet others enigmatically connote both of them together: the son of man will suffer and die, and he will also be raised up (4, 8, 9). The son of man in these stories is both human and nonhuman at once. He is a humanoid being. In addition, the relation in the gospel of Mark between the son of man and Jesus never comes entirely clear. Like the son of man, Jesus is betrayed, suffers at the hands of his enemies, and dies. Although his resurrection is announced at the end of the story, he never appears in supernatural glory with clouds and armies of angels. The human side of Jesus' "son of man" story comes true in Mark's story, more or less,

---

18. Tödt, *Son of Man,* 120 n. 3.
19. See Todorov, *Fantastic,* 24–40.

for Jesus himself, but the truth or denotation of the supernatural side of the story is left in doubt.[20]

It is not clear whether Jesus tells a single story of the son of man in Mark's gospel or two stories. It would solve a great deal to think that Jesus' words in this gospel connote two distinct sons of men, one human and one supernatural, and that these two separate stories have somehow been fused together into one story told by Jesus. Then only one of the stories might denote Jesus. This option, however, is not ideologically attractive to many Christian readers, who want to think that there is only one story of the son of man and that the son of man in each lexia of that story is just one person, Jesus. For these readers, the conflict between the two stories is resolved by the claim that they connote, respectively, two Natures in one Person, "truly God and truly man," as Christ is understood in post-Nicean, post-Chalcedonian, orthodox Christianity. These readers want to believe that although Jesus was a suffering human being, he is also the supernatural son of God. For them, the ideological influence of the New Testament canon is hard at work. The New Testament canon rewrites Mark's double story of the son of man, not by physically changing it, but by placing it in an intertextual context in which many of its ambiguities are clarified.

Many of the parallels in the gospels of Matthew and Luke to Jesus' "son of man" story in Mark do little more than reiterate lexias in Mark.[21] Some of these sayings, as in Mark, connote a human son of man, some of them connote a supernatural one, and some connote both. Thus the double "son of man" story appears again in Matthew and Luke. Likewise, in Matthew and Luke, Jesus' relation to the son of man remains unclear. However, each of these gospels begins with a miraculous birth story and concludes with the appearance of the resurrected Jesus (see also Acts 1; 7; John 1; 20–21). As a result, in both Matthew and Luke, the supernatural connotation of the son of man is emphasized, and at least some of the supernatural lexias do come true for Jesus. There is thus a distinct tendency in the narratives of Matthew and Luke-Acts, as in John, to clarify the meaning of the "son of man" sayings in favor of a supernatural reading that applies only to one being, Jesus. Jesus is *the* son of man, the unique human being whose mortal suffering redeems those who believe that he is also the nonhuman, heavenly being whose *parousia* will occur at the end of days.

Several seemingly minor differences between the gospel of Mark's story of the son of man and the versions in Matthew and Luke are nonetheless significant in this regard. Neither Matthew nor Luke parallels Mark

---

20. I consider the gospel of Mark to end at 16:8. The two endings added to Mark resolve doubts regarding the relation between Jesus and the son of man. The anarthous "son of man" phrases in the book of Revelation are also linked intertextually within the New Testament canon to the supernatural connotations of the gospels' "son of man" stories.

21. See Matthew 9:6; 12:8; 17:9, 12, 22; 20:18, 28; 26:2, 24, 45, 64; and Luke 5:24; 6:5; 9:22, 26, 44; 21:27; 22:22, 69; 24:7.

2:27, and this eliminates the apposition in lexia 2 between "man" and "son of man." Luke has no parallel to Mark 9:9 (lexia 6), and Matthew 17:9 changes Mark's "what they had seen" (*eidon*) at the transfiguration to "the vision" (*horama*), emphasizing the supernatural nature of that event. Luke also does not parallel Mark 9:12–13 (lexia 7), and Matthew 17:11–12 inserts "so also" (*outōs kai*) between "Elijah" and "son of man," reducing the possibility of confusing these two figures. Matthew also eliminates the self-referential "it is written" brackets from this saying. Instead of lexia 10 (Mark 10:45), Luke 22:27 has simply, "I am among you as one who serves," and Luke omits any parallel to lexia 13 (Mark 14:41). The effect of these small variations in individual sayings in both Matthew and Luke is consistently to reduce the ambiguity that appears in Mark regarding the nature of the son of man and regarding his relation to Jesus. The supernatural character of the son of man is further reinforced, as is his identity with Jesus.

"Son of man" sayings also appear in material that appears only in Matthew or in Luke. In Matthew 16:13, the identity of the son of man is questioned. In every other saying that is unique to Matthew, the son of man connotes a supernatural being.[22] Luke also includes unique additional statements that can be read in both ways, as well as statements more clearly connoting a supernatural being.[23] Of the unique material, only Luke 22:48 connotes a human being. Luke also uses the phrase "the sons of this age (*aiōnos toutou*)" at 16:8 and 20:34 to connote human beings, but the change in the signifiers in these phrases prevents any confusion with the son of man.

Additional "son of man" statements that are not in the gospel of Mark's story appear in the hypothetical common sayings source, Q, and several of these sayings can also be read as connoting a human being. Luke 12:10 (= Matthew 12:32) is discussed below, and I omit Luke 10:22 (= Matthew 11:27) as this is not clearly a "son of man" saying. Other "son of man" sayings in Q are supernatural in connotation.[24] Once again the double story appears. However, the absorption of Q material into the larger stories in Matthew and Luke, along with other material unique to either Matthew or Luke (including the birth stories and postresurrection appearances), has reduced the ambiguity of Q's version of the "son of man" story. The son of man is indeed Jesus, and the nonhuman, supernatural aspect of the son of man coexists with the human aspect but also dominates it and resolves any conflict.

---

22. Matthew 10:23; 13:37, 41; 16:27–28; 19:28; 24:30; 25:31.
23. The son of man as both human and supernatural: Luke 18:31; 19:10. The son of man as supernatural only: Luke 17:22; 18:8; 21:36.
24. I follow the reconstruction of Q in Kloppenborg et al., *Q-Thomas Reader*. The son of man as a human being: Luke 6:22; Luke 9:58//Matthew 8:20; Luke 11:30//Matthew 12:40. The son of man as a supernatural being: Luke 12:8; Luke 12:40//Matthew 24:44; Luke 17:24–30//Matthew 24:27, 37–39.

When the Christian churches canonized the New Testament, the multiple gospels were accepted with the rationalization that they were four versions of one story, the single true story of Jesus. Each gospel text was understood to be the "gospel according to...," not the "gospel of...," and the four gospels all together were believed to denote only one truth.[25] Likewise, the gospels' "son of man" stories are understood within the intertextual, canonical frame as four versions of the one story that Jesus tells about the son of man. Because of their canonical juxtaposition, the gospels of Matthew and Luke-Acts consistently clarify the ambiguous connotations of Jesus' "son of man" stories in Mark.

The gospel of Mark's "son of man" story has been neutralized intertextually, and Q's "son of man" story has been disposed of intratextually. Both Matthew and Luke decide the undecidability of the stories in Mark or Q in favor of a son of man who was a human being during the course of his earthly life but who is also ultimately and forever a supernatural being. This son of man is also a humanoid, but the "mix" of human and nonhuman in this canonized version of the story is more smoothly blended, and the supernatural side is dominant. Although its own "son of man" story is quite different from the synoptic versions, the gospel of John further supports this canonical reading.

The Sons and the Son

A serious obstacle to the canonical reading of Jesus' "son of man" story appears in Mark 3:28–29, " 'Truly, I say to you, all sins will be forgiven the sons of men, and whatever blasphemies they utter; but whoever blasphemes against the Holy Spirit never has forgiveness, but is guilty of an eternal sin.' "[26] This is lexia 3 in the gospel of Mark's "son of man" story as described above. The sons of men mentioned in this saying are evidently human, not supernatural, beings. They sin and blaspheme, and they require forgiveness. In this regard, Mark 3:28 is quite consistent with every other instance in the Bible of the plural phrase. The phrase "sons of men" in this saying does not appear to be a title, messianic or otherwise. If Mark 3:28 denotes Jesus as one son of man among others, then the saying also implies that Jesus himself might be guilty of sins and blasphemies. This alone is reason enough, according to the canonical control of meaning, to rule out this lexia as a "son of man" saying.

However, that is not the only difficulty presented by this saying. Mark 3:28 differs from all of the other "son of man" sayings in the gospel of

---

25. Gamble, *New Testament Canon*, 76.

26. Although there is some variation in the oldest manuscripts of the word order of Mark 3:28, they all contain the plural phrase "sons of men." *Nomina sacra* contractions of *anthrōpos* (but not *huios*) in this verse suggest that ancient scribes read the phrase as connoting human beings.

Mark, or indeed in any biblical gospel, in that the "son of man" phrase is stated in the plural: the saying concerns the *sons* of *men*, not a singular son of man. On grounds of arithmetic alone, Mark 3:28 cannot refer *only* to Jesus. Jesus may be a son of man, but he is merely one of several. Whatever their metaphysical status, the sons of men are not unique beings. In addition, if this saying is indeed one part of a larger, coherent "son of man" story, then the other "son of man" sayings in Mark may also not concern a unique being, even though they are phrased in the singular. The possibilities that appear in this single lexia contaminate Mark's entire story of the son of man, and thus also (if the son of man is Jesus) Mark's entire story of Jesus. If Jesus tells only one story of the son of man, this lexia makes it impossible to read the entire story of the son of man as exclusively denoting a unique being, who is human but also superhuman—that is, according to the Nicean-Chalcedonian ideology that Christians prefer.

This "sons of men" saying has been troublesome to many readers of the gospel of Mark, beginning already with the gospels of Matthew and Luke. The gospels of Matthew and Luke each deviate significantly from Mark's story of Jesus' story of the son of man in their treatment of the material in Mark 3:28. Matthew presents a parallel (12:24–32, 46–50) to the episode in Mark 3:19b-35 that provides the narrative context for the saying. However, in Matthew's account, a significantly different version of Jesus' saying appears:

"Every sin and blasphemy will be forgiven men, but the blasphemy against the Spirit will not be forgiven. And whoever says a word against the Son of man will be forgiven; but whoever speaks against the Holy Spirit will not be forgiven, either in this age or in the age to come." (Matthew 12:31–32)

The gospel of Luke omits the saying from its dispersed parallels (11:15–23; 8:19–21) to Mark's episode, but Luke 12:10 presents a version of the saying that is nearly identical to Matthew's saying in a different narrative context. Luke's version omits the unforgivable sin. Both Matthew and Luke draw on the common sayings source Q, which describes a word (of blasphemy?) spoken *against* the singular son of man, in considerable contrast to the blasphemies uttered *by* the plural sons of men described in Mark.

In their presentations of this saying, Mark and Q part company regarding the son of man. Even if the differences between the saying in the gospel of Mark and the saying in Q result from two different but equally legitimate translations from a hypothetical single Aramaic original, as some scholars have argued,[27] it remains true that the statement in either Matthew or Luke and the statement in Mark are *not* equivalent to each other. The contrast between these two quite different sayings highlights the distinction between the son of man who might be spoken against and the sons of men who might blaspheme. This difference emphasizes the supernatural characteristics of the son of man for Matthew or Luke, especially if the phrase "speak a word against" is equivalent to the word "blaspheme."[28] In addition, the difference between the sayings distinguishes a singular, probably unique son of man from plural sons of men. In these ways, both Matthew and Luke avoid the difficulties that Mark 3:28 presents.

No other "son of man" saying in either Matthew or Luke presents anything resembling Jesus' "sons of men" saying in Mark 3:28. Only one additional "son of man" saying in the gospels of Matthew and Luke, once again from Q, is at all comparable to Mark 3:28 in describing the son of man in terms that are not only distinctively human but also less than optimal. Luke 7:34 (= Matthew 11:19) states, "The Son of man has come eating and drinking; and you say, 'Behold, a glutton and a drunkard, a friend of tax collectors and sinners!'" This sentence is part of a larger saying (Luke 7:24–35) that distinguishes between John the Baptist and the son of man, quite unlike Mark, and that associates the son of man with Jesus. However, here the decidedly human description of the son of man is quoted by Jesus in the words of his enemies. It is not his own description of the son of man. Perhaps more important, the saying speaks of a singular son of man, and thus the arithmetical difficulty presented by Mark 3:28 does not appear.

In the entire New Testament, there are only two plural "sons of men" phrases, and they both connote human beings, as such phrases do in the Old Testament. In contrast, the cumulative effect of the many singular "son of man" phrases in the New Testament canon is to connote a particular being, humanoid but ultimately supernatural, who is identified as Jesus. Daniel 7:13 provides the intertextual junction through which the New Testament transforms the connotation of the singular phrase in the Old Testament. Christian readers have a strong desire to read all of the "son of man" sayings in the gospels as connoting a unique being, at once human and divine, and denoting Jesus only, and the intertextual mechanism of the Christian canon attempts to satisfy this desire. For such a reading, the phrase "son of man" serves as an alternative messianic designation for the "son of God." However, if Mark 3:28 is regarded as part of Jesus' "son of man" story, then that story cannot be read in this way. Therefore this saying threatens the canonical control of meaning.

I argue in chapter 1 that extracanonical commentary inevitably stands

3:28 originally contained the singular phrase "son of man" (Tödt, *Son of Man*, 312 ff.). Dunn disagrees with Tödt about the priority of the Q version. See also Nickelsburg, "Son of Man."

28. Dunn notes that if there is an Aramaic original, "blaspheme" would be a legitimate translation alternative to "speak against" (*Jesus*, 50). Tödt sees this difference in wording as evidence for the priority of the Q version of the saying (*Son of Man*, 315–17).

in an awkward relationship to the biblical canon. The canon seeks to provide its own commentary, but the canon also inevitably fails to control the meaning of its constituent texts, and thus it needs to be rescued by external commentaries. The commentaries recognize the authority of the canonical texts. Commentators represent the believing community, and thus they reinforce the canonical control of meaning. This is probably why I have yet to find any biblical scholar who considers the plural phrase "sons of men" as it appears in Mark 3:28 to be a "son of man" saying. Some scholars simply ignore the plural phrase entirely.[29] Others retranslate the saying from a presumed Aramaic original in order to rewrite the phrase as a singular one, much as in the gospels of Matthew and Luke. The supposed Aramaic original replaces a difficult text that actually exists with an imaginary text that is more readily interpreted. Both the refusal to recognize this passage as a "son of man" saying and the presumption of an original text containing the singular phrase rescue the logocentric understanding of the message produced by the semiotic mechanism of the Christian double canon. These two strategies maintain the story of the God-man who saves sinners, although they do so in somewhat different ways.

The tendency among both scholarly and ordinary Christian readers is thus to disregard the plural "sons of men" saying in Mark 3:28. A great many of the "son of man" passages in the New Testament appear to support this tendency. In contrast, no passage in the Old Testament, with the possible exception of Daniel 7:13, supports such a reading. As a result, the "sons of men" statement in Mark 3:28 occupies a peculiar semiotic position in the New Testament. In this lexia, and in Ephesians 3:5, the phrase retains its Old Testament connotation. However, unlike Ephesians 3:5, Mark 3:28 appears to be part of a larger arrangement of "son of man" sayings in the gospel of Mark—that is, part of Jesus' story of the son of man. This is ideologically unacceptable to Christians. The cumulative force of the New Testament canonical meaning of "son of man," as an exclusive designation for Jesus, requires the rejection of Mark 3:28 as part of Jesus' "son of man" story. Given the ideological desire to see Jesus' "son of man" sayings as significant christological designations for himself alone, the theologically acceptable solution requires exclusion of the saying in Mark 3:28 from consideration as a "son of man" saying.

There is in any case no conclusive reason to regard all of the "son of man" sayings in a single book, such as the gospel of Mark, as denoting the same object or belonging together in a single story. The alphabetical differences

---

29. Fowler, *Let the Reader Understand,* and Kmiecik, *Menschensohn,* omit any reference to Mark 3:28 from their extensive discussions of Mark's "son of man" language. *The Anchor Bible Dictionary* mentions Mark 3:28 in relation to various topics, but it is omitted from Nickelsburg's lengthy article on "Son of Man." Tödt argues that Mark's version of the saying is incoherent (*Son of Man,* 118 ff.). See also Dunn, *Jesus,* 52–53; Nineham, *Saint Mark,* 124–25; and Johnson, *Commentary,* 83–84.

between "son of man" and "sons of men" may be sufficient evidence that
the two phrases mean different things. In fact, the Revised Standard Version
translation of Mark 3:28 uses a lowercase *s* to begin the phrase "sons of
men," as it does everywhere else in the Bible, even though the RSV uses an
uppercase *S* to begin the singular, articulated phrase "son of man" wherever
it appears in the New Testament—that is, in the gospels and Acts. Although
the RSV is usually "literal," this variation of the signifier also functions as
commentary. The NRSV, as noted above, avoids the gender-exclusive term
"sons of men" in Mark 3:28 altogether.

The episode in which this troublesome saying appears, Mark 3:19b-35,
centers on the question of who Jesus is, and in that story several parties
lay claim to Jesus.[30] The "sons of men" in Mark 3:28 might denote any
of these groups. According to Mark 3:30, Jesus utters the saying because
"they had said, 'He has an unclean spirit.' " Who "they" are or how they
have blasphemed against the Holy Spirit is not entirely clear. Jesus may
be addressing the saying to his family, who have come to seize him, "for
people were saying, 'He is beside himself' " (3:21). Or perhaps he says these
words to the scribes from Jerusalem, who maintain that he is possessed by
Beelzebul, the "prince of demons" (3:22). Or Jesus may even be addressing
the crowd of people jammed together in the house around him (3:20), those
whom he will soon claim as his "brother, and sister, and mother" (3:35).
All of these people are "the sons of men." All of them will eventually be
betrayed and give their lives, be ashamed in this sinful generation, suffer
like Elijah and die, and they are all even lords of the sabbath. If Mark 3:28
is part of Jesus' "son of man" story, then Jesus also says that these women
and men will all be raised up and come in judgment with clouds and power.

Ideology and the Son of Man

Mark 3:28 appears in a text included within the Christian canon, but the
Christian canon excludes this lexia from the collection of recognized "son
of man" sayings. The saying is therefore simultaneously canonical and noncanonical. A reading of Mark's "son of man" story that would include Mark
3:28 as a "son of man" saying is rejected already in the gospel of Mark itself
by Jesus' followers, who either ignore Jesus' "son of man" sayings or else
are disturbed by them in the course of Mark's story. This reading is also
rejected by the gospels of Matthew and Luke, which present instead theologically orthodox substitutes for the troublesome saying and whose "son
of man" stories are therefore not simply different versions of "the same
story." They are significantly *different stories*. Despite their own variations,
the stories in Matthew, Luke-Acts, and John of a unique, predominantly
supernatural son of man have all been preferred by Christian readers ever

---

30. See Aichele, "Jesus' Uncanny 'Family Scene.' "

since they appeared. Finally, modern biblical scholarship also rejects this alternative reading of Mark's "son of man" story.

This ideological exclusion of Mark 3:28 from the accepted canon of "son of man" sayings encourages the reader to ignore an alternative reading of Jesus' "son of man" story. This reading would allow the reader to include Mark 3:28 in a single story that runs through all fourteen of Mark's "son of man" lexias. For this alternative reading, Jesus' story of the son of man in the gospel of Mark connotes a being who is simultaneously human and supernatural—that is, a fantastical, humanoid being. As such, this son of man might be canonically acceptable. However, this son of man is not the unique God-man of orthodox Nicean-Chalcedonian christology, the theological position adopted by the "great church" at approximately the same time that the Christian canon was closed. According to this reading, Mark's Jesus' son of man is not the single being, Jesus Christ, who is eternally fully divine and fully human. Instead, this son of man is *any person whatsoever:* it is the plural being, the sons of men, all of humanity.

This alternative reading highlights the ideology behind the tendency to exclude Mark 3:28 from the "son of man" story in the gospel of Mark. If the troublesome "sons of men" saying in lexia 3 is a "son of man" saying that belongs with the others in Mark, then Mark's Jesus' "son of man" story implies a distinctly non-Christian anthroposophy of enlightenment available to any human being "who has ears to hear." *Every* son of man—that is, every human being—may be *the* son of man, and vice versa. Tödt asks, "Is it perhaps a specific interest of Mark's to speak of 'man' or 'men' in general?"[31] Tödt also quotes Ernst Lohmeyer's comment that Mark 3:28 is "a monstrous saying from which it would follow that all discernment of sin and all final judgement would be eliminated."[32] The sons of men in Mark 3:28 are humanoids, but they are also monsters, beyond good and evil.

This alternative reading is also suggested by Thomas Lambdin's translation of saying 106 of the gospel of Thomas: "When you make the two one, you will become the sons of man, and when you say, 'Mountain, move away,' it will move away."[33] This same passage, which I noted at the beginning of this chapter in the gender-inclusive translation of Marvin Meyer, is not found in the fragmentary Greek texts of the gospel of Thomas. However, Oxyrhynchus Papyrus 1 (= Thomas 28) does contain the phrase *tois huiois tōn an[thrōp]ōn,* "the sons of men." In Thomas 106, Jesus seems to be telling his listeners that they can develop supernaturally magical speech, and if they do so, then they will achieve the status of "sons of man."

I know of no historical connection between the gospels of Thomas and Mark. In addition, the support offered to my suggested alternative reading

---

31. Tödt, *Son of Man,* 131 n. 2.
32. Ibid., 120 n. 3, quoting Lohmeyer, *Das Evangelium des Markus,* 80.
33. In Cameron, *Other Gospels,* 36.

of Mark's story by a noncanonical and allegedly heretical gospel may not be especially persuasive. In any case, the power to move mountains by speaking also appears in Mark 11:23–24, where Jesus says,

> "Whoever says to this mountain, 'Be taken up and cast into the sea,' and does not doubt in his heart, but believes that what he says will come to pass, it will be done for him. Therefore I tell you, whatever you ask in prayer, believe that you have received it, and it will be yours."

Belief gives one the godlike power to make desired things happen. Specific instances of belief producing actions or words with supernaturally magical results appear in Mark 5:34 and 7:29, where no "son of man" language appears. Nevertheless, in light of these instances, as well as sayings such as Thomas 106, the suggestion does not seem so strange that Mark's Jesus' "son of man" story, including and because of the saying at Mark 3:28, teaches that any human being can realize that she or he is a supernatural son of man.

One reason that the saying in Thomas 106 seems odd is because, unlike Mark 3:28, it is found outside of a canonical context that would help to "clarify" it ideologically. This saying need not be taken seriously because it is not canonical—indeed, it may even be heretical. The sayings in Mark 3:28 and 11:23–24 would seem just as odd, and perhaps also heretical, if these lexias were not "protected" from readings such as this alternative one by their inclusion in the canonical intertext provided by the Christian Bible and by the history of Christian theology. The "son of man" stories in Matthew, Luke, and John secure the canonized, authoritative understanding of the "son of man" phrase in the New Testament, including the gospel of Mark.

This understanding of the New Testament provides the canonical context that supports the Christian reading of Daniel 7:13 as connoting a supernatural being. Frank Kermode describes how the authoritative, canonical intertext of the New Testament leads Christians to read the Old Testament in different ways than Jews read their scriptures:

> The expression *Son of man* occurs in Psalm 8:4, and modern scholars agree that it means simply "man," and that it ought not to be thought of in relation to the apocalyptic sense of the phrase in Daniel or the passages in the New Testament which seem to derive from Daniel. But, as John Barton says, the case would be different if the New Testament had happened to cite the passage from the psalm for christological purposes.[34]

Perhaps an even better example of this would be Psalm 80, with its references not only to a ravaged vineyard but to "the man (*andra*) of thy right hand, / the son of man (*huion anthrōpou*) whom thou hast made strong for

---

34. Kermode, "Plain Sense," 182.

thyself" (LXX 79:18). This anarthous son of man sounds rather like the son who appears in Jesus' vineyard parable (Mark 12:1–12; Matthew 21:33–46; Luke 20:9–19; see further chapter 8), the son of the vineyard owner, who is, according to Christian interpretation, the son of God. In that parable, Jesus cites "scripture" (Mark 12:10; Matthew 21:42; Luke 20:17) in a passage that quotes Psalm 118 verbatim, but whether the parable also alludes to Psalm 80 "for christological purposes" is less clear.

In the case of Mark's "son of man" story, another sort of canonical pressure has been brought into play. Christian readers have a strong interest in distinguishing Mark 3:28 from the other "son of man" sayings in the gospel of Mark and indeed anywhere else that they appear in the words of Jesus—that is, anywhere in the gospels. If lexia 3 is included in the "son of man" story, the son of man is sinfully, blasphemously human. Perhaps more important, the son of man is not a unique being. Jesus tells the story of the son of man, and Jesus appears to be a son of man, but he has many brothers and sisters and mothers (Mark 3:34–35). Any human being, every human being, may be the son of man. Christianity cannot tolerate this reading, and so the saying in Mark 3:28 is either ignored or dismissed, or else the variation on the saying in Q or the hypothesis of an Aramaic original provides the context in which the saying is rewritten in an orthodox way.

Conversely, to read Mark 3:28 as a "son of man" saying is in effect to break the gospel of Mark free from the Christian double canon. This reading requires the reader to comprehend the fantastical unity of Jesus' seemingly incoherent "son of man" story and to recognize herself as a son of man. Read in this light, Mark's supernatural "son of man" lexias (1, 5, 11, and 14) shift considerably in meaning. The supernatural reality that is the "kingdom of God" is not then some other, mythical world, but it is real, nearby, and paradoxically quite human.

Could this reading even result in belief that moves mountains? Mark's story *produces* the son of man by enlightening the reader ("let the reader understand," 13:14), and this reader becomes, as Lohmeyer suggests, something monstrous, human and yet also supernatural. The reader transvalues "man" and becomes what Davies calls "humanoid." Indeed, in some ways, this reader very much resembles the humanoid being that Davies perceives in Daniel 7, perhaps even more so than Davies himself would prefer:

> Daniel can indeed be read as a highly postmodern text, a celebration ... of the dispersal of authority, and with it the abolition of any certain knowledge, of confidence and determinate meaning, even of history as a process rather than a sequence. The only difference from Daniel is that the [postmodern] world is ruled not by deities in human guise but by humans acting like deities.[35]

---

35. Davies, *Whose Bible,* 140.

Each of the synoptic gospels juxtaposes in what seems to be a single story two contrary stories of the son of man: that of an ordinary human being and that of a marvelous, supernatural being. However, one troublesome verse, Mark 3:28, especially emphasizes that the potential for this paradoxical narrative union is found not just in one unique individual, Jesus, but in any human being.

I do not think that Mark's character Jesus is talking about science-fiction cyborgs, genetic or cybernetic transformations of humanity, in his "son of man" story. Nevertheless, I do think that Mark's story of Jesus' story of the son of man belongs to the genre of science fiction. The son of man in the gospel of Mark is a humanoid because the son of man is also the sons of men, and vice versa. Although the sons of men are human beings, they are also monsters, and they are gods. Read in this light, not only Mark 3:28 but Mark's entire "son of man" story and indeed Mark's entire story of Jesus acquire different meaning—that is, distinctly noncanonical meaning.

Chapter 8

DAVID RECONFIGURED

Then came David to Nob to Ahimelech the priest; and Ahimelech came to meet David trembling, and said to him, "Why are you alone, and no one with you?" And David said to Ahimelech the priest, "The king has charged me with a matter, and said to me, 'Let no one know anything of the matter about which I send you, and with which I have charged you.' I have made an appointment with the young men for such and such a place. Now then, what have you at hand? Give me five loaves of bread, or whatever is here." And the priest answered David, "I have no common bread at hand, but there is holy bread; if only the young men have kept themselves from women." And David answered the priest, "Of a truth women have been kept from us as always when I go on an expedition; the vessels of the young men are holy, even when it is a common journey; how much more today will their vessels be holy?" So the priest gave him the holy bread; for there was no bread there but the bread of the Presence, which is removed from before the LORD, to be replaced by hot bread on the day it is taken away. (1 Samuel 21:1–6)

David in the New Testament

The New Testament continues the Old Testament story of King David of ancient Israel, and like many literary sequels, it takes that story in directions that may not have been previously anticipated. This is one of the ways that the New Testament canon transforms the Jewish scriptures into the Christian Old Testament. The David of the Christian canon of the Old Testament is significantly different than the David of the Jewish scriptures, even though the texts in which he appears are verbally identical. He is one whose full significance does not come clear until it is revealed in the New Testament texts.

The Old Testament David continues to "live" in the New Testament, not as a character in the primary narrative "level of reality," but in a tertiary level,[1] as a character in stories told by the New Testament stories' characters

---

1. See Calvino, "Levels of Reality."

173

and also as a characteristic of the New Testament narrative world. In that world, Bethlehem is the "city of David" (Luke 2:4, 11; see also John 7:42), Jesus and his father Joseph belong to the "house (or lineage) of David" (Luke 1:27; 2:4), and Israel is the "kingdom (or dwelling) of . . . David" (Mark 11:10; Acts 15:16).

David also appears more covertly in numerous intertextual (and inter-testamental) reverberations in the New Testament, such as unmarked quotations from "Davidic" psalms and narrative echoes of Davidic deeds. For example, the accounts of Jesus' entry into Jerusalem on Palm Sunday resonate, although perhaps by way of parody, with the story of David's entry into Jerusalem preceding the ark of the covenant (2 Samuel 6:12–19). The gospel of Matthew states that the crowd explicitly describes Jesus on that occasion as the "Son of David" (21:9, 15). In other versions of the story, the intertextual echoes are less explicit: Mark 11:10 mentions "the kingdom of our father David," and Luke 19:38 refers to "the King who comes in the name of the Lord."

An even more subtle Davidic resonance may be found in Jesus' vineyard parable (Mark 12:1–12; Matthew 21:33–46; Luke 20:9–19). The "son" in that parable invites interpretation as the son of God, by way of Isaiah 5, but within biblical tradition, the "son of David" might well also be "the son of God"—that is, the king, according to Psalm 2. Acts 13:33–36 comes close to saying as much, associating the son of God in Psalm 2 with the blessings of David (Isaiah 55:3). The vineyard parable in the gospels also concludes with a citation from Psalm 118:22–23: "The stone which the builders rejected / has become the head of the corner. / This is the LORD's doing; / it is marvelous in our eyes." Another quotation from the same psalm appears in the story of Jesus' entry into Jerusalem ("Blessed be he who enters in the name of the LORD," 118:26). This is the passage to which Matthew 21:9 attaches the phrase "son of David," noted above.

There are a great many of these implicit references to David in the New Testament. The reader will find more or less of them depending on her willingness to play with the texts. In any case, these intertextual suggestions and allusions are not surprising, as David is one of the more important characters in the stories of the Old Testament. David is the shepherd-musician who becomes a great warrior and the second king of the Israelites. He is the conqueror of Jerusalem (commonly described as the "city of David" in the Old Testament) and the progenitor of the "house of David," including kings of Israel and later Judah. In the Old Testament, David also occasionally serves as the model and archetype of the messianic warrior-king who will save the people of Israel from their enemies and who will establish in the promised land the kingdom of God (for examples, see Isaiah 9:7; Jeremiah 23:5; Ezekiel 37:24; and Amos 9:11).

However, my concern in this chapter is not with unidentified suggestions of or allusions to the Old Testament character David nor with other sorts of

Book	Verse(s)
Matthew	1:1, 6, 17, 20; 9:27; 12:3, 23; 15:22; 20:30, 31; 21:9, 15; 22:42, 43, 45
Luke	1:27, 32, 69; 2:4, 11; 3:31; 6:3; 18:38, 39; 20:41, 42, 44
Mark	2:25; 10:47, 48; 11:10; 12:35, 36, 37
John	7:42
Acts	1:16; 2:25, 29, 34; 4:25; 7:45; 13:22, 34, 36; 15:16
Romans	1:3; 4:6; 11:9
2 Timothy	2:8
Hebrews	4:7; 11:32
Revelation	3:7; 5:5; 22:16

nonexplicit intertextuality involving David in the New Testament, but with the fifty-nine times that David is mentioned by name (see chart). Of the explicit references to David in the New Testament, over half of them appear in the gospels of Matthew (seventeen times) and Luke (thirteen times). The Acts of the Apostles is also a source of frequent references to David (eleven times). Luke-Acts contains twenty-four (over 40 percent) of the explicit references to David. In contrast, the gospel of Mark uses the name "David" seven times, and the gospel of John uses "David" only twice, both times in a single verse. Outside of the gospels and Acts, the name "David" is rare in the New Testament. The gospels and Acts, and especially Matthew and Luke-Acts, are therefore the principal sources for references to David in the New Testament. None of the references to David in Matthew or Luke comes from their common source (Q), nor does the name "David" ever appear (nor is it ever omitted) in any of the "minor agreements" of Matthew and Luke against Mark.[2]

Once again, denotation and connotation play important roles in the analysis of the transformations of this name. I noted in chapter 3 that proper names usually are quite weak in connotation. In a story, the proper name denotes a character and functions as a "linchpin" to which connotative phrases are attached in the course of the narrative. The denotation of "David" in the Christian Bible is much the same as it is in the Jewish scriptures, but the connotations of the name have changed. One change in the connotation of "David" in the New Testament is that it includes "father of Joseph and by 'adoption' of Jesus." In addition, various Old Testament connotations of the name "David" are reconfigured in New Testament texts. New connotations

---

2. See Neirynck, *Minor Agreements*. Matthew 21:9 substantially rewrites Mark 11:9–10. Otherwise Matthew's version of the story of Jesus' entry into Jerusalem would agree with Luke (against Mark) in omitting David's name.

are attached in a variety of ways, and they usually serve to denote Jesus in one way or another.

The New Testament reconfigures David as the ancestor, the warrior-king, and the singer of psalms. All of these characterizations of David have ample precedent in the Old Testament, but the further transformations of them in the New Testament writings are of special interest to the study of articulations and tensions between the two canons. More specifically, within the synoptic gospels there is a core set of texts in which the gospels of Matthew and Luke closely follow Mark's use of the name "David." With the exception of Mark 11:10, each of Mark's usages of the name "David" appears in variants in Matthew or Luke. These texts are of particular interest for my study because in them the use of David's name counters the general tendency of the New Testament canon to identify Jesus as the supernaturally powerful savior.

David the Ancestor

The name "David" appears as part of a genealogical sequence thirty times in the New Testament. Not surprisingly, the great preponderance of references to David as the "father" of the messiah, Jesus, are in the gospels, and almost all of them are in Matthew and Luke. In the gospel of Matthew, fourteen of the seventeen references to David describe him as Jesus' ancestor, or Jesus as the son of David. In the gospel of Luke, eight of the thirteen references identify David in the same way. I include among these genealogical references Matthew 1:20 and Luke 1:27 and 2:4, which describe Jesus' father Joseph as the son of David or belonging to the house of David. John 7:42, the only verse where the name "David" appears in the gospel of John, identifies Christ as "descended from David." In the gospel of Mark, Jesus is described as the son of David twice, in a single passage (10:47–48), and the phrase appears one other time (12:35). Further New Testament language identifying Jesus as a descendant of King David appears in Acts 13:22–23; Romans 1:3; 2 Timothy 2:8; and Revelation 5:5 and 22:16. The obscure language of Revelation 3:7 (" 'The words of the holy one, the true one, who has the key of David, who opens and no one shall shut, who shuts and no one opens' "), with its allusions to Isaiah 22:22 ("the key of the house of David"), should perhaps also be included in this category.

In the Old Testament, phrases such as "son of David" frequently denote male descendants of King David, often Solomon. Although various connotations are also important in determining the meaning of these phrases as they appear in the Old Testament, the identification of David as natural, genetic ancestor of these people is also relevant in these passages. However, in the New Testament, references to David as father serve as symbols of something quite different. These references to David as father do not actually connote anything about the Old Testament character, not even that he is a parent.

The phrase "son of David" often denotes Jesus in the New Testament, but it tells the reader nothing about either David or Jesus, or about any familial relation between them. Instead, the phrase serves as an authorization, a brand name or trademark that marks its bearer, not at all unlike the advertising message that connotes merely, "Buy this."[3] In other words, the phrase "son of David" in the New Testament is strongly connotative, but even in the genealogies of the gospels of Matthew and Luke that claim descent for Jesus back through Joseph to King David (and beyond), this language is not about ancestry. This is especially clear from the theological and especially christological difficulties that would otherwise accompany these genealogies. The miraculous virgin-birth stories in the gospels of Matthew and Luke—the very same books that record the genealogies—effectively deny that Joseph, the descendant of David, is the biological father of Jesus. In other words, these gospels claim both that Jesus is the son of David because he is the son of Joseph and also that Jesus is not really the son of Joseph because he is the supernatural son of God. Therefore, Jesus' status as "son of David" has nothing to do with David as a biological father. To borrow language from the apostle Paul, Jesus is a son of David "according to the Spirit," not "according to the flesh" (Galatians 4:29).

Further indications of the metaphorical status of son of David language in the New Testament appear in both Mark 11:10 and Acts 4:25, where David is described by various groups of people as "our father David." These instances of the phrase do not denote Jesus, but they do indirectly imply that Jesus is not a unique son of David. Both Matthew and Luke omit the phrase in Mark 11:10 from their Palm Sunday stories. In the gospel of Mark, the denoted objects of the phrase (the self-proclaimed descendants of David) are people who accompany Jesus as he enters Jerusalem. They have just quoted Psalm 118 in messianic reference to Jesus (Mark 11:9). In the Acts of the Apostles, the objects of the phrase are the disciples Peter and John and their companions. These people then quote Psalm 2 in messianic reference to Jesus (Acts 4:25–27).

Despite the proximity of psalm quotations in each case, in neither case is the phrase's connotation messianic. Although these people claim David as their father, neither Peter and John and their friends nor the crowd that accompanies Jesus is claiming to be the messiah. Nor are the speakers claiming for themselves direct genealogical descent from David. Instead, in both cases this rather unusual phrase connotes a sense of social solidarity, something on the order of participation in the messianic kingdom traditionally associated with David. In each use of the phrase, the people identify themselves in effect as those who continue (or revive) the Davidic, messianic kingdom.

The preponderant tendency of the usages of the phrase "son of David" is to describe Jesus as the heir to the royal throne of Israel. He is the messiah or

3. Barthes, *Semiotic Challenge*, 173–78.

Christ, the "anointed one" or king who rules over the kingdom of God. In Matthew 1:1, 17 and 22:42, as in Luke 1:32, 69, the messianic connotation of the phrase "son of David" is made explicit. For example,

> Now while the Pharisees were gathered together, Jesus asked them a question, saying, "What do you think of the Christ? Whose son is he?" They said to him, "The son of David." (Matthew 22:41–42)

According to these texts, being the son of David is one of the criteria that anyone must meet in order to be the Christ, and Jesus meets this criterion. Logocentric understanding of the messianic message of the gospels of Matthew and Luke (and probably also John) is underlined through these references to David, as well as in other ways. In these texts, Jesus is recognized as the messiah by his followers and other people, even as he changes the ground rules of messiahhood.

In contrast, in Mark 12:35 Jesus brings the two titles together but does so in order to question the equation: "How can the scribes say that the Christ is the son of David?" Luke 20:41 presents a similar question, but Matthew 22:42 separates the two titles into question and answer (see above), transforming theological challenge into affirmation. Jesus' question in Mark 12:35 subverts the identification of the son of David with the Christ. Indeed, the rhetoric of Jesus' question, as well as his discussion of Psalm 110 in the verses that follow, seems to deny that the messiah must be the son of David, contrary to the tendency of Matthew and Luke noted above. The ambiguities of the passage in the gospel of Mark in which this saying appears will be discussed further below. Unlike Matthew and Luke, the gospel of Mark has neither birth story nor extended genealogy, and it never mentions Jesus' human father, Joseph, who in Matthew and Luke provides the connection to David's lineage. Instead, Mark alone describes Jesus as the "son of Mary" (6:3), and if this phrase implies that his paternity is unknown, it also challenges any identification of Jesus' ancestry.

The two other places in Mark where the phrase "son of David" appears are both in the Bartimaeus story (Mark 10:46–52; Matthew 20:29–34; Luke 18:35–43), and in that story the phrase is not obviously messianic. Why Bartimaeus would call Jesus "Son of David" is not clear. Joel Marcus claims that Bartimaeus's words play a crucial part in signifying Jesus' messianic procession to Jerusalem and the temple,[4] but if this is the case, the signification is a paradoxical one. When Bartimaeus hails Jesus as "Son of David," he is "rebuked" (*epetimōn*, Mark 10:48) by the bystanders. This term is used elsewhere in Mark to refer to Jesus rebuking demons, storms, and thick-headed disciples, and it suggests more than a mere "hushing" of an unruly member of the crowd.

---

4. Marcus, *Way of the Lord*, 137–41. Compare Johnson, *Commentary*, 182.

In addition to calling Jesus "Son of David," Bartimaeus also calls him "master" (*rabbouni,* Mark 10:51), perhaps a more significant designation from someone seeking to be healed. Nevertheless, compared to Jesus' healing of a blind man in Mark 8:22–25, it is not certain that Jesus does anything at all to heal Bartimaeus. Unlike Matthew 20:34, in Mark and Luke there is no reference to touching or spittle. Mark's story itself suggests that Jesus does nothing at all, for it concludes when Jesus announces that Bartimaeus's own faith has effected the miracle (10:52). The gospel of Luke again follows Mark in this (18:42), but Matthew omits this sentence. If Bartimaeus's faith has made him well, then Jesus does nothing except serve as the occasion for it (see further chapter 9). In several other miracle stories in the gospel of Mark, Jesus attributes supernatural power to the human believer, who apparently heals himself or herself through the power of his or her own faith (5:34; 7:29; see also 11:23–24). These same verses also resonate curiously with Jesus' "son of man" story (see further chapter 7).

Lacking the explicit language of the gospel of John, and the elaborate genealogies and birth stories of Matthew and Luke (which contain much of their "son of David" language), the two appearances of the phrase "son of David" in a single episode do not have sufficient narrative context in the gospel of Mark alone to clarify their meaning. The connotations are uncontrolled. In addition, Jesus' questioning of the identity of the son of David and the messiah in Mark 12:35 does nothing to remedy this situation. The phrase "son of David" contributes nothing to the understanding of the story of Bartimaeus in Mark, except to serve as a marker of Jesus' special status. Even so, in order to make sense of the phrase in Mark's story of the healing of Bartimaeus, the reader must look to the larger canonical context provided for the gospel of Mark by other New Testament texts.

In other ways, the versions of the story of Bartimaeus in the gospels of Matthew and Luke both follow Mark's account closely. The most significant difference between the versions appears to be that Matthew and Luke both replace Mark's named character, Bartimaeus, with either one or two unnamed blind men. Each version includes the "son of David" phrase twice, as in Mark. Nevertheless, both of these gospels have previously and clearly identified Jesus as the son of David, and they have also already identified the son of David as the Christ. In this way the connotations of the versions of the "Bartimaeus" parallels in Matthew and in Luke are both better controlled by the larger narratives. For both Matthew and Luke, Jesus here and elsewhere reveals himself to be a messiah who is different from the ancient Israelite warrior-king David. This son of David is not a conqueror of cities and peoples. He does not heal the nation in a political fashion. Instead, this reconfigured messiah conquers demons and heals those who are afflicted in body and spirit. This reconfiguration of David plays an important part in the logocentric message of the Christian Bible.

There may be precedent for this reinterpretation of the messiah in the Old

Testament itself, such as the "servant songs" of Isaiah. David is frequently identified as the servant of Yahweh in the Old Testament, but the Old Testament references to David do not invite a messiah concept such as that suggested by healing stories in the gospels. The Old Testament precedents for a merciful and spiritual messiah are not explicitly Davidic.

"Son of David" becomes for the gospels of Matthew and Luke (and to a lesser extent John) a textual linchpin that connects Jesus to the Old Testament messiah concept but that also connotes a significantly different version of the concept. "Son of David" in these texts connotes Jesus as a different kind of messiah. It resignifies the messiah as a savior, not of kingdoms, but of individual persons. This is made clear in the detailed temptation narratives in Matthew (4:3–10) and Luke (4:3–12). The gospels' temptation stories make no mention of David, but the devil's offer of "the kingdoms of the world and the glory of them" (Matthew 4:8; compare Luke 4:5) suggests a messiah rather like the Old Testament David. When Jesus rejects the devil's offer, he implicitly rejects that messiah concept.

This may also be the case in the gospel of Mark, but Mark by itself gives the reader no reason to think so. Mark does not include detailed temptation stories. The connotation of the phrase "son of David" is not well established in Mark, as it in Matthew and Luke. The few other appearances of "David" in Mark and the only other appearance of "son of David" (12:35) do not support a messianic reading of the Bartimaeus story—neither one connoting a Davidic warrior-king nor otherwise. Mark also is rewriting the Old Testament David, to be sure, but to what point is much less clear. This is consistent with the overall level of connotative indeterminacy in Mark, especially in regard to the identity of Jesus. Mark is consistently ambiguous about Jesus' identity in narrative passages where the other canonical gospels state relatively clearly that he is the messiah.[5] As is often the case, the canon of the New Testament rescues Mark from ambiguity by encouraging a reading of that gospel in the light of Matthew or Luke so that Mark in turn, but only with this intertextual assistance, can reconfigure David as the other gospels do.

David the Psalm(ist)

The Old Testament character David is often identified as a musician and composer of psalms. "David" also appears a number of times in the New Testament as a marker connoting psalms or songs. The name "David" appears in phrases such as "David says" in conjunction with a quote from the Psalms. Nevertheless, just as with the phrase "son of David," here too the phrase connotes nothing about the Old Testament character. Nor does

---

5. This ambiguity is explored in some detail in Aichele, *Jesus Framed;* and *Sign, Text, Scripture.*

"David" denote an author or performer of the psalm, although as heirs of
the modern, print-culture ideology of intellectual property, contemporary
readers are probably inclined to read the name in that way (see further
chapter 2). Instead, "David" metonymically connotes the text of the song
itself. Compare John 7:22: " 'Moses gave you circumcision (not that it is
from Moses, but from the fathers).' " In this verse, the first iteration of the
name "Moses" connotes the Torah, and the second one denotes the character Moses. For this reason, Luke 20:42 (" 'David himself says in the Book
of Psalms' ") is redundant. In the New Testament, the character David never
speaks or says anything. Instead, whoever is quoting the psalm speaks.

There are a great many quotations of Old Testament psalms in the New
Testament, only some of which are marked as such. Explicit use of the name
"David" to refer to songs from the book of Psalms occurs thirteen times in
the New Testament. In the Acts of the Apostles, Peter cites the "scripture"
spoken by the Holy Spirit through the "mouth of David" but also "the
book of Psalms" in regard to the fate of Judas, quoting Psalms 69 and 109
(Acts 1:16–20; compare Luke 20:42). In his Pentecost speech, Peter again
cites David the "prophet,"[6] with quotes from Psalms 16; 110; and 132, to
the effect that the crucified and resurrected Jesus is "both Lord and Christ"
(Acts 2:29–36). Together with John, Peter cites Psalm 2 as from "the mouth
of our father David . . . by the Holy Spirit" (Acts 4:25). The two apostles use
the psalm in support of their claim that Jesus is the messiah and that God is
with them (Acts 4:24–30). Here "David" does double duty, connoting both
psalm (mouth) and ancestor (father). Finally, in Acts 13:34 Paul mentions
the "blessings of David," quoting Isaiah 55, in which God's covenant with
Israel ("my steadfast, sure love for David," 55:3) draws the nations to Israel.
Then Paul goes on to quote David in "another psalm," citing Psalm 16 in
support of his claim that the resurrected Jesus is superior to the unresurrected
David (Acts 13:34–39).

All of these quotations appear in public sermons or prayers narrated in
the Acts of the Apostles. However, the name "David" also appears as a
designation of psalms in two New Testament letters. The blessing of David
appears again in Romans 4:4–8, with a quote from Psalm 32, in reference to
Paul's distinction between faith and works. In Romans 11:5–10, discussing
righteousness through grace and works, Paul also quotes Psalm 69 under
the name of David. In addition, in a discussion of faith and salvation in
Hebrews 4:7, Psalm 95 is quoted as coming from David. In each of these
uses of "David" to signify various psalms, the canonical New Testament
message of salvation brought to people by Jesus Christ is further reinforced.
In these passages, "David" announces salvation of the spirit, a salvation

---

6. Identification of David (the book of Psalms) as a prophet is evidence that the "Prophets"
portion of the Jewish canon was not yet clearly distinguished from the "Writings" (Barton,
Oracles of God, 40). In other words, the Jewish canon was still "open" when the Acts of the
Apostles was being written.

that endures and survives death and thereby unites the faithful person with God. Salvation is not the physical, political defeat of our enemies here in this world, in these bodies, but rather it is the otherworldly exaltation of Jesus and through him, of those who have faith in him. These usages of David's name conform to and clarify further the overall tendency noted above in relation to the phrase "son of David" in the New Testament.

There is a strong difference between use of David's name to refer to psalms in the Acts and New Testament epistles and its use in the gospels. In the gospels, although "David" is also used to connote a psalm, that usage is ambiguous and paradoxical. The name "David" used to connote a psalm appears six times in the gospels, used twice in each of the three synoptic gospels in versions of a single statement of Jesus:

> "How can the scribes say that the Christ is the son of David? David himself, inspired by the Holy Spirit, declared,
>
>> 'The Lord said to my Lord,
>> Sit at my right hand,
>> till I put thy enemies under thy feet.'
>
> David himself calls him Lord; so how is he his son?" (Mark 12:35–37)

The gospel of Mark's version of this saying is closely paralleled by Matthew 22:41–46 and Luke 20:41–44. I have already noted the rhetorical effect of the opening question in Mark 12:35 in relation to the following statements of Jesus. Jesus quotes the Davidic Psalm 110, but unlike the Pentecost speech in which Peter cites this psalm to glorify Christ, Jesus here uses the psalm to create a parabolic puzzle that disputes an equation of the Christ to the son of David.

Jesus seems to be playing with language here, and with popular beliefs about the Christ. He is playing with messianic ideology. Jesus' puzzle about David's Lord makes at least two assumptions:

1. David's "Lord" is the Christ.

2. A father is superior to his son.

It does not follow that Jesus accepts (or rejects) either of these assumptions, but presumably some member of his audience accepts them both. Otherwise the puzzle ceases to be a puzzle. However, according to Mark, "the great throng heard him gladly" (12:37). I noted above a text in which "David" connotes both father and psalm (Acts 4:25). In Mark 12:35–37 and its parallels, Jesus' invocation of "David himself," who both says in the psalm, "my Lord," and who has a son, also draws on these same two connotations. In contrast to Peter and John's language in Acts 4:25, the two meanings of "David" in Mark 12:35–37 produce conflicting and exclusive conclusions: David's Lord cannot be his son.

Despite this, Jesus is not just playing with words here. Instead he seems quite serious. The saying in Mark 12:35–37 is one in a string of verbal sparring matches between Jesus and his opponents that appears in Mark 11–12. The stakes apparently are high, and Jesus' questions are not merely hypothetical ones. Jesus says these troubling words in the temple, and the Passover is near. The priests, elders, Pharisees, Herodians, Sadducees, and scribes have been trying to outwit him in a series of dialogues and verbal contests, "to entrap him in his talk" (Mark 12:13). With the exception of a single scribe, with whom Jesus appears somewhat surprisingly to come to agreement ("You are not far from the kingdom of God," 12:34), he has outwitted all of these people. Indeed, Jesus has scored especially well against his opponents with the vineyard parable noted at the beginning of this chapter. After speaking the words in 12:35–37, Jesus attacks the scribes one last time, and then he sits down and watches outside of the temple treasury, like a robber "casing" a bank.

The gospels of Matthew and Luke follow the larger story in Mark 11–12 fairly closely, with the exception of the cursing of the fig tree and cleansing of the temple. Matthew inserts several additional parables. Numerous other discrepancies in the sequences and versions of the stories are not particularly relevant to the reconfiguration of David. However, a few points of difference from the gospel of Mark are worth noting, in each of which Jesus' identity as messiah is emphasized in the other gospels. In connection with the story of Jesus' entry into Jerusalem, Matthew 21:5 quotes Zechariah 9 and Isaiah 62, suggesting that Jesus is the king of Zion or Jerusalem. As I noted above, in Matthew 21:9 the crowd refers to Jesus as the son of David. In Matthew 21:15–16, the children in the temple also describe Jesus as the son of David, and Jesus approves of this designation. Luke and Matthew both rewrite Mark's story of the scribe asking which commandment is greatest, and they both state that this scribe also is trying to trap Jesus (Matthew 22:35; Luke 10:25), quite unlike the version in Mark.

In the saying in Mark 12:35–37 and its parallels in Matthew and Luke, Jesus offers his opponents an unpleasant choice. If the messiah is David's lord, then he cannot be David's son, and vice versa. This choice is also an unpleasant one for Christian readers of these passages. This saying is the last time that the name "David" appears in each of the synoptic gospels, and Jesus seems to deny with these words that the messiah is the son of David. In addition, Jesus' own ignominious death appears to confirm that he is not a Davidic messiah. This creates serious problems for the gospels of Matthew and Luke, each of which emphasizes both that Jesus himself truly is the son of David and also that Jesus truly is the Christ. In contrast, the gospel of Mark questions the correctness of both "Christ" and "son of David" as designations for Jesus at various points in its narrative. This brief but puzzling passage continues the Markan interrogation of both of these titles by economically setting them against each other.

The double connotation of "David" (as father and psalm) in Mark 12:35–37 and its parallels also entails a second consequence, which is perhaps even more disturbing, at least for Christian readers. Given the two assumptions noted above, either the messiah is not the son of David, or else "David" did not speak truly in Psalm 110. Jesus' puzzle interrogates not only the identity of the messiah but also the scriptural status of the psalm. In order to affirm that Psalm 110 is authoritative, the reader must deny that the messiah is the son of David. Conversely, if the reader affirms that the messiah must be David's son, then Jesus' argument requires that she deny the authority of scripture—even though this denial is itself prompted by a passage in another scripture. Scripture turns against scripture, and thus the gospel of Mark once again offers an "aesthetic" text.

One of the semiotic functions of canon is to suppress this sort of inconsistency when it occurs. Thus the identity of the messiah becomes, indirectly at least, a question of canon. The nonscriptural status of Psalm 110 is unacceptable to the New Testament's Christian readers, unless they are Marcionites. Many probably are, in effect. However, other readers will want to retain the canonical status of the psalm's messianic and eschatological overtones, and for them these puzzles must be resolved.

A more "orthodox" solution, which appears already in the texts of both the gospels of Matthew and Luke, is to affirm that Jesus the messiah is not the natural, biological descendant of David at all. Therefore it is not important that Jesus' apparent human father, Joseph, who provides his connection to the lineage of David, according to the genealogies, is not actually his father. Jesus is the supernatural son of God by way of his miraculous virgin birth, according to both Matthew and Luke, and Jesus only becomes the son of David "by adoption," as it were—that is, through Joseph's acceptance of him (Matthew 1:20–25; note also Luke 3:23). In this way, both of these gospels further emphasize the supernatural dimension of Jesus' identity.

Again this stands in contrast to Mark 1:11, where Jesus, the son of Mary, may become God's son, but only by way of supernatural adoption. Jesus' divine sonship is problematic throughout the gospel of Mark. There is no Christmas story. The spirit that comes upon Jesus at his baptism is not clearly identified as God's Spirit (Mark 1:10; compare Matthew 3:16; Luke 3:22), and the voice from the sky that calls Jesus "my beloved Son" (Mark 1:11; 9:7) is not further identified. In Gethsemane, "Abba, Father" has nothing to say to Jesus' prayers (14:35–41), and Jesus dies abandoned by God (15:34).

According to the gospels of Matthew and Luke, Jesus the king of Israel is a son adopted, not by God (as in Psalm 2), but by man. The Christmas stories make it clear that Jesus is already the divine son. This strategy not only saves the authority of David, the psalm(ist), but it also maintains Jesus' identity as the son of David. The messiah, Jesus, both is and is not the son of David.[7]

---

7. See Nineham, *Saint Mark,* 329–31; and Taylor, *Saint Mark,* 492–93.

He is metaphorically the son of David, but he is actually much greater than David. This "solves" Jesus' puzzle about David's Lord and David's son in a way that is attractive to Christianity. The paradox disappears. Because of this, Matthew and Luke can include in their stories Jesus' apparent denial that the Christ is the son of David without that denial threatening to tear the stories apart. For Mark, which lacks these narrative resources, the problem remains unresolved, except insofar as the canonical proximity of the other gospels encourages readers to overlook it.

David the Warrior

A final group of references to David in the New Testament do refer to stories about King David from the Old Testament canon. This usage of the name "David" appears in the New Testament eight times. Unlike the previous two uses of the name, "David" is in these cases more than merely a sign of authority, a brand name. The character David is rewritten by its inscription in a different story, that of apostolic belief in Christ, and placed in a subservient role to that of Jesus. These New Testament references to Old Testament stories of King David bring the reader closer to the Old Testament character David than do the references to David as father or as psalm(ist), but these sketchy descriptions still use David as little more than a pointer to Christ. They are quite brief and summary in character.

Once again, a distinct division appears between the way David's name functions in the synoptic gospels and its usage elsewhere in the New Testament. John 7:42 identifies Bethlehem as "the village where David was." Hebrews 11:32 refers to David, among other heroes of the Israelites, as one "who through faith conquered kingdoms" (11:33). The Acts of the Apostles mentions David along similar lines three times: he became king of Israel by the favor of God and wanted to build a temple (7:45), and he died and was buried, but not resurrected (2:29; 13:36). Each of these descriptions of David in the book of Acts appears in a speech by Peter, Stephen, or Paul, and the significance of each of these moments in David's life is determined in relation to the apostolic preaching of Christ. David is a "prophet" (2:30) who foresees the resurrection of the Christ, but also one to whom the Christ is superior (13:37).

However, this is not the case in three passages that appear in the synoptic gospels, the only other New Testament passages where reference to an Old Testament story about David occurs. Again, all three instances are variants of the same story:

> "Have you never read what David did, when he was in need and was hungry, he and those who were with him: how he entered the house of God, when Abiathar was high priest, and ate the bread of the Presence,

which it is not lawful for any but the priests to eat, and also gave it to those who were with him?" (Mark 2:25–26)

Once again, the versions in Matthew 12:3–4 and Luke 6:3–4 are quite similar to Mark's story, except that Matthew adds additional references to the Torah regarding violation of the sabbath. In all three versions, Jesus addresses Pharisees who have criticized the disciples for plucking heads of grain on the sabbath. Also in all three versions of the little story, Jesus concludes by saying, " 'The Son of man is lord even of the sabbath' " (Mark 2:28; Matthew 12:8; Luke 6:5). However, only in the gospel of Mark does Jesus speak the preceding words, " 'The sabbath was made for man, not man for the sabbath' " (2:27), which together with the saying in 2:28 suggests that "man" and "son of man" both connote the same thing (see further chapter 7).

The sayings in Mark 2:25–28 display several important features:

1. Much as in Mark 12:35–37 and its parallels, discussed above, Jesus uses these sayings as a way to reply to opponents, in this case the Pharisees. Like the references to David as warrior-hero in Acts and Hebrews, Mark 2:25–26 refers to a specific incident in the life of David, one that is recounted in the Jewish scriptures (1 Samuel 21:1–6). However, the story that Jesus tells here is more intricately detailed than are the references to David in Acts or Hebrews. Indeed, the narrative detail of this story rewrites the scriptures.

2. The story does not compare David to the Christ directly, as the statements in Hebrews and Acts do, but it suggests instead that David is a "son of man." Given Jesus' questioning of the relation between the son of David and the Christ, discussed above, this association of David with the son of man is especially interesting. In the gospels, Jesus never speaks about the Christ, but he often uses the phrase "son of man," sometimes apparently to refer to himself. Yet "son of man" is here also (in Mark) in apposition to "man."

3. Jesus takes considerable liberties in his presentation of the story from 1 Samuel. According to that story, Abiathar is not yet the high priest when David takes the bread, and indeed Mark's reference to Abiathar is dropped by both Matthew and Luke. The Old Testament story also emphasizes that David is "alone, and no one with you [David]" (LXX: *monos kai outheis meta sou,* 1 Samuel 21:2). Finally, the story in 1 Samuel takes place immediately after David has fled from King Saul. He is on the verge of becoming a rebel or renegade. David conceals this information from the priest.

Jesus' use of the story creates a parallel between Jesus and his disciples (plucking grain on the sabbath) and David and his companions (taking the holy bread from the priest). The son of man as lord of the sabbath is the narrative linchpin through which these textual elements are connected. Perhaps the story's author knows a somewhat different version of 1 Samuel than the texts that have survived, and indeed, "according to the *Midrash* on 1 Sam. 21, David's action was performed on a sabbath."[8] Nevertheless, the story in 1 Samuel that survives in biblical texts makes no mention of keeping the sabbath, and thus the "fit" of Jesus' statement about David's deed within the narrative context of the dispute in Mark 2 is poor.

Commentators claim that the point of this story is that Jesus, like David the king, is superior to the Jewish law.[9] However, the story can also be read as asserting that Jesus, like David the outlaw, must break the Old Testament law (Exodus 20:10; Leviticus 24:5–9; Deuteronomy 5:14). Indeed, Jesus' version of the story itself "breaks the law" of accurate quotation. According to the latter reading, the story supports the Pharisees' reasons for disapproval of Jesus, even though it does not support their disapproval itself.

The phrases *hoi met' autou* in Mark 2:25 and *tois sun autō ousin* in 2:26 ("those who were with him"), used to denote David's followers, suggest a band of supporters, perhaps even a group of warriors.[10] These phrases heighten the parallel between Jesus and David, as Jesus has redescribed David in the saying, but conversely they also connote that Jesus' disciples are not unlike a band of rebels following an otherwise unacknowledged king. This particular distortion of the story from 1 Samuel, unlike the trivial Abiathar/Ahimelech confusion, is not accidental. If Jesus had told the story "correctly," then the similarity between Jesus and David would have been seriously weakened.

In that case, this story then joins a handful of other stories in the gospels that look like nearly obliterated fragments of a story in which Jesus appears as a violent outlaw, accompanied by a band of brigands. This story tells how the outlaw Jesus is eventually caught and executed for his crimes, while his followers flee. Elsewhere I have argued that the gospel of Mark and to a lesser degree other gospels present a puzzle that can be solved by recognizing that Jesus is a man of violence.[11] This story of Jesus' violence is a much better kept secret than is Mark's so-called messianic secret. I do not claim that this story ever actually existed as an independent text, written or oral, nor that it is a true story. The evidence for it is at best fragmentary and sketchy, but there are enough apparent bits and pieces of it scattered throughout the gospels to be worthy of consideration.

---

8. Nineham, *Saint Mark*, 107 n.

9. Ibid., 105–6; and Johnson, *Commentary*, 67. Contrast Fowler, *Let the Reader Understand*, 106.

10. Some commentators suggest that these phrases connote a eucharistic meal; see Robinson, *Problem of History*, 131 n. 1. Nineham disputes this view (*Saint Mark*, 108).

11. Aichele, "Jesus' Violence."

Some of these narrative fragments appear in sayings of Jesus that approve of violence. Several of the parables carry strong overtones of violence or suggest revolutionary or criminal actions, including among others the parables of the assassin (gospel of Thomas 98), the treasure in the field (Matthew 13:44), the unrighteous steward (Luke 16:1–9), and the unjust judge (Luke 18:2–5). The saying in Mark 3:27 (Matthew 12:29; Luke 11:21–22) about binding the strong man and stealing his goods also appears in another controversy with Pharisees. In this saying, Jesus' words favor the robber and the theft. The vineyard parable (Mark 12:1–12; Matthew 21:33–46; Luke 20:9–19), discussed earlier in this chapter, is another story about theft of property (withholding of payment) and violence set in a context of dispute, and although the son in this case is on the side of due payment, the story suggests imminent violence, perhaps of a revolutionary sort—that is, an insurrection.

Other fragments of this nearly invisible story may be inferred from connotations of various episodes. The miraculous feeding of five thousand men, seated "in groups, by hundreds and by fifties," sounds rather like a military encampment (Mark 6:40; Luke 9:14; compare Exodus 18:21). Military connotations appear also in Jesus' miraculous defeat of the Gerasene demons, whose collective name is "Legion," a transliterated Latin word for a unit of Roman soldiers. Jesus sends Legion into unclean pigs, which then stampede to their death (Mark 5:1–20; Matthew 8:28–34; Luke 8:26–39). With the exception of the former demoniac, the local people respond to this event not with gratitude but by asking Jesus to leave their neighborhood. This request suggests that they fear some further consequence of the destruction of Legion—perhaps military reprisal.

Whether that episode alludes to a violent military encounter or not, the passion stories indicate that the Romans perceive Jesus as a violent outlaw and a political threat to themselves. Jesus is scourged and crucified by the Romans as the "King of the Jews" (Mark 15:26; Matthew 27:37; Luke 23:38). He dies in the place of Barabbas, a rebel "who had committed murder in the insurrection" (Mark 15:7; Matthew 27:16). The name "Barabbas" suggests "son of Abba," and Barabbas is surnamed "Jesus," according to a variant on Matthew 27:17. In this way, Jesus' own revolutionary responsibility may be displaced onto another, an uncanny double who is released.

Still other episodes require less speculation on the reader's part. Jesus attacks the temple in Jerusalem, calling it "a den of robbers" (Mark 11:17; Matthew 21:13; Luke 19:46).[12] In effect, he acts out a variation on the conclusion of the vineyard parable. As I noted above, not long after he questions the equation of David's son to David's Lord, Jesus sits and watches as people

---

12. Both Matthew's and Luke's alterations of Mark's intercalation of the fig tree and temple cleansing stories eliminate (in different ways) Mark's suggestion that Jesus' violence in the temple is as irrational as his cursing of the fig tree ("for it was not the season for figs," 11:13).

donate money to the temple treasury (Mark 12:41; Luke 21:1), almost as though he were contemplating a robbery. Jesus' saying about the widow's mite (Mark 12:43–44; Luke 21:3–4) emphasizes her great generosity, but it also implies that rich donors can easily afford their large contributions. Just prior to that, Jesus also notes how the scribes prey on widows (Mark 12:40; Luke 20:47). The gospel of Matthew omits Jesus' final harsh words in the temple regarding the scribes, and also the scene where Jesus watches outside the treasury, but in Mark and Luke, Jesus seems rather like a Galilean Robin Hood. Later on, some of Jesus' followers become indignant at the "waste" of expensive nard that is poured over his head (Mark 14:4; Matthew 26:8).[13]

Jesus already has contacts in Jerusalem before he enters the city. A colt is provided without question for his triumphal entry (Mark 11:1–7; Matthew 21:1–7; Luke 19:29–35), and his followers also have no difficulty in securing the room for the Passover meal (Mark 14:12–16; Matthew 26:17–19; Luke 22:7–12). According to the synoptic gospels, the priests are fearful of the hold that Jesus has over the crowds (Mark 12:12; 14:1–2; Matthew 21:45–46; 26:3–4; Luke 20:19; 22:2), and he is eventually arrested at night by an armed crowd "as if I were a highwayman": (Mark 14:48; Matthew 26:55; Luke 22:52). D. E. Nineham claims that *lēstēn* (highwayman) can also be translated as "insurrectionist."[14] One of Jesus' followers even draws a sword and cuts off a man's ear (Mark 14:47; Matthew 26:51; Luke 22:49–50). In other words, the gospels present Jesus as a man with an armed gang that wanders around at night in lonely places.

The name "David" does not figure directly in the bits and pieces of this story of Jesus' violence. Nevertheless, the parallel established between Jesus and the outlaw David in the saying at Mark 2:25–26 and its variants establishes a fundamental theme of this fragmentary story. It gives Jesus the title of the new David, only not as established king, but rather the rebel or criminal on the run.[15] However, in this case, instead of the New Testament rewriting the Old Testament story of David, the reverse happens. The Old Testament story of David the king who is not yet a king briefly invades the New Testament stories of Jesus the messiah, the son of David, and pulls those stories "back" in the direction of a political messiah, a violent warrior-king. The Old Testament connotations of David, the conqueror of Jerusalem, threaten to overpower the New Testament connotations of Jesus, the spiritual savior.

This connotative threat to the New Testament message occurs only three times, once in each of the synoptic gospels. The threat is more evident in the gospel of Mark than in any other gospel because the references to David are skimpier and the identity of Jesus is more ambiguous throughout Mark.

---

13. In the gospel of Mark, the stories of the poor widow's mite and the wealthy woman's nard are separated only by the apocalyptic discourse. Jesus speaks approvingly of both women.

14. Nineham, *Saint Mark*, 396.

15. David (and Jesus) in these stories is the nomadic warrior, not the sedentary monarch. See Deleuze and Guattari, *A Thousand Plateaus*, 351–423.

Even if it were not so fragmentary and dispersed, the story of Jesus' violence would not replace the prevailing New Testament identification of Jesus as a supernatural messiah with a clear, alternative identification of Jesus. The New Testament canon again comes to the "rescue" of these otherwise disturbing narrative fragments with its message of a gentle, nonrevolutionary messiah whose kingdom is a heavenly one, a savior who comes to rescue your immortal spirit, who is a healer and not a fighter.

The semiotic machine that is the New Testament canon manages this christological damage control in a variety of ways. Elsewhere in the New Testament, both the gospel of John and Paul's "gospel" in various ways emphasize a Jesus who brings salvation and a kingdom "not of this world" (John 18:36; see also 1 Corinthians 15:49–50; Romans 14:17). Even within the synoptic gospels, the "son of David" language noted earlier, especially in Matthew and Luke, rewrites David's son as a supernatural healer, not a political rebel. In addition to the Bartimaeus parallels already noted, this is emphasized in Matthew 12:23 ("all the people were amazed, and said, 'Can this be the Son of David?' " following a servant song quote from Isaiah). Both of the "trials" of Jesus, before the council of priests and before Pilate, in all of the gospels, emphasize Jesus' innocence.

The resurrection appearances in the gospels of Matthew, Luke, and John further de-emphasize Jesus' political interests. To be sure, the apocalyptic figures that appear in some of Jesus' "son of man" sayings (such as Mark 13:26–27) and in the book of Revelation are fighters, but they will appear only at the end of the age. They do not fight in any present struggle, and thus they too are quite different from the Davidic warrior-messiah. According to all of these stories, Jesus is neither outlaw nor political claimant.

Resignifying David

James Sanders describes how canon arises as a process of resignifying texts that have been selected by the reading community. Over time, these paradigmatic texts have been adapted to new situations and experiences; in other words, the reasons that people continue to read the texts have changed. The texts have come to mean something different than they originally did. According to Sanders, "canonical criticism" is not so much interested in the original meaning of the texts, nor in their "final form," as it is in the "canonical process" by which meaning is transformed in the communities that continue to use the texts, for whatever reason.[16]

Within the intertextual frame of the Jewish scriptures, the name "David," like the phrase "son of God," tends to connote political, this-worldly sal-

---

16. Sanders, *Canon and Community,* 22, 33–34. Sanders's understanding of canonical criticism is significantly different than that of Brevard Childs. See also Barr, *Holy Scripture,* 75–104.

vation. With regard to the resignification of David in the New Testament canon, two options are evident. The first resignification option, and the most common usage of David's name, refers in one of several ways—by means of an ancestor, a psalm, or a character in a story—to Jesus. It reads the story of David in the story of Jesus. This is the mainstream, canonical Christian reading. The cumulative tendency of the New Testament is to transform David's name into a signifier of spiritual, other-worldly salvation. Jesus is described through his association with David as a spiritual savior, a supernatural being who overcomes death by passing through it. As I noted above, the temptation stories in the gospels of Matthew and Luke, and especially Jesus' rejection in them of the temptation of the kingdoms of this world, suggest a turning away from the path of the political messiah and adoption of a different path in its stead.

The curious saying of Jesus at Matthew 23:37–39 (Luke 13:34–35) reflects a further aspect of this transformation of the messiah concept:

"O Jerusalem, Jerusalem, killing the prophets and stoning those who are sent to you! How often would I have gathered your children together as a hen gathers her brood under her wings, and you would not! Behold, your house is forsaken and desolate. For I tell you, you will not see me again, until you say, 'Blessed is he who comes in the name of the Lord.' "

The saying refers once again to Psalm 118. The gospel of Matthew's version of this saying from Q comes at the very end of Jesus' visit to the temple, and it concludes his "woes" upon the scribes and Pharisees. Luke's version is set earlier in that gospel's story and also is spoken in response to Pharisees who threaten Jesus. In both versions, Jesus seems to speak with the voice of God. "Your house," now forsaken and desolate (with reference to 1 Kings 9 and Jeremiah 22), may refer to the Pharisees and scribes only, but it also suggests all of Israel, and thus also the kingdom of David. Jesus abandons "Jerusalem," the city of David, and apparently resigns himself to death. Luke makes this clearer: " 'I must go on my way today and tomorrow and the day following; for it cannot be that a prophet should perish away from Jerusalem' " (13:33).

The spiritual resignification of the messiah in the New Testament opens the way for a universalizing of the messiah. For this resignifying process, David the Israelite warrior-king cannot be sufficient. His story is too localized, too particular. It can never be more than a "micronarrative" (see further chapter 4). In order to be taken up into the logocentric understanding of the message of the Christian Bible, the name "David" must be relegated to the semiotic function of a pointer, a trademark for a savior who will not be limited to Jerusalem (much less Galilee!) but who belongs to the whole world. This change in David's status corresponds to the spiritualizing and de-Judaizing of Jesus as the Christ, which is one of the more important ideological effects of the New Testament canon.

The second resignification option for David's name in the New Testament appears only in the distinct minority of passages that I have focused on in this chapter, passages where the gospels of Matthew and Luke follow Mark's usage of "David" fairly closely. It is perhaps misleading to call what appears in these passages an "option," or even a "resignification," because these references to David do not present a clearer identification of Jesus, as the first option does, but rather they interfere with his identification. These passages confuse the reader by

1. presenting Jesus as the "son of David" but without a clear context for that phrase,

2. challenging the common assumption that David's son is the messiah,

3. and comparing Jesus and his disciples to the renegade David and his warriors.

There is no cumulative tendency in these passages, as there is in the others. Instead of helping to identify Jesus' messianic status, these references to David interfere with the desire of the reading community, the canonical desire for meaning. They undercut settled answers to the question of Jesus' identity.

However, the ideological problems presented by the passages discussed above are not as great as they might otherwise be for readers of the New Testament, because within the New Testament canon, support for the first resignification option for "David" considerably outweighs support for the second one. Extended passages describing the spiritual salvation attributed to Jesus, such as John 1:1–14 and Philippians 2:1–11, are well known, and the intertextual accumulation of David references throughout the New Testament canon establishes a tendency that is consistent with these passages. The canonical New Testament resignification of David includes these texts quite comfortably. They are what Roland Barthes would call "readerly" texts, and they satisfy the desire for meaning. As a canon, the New Testament overcomes the threat to its readerly message about Jesus as the spiritual savior—that is, the threat posed by the "writerly" passages described above.[17] The success of the cumulative tendency toward the first option is evidenced in the way that these troublesome gospel texts about David and Jesus are usually read, both by ordinary readers and by biblical scholars.

In fact, it appears that one effect of the close parallels in the gospels of Matthew and Luke to Mark's troublesome references to David is also to support the first resignification option. Matthew and Luke "rescue" the problematic texts in Mark and show the reader that these texts do after all

---

17. Barthes, *S/Z*, 4–9.

fit into the larger canonical message about Jesus. Regardless of what the authors of Matthew and Luke had in mind when they drew so heavily on Mark's references to David, the result of their rewritings of Mark's gospel in the context of the New Testament's semiotic canonical process is to tame the "wild connotations" that Mark releases. The gospel of Mark does not include a Christmas story or Davidic genealogy, but wedged in between the other two gospels as it is, it does not need them.

Even though Matthew and Luke otherwise follow Mark's "David" texts closely, in each case the other synoptic gospels also present a great deal of additional, non-Markan material that serves in various ways to emphasize the prevailing New Testament message that Jesus is a spiritual, supernatural savior. They fill in Mark's semiotic gaps. Their parallels do what Mark itself does not—that is, they place the difficult texts in larger narrative contexts that change or clarify their meaning. These indirect but quite effective rewritings permit the ambiguities and uncertainties of the Markan text to be overlooked or explained away. Again, they satisfy the reader's desire for coherent meaning.

The spiritualization of the messiah concept associated with the name "David" in the New Testament belongs to the signified message that is conveyed through the signifying texts of the Christian canon (see further chapters 3 and 4).[18] Both the spiritual messiah and the logocentric message establish binary oppositions between inside and outside, contained and container—that is, spirit and flesh for the messiah, signified and signifier for logocentrism. In each case, the opposition concerns the incarnate word of God. Each of these concepts privileges the nonmaterial member (supernatural spirit, signified message) of the binary structure at the expense of the material member (fleshy human body, physical text). The Christian canon requires a spiritual savior in the same way that it requires a logocentric understanding of language and in the same way that it requires dynamic equivalence in translation and the historical "empire" of the classic.

In the accumulation of New Testament references to David, the double canon's semiotic machine does what a canon is supposed to do. By rescuing Mark's texts about David for the New Testament, the gospels of Matthew and Luke eliminate the threat posed by the gospel of Mark to their own appropriations of the Old Testament's David. For not only does the New Testament, as a canon, seek to secure its own internal unity, but it also, as the privileged member of the double Christian canon, seeks to demonstrate its unity with the Old Testament—that is, it controls the meaning of the Old Testament as part of its own control of meaning. Thus at one stroke, Mark's difficult passages are explained, and the Bible's coherent and universal message is reinforced.

---

18. See also Ong, *Interfaces*, 265–67.

Chapter 9 _____

SIGNIFYING JESUS

[O]nly writing can be deployed *without a site of origin;* only writing can baffle every rhetorical rule, every law of genre, every arrogance of system: writing is *atopic;* ... writing anticipates a state of reading and writing practices where it is desire which circulates, not domination.
—Roland Barthes, *The Rustle of Language*

Resistance to Canonical Control

The previous two chapters both ended with texts from the gospel of Mark that tend to resist canonical control of meaning and to shatter the ideological and semiotic integrity of the Bible. I do not want to suggest that Mark cannot be given a canonical reading—that is, one that extracts a properly logocentric, and orthodox Christian, message from within the material, textual husk. Christians have apparently been reading the gospel of Mark, as they have read all of the biblical gospels, in such ways ever since it was first regarded as "scripture." You need only to browse through any of the numerous commentaries on Mark or introductions to the New Testament to see examples of such readings.

Nor do I want to suggest that the gospel of Mark is unique in its resistance to canonical control. Numerous other texts within the Bible also resist the semiotic control of the canon in ways similar to Mark's, as well as in other ways. Other biblical books that resist canonical control include those that, for any reason, were debated or considered doubtful by the people who were involved in the historical canonization processes. The rabbis hesitated over the Song of Songs and Ecclesiastes because they "did not make the hands unclean." Christians also disputed the Old Testament book of Esther for similar reasons. John Barton has shown that this designation does not simply equate to the claim that the books in question were noncanonical; rather, it means that the holy name does not occur in them.[1] Not every book with God's name in it is canonical, to be sure. Nevertheless, the absence of

---

1. Barton, *Holy Writings, Sacred Text,* 108–21, esp. 116.

the name of God from a text might be one way in which that text contested the canonical message.

Patristic records indicate that the canonical status of several New Testament books was disputed, in large part, because the book's "apostolic" character was in doubt. Disputed books that eventually were accepted into the New Testament include Revelation, Hebrews, James, 2 Peter, Jude, and 2 and 3 John.[2] Other books were included in early canonlike lists but later excluded from the New Testament, for similar reasons. This question of apostolicity cannot be settled by "objective" procedures such as fingerprints or carbon dating. Nor is it settled by showing that a text came, or did not come, from one of the apostles. Gospels associated with the disciples Peter and Thomas were eventually rejected by the early Christians, not because they were proved to be nonapostolic in origin, but because they were judged to be theologically unacceptable. In other words, the apostolic character of a book becomes a problem if its orthodoxy is doubted.

Identifying the apostolicity of a text necessarily involves the reader's beliefs and interests. It is an exercise of power. The question of apostolicity is an ideological one, and therefore it is closely related to the question of orthodoxy (see further chapter 4). Harry Gamble argues that orthodoxy is not a suitable canon criterion because that would create a logical circle, since the canon also in effect defines orthodoxy.[3] This is true, but it is more relevant to texts that were accepted into the New Testament than it is to those that were rejected. Because ideological difference is a factor in the rejection of some texts, ideological conformity is also, at least implicitly, a factor in the acceptance of others. Logical circles sometimes define practical realities.

Traditional usage may be a more important, and more practical, determinant of the canonical status of a text than is its apostolicity. However, traditions change, and what counts as "usage" (or even "authority") varies from one reading context to another. The biblical canon's continuing ability to generate new interpretations is part of the enduring strength of the Christian Bible—that is, its ability to continue to "speak" in new times and contexts. In this way it functions as what Frank Kermode calls a "modern classic."

In addition, precisely who is using which texts is very much to the point. Insofar as the canonical status of books both inside and outside of the biblical collection continues to be disputed, the Christian canon has never been finally closed. Old Testament apocryphal books continue to be disputed by Christians, and other texts from both testaments are almost never read—in effect, they are no longer being used. At the same time, Mormons and Christian Scientists claim additional books as part of their canon, and some contemporary scholars wish to add recently discovered ancient texts, such

---

2. Gamble, *New Testament Canon*, 67–72.
3. Ibid., 69–70.

as the gospel of Thomas, to the New Testament. Still others may wish to make even more radical changes in the composition of the biblical canon. The addition of a text to the canon, or the deletion of a text from it, changes the meaning of the whole because it reconfigures the entire collection, but it does not change the semiotic and ideological operation of the canon. As long as the semiotic mechanism of canon is retained, the phenomenon of tensions between the canon and its component texts will also remain.

In any case, the disputed character of a given book may or may not have anything to do with tension between that text and the intertextual effect of the canon. Not all of the disputed books noted above contain "difficult" passages like those that appear in the gospel of Mark. Furthermore, anyone familiar with the Bible can come up with a list of other equally difficult texts in a wide variety of biblical books, including books that were not disputed in early canon discussions and that have not been disputed since. The story of Zipporah in Exodus 4, discussed in chapter 6, would be one such text. Indeed, the canonical status of the gospel of Mark itself was not disputed by early Christians. Mark is always mentioned in the early canon lists identified by Bruce Metzger, although the beginning of the Muratorian Canon is damaged and Mark is not cited in that list by name.[4]

Despite this, there is reason to think that the early churches were uncomfortable with Mark's gospel. Clifton Black notes both "the diffidence with which the fathers regarded Mark the Evangelist and their own rather chilly reception of the Gospel of Mark."[5] Of the four biblical gospels, Mark is the least often cited by early Christian writers, and it is the only one not to have a line-by-line commentary written for it during the first seven centuries of the common era.[6] In addition, the elaboration of Christian legends about Mark's author is more extensive than for any other gospel.[7] This suggests a heightened desire in the early churches to confirm that Mark's authority was truly apostolic and a corresponding fear that perhaps it was not. For example, the early Christian writer Papias's source, "John the elder," insists that the gospel of Mark accurately presents the teachings of the apostle Peter, although John admits that Mark is not written in correct order.[8] Papias's claim (like John's) suggests an uncomfortable awareness that Mark diverges in significant ways from the other gospels, and perhaps even that Mark creates problems for the reader that do not appear in other writings or traditions about Jesus.

---

4. Metzger, *Canon of the New Testament,* 305 ff.

5. Black, *Mark,* 213.

6. The so-called commentary of Victor of Antioch, at the end of the fifth century, "is itself an early catena whose main sources are the homilies on Matthew" by various early Christian writers (Oden and Hall, *Ancient Christian Commentary,* xxxi).

7. Black, *Mark,* 77, 200.

8. Eusebius *Church History* 3.39.14–17, quoted in Black, *Mark,* 83. John the elder apparently thinks that the gospel of Matthew was written in correct ("systematical") order.

It would have been much easier for the early apologists if the gospel of Mark's text had at least been associated by name with one of the apostles. The gospel of Luke also was not named after an apostle, but Luke begins with a reassuring prologue (1:1–4) that specifically addresses the matter of its own reliability. Mark lacks such a prologue, just as it also lacks a Christmas story to assure the reader in advance of Jesus' identity. In fact, Mark begins quite suddenly. The equally abrupt end of the gospel of Mark at 16:8 also presents serious theological difficulties. The early addition of two separate endings to supplement Mark's conclusion, as well as the physical absorption and rewriting of the entire gospel by two distinctly different texts, Matthew and Luke, also suggests that these problems were perceived by Christian readers very early on. In addition, Mark's many ambiguities, non sequiturs, and various other semiotic difficulties have long been noted. Epiphanius faintly praises Mark for being written "without . . . verbal precision" so that it clouds the minds of heretics.[9] However, the evidence suggests that Mark also clouded the minds of orthodox Christians. Manuscripts of Mark are the most heavily "corrected" of the gospels,[10] and few very early ones have survived.[11] If the letter that is ascribed to Clement of Alexandria and that describes the "secret gospel of Mark" is authentic and even remotely correct, still other physical modifications were also made to Mark's text to reduce its susceptibility to heretical readings.[12]

Nevertheless, even these rewritings of the text of Mark were not sufficient to bring that gospel fully into semiotic coherence with the biblical canon. I propose a thought experiment: let us imagine that the gospel of Mark had simply disappeared long ago, as so many ancient texts disappeared, including Q, the other common source for Matthew and Luke. In other words, let us imagine that only three gospels were accepted into the New Testament by the early churches. (Irenaeus would no doubt be quite disturbed by this! It is also unthinkable for those who believe that canonicity is somehow inherent in the biblical texts. See the introduction.) Would the message of the Bible be changed in any way by Mark's absence? I submit that it would not. Mark contributes nothing to the orthodox Christian message of the canon.

Let us imagine further that a copy of Mark has recently been found again, lying long ignored in some dusty archive, or perhaps buried in an Egyptian garbage dump. Although the text's value as a historical object would be immense and unquestioned, it is unlikely that this newly discovered gospel would have any greater chance of being admitted to the Christian canon

---

9. Epiphanius *Panarion* 51.6.10–13, quoted in Black, *Mark*, 163.

10. Moule, *Birth*, 194. Moule infers from this that Mark circulated independently of the other gospels "for a considerable period."

11. According to Aland and Aland, only one manuscript of Mark has survived from the period prior to the fourth century, compared to eight of Matthew, four of Luke, and nine of John (*Text*, 85).

12. The letter appears in Cameron, *Other Gospels*, 67–71.

now than the gospel of Thomas has—that is, it would have no chance at all! Scholarly arguments against Markan priority would be more widespread than they are now, and perhaps Mark's derivative character would be generally assumed (much as the gospel of Thomas is now often considered to be derivative). Scholars might even dispute whether or not Mark was produced by heretics.

As it is, the gospel of Mark did not disappear, and it was accepted into the Christian canon. In contrast, the document now known as "Q" was not accepted into the canon or even mentioned by the early Christians. Or rather, the Q text was accepted, but at the price of its total absorption into Matthew and Luke. Unlike Mark, Q did not survive as a distinct text, and the non-canonical gospel of Thomas, which is similar to hypothetical reconstructions of Q, was itself only recently found again after being "lost" for many centuries. The disappearance of Q as a separate written text and the lack of fragmentary or indirect evidence for it, apart from passages shared by Matthew and Luke, lead some to doubt whether Q ever existed as a written text at all. In this book, I am not concerned with the Q hypothesis or with claims of Markan priority. I assume the truth of both of these theories for practical purposes, whenever some assumption must be made, but I doubt that my own readings of any of the biblical texts require either theory. More to the point of the present study is the question of why the gospel of Mark was accepted at all into the Christian canon, if my conclusions about Mark's resistance to the canon are correct.

I have argued in this book that the Christian canon was produced in conjunction with the acceptance of Christianity by the emperor Constantine and the consequent pressure toward standardization of the Christian faith along "early Catholic" lines (see further chapters 1 and 4). This standardization included the negotiation of Christian orthodoxy as a compromise between divergent theologies, resulting in the fourth-century credal statements and lists of accepted books. If this was the case, then perhaps the Bible's canonizers feared the consequences of abandoning such a potent text as the gospel of Mark to their opponents.

In one version or another, Mark was attractive to heretical groups, as the "secret Mark" letter states and as Epiphanius implies. Nevertheless, despite its differences from the gospels of Matthew and Luke, including many troublesome points of tension with the canon, Mark's text is clearly similar to these more orthodox texts. Perhaps the canonizers also feared that rejection of Mark as heretical would imply that Matthew and Luke had also been contaminated by heresy. In any case, within the compromise situation of canon formation, it might have been preferable to accept Mark if that made it easier to accept the more attractive gospels of Matthew and Luke.

If these speculations are at all correct, then Mark was too similar to the more clearly orthodox gospel texts to be dismissed as heretical and too different from them to be ignored entirely. If it were left outside of the canon,

Mark's gospel would be beyond the churches' semiotic control. My suspicion is that the canonizers hoped to clamp down on Mark's "wild connotations" by placing that gospel in proximity to the other gospels, within the canon. If Mark was indeed accepted into the Bible for reasons of this sort, then in large part the strategy of the canonizers has succeeded.

The gospel of Mark's wild connotations and the accompanying threat of unlimited semiosis produce a great deal of tension between that text and the canon. In the "aesthetic messages" that appear in Mark, the sheer physicality, or *hulē*, of the signifier becomes visible (see further chapter 5). Like other "aesthetic" texts, Mark is dominated by the poetic function of language, in which "similarity is superimposed on contiguity."[13] The poetic function surfaces in the text's resistance to canonical control. Signification is disrupted, and the reader becomes aware of the text primarily or even exclusively as a physical object, and not as a meaningful one.

The remarks of Epiphanius and of John the elder noted above may reflect awareness of Mark's aesthetic quality. Aesthetic messages appear in what Roland Barthes calls "writerly" texts—that is, texts that both demand and refuse meaning.[14] The effect of Mark as well as other writerly texts, both in the Bible and elsewhere, is to frustrate the reader's desire for coherent meaning, not to present a coherent meaning of its own. Such texts evade any semiotic control, including that of the canon. Therefore, it is not at all the case that the gospel of Mark points in one meaningful direction and that the rest of the New Testament points in another direction.

Mark is a writerly text, but it is by no means unique in the Bible. Different forms of this frustration of meaning can be found elsewhere in both testaments of the Bible. Furthermore, Mark is not fundamentally different than any other text in this regard. One important discovery of postmodern philosophy and literary theory has been that all texts to one degree or another resist the reader's desire for meaning. *Every* text is at least somewhat aesthetic, and every narrative is at least somewhat self-referential. These terms are contemporary ones, and to a considerable degree awareness of the phenomena that they name is relatively recent, but the phenomena themselves are very old, perhaps as old as language itself.

The material *hulē* of the signifier, the physical text, is always in tension with the desire for meaning, and thus it is always in tension with the ideological attempt to control meaning through a canon. No text is inherently canonical, although some pretend to be. The converse is also true: no text is inherently noncanonical. The intertextual control exercised by the canon derives from the collection of texts *as a whole*, not from its parts, and is determined by the ideological configuration of the entire collection. Every one of the various texts that make up a canonical collection stands in greater

---

13. Jakobson, *Language and Literature*, 86.
14. Barthes, *S/Z*, 4–6.

or lesser tension with the meaning of the whole. In other words, every text in the Bible resists the canon's semiotic control to one degree or another. There are texts in the gospels of Matthew, Luke, and especially John that also stand in tension with the canonical message. However, instances of this resistance are more readily found in Mark, as compared to the other gospels.

Like the canon itself, the tension between any text and the canon is a product of ideology, and therefore it also changes from one era or culture to another, and even from one reader to another. Likewise, the success with which the canonized collection controls the meaning of the individual text will vary from one text to another. In the Christian Bible, this control takes the form of two testaments and especially their asymmetrical relation to one another. One purpose of the double canon is to render the disturbing features of these texts invisible by controlling the wild connotations that might be generated in relation to them. In other words, the canon authorizes a "natural" or obvious reading in which the materiality of the text is overlooked in favor of the logocentric message. In the remainder of this chapter, I describe two additional cases of this phenomenon.

The Name of the Name

In the gospels, the phrase "son of man" in the words of Jesus is often read as though it were an alternative way to say "I," even though the connotation of this phrase, as well as its relation to Jesus himself, is often unclear (see further chapter 7). Similarly, Jesus seems to use the phrase "my name" rather frequently as another way to say "me." However, there is something strange about this discourse regarding the name, especially when it appears in the words of Jesus. Just as it is peculiar for Jesus (or anyone) to refer frequently to himself as "the son of man" instead of simply saying "I," so it is also odd for Jesus repeatedly to say "my name" instead of simply saying "me."

Several other sayings of Jesus in the gospels include different phrases with connotations that may be similar to the "my name" phrase, but without its grammatical strangeness. These include the phrases "for my sake" (*eneken emou*), which appears in the synoptic gospels only, and "because of me" (*dia emou*), which appears in the gospel of John only.[15] In these sayings, the word "name" (*onoma*) does not appear. The availability of the signifying options provided by these alternative phrases emphasizes the oddity of Jesus' intense interest in "my name."

Robert Fowler argues that "son of man" in Jesus' words is an instance of ideological commentary by the narrator.[16] Fowler does not discuss the

---

15. "For my sake": Matthew 5:11; 10:18, 39; 16:25; Mark 8:35; 10:29; 13:9; Luke 9:24. "Because of me": John 6:57; 10:9; 12:30; 14:6; and elsewhere in the New Testament to denote other persons.

16. Fowler, *Let the Reader Understand*, 127–54.

phrase "my name," but it seems likely that something similar is going on when these words appear. To do something "in my name" or "for my name's sake" is to do it in relation to "me," perhaps as a disciple or follower. This suggests that there might be special ideological significance to this phrase, just as there is with "son of man." In other words, if the phrase "son of man" is a special term or even a title in the New Testament, then so is the phrase "my name." The name of Jesus is central to the narratives of the biblical gospels, and thus it plays a crucial role in the logocentric understanding of the message of the New Testament, and of the Christian Bible, as canonical wholes.

The phrase "my name" (*onoma mou* and variants) occurs at least 116 times in the Septuagint and 33 times in the New Testament. Because there is considerable variation in the wording of the Greek phrases, parsing software has trouble counting every occurrence. I am here overlooking certain physical differences in these texts since the English phrase "my name" is itself signified in the Greek texts in various ways. This will no doubt affect my analysis.

In the Greek Old Testament (LXX),[17] *onoma mou* and variants of the phrase are used frequently, but not always, to denote the proper name of God, which may or may not be explicitly stated along with the phrase. The holiness and power of the name of God are immensely important in Judaism and in the Jewish scriptures, and the typical usage of this phrase in those scriptures strongly reinforces that importance. Since God's proper name is holy and forbidden (Exodus 20:7), "my name" becomes one of several ways to signify God without saying his name. In that sense, the divine name itself is not, strictly speaking, a signifier in these writings since it is effectively identical to its signified, God. "My name" not only denotes God's proper name, but it connotes God's actuality—that is, "who I am." In Exodus 3:13–15, Moses asks for God's name, and God replies, "I am who I am" (LXX: *egō eimi hō ōn*). God then continues,

> "Say this to the people of Israel, 'I am (LXX: *hō ōn*, "the being") has sent me to you.' " . . . " 'The LORD, the God of your fathers, the God of Abraham, the God of Isaac, and the God of Jacob, has sent me to you': this is my name (LXX: *touto mou estin onoma*) for ever, and thus I am to be remembered throughout all generations."

---

17. Genesis 21:23; 32:30; 48:16; Exodus 3:15; 6:3; 9:16; 20:24; 23:21; 33:19; Leviticus 19:12; Numbers 6:23; 14:21; Deuteronomy 18:19, 20; Judges 13:18; 1 Samuel 24:22; 25:5; 1 Samuel 7:13; 12:28; 1 Kings 5:19; 8:16, 18, 19, 29; 9:3, 7; 11:36; 2 Kings 21:4, 7; 23:27; 1 Chronicles 22:8, 10; 28:3; 2 Chronicles 6:5, 6, 8, 9; 7:14, 16, 20; 33:4, 7; 35:19; 1 Esdras 8:85; 2 Esdras 11:9; Esther 8:8; Job 19:14; Psalm 88:25; 90:14; 102:1; Isaiah 29:23; 41:25; 42:8; 43:7; 48:9, 11; 49:1; 51:15; 52:5, 6; 65:1; 66:19; Jeremiah 7:10, 11, 12, 14, 30; 12:16; 14:14, 15; 16:21; 23:25, 27; 32:29; 34:15; 36:9, 23, 25; 39:34; 41:15, 16; 51:16, 26; Ezekiel 20:9, 14, 22, 39, 44; 36:20, 21, 22, 23; 39:7; 43:7; Amos 9:12; Zechariah 5:4; 13:9; Malachi 1:6, 11, 14; 2:2, 5; 3:5, 20; Tobit 3:15; Wisdom of Solomon 2:4; Baruch 2:32.

Elsewhere in the Old Testament, "my name" sometimes denotes the name of a human being, such as Jacob (Genesis 48:16), David (1 Samuel 25:5), the "servant" of Isaiah (49:1), the Persian king Ahasuerus (Esther 8:8), the man Job (Job 19:14), or Sarah, the daughter of Raguel (Tobit 3:15). Nevertheless, such uses comprise a small minority of the total number of times that the phrase appears. In nearly every other appearance of "my name" in the Old Testament, the phrase denotes the divine name. For example:

Genesis 32:29—Then Jacob asked him, "Tell me, I pray, your name." But he said, "Why is it that you ask my name?" And there he blessed him.

Numbers 6:27—"So shall they put my name upon the people of Israel, and I will bless them."

Judges 13:18—And the angel of the LORD said to him, "Why do you ask my name, seeing it is wonderful?"

1 Kings 8:16—"Since the day that I brought my people Israel out of Egypt, I chose no city in all the tribes of Israel in which to build a house, that my name might be there; but I chose David to be over my people Israel."

Psalm 89:24—"My faithfulness and my steadfast love shall be with him, / and in my name shall his horn be exalted."

Ezekiel 20:9—"But I acted for the sake of my name, that it should not be profaned in the sight of the nations among whom they dwelt, in whose sight I made myself known to them in bringing them out of the land of Egypt."

Malachi 1:11—"For from the rising of the sun to its setting my name is great among the nations, and in every place incense is offered to my name, and a pure offering; for my name is great among the nations, says the LORD of hosts."

Baruch 2:32—"[T]hey will praise me in the land of their exile, and will remember my name."

In contrast, the New Testament, with two exceptions, does not use the phrase "my name" to denote the divine name.[18] The two exceptions both involve quotations from the Greek version of the Jewish scriptures. The first exception appears in Acts 15:17, ' "The rest of men may seek the Lord, / and all the Gentiles who are called by my name, says the Lord," quoting

---

18. "My name": Matthew 10:22; 18:5, 20; 19:29; 24:5, 9; Mark 5:9; 9:37, 39; 13:6, 13; 16:17; Luke 9:48; 21:8, 12, 17; John 14:13, 14, 26; 15:16, 21; 16:23, 24, 26; Acts 9:15, 16; 15:17; Romans 9:17; 1 Corinthians 1:15, Revelation 2:3, 13; 3:8, 12.

LXX Amos 9:12. The second exception is Romans 9:17: "I have raised you up for the very purpose of showing my power in you, so that my name may be proclaimed in all the earth," where LXX Exodus 9:16 is quoted.

Several other instances of the phrase in the New Testament do not denote God but nevertheless do suggest a supernatural connotation for "my name." In Mark 5:9, Jesus asks the Gerasene demoniac, " 'What is your name?' " The demoniac replies, " 'My name is Legion; for we are many.' " In the demoniac's answer, the phrase is uttered by a supernatural being (or beings), even though that being is not God. The gospels of Matthew and Luke both rewrite their parallels to this story so that the phrase "my name" is not stated by Legion. In 1 Corinthians 1:15, Paul sternly rejects the thought that he baptizes people "in my name"—that is, in his own name. It appears that Paul believes that baptism "in my name" is not permitted, except perhaps to Christ himself ("For Christ did not send me to baptize," 1 Corinthians 1:17). Elsewhere in the New Testament, the book of Revelation opens with letters from "one like a son of man" (1:13) to seven churches. These letters include four references to "my name" (2:3, 13; 3:8) or "my own new name" (3:12). This "son of man" is apparently the humanoid being of Daniel 7:13 (see further chapter 7), who is presented as both human and divine. Revelation indicates that this being is the resurrected Jesus (" 'I died, and behold I am alive for evermore, and I have the keys of Death and Hades,' " Revelation 1:18).

The phrase "my name" also appears three times in postresurrection statements by Jesus, where the usage of "my name" again connotes something supernatural. In the longer ending of the gospel of Mark, the resurrected Jesus says to the disciples, " 'These signs will accompany those who believe: in my name they will cast out demons; they will speak in new tongues' " (16:17). In Acts 9:15–16, the resurrected Jesus speaks to Ananias in a vision and informs him that Paul will " 'carry my name before the Gentiles and kings and the sons of Israel' " and " 'suffer for the sake of my name.' "

The remaining twenty-two appearances of the phrase "my name" in the New Testament are all in the gospels, and in each instance, this phrase again appears in the words of Jesus. Each of these instances is situated during Jesus' earthly life, but even so Jesus' use of the phrase seems to parallel God's use of the phrase in the Old Testament, at least in the sense that "my name" acquires a special connotation, a narrative reality and significance of its own. For example:

Matthew 18:5—"Whoever receives one such child in my name receives me."

Mark 13:6—"Many will come in my name, saying, 'I am he!' and they will lead many astray."

Luke 21:17—"You will be hated by all for my name's sake."

John 16:24—"Hitherto you have asked nothing in my name; ask, and you will receive, that your joy may be full."

In the discourse of Jesus, "my name" would appear to possess power and reality of its own, which may be used for good or which may be abused, as Mark 13:6 indicates. The phrase does not simply denote someone's name, one proper name among many others, such as Joshua or Jesus. All of these uses of the phrase also connote something supernatural. Jesus' use of the phrase "my name" appears to denote not merely "me, Jesus" but "me, God." This New Testament usage "translates" the Old Testament phrase, and like all translations, this one makes an ideological move. Through "my name" in the words of Jesus, the New Testament canon appropriates the Old Testament, and in so doing it identifies Jesus as a divine being.

The usage of a larger group of phrases in the New Testament in which the word "name" also appears confirms this observation. In the English translation of the Revised Standard Version, these phrases take the general form of "the name of (X)" (Greek *onoma* plus genitive).[19] Although the "my name" phrases are a logical subset of this larger group, I treat them separately for the purpose of this discussion. In the synoptic gospels, in comparison to the rest of the New Testament, phrases in the form "the name of (X)" (excluding the phrase "my name") do not often designate Jesus. When they do denote Jesus, they are usually stated in the third person and spoken by another character or the narrator, and they usually connote the name of a human being. For example:

Matthew 1:25—[Joseph] called his name Jesus.

Mark 6:14—King Herod heard of it; for Jesus' name had become known.

Elsewhere in the New Testament, the phrase "the name of (X)" once again tends to signify a supernatural being. In the gospel of John, the theme of belief "in his [Jesus'] name" plays an important role. John 3:18, which mentions "the name of the only Son of God," appears to be a variant on this. In the Acts of the Apostles, "the name of (X)" appears twenty-seven times—far more than in any gospel—and there this phrase is almost always completed by "the Lord" (connoting Jesus), "Jesus Christ," "Jesus," or "the Lord Jesus." In the Pauline writings (both genuine and disputed), the phrase

---

19. "The name of (X)," but not including "my name": Matthew 1:21, 23, 25; 6:9; 10:2, 41, 42; 12:21; 21:9; 23:39; 28:19; Mark 6:14; 9:38, 41; 11:9; Luke 1:5, 13, 27, 31, 49, 59, 63; 2:21; 6:22; 9:49; 10:17, 20; 11:2; 13:35; 19:38; 24:47; John 1:12; 2:23; 3:18; 5:43; 10:25; 12:13; 17:11, 12, 26; 20:31; Acts 2:21, 38; 3:6, 16; 4:10, 18, 30; 5:40; 8:12, 16; 9:14, 27, 28; 10:43, 48; 13:6, 8; 15:14, 26; 16:18; 18:7; 19:5, 13, 17; 21:13; 22:16; 26:9; Romans 1:5; 2:24; 10:13; 15:9; 1 Corinthians 1:2, 10, 13; 5:4, 11; 6:11; Ephesians 1:21; 5:20; Philippians 2:10; Colossians 3:17; 2 Thessalonians 1:12; 3:6; 1 Timothy 6:1; 2 Timothy 2:19; Hebrews 2:12; 6:10; 13:15; James 5:10, 14; 1 Peter 4:14; 1 John 2:12; 3:23; 5:13; Revelation 3:1, 5, 12; 8:11; 11:13, 18; 13:1, 6, 8, 17; 14:1, 11; 15:2, 4; 16:9; 17:3, 5; 19:13; 21:12, 14; 22:4.

is sometimes completed by reference to God or human beings such as Paul himself, but more frequently the phrase is completed by "our Lord Jesus Christ" or variants on those words. In the letter to the Hebrews, the phrase is used with reference to God. The letter of James completes the phrase with "the Lord" (connoting Jesus), and 1 Peter completes it with "Christ." First John uses "Son of God" and "his [God's] son Jesus Christ." Revelation completes the phrase by reference to various objects, including God and the beast. The book of Revelation is thus exceptional in its usage of both of the phrases "my name" and "the name of (X)."

In summary, the phrase "my name" appears more frequently in the gospels than it does in the rest of the New Testament, and in the gospels this phrase is used almost exclusively by Jesus to denote a human name but also to connote something supernatural. It differs from the Old Testament use of the phrase in denotation but not in connotation. In contrast, the phrase "the name of (X)" (excluding "my name") appears more frequently outside of the gospels in the New Testament. Many of these instances are followed by some designation for Jesus that emphasizes his divine or messianic qualities. The intertextual accumulation of these additional passages within the New Testament canon effectively determines the connotation of Jesus' phrase "my name" to be something like "a supernatural being," in parallel to God's use of the same phrase in the Old Testament. This accumulation of connotations reinforces the logocentric understanding of the message of the Christian double canon—namely, the story of the God-man who saves those who call on his name or live in his name or suffer and die for his name's sake.

However, at the same time that the biblical canon is working to control the meaning of the phrase "my name," its component texts are subverting that control. In the gospels, Jesus' use of phrases such as "son of man" and "my name" indicate points at which the reference of the text is "split" (see further chapters 3 and 5). The words point not only to some conceptual content—that is, a message about Jesus—but also back to themselves as signifiers. This results in an aesthetic message in which the materiality of the signifiers interferes with the transmission of meaningful content.

An example of split reference appears in Mark 9:38–41. In Mark 9:38 and Luke 9:49 (see also Luke 10:17), Jesus' disciples prevent a man from casting out demons "in your [Jesus'] name" (*en tō onomati sou*). In the gospel of Mark, Jesus responds to this "name of (X)" saying with a "my name" saying: " 'Do not forbid him; for no one who does a mighty work in my name (*epi tō onomati mou*) will be able soon after to speak evil of me' " (Mark 9:39). "My name" does not appear in Luke 9:50. Jesus then says, " 'Whoever gives you a cup of water to drink because you bear the name of Christ (*en onomati hoti Christou este*), will by no means lose his reward' " (Mark 9:41). This saying is substantially rewritten in Matthew 10:42, and it is omitted entirely from the gospel of Luke.

The substitution of prepositions (*en* → *epi* → *en*) and qualifiers (*sou* → *mou*

→ *Christou*) of the repeated word "name" in this sequence of verses in Mark calls attention to the textual awkwardness concerning the name. In effect, the text folds back upon itself—that is, it stutters. As usual in the Bible, "my name" in Mark 9:39 has supernatural overtones, for someone does a mighty work in it, but both "your name" in 9:38 and "the name of Christ" in 9:41 are less clear in connotation. Indeed, it is not at all clear what it means to "be in" (*en . . . este*) the name of Christ. D. E. Nineham describes Mark 9:41 as "a phrase as odd in Greek as it is in English."[20] Richmond Lattimore translates this awkward phrase as "because you are named as being Christ's," focusing on "your" name rather than Christ's name. The RSV translation, "because you bear the name of Christ," reduces the oddity of Jesus' words.

In Mark 9:40, Jesus says, " 'He that is not against us is for us,' " and this may imply that being in the name of Christ involves no more than not being "against us." Alternatively, "bear the name of Christ" may simply be a bizarre way to say, "do something in the name of Christ," although other elements in Jesus' words (doing mighty works, receiving a cup) indicate more than ordinary deeds. "Because you are in the name of Christ" cannot be simply assumed to mean the same as "because you are a Christian." Nor can "your name/my name" be simply assumed to be "Christ." Indeed, given the ambivalence that the gospel of Mark elsewhere displays in regard to Jesus' relation to the Christ, and especially the crucial dialogues with the disciples on the way to Caesarea Philippi (8:27–33) and with the high priest at his trial (14:61–62), the apparent equation of "the name of Christ" with "your name/my name" in this dialogue, also with the disciples, must be regarded with suspicion.

Once again the gospel of Mark serves as a symptom of a larger textual phenomenon. The awkwardness and uncertainty of "your name/my name/the name of Christ" that is evident in Mark 9:38–41 also appear whenever Jesus refers to his name in the gospels. The canonical message of supernatural salvation is not the only thing signified by Jesus' use of the phrase "my name." Just as Jesus never explicitly says in the synoptic gospels that he is the son of man, so he also never says what "my name" is. In itself, that omission may not be so odd, but added to Jesus' repeated use of the phrase "my name," it raises a question: What name does he have in mind?

In this discussion, I have assumed that the denoted object of Jesus' words "my name" is the proper name "Jesus."[21] In other words, in addition to the profoundly ideological connotation of "my name" produced by the accumulation of New Testament passages, "my name" is also the sign by which

---

20. Nineham, *Saint Mark*, 257. See also Taylor, *Saint Mark*, 407–8.
21. Or in the Greek texts, *Iēsous*. On the translatability of proper names, see chapter 3. In the English translation of the gospels, other characters do refer to "his name" as "Jesus" (Matthew 1:21, 25; Luke 1:31; 2:21).

Jesus denotes his quite ordinary, human name. If "my name" is something else, such as "Christ" (as some might prefer to read Mark 9:38–41), then my analysis is mistaken. The fact that the reader must make some assumption in this matter also indicates the oddity of the linguistic situation.

Jesus' name is not holy in the way that God's name is holy in Judaism.[22] Therefore, the difference between Jesus' name (as signifier) and the character Jesus himself (as signified) does not disappear, as it does for God in the Jewish scriptures. The New Testament reconfigures the Old Testament usage, and "my name" denotes, no longer the forbidden holy name, but the ordinary human name of Jesus instead, even though the supernatural connotation remains much the same. Mark 13:6 (see also 13:21–22; Matthew 24:23–24) does suggest practical concern about abuse of "my name," but in John 16:24, Jesus even encourages his followers to ask in his name (" 'Hitherto you have asked nothing in my name; ask, and you will receive, that your joy may be full' ").

Like all words, names are signifiers, and like all words, names too can be signified. The phrase "my name" is not itself strictly speaking a proper name, but it does behave somewhat like one. Proper names are what C. S. Peirce calls indexes, and the pronoun "my" is also an index (see further chapter 6). Until the reader knows who says the phrase "my name," she does not know what the name is. "My name" is therefore effectively the name of someone's name. The phrase "my name" is a way that Jesus in the gospels, like God in the Old Testament, signifies his name. "My name" usually names Jesus' name. In the words of the White Knight in Lewis Carroll's novel *Through the Looking Glass,* "my name" is what Jesus' name is "called." The White Knight develops this distinction in a discussion with Alice:

"The name of the song is called '*Haddocks' Eyes*' " [the Knight said].

"Oh, that's the name of the song, is it?" Alice said, trying to feel interested.

"No, you don't understand," the Knight said, looking a little vexed. "That's what the name is *called.* The name really *is* '*The Aged Aged Man.*' "

"Then I ought to have said, 'That's what the *song* is called'?" Alice corrected herself.

"No, you oughtn't: that's quite another thing! The *song* is called '*Ways and Means*': but that's only what it's *called,* you know!"

"Well, what *is* the song, then?" said Alice, who was by this time completely bewildered.

"I was coming to that," the Knight said. "The song really *is* '*A-sitting on a Gate*': and the tune's my own invention."[23]

---

22. See Barton, *Holy Writings, Sacred Text,* 113–15.
23. Carroll, *Through the Looking Glass,* 273–74, his emphases.

The White Knight distinguishes in good semiotic fashion between the signified object (the song) and the signifying representamen (its name). Then he takes his analysis one step further and distinguishes between the song, its name, and a third item, what each of them is "called." (According to the Knight there are actually four items, but the last two items [what the name is called and what the song is called] can be lumped together for my purposes.) This third item is the name of the name. It is the connotation or Peircean interpretant, a further level of signification that both separates and connects the signifier (the name as representamen) and the signified (the song as object).

The Knight's language becomes strange and amusing, in typically Carrollian fashion, because he insists on treating the name of the name ("what it's called, you know") as though that actually were another proper name—in other words, as though words were like other objects in the world, needing names, and as though names were like other words. It would be strange indeed if the name of my own name (George) were to be some other proper name (let's say, Homer), which in turn would have its own name, and so on. If each name has its own name, then there is no end to the names of the names.

Underlying the humor of all this is in fact the quite serious principle of unlimited semiosis. Endless semiotic slippage subverts the ideological function of the phrase "my name" in the canonical message. Within the New Testament gospels, the phrase "my name" is connotation itself, signified in the text. "My name" is not the name of Jesus. It is the name of his name. Again, the text folds back upon itself. By naming his name, Jesus releases multiple layers of signification, wild connotations, unlimited semiosis. "Christ" or "Lord" may be names of Jesus' name, as indeed may "son of God," "son of David," or "son of man," as indeed may be any word or phrase whatsoever.

The *hulē* of the signifier appears in the biblical texts in various phrases that are translated as "my name" in the RSV. Jesus' use of "my name" may connote supernatural power, but it also is a point at which the semiotic control mechanism of the canon becomes visible, a point where the reader sees a distinctly nonsupernatural man behind the curtain, as it were, if she pays enough attention. The name of the name "my name" denotes the connotation-poor proper name. For a character in a story to refer to "my name," as Jesus does in the gospels, is to open up a self-referential loop, to turn on the poetic function of language at a point where the truth value or relation to reality of the narrative is quite vulnerable. Narratives draw heavily upon proper names because proper names connect phrases, allowing different connotations to be attributed to the same denoted object. The distribution of proper names in the story allows a fictional illusion of realism to be established. By emphasizing "my name," the character named Jesus denotes points of narrative construction sustaining the gospels. He points to the fictionality of the very story in which he is a character.

The Sign of Jonah

Through Jesus' usage of "my name" in the gospels, the New Testament reconfigures Old Testament texts into its canonical message of salvation. At the same time, these same New Testament texts open up unlimited semiosis, allowing the materiality of the text to appear in the name of the name. The word "sign" (Greek *sēmeion*) also appears in some texts with both of these characteristics. These passages similarly reinforce the logocentric understanding of the message of the Christian canon even as they threaten to undo all signification by exposing the materiality of the text.

In some instances of "sign" in the New Testament, the metaphysical status of the sign is not clear. For example, in the gospel of Mark, several disciples beg Jesus to tell them what the signs of the destruction of the temple will be (13:3–4). Some of the apocalyptic portents listed by Jesus in his lengthy reply are supernatural events, but most of them are not. Luke's version of the disciples' request (21:7) stays fairly close to Mark, but Mark's language, " 'the sign when these things [the destruction of the temple buildings] are all to be accomplished,' " is replaced by " 'the sign of your [Jesus'] coming and of the close of the age' " in Matthew 24:3. The disciples' request in either Mark or Luke concerns what appears to be a natural or historical event, but in Matthew it concerns a supernatural event.

Indeed, the word "sign" is frequently used in the New Testament to connote miracles or other supernatural events.[24] Signs of the miraculous sort figure prominently in the gospel of John, where the word "sign" is John's special term for miracles. In John, Jesus' miracles are signs of his authority and even divinity, and they are of special importance in the first half of the gospel. Of the seventy-seven times that the word "sign" appears in the New Testament, seventeen of them are in John, and it is arguable that each of these appearances of the word has the connotation of miracle. For example,

> John 2:23—When he [Jesus] was in Jerusalem at the Passover feast, many believed in his name when they saw the signs which he did.

> John 3:2—"No one can do these signs that you [Jesus] do, unless God is with him."

For John, Jesus' ability to perform miraculous signs is significant evidence that he is the son of God. Jesus' miracles cause people to believe in him. As Jesus himself says, " 'Unless you see signs and wonders you will not believe' " (4:48; see also 2:23 above).

---

24. "Sign" as supernatural event: Matthew 12:38, 39; 16:1, 4; 24:3, 24, 30; Mark 8:11, 12; 13:22; 16:17, 20; Luke 11:16, 29; 21:11; 23:8; John 2:11, 18, 23; 3:2; 4:48, 54; 6:2, 14, 26, 30; 7:31; 9:16; 10:41; 11:47; 12:18, 37; 20:30; Acts 2:19, 22, 43; 4:16, 22, 30; 5:12; 6:8; 7:36; 8:6, 13; 14:3; 15:12; Romans 15:19; 1 Corinthians 14:22; 2 Corinthians 12:12; 2 Thessalonians 2:9; Hebrews 2:4; Revelation 12:1, 3; 13:13, 14; 15:1; 16:4; 19:20.

In diametrical opposition to the gospel of John's treatment of signs, the synoptic gospels all explicitly present belief or trust in Jesus as that which produces miracles, not that which is produced by them. For example,

Mark 5:34 (Matthew 9:22; Luke 8:48)—the hemorrhaging woman's willingness to touch Jesus' garment leads to her cure.

Mark 7:29 (Matthew 15:28)—the Syrophoenician woman's clever words in dialogue with Jesus result in the cleansing of her daughter.

Mark 9:24–25—the father's desperate statement of faith is directly followed by Jesus' exorcism of his son.

Mark 10:52 (Luke 18:42)—Bartimaeus regains his sight because of the faith he shows in calling out to Jesus.

A contrary instance may be Luke 10:13//Matthew 11:21: " 'Woe to you, Chorazin! woe to you, Bethsaida! for if the mighty works done in you had been done in Tyre and Sidon, they would have repented long ago, sitting in sackcloth and ashes.' " However, this statement is hypothetical and concerns repentance, not belief. Another text from Q, Luke 7:18–23//Matthew 11:2–6, may or may not concern belief. The gospel of Mark has no parallel to either of these texts, and in Mark 6:1–6 (Matthew 13:53–58), Jesus is apparently prevented from performing miracles by the local people's unbelief.

Nevertheless, supernatural signs are invoked in the synoptic gospels, in discussions of the authentication of Jesus. Opponents of Jesus, such as the Pharisees, ask him for proof that he should be listened to or followed.[25] They desire a miracle or some other evidence of Jesus' authority. Not surprisingly, and in contrast to the gospel of John, in the synoptic gospels Jesus responds to the opponents' request for a miraculous sign by refusing to grant one. Jesus apparently refuses to give a sign because his opponents do not believe in him. In the synoptic gospels, Jesus performs many miracles, but he does not use them as signs of anything.

Jesus' refusals to give a sign appear in several texts in which "the sign of Jonah" is mentioned, as well as variant texts in which it is not. Four of these texts reflect two distinct but related passages in Q. In Matthew 12:39–41, in response to a request from scribes and Pharisees for a sign, Jesus says,

"An evil and adulterous generation seeks for a sign; but no sign shall be given to it except the sign of the prophet Jonah. For as Jonah was three days and three nights in the belly of the whale, so will the Son of man be three days and three nights in the heart of the earth. The men of Nineveh will arise at the judgment with this generation and

---

25. Matthew 12:38; 16:1; Mark 8:11; Luke 11:16; 23:8. Compare John 2:18.

condemn it; for they repented at the preaching of Jonah, and behold, something greater than Jonah is here."

The only sign that Jesus gives here is a linguistic one, the saying itself. Like René Magritte's famous Dadaist painting of a pipe under which the words "Ceci n'est pas une pipe" ("this is not a pipe") are written, Jesus offers a saying about a miracle, not the miracle itself. This is also the case for the supernatural signs in Jesus' apocalyptic discourse in Mark 13 and parallels, noted above.

In the Old Testament story of Jonah, the people of the gentile city of Nineveh repent immediately upon hearing the warning given to them by the reluctant prophet (Jonah 3:3–9). In contrast to Jesus' comment in Luke 10:13//Matthew 11:21 (see above), no "mighty works" are required to secure their repentance. Numerous miracles occur in the story of Jonah, but the Ninevites do not require a sign from God, miraculous or otherwise. Instead, they take Jonah at his word. Once again, belief is not caused by the sign or miracle; instead, the Ninevites' belief in Jonah's words enables them to accept his preaching and to repent (Jonah 3:4–5). This is one of the more remarkable elements in the parabolic fantasy that characterizes the book of Jonah: the Ninevites' response to Jonah is itself the sign. Jesus implies that his opponents' request for a sign results from their failure, unlike the Ninevites, to understand that they must become the miracle. Once again, belief is necessary in order for the miracle to happen.

Jesus compares the son of man to Jonah, and he specifies "the sign of Jonah" as the only sign that he will give to the evil generation. The comparison centers around the burial of the son of man for three days and nights, which appears to be a prophecy by Jesus of his own death and resurrection. That a man might survive three days in the belly of a "whale" (Greek *kētos*, "sea monster") and then be "vomited out" on solid ground would surely be a miracle (Jonah 1:17; 2:10). Men and women die and are buried all the time, but they are not spewed out of "the heart of the earth" without a miracle.

Read in this way, this "sign of Jonah" saying is ironic at best since Jesus, at the time that he utters these words, has not yet died, and thus the sign has not yet occurred. In order to recognize Jesus as a Jonah-like sign, the listeners have to be able to foresee the future! At this point in the gospel of Matthew, Jesus has not even foretold his death and resurrection to his followers, unless the present passage counts as the first foretelling. Nor will he do so for four more chapters in Matthew. Therefore only those narrative characters or gospel readers who already believe that Jesus is the son of man and who understand what will happen to him are able to interpret Matthew's version of the saying. The "sign" then is Jesus' cryptic foretelling of his own death and miraculous resurrection and the believers' ability to decode it.

In other words, Jesus' apparent refusal to grant a sign itself becomes a sign, but only for those who need no sign because they already believe. According to J. C. Fenton, "The reader knows that the healing miracles [previously in Matthew] have been signs."[26] Some readers know this, and perhaps some characters in the story do as well. However, such people are even more fortunate than the Ninevites, and they are not an evil and adulterous generation, for they need no further sign. In contrast, the ones to whom Matthew's Jesus offers the sign of Jonah—that is, the evil and adulterous ones who ask for a sign—are the ones who cannot interpret it because they do not believe. For them it will always be a meaningless sign.

I have already noted that not all uses of the word "sign" in the New Testament signify a supernatural or miraculous event. The word can also be used to connote words or other artificial or natural signifiers, whether portents of things to come or signals of present states.[27] In a variant on Matthew's "sign of Jonah" saying in the gospel of Luke, Jesus says,

> This generation is an evil generation; it seeks a sign, but no sign shall be given to it except the sign of Jonah. For as Jonah became a sign to the men of Nineveh, so will the Son of man be to this generation. . . . The men of Nineveh will arise at the judgment with this generation and condemn it; for they repented at the preaching of Jonah, and behold, something greater than Jonah is here. (Luke 11:29–30, 32)

Here the "three days and three nights" do not appear, and instead Jonah himself is the sign that the Ninevites interpret.[28] No miracle appears in Jesus' saying in Luke, even though some people have requested "a sign from heaven" in order "to test him" (11:16). Instead, the saying merely presents the real-life problem of determining whether or not the person standing in front of you is a sign of something.

Once again, the belief of the Ninevites in Jonah and their miraculous repentance stand in sharp contrast to the nonrepentance and unbelief of Jesus' opponents. Luke 11:31, omitted in the quote above, concerns the queen of the South, who " 'came from the ends of the earth to hear the wisdom of Solomon, and behold, something greater than Solomon is here.' " A parallel passage regarding the queen of the South and Solomon follows the "sign of Jonah" saying in Matthew 12:42. Like the Ninevites, the queen of the South knows how to interpret the signs.

Although it does not describe a miracle, in Luke's version of the "sign of Jonah" saying, the same dilemma arises as in Matthew's version—namely, the only ones who could benefit from understanding the sign of Jonah are

---

26. Fenton, *Saint Matthew,* 203. See also Matthew 11:2–6.

27. "Sign" as nonsupernatural event: Matthew 16:3; 26:48; Mark 13:4; Luke 2:12, 34; 11:30; 21:7, 25; Romans 4:11; 1 Corinthians 1:22; 2 Thessalonians 3:17.

28. Fenton suggests that Matthew's author added the "three days" part of the saying (*Saint Matthew,* 203).

the very ones who do not benefit from it. Only those who already believe in the sign will see and understand it. For the opponents, or any unbelievers, the sign of Jonah in the words of Jesus never functions as a sign, miraculous or otherwise. The transmitted message cannot be received. This semiotic failure applies just as well to the extratextual reader of the gospel as it does to the audience-characters within the story.

For this reason, both versions of this saying are reminiscent of Jesus' words to his disciples in regard to the secrets of the kingdom of God in the gospel of Matthew, in which Isaiah 6:9–10 is quoted. Jesus' parables separate his followers, who possess these secrets, from all others, who do not possess them: " 'because (*hoti*) seeing they do not see, and hearing they do not hear, nor do they understand' " (13:13). These others, described as "great crowds" (Matthew 13:2; Luke 8:4), are "those outside" (Mark 4:11), the ones who do not perceive or understand the sign. Jesus' disciples, in contrast, are insiders, and they do perceive and understand.

Both the "sign of Jonah" saying in Matthew and the one in Luke are initiated by requests from Jesus' opponents for a sign, probably a miracle. These two versions of the "sign of Jonah" saying themselves suggest two different possible signs, or perhaps they are themselves two different interpretations of one sign.[29] The audience-characters who hear Jesus' sayings, like the extratextual reader of the gospel texts, must interpret the parabolic sign of Jonah. They must decide, and in order to decide, they must have some belief. If they do not believe, then they are outsiders, and there can be no understanding of the sign, no interpretation. As a result, they cannot repent and be forgiven.

The desire for a sign, whether that of character or reader, is identified with "an evil and adulterous generation"; that is, it is the desire of the opponents of Jesus. The evil generation is unable to interpret the only sign that it has already been given, unlike the "men of Nineveh." Jesus responds to the opponents' request for an action that would constitute a miraculous sign by offering them, not a miracle, but a text to be understood: that text which is the "sign" of Jonah because it is the book of Jonah. The Old Testament book of Jonah itself suggests other possible "signs," some of them quite marvelous ones. A. K. M. Adam's sketch of the history of interpretation of the "sign of Jonah" sayings in these two gospels indicates that the range of readings of these sayings has been wide.[30] The intertextual juncture between the canons is quite loose at this point. As a result, Jesus' response to his questioners is all the more obscure.

Further on in the gospel of Matthew, Jesus again brings together in one saying an evil and adulterous generation, the task of interpretation, and

29. Adam, "The Sign of Jonah," 182.
30. Ibid., 182–85.

the sign of Jonah. Once again the Pharisees, this time together with the Sadducees, test Jesus by asking for "a sign from heaven" (16:1). He replies,

> "When it is evening, you say, 'It will be fair weather; for the sky is red.' And in the morning, 'It will be stormy today, for the sky is red and threatening.' You know how to interpret the appearance [Greek *prosōpon,* "face"] of the sky, but you cannot interpret the signs of the times. An evil and adulterous generation seeks for a sign, but no sign shall be given to it except the sign of Jonah." (16:2–4)

Fenton suggests that Matthew has added the "sign of Jonah" language to this saying in order to achieve consistency with the earlier saying.[31] Here the "signs of the times" are apparently purely natural phenomena, like "the appearance of the sky," and thus this saying also resonates with Luke's version of the "sign of Jonah" saying. Furthermore, embedded in the saying itself is an example of a single text with multiple meanings, for according to Jesus, "red sky" under different circumstances—that is, different reading contexts—denotes different types of weather coming.

Matthew 16:2–4 also has a parallel in Luke 12:54–56:

> "When you see a cloud rising in the west, you say at once, 'A shower is coming'; and so it happens. And when you see the south wind blowing, you say, 'There will be scorching heat'; and it happens. You hypocrites! You know how to interpret the appearance (*prosōpon*) of earth and sky; but why do you not know how to interpret the present time?"

There is no mention of signs or of Jonah in Luke's passage, the poly-significance of the sign does not appear, and the evil generation is replaced by hypocrites. However, this passage is still talking about signs and especially about their interpretation, as the phrase "the appearance (*prosōpon*) of earth and sky" makes clear. Yet another parallel to these sayings in Luke 12 and Matthew 16 appears in the noncanonical gospel of Thomas, saying 91:

> They said to Him, "Tell us who You are so that we may believe in You." He said to them, "You read the face of the sky and of the earth, but you have not recognized the one who is before you, and you do not know how to read this moment."[32]

---

31. Fenton, *Saint Matthew,* 261.

32. Cameron, *Other Gospels,* 35. The problem of interpretation is fundamental to the gospel of Thomas, although a sign is only mentioned once, in saying 50. Interpretation is focused on "the secret sayings which the living Jesus spoke and which Didymos Judas Thomas wrote down." Already in this introductory logion, the hermeneutical problem of the written text appears, and in sayings 1 and 2, this problem is made central to the entire gospel. The self-referential theme of the difficulty of understanding this text appears in several other sayings of Jesus in the gospel of Thomas, and many of the other sayings seem very "mysterious" and appear to conceal some hidden meaning.

In the Q version of both Luke and Matthew, the sky's face in the present is a portent or warning of some event to come. In contrast, in the gospel of Thomas's version, the face concerns something that is already present "before you." In none of these versions of the saying is the sign or face a miracle.

A natural sign such as the face of the sky is yet another instance of what Peirce calls an index. An index (the face of the sky) requires no interpretant, no connotation or further level of mediation, in order to denote a meaningful object (the weather). The connection between signifying representamen and signified object is entirely natural—that is, it is not culturally or ideologically produced. If "red sky in morning" is a reliable sign of something, it is because its appearance correlates strongly with certain types of weather. Interpretation of the face of the sky is a matter, not of identifying an interpretant, but of knowing how the natural world works. The face of the sky is a sign that is in front of you, and you do not need any further signs in order to interpret it. The necessary knowledge is immediately present in your experience of the everyday world, and thus no miracle is involved.

Faces are signs, and signs also have faces. The face of the sign appears in sayings that cluster around "the sign of Jonah" in the gospels. In the face of the sign, the meaningless matter of the sign begins to signify.[33] Merely to recognize red sky as a sign is already to see it as potentially meaningful, even if you have no idea what the sky's color signifies. Even a meaningless sign signifies at minimum that it is a signifier, just as a proper name connotes at least "the name of (X)." In other words, the face of the sign is a mechanism of desire, at once a function that desire produces and in which desire is produced. The face is both the meaningless, hyletic matter from which the sign is formed and the fact that as a signifier, the sign already signifies. As with the phrase "my name," described earlier in this chapter, the reference is split, and the text presents an aesthetic message. That is why interpretation is both demanded by and rejected in these sayings.

Even a meaningless sign signifies more than no sign at all. In the gospel of Mark, when the Pharisees request "a sign from heaven, to test him," Jesus replies, " 'Why does this generation seek a sign? Truly, I say to you, *no sign* shall be given to this generation' " (8:11–12, emphasis added). In Mark's saying, the opponents are described simply as "this generation," but "this adulterous and sinful generation" appears soon afterward, in Mark 8:38. This saying corresponds in part to Q's "sign of Jonah" saying described above, but in Mark there are no sayings featuring Jonah. In contrast to the Q versions of the saying, with their paradoxical, ambiguous, or indexical signs, in Mark Jesus offers no sign at all.

---

33. Deleuze and Guattari describe the face of the sign as the threshold where nonsignifying matter begins to signify, where sheer hyletic stuff becomes significant—that is, where meaningful language appears (*Anti-Oedipus*, 36). On the "faciality of the sign," see especially Deleuze and Guattari, *A Thousand Plateaus*, 167–91, which focuses on the face of Christ.

It is not surprising that Mark's version of the saying omits the sign of Jonah. In the gospel of Matthew (13:10–17), Jesus' use of parables maintains clear lines of division between insiders, who know the secrets of the kingdom, and outsiders, for whom everything is in parables. The saying about the secret of the kingdom is harsher in the gospel of Mark than it is in Matthew, for in Mark's version, Jesus claims to teach in parables "so that" (*hina*) the outsiders will neither perceive nor understand, "lest they should turn again, and be forgiven" (4:12).[34] The parables are not a response to the outsiders' ignorance of the sign, but the cause of that ignorance. Furthermore, according to Mark's story, the disciples remain ignorant and thus outside, whereas some nondisciples do show understanding and come inside. In Mark, the clear opposition between belief and unbelief is subverted, and as a result the operation of signs is also problematic.

The "sign of Jonah" passages in Matthew and Luke divide repentant followers of Jesus, insiders, from unrepentant nonfollowers, outsiders. For the insiders, the sign of Jonah presents no difficulty, but for the outsiders, it is inscrutable. The insiders "get" the sign, and therefore they get the message. For the gospel of Mark, even the disciples are on the outside and cannot understand (4:10–13). Likewise, in Jesus' saying in Mark 8:11–12, there is no understanding, no interpretation, for anyone because *there is no sign.* This difference is consistent with Mark's treatment of the outsiders. Neither insiders nor outsiders can receive a message without a sign.

However, Jesus' refusal to give a sign itself makes no sense because the gospel of Mark, like every other text in the Bible, is made up of nothing but signs. Even to give "no sign" is to signify something. Commentators note the contrast between the saying in Mark 8:11–12 and the immediately preceding story of the feeding of the four thousand (8:1–10), which appears to be a spectacular "sign." Nevertheless, as Temma Berg says, "words are all we have in Mark's Gospel; we have signifiers, not signifieds."[35] A signifier without a signified is not a sign—indeed, it is not even a signifier. It is at best merely the face of the sign. Berg continues: "[T]hese signifiers, including the important 'kingdom of God,' continue to hover loosely above the narrative.... The series of metaphoric/metonymic condensations stretched before me, like any signifier or series of signifiers, capable of endless supplementarity." Once again, the prospects of wild connotation or unlimited semiosis associated with the poetic function of language jeopardize the desire for a coherent reading—the desire for a canon—in the self-referentiality of the sign.

The biblical canon is itself an important sign of the Christian message, and as the word of God it also signifies the truth and coherence of that message.

---

34. See Kermode, *Genesis of Secrecy,* 23–47. Of the synoptic gospel quotations of Isaiah 6:9–10, Mark comes closest to the LXX. Luke 8:10 uses *hina,* like Mark, but it omits the "lest they" clause.

35. Berg, "Reading," 200–201.

The gospel of John, along with much of the rest of the New Testament, offers a sequence of miraculous signs connoting Jesus as the son of God, the divine *logos,* who offers salvation to those who believe in him. That this message may itself be believed is the desired result of these signs.

In the gospels of Matthew and Luke, Jesus offers the sign of Jonah, which can be read with understanding only by those who already believe, and in Mark he offers no sign at all. The poetic function is strong in these passages. The canon fails to control these sayings because the signifiers themselves expose the desire for meaning that generates the canon, and therefore they interfere with the logocentric transmission of the message. Nevertheless, the canon succeeds after all because, as canon, its texts are read only by those who already believe, like the Ninevites, and who therefore need no further sign. As Jesus says, 'To him who has will more be given; and from him who has not, even what he has will be taken away' " (Mark 4:25; Matthew 13:12; 25:29; Luke 8:18; 19:26).

Conclusion _____

THE FUTURE OF
THE CHRISTIAN CANON

I'm not sure that the notion of canon can survive postmodernity. Whatever canon may have meant in antiquity, has it not become in modernity one of those figures of totality and completeness that is so distrusted by the postmodern?
— Robert Fowler, *Let the Reader Understand*

The word is now a virus.
— Williams Burroughs, *The Ticket That Exploded*

The End of the Canon

The ideal of the canon of scriptures is a collection of writings that produces and enforces the ideology or system of beliefs and values of the community that regards this collection as authoritative. The canon is produced by the community's desire for a semiotic mechanism that controls the meaning of its constituent texts, and indirectly the meaning of any text. This intertextual mechanism supports the believing community's desire for a reading context through which the component texts can be understood correctly. The Bible as a canon is indispensable to Christian faith because it transmits "the word of God." Therefore the biblical canon must be understood within a logocentric framework; in other words, it is the transmitted message or conceptual signified of the collection of texts that is holy and eternal, and not the signifying container, the physical texts themselves. The message of the canonical books must be clear and coherent, universal, and perfectly translatable.

I have tried to show in this book that in actual practice, the ideological control provided by the canon is extremely powerful but never complete. The purpose of the canon is to colonize and transform the meaning of individual component texts. Nevertheless, each of these texts also, to a greater or lesser degree, resists the canonical control of its meaning, not actively, as one concept or message might counter another in a disagreement of views, but passively, as an inert, meaningless, material substance, the *hulē* of the signifier—that is, the physical text that logocentrism disregards. This resistance appears in those situations in which the text becomes ideologically troublesome, in various ways. I have identified several cases of control by the canon and also different ways that resistance to canonical control may appear. My survey is by no means exhaustive, and it only identifies some of the more evident kinds of control and resistance.

The technologies of text, including oral, manuscript, print, and electronic texts, the concept of the classic, and the problem of translatability all play crucial roles in defining both the possibility of and the desire for the canon as a semiotic control mechanism. Up until recent times, human cultures were limited in space by geography, language, and relatively primitive technologies of communication and transportation. It was under these circumstances that the Christian Bible came into existence as a canon. Writing and the codex made the canon thinkable and feasible. Exile and empire made the canon desirable. However, further transformations in technology and ideology have challenged the canon, and they now threaten its viability.

The speed with which new technologies have affected human culture has dramatically increased. It took a thousand years or more for writing to be accepted as a suitable medium for the sacred traditions of the Jews and the Greeks. At that point the scriptures began to be recognized. Then further hundreds of years were required for the codex format of the book to replace the scroll in the early common era. This made the canon possible in a single volume. Considerably later on, print culture did not spring into full-blown existence with the introduction of the first movable-type printing press. Instead, universal literacy was not widely regarded as highly desirable until several hundred years later. Considerable (but decreasing) amounts of time were required to realize the effects of each of these technological innovations. In contrast, the telephone has been in existence for only a hundred years or so, the microcomputer for only a few decades, and the World Wide Web for much less than that, and already this electronic technology is transforming the human world in ways that are not yet fully understood but that are already and clearly profound.

The five-hundred-year-old culture of the printed text is rapidly giving way to another culture, a new mediation of power and knowledge. Alternative means of reading, writing, and publishing now threaten to eliminate the printed codex, or at least radically transform its function, just as printing eliminated the manuscript and the codex itself effectively eliminated the handwritten scroll. As with each of the preceding stages of development, no specific persons or groups control the latest technological changes; instead, the transformations have their own "life" and make their own rules: "[T]he system seems to be a vanguard machine dragging humanity after it, dehumanizing it in order to rehumanize it at a different level of normative capacity."[1] There is considerable resistance to this new technology, just as there was to each of the earlier transformations of linguistic medium. However, the increased rate of change since writing was first introduced suggests that resistance to new technologies of the text has become less and less effective.

Thanks to the new technology, human beings already live in a world for which traditional cultural and political borderlines hardly matter any more. It costs no more, in either time or money, to send e-mail messages between Detroit, U.S.A., and Sydney, Australia, than it does to send e-mail between Detroit and Ann Arbor. I can access newspapers in Johannesburg or Tel Aviv or Lima or Tokyo via the World Wide Web as easily as the one in my small hometown. I can download text, data, graphics, and music from anywhere in the world in a matter of minutes, or less, and at minimal cost. Given the escalating value of "information" in the contemporary world, this ease of transfer becomes even more significant. You can shop, gamble, fall in love, or commit a crime almost anywhere in the world, without leaving your own house. If you can't afford your own computer, then (in the United States, at least) you can go to a public library and do these things from terminals there. Electronic culture is the first truly global culture.

Nevertheless, electronic culture will not give rise to a single global, electronic empire. "Empire," like "canon," implies a totalizing, unifying principle of self-sufficiency and completeness (see further chapter 4). The old colonial empires were driven by the hierarchical dream of monolithic universal control. In contrast, the contemporary equivalent to empire is no longer the nation-state or nationalistic structure, and the old colonial establishments, outmoded and despised, are rapidly disappearing. The multiple empires of our time, and for the foreseeable future, will take on the very different forms of huge transnational corporations such as Microsoft, Disney, McDonald's, and General Motors.

The modern nation-state will eventually be parceled out, reconfigured, and perhaps even dissolved entirely by the transnational corporate entities that already dominate what Fredric Jameson calls the culture of "late capitalism." Whether the resulting corporate empires will form either eternal or historical empires remains to be seen, but it is doubtful in either case. Already many different ideologies and paralogistic micronarratives contend for the loyalties and the lives of human beings. Perhaps the very partiality and multiplicity of the new corporate empires allow them to coexist, like the components in a bizarre Dadaist mobile, constantly shifting and reconfiguring themselves and their relations to one another.

Whether any canon of texts can speak universally or authoritatively in this brave new world is also doubtful. Frank Kermode claims that the latest phase in the historical understanding of the classic text encourages a

---

1. Lyotard, *Postmodern Condition*, 63.

plurality of understandings that will in fact increase over time.[2] In the post-modern world, no text can any longer stand unequivocally connected to a monolithic empire, whether eternal or historical. Instead, an indefinite number of possible meanings will be simultaneously signified by each "classic" work. According to Jean-François Lyotard, postmodernism "contributes to elevating all language games to self-knowledge, even those not within the realm of canonical knowledge."[3] In the pluralistic world of electronic culture, biblical texts may continue to be revered by Christian communities, but those communities will be less and less able to pretend that the message of the biblical canon is a universal one. For Christianity, this will constitute in effect a return to a pre-Constantinian situation—that is, a church, or rather multiple churches, without a canon. The biblical stories will then be understood as limited and fragmentary micronarratives, not the components of a universal metanarrative.

Indeed, the whole question of ideology and the Bible may already be moot. The biblical canon plays a significantly diminished role in the contemporary world. It is arguable that the Bible no longer has any genuine canonical hold over anyone today, no matter how loudly some people might protest. Indeed, the loudness of the believing communities' protests is itself a symptom of the failure of the canon's authority.

The biblical canon began to lose its hold over its component texts quite a long time ago. The Christian double canon has failed to control the meaning of the Bible ever since the emergence of print culture. Elizabeth Eisenstein concludes her monumental study of the emergence of print culture by puzzling over the simultaneous rise of Christian fundamentalism and modern science, each of them apparently a product of the transition during the Renaissance from handwritten to printed texts.[4] Both science (directly) and fundamentalism (indirectly) are effects of the technology of the printing press, and both movements serve as symptoms of the damage done by print culture to the authority of and desire for the canon.

Eisenstein demonstrates how economic and technological consequences of printing took over canonical functions of stabilizing and securing the written text and thereby diminished the need for a canon of the scriptures. She also claims that the emerging printing industry promoted critical historical and philological studies of the original languages and the manuscript history of the Bible's texts. Both a "scientific" attitude toward biblical texts and belief in the right of individual readers to make up their own minds ("the priesthood of all believers") were strongly encouraged by the development of print technology and associated economic changes, and these played considerable roles in the growing diversity of ways to read the Bible.[5]

---

2. Kermode, *The Classic*, 121 ff.
3. Lyotard, *Postmodern Condition*, 62.
4. Eisenstein, *Printing Press*, 2:704 ff.; see also ibid., 1:130.
5. Ibid., 1:321, 336–37.

Both the Renaissance and the Reformation (and Counter-Reformation) were deeply implicated in the rise of print culture, and they depended heavily on print technology. The increased awareness of religious difference and the rise of humanistic tolerance of differences of culture and lifestyle promoted a willingness to question the authority of the canon. As a result, skeptics and freethinkers were more willing to reject the metatextual message of the biblical canon and to identify the contradictions that the canon was supposed to conceal.

Print technology weakened the traditional authority of the canon of the Bible, even as it strengthened the position of science. Eisenstein shows in detail how print technology made possible the standardized texts (including maps, charts, and diagrams) that are essential to the development of modern science. Scientific examination of the "book of Nature" was also freed by the diminished authority of the biblical canon, especially in regard to topics on which the Bible might be taken to contradict science, such as the creation of the universe or miracle and natural law.

Christian fundamentalism arose as a reaction against these modern scientific and humanistic challenges to the Bible's authority. Fundamentalism attempts to control ideological diversity through rejection or severe limitation of critical examination of the canonical texts, on the one hand, and through doctrines of an infallible Bible, on the other. Fundamentalists may want the Bible to be read widely, but they also want it to be read in the one correct way—that is, according to their own perceptions of the single coherent message of the canon. Christian fundamentalists adopt a logocentric view of the biblical texts, and thus in effect they support dynamic equivalence, even though they may object to modern translations of the Bible.

The rise of modern Christian fundamentalism is a consequence of print culture and a symptom of the decline of the canon. However, fundamentalism is a deeper and a more widespread feature of modern print culture than is usually recognized. Even modern science itself tends to be "fundamentalist" in its attitude toward truth and authority. Scientists believe that there is just one correct interpretation of "the facts" and that the scientific method authorizes the scientist's conclusions. Science is also very careful to control skepticism. Science encourages some skepticism, but it is intolerant of skepticism directed against its own prevailing theories and assumptions.[6] In other words, modern science is fundamentalistic natural philosophy.

The damage to the canon caused by print culture is evident in the freedom with which popular mass media take over and rewrite biblical stories in a wide variety of ways. This applies both to the original mass media—printed books, magazines, and newspapers—but also, and perhaps even more so, to

---

6. On the relation between "normal" science and the paradigm shifts that occur during scientific "revolutions," see Kuhn, *Structure*.

the newer, electronic media of telephone, cinema, television, and now the World Wide Web.[7] It would not be difficult to trace this phenomenon back to the influence of the printing press. Thus it is not surprising that Christian fundamentalists are actively involved in modern media transformations of biblical texts, using them to tighten their control over the meaning of the scriptures. This control is effective insofar as the "average person" tends to think that fundamentalist interpretation of biblical texts is the only possible interpretation. Other media producers with less readily identifiable theological interests are also quite willing to use biblical images, themes, and entire stories, alongside material drawn from a wide variety of other sources, to create works in which biblical material is not treated as authoritative or otherwise canonical.[8] As a result, the mass-media audience is presented with a wide variety of intermedial translations and interpretations of biblical texts. These different translations of biblical texts in the new media become in effect a diverse paralogy of micronarratives.

The canon plays a crucial role in defining and identifying its reading community, and vice versa. The loss of significance of the biblical canon in the contemporary world is therefore a symptom of the failure and disintegration of the believing community. To be sure, believing communities will continue to exist in isolated clusters here and there, not unlike the Amish or ultraorthodox Jews. As the global, electronic, postmodern culture engulfs the contemporary world more and more, these outposts of Christianity, Judaism, and other religions will be less and less engaged in the world. They will withdraw more and more into reactionary enclaves. The canons of these communities will be, of necessity, partial canons—that is, nonuniversal and therefore failed canons.

Postmodern Semiotics

This book has argued that the canon constructs and controls the meaning of the Bible. The biblical canon appears because a religious community desires

---

7. "Up to now it has been thought that the Christian myth-building during the Roman Empire was possible only because printing had not yet been invented. The truth is altogether different. The daily press and the telegraph, which spread their inventions over the whole earth in a second, fabricate more myths (and the bourgeois cattle believe and spread them) in one day than could formerly have been done in a century" (Marx, *Letters*, 282). See also Benjamin, *Illuminations,* 217–51. The articles in Aichele, ed., *Culture, Entertainment,* explore transformations of biblical texts in relation to popular film, television, literature, music, visual art, and journalism.

8. For example, recent movies such as *Michael* or *Dogma,* TV shows such as *The X-Files* or *Buffy the Vampire Slayer,* or the "Godhead trilogy" of novels by James Morrow. Neal Stephenson's novel *Snow Crash* is discussed below. See also Aichele, *Culture, Entertainment.* Recent boycotts by fundamentalist Christian groups of secular mass media producers such as Disney suggest that the competition for control over popular media will become more intense. Unfortunately, many secular film and TV producers (including Disney) typically interpret the Bible and other "classic" texts in maudlin, highly sentimentalized ways.

an intertextual web through which the scriptures completely explain each other. All writing requires interpretation, but canon makes evident the need for explanation, both implicitly (as does any written text) and explicitly, as in Acts 2:12, when the Pentecost witnesses ask, " 'What does this mean?' " Canon serves as commentary on its component texts, but canon also requires extracanonical commentary, interpretive practices whose ideological function is to keep the canonical texts relevant to new historical situations, as well as to provide for, and to limit, different possible readings. This has been the case for as long as there has been a canon, but it is only in the new world of electronic culture that we have become continually conscious of this situation—that is, of both the need for meaning and the constructed character of meaning. Electronic culture makes it possible to raise in a new way the question of the canon.

Digitizing a text does not automatically make it postmodern. Nor are nonelectronic texts necessarily modern or premodern. Many predigital texts are also postmodern texts—for example, Laurence Sterne's *Tristram Shandy* and James Joyce's *Finnegans Wake,* as well as the stories of Franz Kafka and Jorge Luis Borges and Lewis Carroll. Older texts, such as the *Arabian Nights,* the *Odyssey,* and portions of the Bible, also contain postmodern elements. What makes a text postmodern is not the time period of its production, but rather the relation of the text to its own signification.

By exposing and explicitly questioning the material stuff that makes possible the positing of meaning, the postmodern text undercuts and interrupts meaningful discourse. It calls attention to the limits of discourse, to that which cannot be said. The postmodern text is a "writerly" text. In other words, it reveals what Julia Kristeva calls (following Plato) the semiotic *chōra,* the meaningless material receptacle that establishes the potential space of meaningful language. In this book, I have referred to this materiality of the text using another Greek word, *hulē,* a term that Kristeva also uses, drawing upon the writings of Edmund Husserl.[9] The postmodern text makes explicit the semiotic paradox that meaning is founded upon meaningless elements (sounds, letters, binary patterns). The postmodern text reveals, self-referentially, that meaningless materiality disrupts *every* text, not just postmodern ones.

Despite this distinction between the digital text and the postmodern one, there is a kind of convergence between the postmodern and the digital that cannot be ignored. This convergence is perhaps most apparent when electronic reproduction (intermedial translation) of a nonelectronic text produces greater awareness of the physical aspect of the signifier.[10] The increased number of technological stages between the sender and the receiver of the digital message also adds to the reader's consciousness of the frailty

9. Kristeva, *Revolution,* 25–37, 88.
10. See Eisenstein, *Printing Press,* 1:16.

of the connecting media. There are more opportunities for the medium to break down and transmission of the message to fail.

When you first learned to read, you were much more aware than you are today of the written medium as an *obstacle* to reading. Once you mastered reading, writing became more or less invisible to you. In time, we will all grow accustomed to electronic media, and these new media too will become invisible to us—at least until some even newer medium should come along. For the moment, the relative unfamiliarity of the new technology brings with it a heightened sense of not only its own artificiality but of the artificiality of every technology of text.

Just as canonizing seeks to render invisible the hyletic material of the text, so conversely the rewriting of the biblical canon in the electronic era, as a result of transformations of the medium, once again brings the materiality of the text into view. Like print culture before it, but even more so, electronic culture threatens the canonical control of meaning. The first readers of printed books (not to mention the first scribes) must have been aware that something rather fundamental had changed, just as readers today may feel uncomfortable when confronted by digital texts. Something has changed, once again. The cultural transformations involved in the shift from print to electronic culture require a postmodern rethinking of semiotics, just as the earlier transitions from oral to print culture required a modernist understanding of semiotics. In the wake of electronic culture, semiotics must become postmodern.

It was in the rethinking of the very first transformation, from orality to writing—a rethinking that begins, at the latest, with Plato, Epicurus, and the Stoics—that semiotics as a field of knowledge was born, at about the same time that the "canon of Torah" was being assembled and written by Israelite exiles returning from Babylon. The present media transformation is happening much more rapidly and simultaneously around the world than that earlier one did, and we are more painfully aware now than we have been for a long time of the physical and ideological transformations undergone by the signifier, and by the phenomenon of signification itself.

Not only does the physical medium of signification change, but signification itself changes. Insofar as they involve electronic culture, these media transformations are still far from complete, and we can only guess (and guess rather wildly at that) what their outcome will be. Contrary to the assumptions of earlier semioticians, signification is not a timeless, unchanging phenomenon. To think, as some biblical scholars do, that digital Bible texts will somehow be the same as printed ones (or even the same as oral ones) implies a logocentric disregard of the violence of translation and of the effects of the physical medium on the message. There is no reason to think that the biblical texts remained somehow "the same" when they passed from oral tradition into written manuscript, nor that they survived the further intermedial translation from manuscript to printed book unscathed. Instead there is quite good reason to suspect, with Socrates, that the texts cannot stay the same after they have been intermedially translated. The digitized Bible is a different Bible.

The canon attempts to satisfy the ideological desire to secure the biblical texts against the threat of loss, to possess the texts, and especially to control their meaning by severely limiting and directing the intertextual play between them. It is an exercise of power, the power to control the meaning of the scriptures. By pointing to intercanonical tensions within the Christian Bible, this book contests that power and contributes to postmodern fragmentation within the canon. However, this same postmodern fragmentation of the canon can be viewed as a movement of liberation. The canon of the Bible is, among other things, an oppressive ideological institution, one that *prevents* people from reading these diverse and ambiguous books or that so controls the reading of these texts that people are in effect blinded and crippled by the canonical constraints. The biblical texts cannot be freed from the ideological effects of intertextuality or ideology as such, for those effects are inevitable in any act of communication. However, the texts can be opened up to a wider and less determinate range of intertextualities. Thus the end of the canon might not be a bad thing at all.

Further News from Nowhere

The prospects presented by contemporary, postmodern, electronic culture will very likely be evaluated differently depending on the evaluator's attachments or hostilities to print culture. In addition, as print culture becomes more and more a thing of the past, all of those involved may well have a different "take" on these matters. One way to explore the terrors and joys of the emerging culture in the present day is through the vivid descriptions of contemporary "cyberpunk" science fiction.[11] Cyberpunk fiction combines a speculative narrative built around imaginary technological innovations in the near future (usually the next century or two) with the gritty urban realism associated with traditional "hard-boiled" detective stories. It contrasts strongly with epic-heroic science fiction of the *Star Trek* or *Star Wars* variety.

Cyberpunk stories generally feature a strong dose of ironic social commentary, and the principal characters are often marginal hustlers and con artists or alienated "street people" who survive in a grim, violent world—often a police state ruled by giant corporations—through their ability to slip through the cracks in a badly disintegrating community order and to manipulate the considerable cybernetic powers that hold that world together. The technological developments that make the cyberpunk story possible involve

---

11. For detailed discussions and examples of cyberpunk, see McCaffery, *Storming the Reality Studio;* and Hayles, *Posthuman,* esp. chaps. 5, 7, and 10.

genetic or cybernetic tools or processes that so modify the human body or mind that questions of human identity and nature are explored as the plot unfolds. Literary style is also very important in cyberpunk fiction, and the story is often narrated from a cynical or even paranoid perspective.

In Neal Stephenson's witty novel *Snow Crash*, a near-future world is threatened by a civilization-destroying linguistic crash. This impending crash is explicitly compared to the biblical story of the tower of Babel, although it seems rather more like a forced global Pentecost event.[12] However, this impending culture collapse will not result from an act of God. Instead, the crash will be caused by a "metavirus" disseminated through a global computer network. The exact nature of this digital viral agent remains playfully ambiguous: "is it a virus, a drug, or a religion? . . . What's the difference?"[13] In any case, the virus erases the mind of the person infected with it, much as some contemporary computer viruses erase data from the hard disks of infected computers. The infected person remains alive and conscious, but her "self" has irrecoverably disappeared. She can only babble strings of nonsense syllables, glossolalia. The human tongues are confused.

Snow Crash depicts a world at once brilliant and degraded, a radically new way to live, and yet a way that contemporary humans already increasingly take for granted. The depicted separation between the rich few and the innumerable poor realistically extrapolates from the current status quo. For "about 99 percent of the people in the world . . . [i]n order to stay alive, you have to spend all day every day doing stupid meaningless work."[14] In the early-twenty-first-century narrative world of this novel, human civilization has become an economic chaos of franchise capitalism gone wild. Not only are all ordinary businesses operated as franchises, but the police, the jails, and even the Mafia are corporately owned and franchised by local operators, not unlike McDonald's, Radio Shack, or Holiday Inn in the contemporary world.

The primary human "reality" of *Snow Crash* consists of a buzzing multiplicity of these franchises in a completely unregulated economic market. Modern nation-states no longer exist as bordered territorial entities, for such entities have ceased to be technologically and economically viable. The decrepit governments have metamorphosed into businesslike entities that combine features of a private club, a neighborhood gang, and an extortion racket. You subscribe to one country or another (whichever one provides the benefits that you want and the rates that you can afford), not unlike the way you subscribe to a telephone service provider or insurance company today. The governments also operate through local storefront franchises (such as "Fedland," the former U.S. government, or "Mr. Lee's Greater Hong

12. Stephenson, *Snow Crash*, 217, 363, 398 ff. (re Babel), 205–8 (re Pentecost). See also Hayles, *Posthuman*, 272–79. See further chapter 5.
13. Stephenson, *Snow Crash*, 200.
14. Ibid., 324.

Kong"). Housing, roads, and presumably all of the schools are corporately owned and franchised. The corporate entities that own the franchises are the major players in this world, but they are largely invisible in the novel. This is not surprising since Stephenson's story is consistently told from the point of view of ordinary people. Religion is also franchised. Rich businessmen own the Christian denominations, which appear in the form of semiautomated pay-to-be-saved chapels (such as "the Reverend Wayne's Pearly Gates") on the street corners. These businessmen also own the graduate schools of religion and archaeology.

Layered on top of this primary narrative world is a secondary, virtual world, produced by the actual world and yet distinct from it. The Metaverse is a huge, immensely powerful computer network that supports an interactive "virtual reality"—that is, a utopia or "no-place" (Greek *ouk topos*)—not unlike the World Wide Web in the contemporary world, but far more potent and extensive than the World Wide Web presently is. The Metaverse takes the form of a fantastical, holographic, multisensory, shared illusion—a three-dimensional illusion of a busy city street with numerous buildings along it. Even though its reality is "only" virtual, the Metaverse is a powerful source of entertainment and education, as well as a major medium for communication and commerce. Indeed, it even provides the means and the medium for distributing the antiviral inoculation software that eventually defeats the metavirus.[15]

In other respects, the Metaverse is far from utopian. A dangerous place, the Metaverse serves as the transmission medium for the potentially catastrophic metavirus. Even apart from that, the illusions of the Metaverse correspond to the economic realities of the actual world. Differences of social class and personal wealth remain apparent, for access to the Metaverse is not free, and those who can afford a faster online connection or custom avatar programming can become much more deeply involved in this parallel world than can others.

Curiously, however, in a world where everything is owned, it appears that no one owns the Metaverse itself. In this respect, the Metaverse is again like the present-day Internet. Even though Microsoft and America Online, not to mention the phone companies, would no doubt love to own the Internet, each of them owns only a relatively small piece of it. The Internet has no center and no periphery; it is a multi-noded, fluid network of computers and telephone lines. In the terminology of Gilles Deleuze and Félix Guattari, it is a rhizome. The Internet depends for its existence on a series of "protocols" that define the possibilities for a wide variety of computers to communicate with one another in a constantly changing network. These protocols of necessity are shared; they cannot be owned.

Likewise, the Metaverse is controlled by the "Global Multimedia Protocol

---

15. Ibid., 456–57.

Group," another invisible agency, whose name suggests neither ownership nor singularity, but rather a many-sided compromise that makes communication possible. Empire survives after all in this postmodern world, but it is not the totalizing, hierarchical empire of old. Instead, the Metaverse is the virtual, digital antiempire that provides a common matrix for the microempires of the corporate franchised actual world. In the last analysis, it is the digital protocols of the Metaverse that provide the universal, Babelian communication medium of the world of *Snow Crash,* not the Pentecostian glossolalia of the virus-infected "Falabalas."[16]

The civilization-threatening metavirus is disseminated by a Christian "cable-television monopolist" in an attempt to take totalitarian control over both the actual and the virtual worlds by artificially producing a Pentecost event.[17] However, the Metaverse is too amorphous and rhizomatic to be owned or controlled by any one party, and the virtual world provides the means by which its own takeover, as well as that of the actual world, is thwarted. Thus the Metaverse is at once the unfallen digital tower of Babel and a postmodern paralogy of fragmented, localized, and diverse micronarratives.

Along the virtual street that is the Metaverse, human users appear in the form of graphic "avatars." The religious connotation of this term is not coincidental. The appearance of the virtual body of each avatar may bear little or no resemblance to the real body of its actual user, but this body provides the interface between the user and the Metaverse. If your Metaverse avatar is killed, your actual body will not be harmed, but if your avatar is exposed to the metavirus, then you will lose your actual mind, forever. In other words, your mind is "really" in the Metaverse while your actual body is temporarily replaced by a virtual one. Thus logocentric ideology also continues to exert considerable influence in the future world of Stephenson's story, but it runs more and more into the troubles that have been described in this book.

Like the World Wide Web, the Metaverse suggests that the concept of "body" needs to be seriously reconsidered.[18] The graphic interface of the virtual world mimics the concrete, steel, and glass world of the actual streets on which the franchises maintain their stores. Even when the human body is digitized, reduced to nothing more than the binary bits that describe the avatar, that avatar still does not exist until it is put into play—that is, until the actual, physical body of the user "logs on" to the actual network. The digital software that generates the virtual body cannot function without physical hardware to support it, including the "wetware" of the user's actual body. The materiality of text may be radically transformed, but it cannot

---

16. Ibid., 25, 177–80.
17. Ibid., 66.
18. This is a major theme of Hayles, *Posthuman,* esp. chaps. 8–11.

be dispensed with. The Metaverse and its avatars are digital beings, not nonphysical ones, and virtual reality (such as the World Wide Web) still requires a material medium.

Traditional cultures no longer exist as such in either the actual or the virtual worlds of *Snow Crash*. They are replaced by a nomadic, tribal society in which fragments of multiple cultures, races, and ethnicities blend together in new and constantly changing configurations. Likewise, there are no more metanarratives, only countless micronarratives, continually being temporarily reassembled out of even smaller narrative fragments. No god is evident in either the actual or the virtual narrative world, although "the Librarian," an extremely powerful database that can be accessed only through the Metaverse, is almost omniscient.

Apart from a few ancient Sumerian clay tablets with writing on them, the only way that texts, including the Bible, are accessed in the world of Stephenson's novel is through the Librarian. The Librarian saves and retrieves bits and pieces of cultural traditions, but it does so like any database, by breaking up the collection into small standardized units that can be accessed and cross-referenced through keywords, phrases, or lexias. In other words, the Bible and all other written texts have been disintegrated into small signifying units—atoms of "information"[19]—so that they can be catalogued and accessed most efficiently.

The traditions and the scriptures are chopped up and shuffled and constantly rearranged, but religion and politics remain at the center of the *Snow Crash* story. Stories from the Bible have not disappeared from this future world, but they have been transformed. In fact, characters in this novel mention biblical texts rather frequently, and these texts play important roles in the story's plot. In addition to the Babel story, stories of Eden and Pentecost, of the Pharisees and Sadducees, and of Jesus are discussed. Bits and pieces of these stories are jumbled together with each other and with other stories from the Sumerians, Babylonians, and Canaanites, stories of Enki and Inanna and of Asherah.[20] Some of the stories are wildly interpreted or significantly altered, perhaps as a result of "secondary orality," in order to play a part in Stephenson's larger story.

The novel's characters access and quote and discuss these stories, and they use them in their arguments, much like present-day readers of the Bible, but they do not appeal to the stories' catholicity or apostolicity. The database does not distinguish between bits of sacred text and other, noncanonical fragments. The arrangement of "hits" is determined by the form of the user's query. The authority of the stories derives only from their ability to speak to readers in specific situations. The written text is standardized, but there

---

19. See Benjamin, *Illuminations*, 83–109. See also Hayles, *Posthuman*, which is subtitled "Virtual Bodies in Cybernetics, Literature, and Informatics."

20. Davies maintains that the Sumerians were the first canonizers (*Scribes and Schools*, 21).

is no canon, no closed collection of texts. The database might identify text fragments as coming from a sacred text or canon of scripture, but that would be merely to list one property alongside other possible properties of the text, such as children's literature, pornography, or law code. It would be one item of information among many others, whose value is determined by the user. Within the Librarian's ever-growing database, all texts are equal, and none is privileged. None of them is able to explain itself. The scriptures have been corrupted, and wild connotations abound.

The world of *Snow Crash* lies beyond the biblical canon. In that world, readers pay no attention at all to some of the formerly canonical texts—their database records are never accessed—and these texts disappear forever into the ever-growing trash heap of forgotten texts. However, other texts continue to be of interest. These formerly canonical texts remain in circulation; they are read and rewritten in all sorts of ways, but they are no longer consulted for "canonical" reasons.

An authoritative canon is no longer possible or meaningful, not even as a "classic," in either the actual or the virtual world imagined in Stephenson's novel. The corporate empires of that world share none of T. S. Eliot's "community of taste" or "common style." Only the Metaverse provides a common space of discourse. That future world has no place for imperial hierarchies; instead, power and speed are the only authorities for constantly changing coalitions of trade and technology. For people in such a world, the biblical canon holds no residual authority, and the formerly canonical status of any of its texts is simply left behind it, part of its past, no longer particularly relevant.

Our grandchildren will probably look back on the technological and social predictions of contemporary science fiction as shortsighted and naive delusions. However, the best science fiction is concerned not so much with prediction of the future as it is with reimagination of the present and even reconsideration of the past. Cyberpunk tells us more about who we are now and who we have been than it does about who we will be. *Snow Crash* ironically and critically recontextualizes the world that we live in today, a world in which the canon of scriptures as an object of desire is very much in question.

The forms and conduits of desire themselves have changed and still are changing, and the conditions and means of power are also changing, sometimes quite radically. The result of these changes is that old imperial forms of power and desire reflected in the biblical canon have become less and less viable. As humanity moves deeper and deeper into the emerging electronic culture, the biblical canon, itself the product of premodern imperialism, will either be radically transformed or else dissolved entirely into something quite different.

GLOSSARY

AURALITY. Hearing as a medium of communication, especially in an oral culture. Complement of ORALITY.

BLIK. Neologism coined by R. M. Hare to refer to a non-falsifiable belief that makes a significant difference in one's perception of the world.

CANON. The catalog or list of books considered to be SCRIPTURE. The canon is both inclusive, in that all scriptural books have been included, and exclusive, in that no scriptural books have been excluded.

CONNOTATION. A second "level" of meaning that arises when a SIGN itself becomes the SIGNIFIER of another SIGNIFIED. Equivalent to the INTERPRETANT, and to Gottlob Frege's concept of meaning as "sense."

DENOTATION. The "obvious" or "surface" meaning of a word. The ability of a word, as a SIGNIFIER, to pick out some SIGNIFIED object. Equivalent to Frege's concept of meaning as "reference."

GENOTEXT. Julia Kristeva's term for the materiality of the signifiers in a text. That which is transformed by codes into a PHENOTEXT.

HULĒ. Greek word for meaningless materiality, used by Kristeva, following Edmund Husserl.

HYLETIC. Partaking of HULĒ.

INDETERMINACIES. Gaps of meaning that appear within any message, such as a story, and that must be filled in by the reader.

INTERPRETANT. C. S. Peirce's term for the component of the sign that connects the REPRESENTAMEN (or SIGNIFIER) to its object. Equivalent to Frege's concept of meaning as "sense," and to CONNOTATION.

LEXIA. Roland Barthes's term for an arbitrarily chosen unit of text (compare Greek, *lexis:* phrase). Equivalent to a "verse" of the Bible.

LOGOCENTRISM. Jacques Derrida's term for a system of thought that privileges nonmaterial meaning (the SIGNIFIED) over the materiality of text (the SIGNIFIER). The predominant mode of thinking in the Western world since Plato.

METACANON. A canon that controls other canons. Especially, the New Testament in relation to the Old Testament.

METAGENRE. A high-level genre (type of narrative) that includes other (sub)genres. For example, comedy, history.

METALANGUAGE. A language (or function of language) that describes another language.

METANARRATIVE. Jean-François Lyotard's term for the great stories, both traditional and modern, that define a culture or epoch. According to Lyotard, the two metanarratives of the modern Western world are the Enlightenment and Hegelianism.

METASTORY. The larger story implied by an arrangement of stories, such as the story of the Bible as a whole.

METATEXT. A text's potential to control its own interpretation, or the comprehensive understanding of a text. Canons are both intertextual and metatextual.

ORALITY. Speaking as a medium of communication, especially in an oral culture. Complement of AURALITY.

PHENOTEXT. Kristeva's term for the text as perceived and understood. The meaningful text.

POLYSEMY. Potential for multiple interpretations. Polyvalence in relation to texts.

READERLY. Barthes's term for texts that do not resist the reader's desire for meaning. The meaning of the readerly text appears to be clear and obvious, and INDETERMINACIES are minimal. Contrast WRITERLY.

REPRESENTAMEN. Peirce's term for the SIGNIFIER or material aspect of the SIGN.

SCRIPTURE. Any writing, but more specifically, writings believed by some group of people to be authoritative.

SEMIOSIS. The process of signification, the binary operation of the sign (SIGNIFIER → SIGNIFIED). "Unlimited semiosis" is the concept that "everything signifies," that every SIGNIFIED is also a SIGNIFIER.

SIGNIFIED. The conceptual aspect of the sign, and any actual or ideal object understood by that concept. Involved in both DENOTATION and CONNOTATION.

SIGNIFIER. The material aspect of the SIGN, composed of HYLETIC matter, but also, insofar as it is perceived as a signifier, understood to be at least potentially meaningful.

TOPOS. Greek word for place. In literature, a topic or theme.

TMESIS. Greek word for cutting or division, used by Barthes to refer to the practice of "skipping" about in the text, reading the linear text in a nonlinear fashion. Encouraged by the codex.

UNIVOCALITY. To possess only one possible interpretation. Opposite of POLYSEMY.

WRITERLY. Barthes's term for texts that resist the reader's desire for meaning. The writerly text demands input from the reader, for INDETERMINACIES are evident. Contrast READERLY.

BIBLIOGRAPHY

Adam, A. K. M. "The Sign of Jonah: A Fish-Eye View." In *Semeia* 51: *Poststructural Criticism and the Bible: Text/History/Discourse.* Atlanta: Scholars Press, 1990.

Adams, Douglas. *The Hitchhiker's Guide to the Galaxy.* New York: Pocket Books, 1979.

Aichele, George. *Jesus Framed.* London: Routledge, 1996.

———. "Jesus' Uncanny 'Family Scene.'" *Journal for the Study of the New Testament* 74 (1999) 29–49.

———. "Jesus' Violence." *Violence, Utopia, and the Kingdom of God.* Ed. George Aichele and Tina Pippin, 72–91. London: Routledge, 1998.

———. *The Limits of Story.* Chico, Calif.: Scholars Press, 1985.

———. "Post-Ecclesiastical Theology." *Explorations* (fall 1992) 5–14.

———. *Sign, Text, Scripture: Semiotics and the Bible.* Sheffield: Sheffield Academic Press, 1997.

———. "The Son of Man and the Sons of Men." *Reading Communities Reading Scriptures.* Ed. Gary Phillips and Nicole Wilkinson. Harrisburg: Trinity Press International, forthcoming 2002.

———. *Theology as Comedy: Critical and Theoretical Implications.* Lanham, Md.: University Press of America, 1980. Digital ed.: *http://gaichele.tripod.com/.*

———. "Translation, Narrative, and Theology." *Explorations* (summer 1991) 61–80.

———. "Two Theories of Translation, with Examples from the Gospel of Mark." *Journal for the Study of the New Testament* 47 (1992) 95–116.

Aichele, George, ed. *Culture, Entertainment, and the Bible: Playing the Parts of God.* JSOT Supplement 309. Sheffield: Sheffield Academic Press, 2000.

Aichele, George, and Gary A. Phillips, eds. *Semeia* 69/70: *Intertextuality and the Bible.* Atlanta: Scholars Press, 1995.

Aland, Kurt, and Barbara Aland. *The Text of the New Testament.* Trans. Erroll F. Rhodes. Grand Rapids: Eerdmans; Leiden: Brill, 1987.

Altieri, Charles. "An Idea and Ideal of a Literary Canon." *Critical Inquiry* (September 1983) 37–60.

Altizer, Thomas J. J. Foreword to *Deconstructing Theology,* by Mark C. Taylor. AAR Studies in Religion 28. Chico, Calif.: Scholars Press, 1982.

Aristotle. *Poetics.* Trans. Gerald Else. Ann Arbor: University of Michigan Press, 1967.

Assmann, Aleida. "The Curse and Blessing of Babel." *The Translatability of Cultures: Figurations of the Space Between.* Ed. Sanford Budick and Wolfgang Iser. Stanford: Stanford University Press, 1996.

Auerbach, Erich. *Mimesis: The Representation of Reality in Western Literature.* Trans. Willard Trask. Princeton, N.J.: Princeton University Press, 1953.

Bailey, Randall C., and Tina Pippin, eds. *Semeia 76: Race, Class, and the Politics of Bible Translation.* Atlanta: Scholars Press, 1996.

Barnstone, Willis. *The Poetics of Translation: History, Theory, Practice.* New Haven: Yale University Press, 1993.

Barr, James. *Holy Scripture: Canon, Authority, Criticism.* Philadelphia: Westminster Press, 1983.

————. *The Scope and Authority of the Bible.* Philadelphia: Westminster Press, 1980.

————. *The Semantics of Biblical Language.* Oxford: Oxford University Press, 1961. Reprint, London: SCM Press; Philadelphia: Trinity Press International, 1991.

Barthes, Roland. *A Barthes Reader.* Ed. Susan Sontag. New York: Hill and Wang, 1982.

————. *Elements of Semiology.* Trans. Annette Lavers and Colin Smith. New York: Hill and Wang, 1967.

————. "From Work to Text." *Textual Strategies.* Trans. and ed. Josué V. Harari. Ithaca, N.Y.: Cornell University Press, 1979.

————. *Image Music Text.* Trans. Stephen Heath. New York: Hill and Wang, 1977.

————. *Mythologies.* Trans. Annette Lavers. New York: Hill and Wang, 1972.

————. *The Pleasure of the Text.* Trans. Richard Miller. New York: Hill and Wang, 1975.

————. *Roland Barthes.* Trans. Richard Howard. New York: Hill and Wang, 1977.

————. *The Rustle of Language.* Trans. Richard Howard. Berkeley and Los Angeles: University of California Press, 1986.

————. *The Semiotic Challenge.* Trans. Richard Howard. New York: Hill and Wang, 1988.

————. *S/Z.* Trans. Richard Miller. New York: Hill and Wang, 1974.

————. *Writing Degree Zero.* Trans. Annette Lavers and Colin Smith. New York: Hill and Wang, 1967.

Barton, John. *Holy Writings, Sacred Text: The Canon in Early Christianity.* Louisville: Westminster/John Knox Press, 1997.

————. *Oracles of God: Perceptions of Ancient Prophecy in Israel after the Exile.* London: Darton, Longman and Todd, 1986.

Bauer, Walter. *Orthodoxy and Heresy in Earliest Christianity.* Trans. Robert A. Kraft and Gerhard Kroedel. Philadelphia: Fortress Press, 1971. Electronic ed.: ed. Robert A. Kraft, 1991–93. German original: Tübingen: J. C. B. Mohr, 1934.

Beckwith, Roger. *The Old Testament Canon of the New Testament Church.* Grand Rapids: Eerdmans, 1985.

Benjamin, Walter. *Illuminations.* Trans. Harry Zohn. New York: Schocken Books, 1968.

————. *Reflections.* Trans. Edmund Jephcott. New York: Harcourt Brace Jovanovich, 1978.

Berg, Temma F. "Reading in/to Mark." *Semeia* 48 (1989) 187–206.

Berquist, Jon L. "Postcolonialism and Imperial Motives for Canonization." *Semeia* 75 (1996) 15–35.

Black, C. Clifton. *Mark: Images of an Apostolic Interpreter.* Columbia: University of South Carolina Press, 1994.

Borges, Jorge Luis. "Kafka and His Precursors." Trans. James E. Irby. *Labyrinths.* Ed. Donald A. Yates and James E. Irby. New York: New Directions, 1964.

———. "Pierre Menard, Author of *Don Quixote.*" *Ficciones.* Trans. and ed. Anthony Kerrigan. New York: Grove Press, 1962.

Boyarin, Daniel. *A Radical Jew: Paul and the Politics of Identity.* Berkeley and Los Angeles: University of California Press, 1994.

———. " 'This We Know to Be the Carnal Israel': Circumcision and the Erotic Life of God and Israel." *Critical Inquiry* (fall 1992) 474–505.

Brumberg-Kraus, Jonathan. "Re: Canon." E-mail to IOUDAIOS-L *http://ccat.sas .upenn.edu/ioudaios/,* 19 October 1995.

Bruns, Gerald. "Canon and Power in the Hebrew Scriptures." *Critical Inquiry* (fall 1984) 462–80.

Bultmann, Rudolf. *History of the Synoptic Tradition.* Trans. John Marsh. New York: Harper and Row, 1963.

Burns, Rita J. "Zipporah." *The Anchor Bible Dictionary.* CD-ROM ed. Ed. David Noel Freedman. New York: Doubleday, 1997.

Calvino, Italo. *If on a Winter's Night a Traveler.* Trans. William Weaver. New York: Harcourt Brace Jovanovich, 1979.

———. "Levels of Reality in Literature." *The Uses of Literature.* Trans. Patrick Creagh. New York: Harcourt Brace Jovanovich, 1986.

Cameron, Ron, ed. *The Other Gospels.* Philadelphia: Westminster Press, 1982.

Carroll, Lewis (Charles Dodgson). *Through the Looking Glass.* New York: Grosset & Dunlap, n.d.

Castelli, Elizabeth. *Imitating Paul: A Discourse of Power.* Louisville: Westminster/ John Knox Press, 1991.

Chatman, Seymour. *Story and Discourse.* Ithaca, N.Y.: Cornell University Press, 1978.

Coote, Robert B., and Mary P. Coote. *Power, Politics, and the Making of the Bible.* Minneapolis: Fortress Press, 1990.

Dan, Joseph. "Midrash and the Dawn of Kabbalah." *Midrash and Literature.* Ed. Geoffrey H. Hartman and Sanford Budick. New Haven: Yale University Press, 1986.

Davies, Philip R. *In Search of "Ancient Israel."* JSOT Supplement 148. Rev. ed. Sheffield: Sheffield Academic Press, 1995.

———. "Loose Canons: Reflections on the Formation of the Hebrew Bible." *Journal of Hebrew Scriptures* 1 (1996) *http://www.ualberta.edu/ARTS/JHS/jhs.html.*

———. *Scribes and Schools: The Canonization of the Hebrew Scriptures.* Louisville: Westminster/John Knox Press, 1998.

———. *Whose Bible Is It Anyway?* Sheffield: Sheffield Academic Press, 1995.

Debray, Régis. *Media Manifestos.* Trans. Eric Rauth. London: Verso, 1996.

Deist, Ferdinand. "Canonical Literature: Some Ideology-Critical Observations." *Concepts of Textuality and Religious Texts.* Acta Academica Supplementum 1. Ed. P. J. Nel and D. J. van den Berg. Bloemfonteine, South Africa: UOVS-SASOL Biblioteek, 1995.

Deleuze, Gilles, and Félix Guattari. *Anti-Oedipus.* Trans. Robert Hurley, Mark Seem, and Helen R. Lane. Minneapolis: University of Minnesota Press, 1983.

———. *A Thousand Plateaus.* Trans. Brian Massumi. Minneapolis: University of Minnesota Press, 1987.

de Man, Paul. *Allegories of Reading.* New Haven: Yale University Press, 1979.

———. *The Resistance to Theory.* Minneapolis: University of Minnesota Press, 1986.

Derrida, Jacques. *Dissemination.* Trans. Barbara Johnson. Chicago: University of Chicago Press, 1981.

———. *The Ear of the Other.* Trans. Peggy Kamuf and Avital Ronell. New York: Schocken Books, 1985.

———. "Living On: Borderlines." Trans. James Hulbert. *Deconstruction and Criticism.* New York: Seabury Press, 1979.

———. *Of Grammatology.* Trans. Gayatri Chakravorty Spivak. Baltimore: Johns Hopkins University Press, 1976.

———. "Shibboleth." *Midrash and Literature.* Ed. Geoffrey H. Hartman and Sanford Budick. New Haven: Yale University Press, 1986.

———. *Speech and Phenomena.* Trans. David B. Allison. Evanston, Ill.: Northwestern University Press, 1973.

———. *Spurs: Nietzsche's Styles.* Trans. Barbara Harlow. Chicago: University of Chicago Press, 1979.

———. "Des Tours de Babel." *Difference in Translation.* Trans. and ed. Joseph F. Graham. Ithaca, N.Y.: Cornell University Press, 1985.

Detweiler, Robert. "What Is a Sacred Text?" *Semeia* 31 (1985) 213–30.

Ducrot, Oswald, and Tzvetan Todorov. *Encyclopedic Dictionary of the Sciences of Language.* Trans. Catherine Porter. Baltimore: Johns Hopkins University Press, 1979.

Dunn, James D. G. *Jesus and the Spirit.* Philadelphia: Westminster Press, 1975.

———. *Unity and Diversity in the New Testament.* Philadelphia: Westminster Press, 1977.

Eco, Umberto. *The Role of the Reader.* Bloomington: Indiana University Press, 1979.

———. *The Search for the Perfect Language.* Trans. James Fentress. Cambridge, Mass.: Blackwell, 1995.

———. *Semiotics and the Philosophy of Language.* Bloomington: Indiana University Press, 1984.

Ehrman, Bart D. *The Orthodox Corruption of Scripture.* Oxford: Oxford University Press, 1993.

Eisenstein, Elizabeth L. *The Printing Press as an Agent of Change.* 2 vols. Cambridge: Cambridge University Press, 1979.

Eissfeldt, Otto. *The Old Testament: An Introduction.* Trans. P. R. Ackroyd. New York: Harper and Row, 1965.

Eliot, T. S. *On Poetry and Poets.* New York: Farrar, Straus and Giroux, 1957.

———. "Tradition and the Individual Talent." *Selected Essays.* New York: Harcourt, Brace, and World, 1964.

Faur, José. *Golden Doves with Silver Dots.* Bloomington: Indiana University Press, 1986.

Fenton, J. C. *Saint Matthew.* Baltimore: Penguin Books, 1963.

Fernhout, Rein. *Canonical Texts: Bearers of Absolute Authority*. Trans. Henry Jansen and Lucy Jansen-Hofland. Currents of Encounter 9. Amsterdam and Atlanta: Editions Rodopi, 1994.

Fishbane, Michael. *Biblical Interpretation in Ancient Israel*. Oxford: Oxford University Press, 1985.

———. "Inner Biblical Exegesis: Types and Strategies of Interpretation in Ancient Israel." *Midrash and Literature*. Ed. Geoffrey H. Hartman and Sanford Budick. New Haven: Yale University Press, 1986.

———. *Text and Texture: Close Reading of Selected Biblical Texts*. New York: Schocken Books, 1979.

Flew, Anthony, and Alasdair MacIntyre. *New Essays in Philosophical Theology*. London: SCM Press, 1961.

Fortna, Robert F. "Signs/Semeia Source." *The Anchor Bible Dictionary*. CD-ROM ed. Ed. David Noel Freedman. New York: Doubleday, 1997.

Foucault, Michel. *The Order of Things*. Trans. A. Sheridan Smith. New York: Random House, 1970.

Fowler, Robert. *Let the Reader Understand*. Minneapolis: Fortress Press, 1991.

———. "Postmodern Biblical Criticism." *Forum* (fall 1989) 3–30.

Frege, Gottlob. *Translations from the Writings of Gottlob Frege*. Trans. and ed. P. T. Geach and M. Black. Totowa, N.J.: Rowman and Littlefield, 1952.

Funk, Robert W. *Jesus as Precursor*. Missoula, Mont.: Scholars Press, 1975.

———. *Parables and Presence*. Philadelphia: Fortress Press, 1982.

Funk, Robert W., Roy W. Hoover, and the Jesus Seminar. *The Five Gospels: The Search for the Authentic Words of Jesus*. Sonoma, Calif.: Polebridge Press; Riverside, N.J.: Macmillan, 1993.

Gadamer, Hans-Georg. *Truth and Method*. Trans. Garrett Barden and John Cumming. New York: Seabury Press, 1975.

Gamble, Harry Y. *Books and Readers in the Early Church*. New Haven: Yale University Press, 1995.

———. "The Codex." *The Anchor Bible Dictionary*. CD-ROM ed. Ed. David Noel Freedman. New York: Doubleday, 1997.

———. *The New Testament Canon: Its Making and Meaning*. Philadelphia: Fortress Press, 1985.

Graham, William A. *Beyond the Written Word*. Cambridge: Cambridge University Press, 1987.

Green, William Scott. "Romancing the Tome: Rabbinic Hermeneutics and the Theory of Literature." *Semeia* 40: *Text and Textuality*. Ed. Charles E. Winquist. Decatur, Ga.: Scholars Press, 1987.

Greenspoon, Leonard J. "Theodotion, Theodotion's Version." *The Anchor Bible Dictionary*. CD-ROM ed. Ed. David Noel Freedman. New York: Doubleday, 1997.

Halpern, Baruch. "Fallacies Intentional and Canonical: Metalogical Confusion about the Authority of Canonical Texts." IOUDAIOS-L Archives *http://ccat.sas.upenn.edu/ioudaios/*, 1990.

Haraway, Donna J. *Simians, Cyborgs, and Women: The Reinvention of Nature*. New York: Routledge, 1991.

Hartman, Geoffrey H., and Sanford Budick, eds. *Midrash and Literature*. New Haven: Yale University Press, 1986.

Hayles, N. Katherine. *How We Became Posthuman: Virtual Bodies in Cybernetics, Literature, and Informatics*. Chicago: University of Chicago Press, 1999.

Hays, Richard B. *Echoes of Scripture in the Letters of Paul*. New Haven: Yale University Press, 1989.

Huizinga, Johann. *Homo Ludens*. Boston: Beacon Press, 1950.

Hurtado, L. W. "The Origin of the *Nomina Sacra:* A Proposal." *Journal of Biblical Literature* (winter 1998) 655–73.

Husserl, Edmund. *Ideas*. Trans. W. R. Boyce Gibson. New York: Macmillan, 1962.

Ingarden, Roman. *The Literary Work of Art*. Trans. George G. Grabowicz. Evanston, Ill.: Northwestern University Press, 1973.

Ingraffia, Brian D. *Postmodern Theory and Biblical Theology: Vanquishing God's Shadow*. Cambridge and New York: Cambridge University Press, 1995.

Jabès, Edmond. "The Key." *Midrash and Literature*. Ed. Geoffrey H. Hartman and Sanford Budick. New Haven: Yale University Press, 1986.

Jaffee, Martin S. "The Oral-Cultural Content of the Talmud Yerushalmi." *The Talmud Yerushalmi and Greco-Roman Culture*. Ed. Peter Schäfer. Tübingen: Mohr Siebeck, 1998.

———. "A Rabbinic Ontology of the Written and Spoken Word: On Discipleship, Transformative Knowledge, and the Living Texts of Oral Torah." *Journal of the American Academy of Religion* (fall 1997) 525–49.

Jakobson, Roman. *Language and Literature*. Ed. Krystyna Pomorska and Stephen Rudy. Cambridge: Belknap Press of Harvard University, 1987.

Jameson, Fredric. *Postmodernism, or the Cultural Logic of Late Capitalism*. Durham, N.C.: Duke University Press, 1991.

Johnson, Sherman E. *A Commentary on the Gospel according to St. Mark*. London: Adam & Charles Black, 1960.

Kafka, Franz. "In the Penal Colony." *The Penal Colony*. Trans. Willa Muir and Edwin Muir. New York: Schocken Books, 1948.

———. *Parables and Paradoxes*. Various trans. New York: Schocken Books, 1958.

———. *The Trial*. Trans. Willa Muir and Edwin Muir; rev. E. M. Butler. New York: Vintage Books, 1956.

Kermode, Frank. *The Classic*. New York: Viking Press, 1975.

———. *The Genesis of Secrecy*. Cambridge: Harvard University Press, 1979.

———. "The Plain Sense of Things." *Midrash and Literature*. Ed. Geoffrey H. Hartman and Sanford Budick. New Haven: Yale University Press, 1986.

———. *Romantic Image*. New York: Random House, 1957.

Kloppenborg, John S., Marvin W. Meyer, Stephen J. Patterson, and Michael G. Steinhauser. *Q-Thomas Reader*. Sonoma, Calif.: Polebridge Press, 1990.

Kmiecik, Ulrich. *Der Menschensohn im Markusevangelium*. Forschung zur Bibel, Band 81. Würzburg, Germany: Echter Verlag, 1997.

Kristeva, Julia. *Desire in Language*. Trans. Thomas Gora, Alice Jardine, and Leon S. Roudiez. New York: Columbia University Press, 1980.

———. *Language: The Unknown*. Trans. Anne M. Menke. New York: Columbia University Press, 1989.

————. *Revolution in Poetic Language.* Trans. Margaret Waller. New York: Columbia University Press, 1984.

Kuhn, Thomas S. *The Structure of Scientific Revolutions.* Chicago: University of Chicago Press, 1970.

Lattimore, Richmond, trans. *The Four Gospels and the Revelation.* New York: Dorset Press, 1979.

Lévi-Strauss, Claude. *Tristes Tropiques.* New York: Atheneum, 1970.

Lyotard, Jean-François. *The Differend.* Trans. Georges Van Den Abbeele. Minneapolis: University of Minnesota Press, 1988.

————. *The Postmodern Condition: A Report on Knowledge.* Trans. Geoff Bennington and Brian Massumi. Minneapolis: University of Minnesota Press, 1984.

Mack, Burton L. *A Myth of Innocence: Mark and Christian Origins.* Philadelphia: Fortress Press, 1988.

Marcus, Joel. *The Way of the Lord: Christological Exegesis of the Old Testament in the Gospel of Mark.* Louisville: Westminster/John Knox Press, 1992.

Marks, Herbert. "Pauline Typology and Revisionary Criticism." *Journal of the American Academy of Religion* (March 1984) 71–92.

Marx, Karl. *The Letters of Karl Marx.* Englewood Cliffs, N.J.: Prentice-Hall, 1979.

McCaffery, Larry, ed. *Storming the Reality Studio.* Durham, N.C.: Duke University Press, 1991.

Metzger, Bruce M. *The Canon of the New Testament: Its Origin, Development, and Significance.* Oxford: Clarendon Press, 1987.

————. *The Text of the New Testament: Its Transmission, Corruption, and Restoration.* 3d ed. Oxford: Oxford University Press, 1992.

Morris, William. *News from Nowhere, or, an Epoch of Rest from a Utopian Romance.* Pocket Edition, New Impression. London: Longmans, Green, 1918.

Morrow, James. *Blameless in Abaddon.* New York: Harcourt Brace, 1996.

————. *The Eternal Footman.* New York: Harcourt Brace, 2000.

————. *Towing Jehovah.* New York: Harcourt Brace, 1994.

Moule, C. F. D. *The Birth of the New Testament.* London: Adam & Charles Black, 1966.

Neirynck, Frans, ed. *The Minor Agreements of Matthew and Luke against Mark.* BETL 37. Louvain, Belgium: Louvain University Press, 1974.

Nickelsburg, George W. E. "Son of Man." *The Anchor Bible Dictionary.* CD-ROM ed. Ed. David Noel Freedman. New York: Doubleday, 1997.

Nida, Eugene, and Charles R. Taber. *The Theory and Practice of Translation.* Leiden: Brill, 1982.

Nietzsche, Friedrich. *Beyond Good and Evil.* Trans. R. J. Hollingdale. London: Penguin Books, 1990.

Nineham, D. E. *Saint Mark.* Middlesex, England: Penguin Books, 1963.

Oates, Whitney J., ed. *The Stoic and the Epicurean Philosophers.* New York: Random House, 1940.

Oden, Thomas C., and Christopher A. Hall, eds. *Ancient Christian Commentary on Scripture, New Testament, II, Mark.* Downers Grove, Ill.: InterVarsity Press, 1998.

Olson, Mark J. "Pentecost." *The Anchor Bible Dictionary.* CD-ROM ed. Ed. David Noel Freedman. New York: Doubleday, 1997.

Ong, Walter J. *Interfaces of the Word.* Ithaca, N.Y.: Cornell University Press, 1977.

———. *The Presence of the Word.* New Haven: Yale University Press, 1967.

Peirce, Charles Sanders. *The Essential Peirce: Selected Philosophical Writings.* Vol. 1 (1867–93). Ed. Nathan Houser and Christian Kloesel. Bloomington: Indiana University Press, 1992.

Petersen, William L., ed. *Gospel Traditions in the Second Century.* Notre Dame, Ind.: University of Notre Dame Press, 1989.

Plato. *Phaedrus.* Trans. Walter Hamilton. Middlesex, England: Penguin Books, 1973.

Quine, Willard Van Orman. *Word and Object.* Cambridge: M.I.T. Press, 1960.

Rabkin, Eric S. *The Fantastic in Literature.* Princeton, N.J.: Princeton University Press, 1976.

Resnick, Irven M. "The Codex in Early Jewish and Christian Communities." *Journal of Religious History* (Spring 1992) 1–17.

Ricoeur, Paul. *Interpretation Theory.* Fort Worth: T.C.U. Press, 1976.

Roberts, Colin. *Manuscript, Society, and Belief in Early Christian Egypt.* British Academy. London: Oxford University Press, 1979.

Roberts, Colin H., and T. C. Skeat. *The Birth of the Codex.* British Academy. London: Oxford University Press, 1983.

Robinson, James M. *The Problem of History in Mark, and Other Marcan Studies.* Philadelphia: Fortress Press, 1982.

Robinson, James M., and Helmut Koester. *Trajectories through Early Christianity.* Philadelphia: Fortress Press, 1971.

Sanders, James A. *Canon and Community.* Philadelphia: Fortress Press, 1984.

Saussure, Ferdinand de. *Course in General Linguistics.* Ed. Charles Bally et al. Trans. Wade Baskin. New York: McGraw-Hill, 1959.

Schneidau, Herbert N. *Sacred Discontent: The Bible and the Western Tradition.* Baton Rouge: Louisiana State University Press, 1976.

Scholem, Gershom. *Kabbalah.* New York: Dorset Press, 1987 (Jerusalem, 1974).

Schüssler-Fiorenza, Elisabeth. *Searching the Scriptures.* Vol. 2. New York: Crossroad, 1994.

Schwartz, Regina, ed. *The Book and the Text.* Cambridge, Mass.: Basil Blackwell, 1990.

Serres, Michel. *The Parasite.* Trans. Lawrence R. Schehr. Baltimore: Johns Hopkins University Press, 1982.

Smith, Jonathan Z. "Sacred Persistence: Toward a Redescription of Canon." *Imagining Religion: From Babylon to Jonestown.* Chicago: University of Chicago Press, 1982.

Spina, Frank Anthony. "Babel." *The Anchor Bible Dictionary.* CD-ROM ed. Ed. David Noel Freedman. New York: Doubleday, 1997.

Steiner, George. *After Babel.* New York: Oxford University Press, 1975.

Stendahl, Krister. "The Bible as Classic and the Bible as Holy Scripture." *Journal of Biblical Literature* (1984) 3–10.

Stephenson, Neal. *Snow Crash.* New York: Bantam Books, 1992.

Sundberg, Albert C., Jr. *The Old Testament of the Early Church.* Cambridge: Harvard University Press, 1964.

Taylor, Vincent. *The Gospel according to Saint Mark*. London: Macmillan, 1953.

Todorov, Tzvetan. *The Fantastic*. Trans. Richard Howard. Cleveland: Case Western Reserve University Press, 1973.

Tödt, Heinz Eduard. *The Son of Man in the Synoptic Tradition*. Trans. Dorothea M. Barton. Philadelphia: Westminster Press, 1965.

Tracy, David. *The Analogical Imagination*. New York: Crossroad, 1981.

———. *Blessed Rage for Order*. New York: Seabury Press, 1975.

———. "Metaphor and Religion: The Test Case of Christian Texts." *On Metaphor*. Ed. Sheldon Sacks. Chicago: University of Chicago Press, 1978.

———. *Plurality and Ambiguity*. San Francisco: Harper and Row, 1987.

Vermes, Geza. "The Use of *Bar Nâsh/Bar Nâshâ* in Jewish Aramaic." Appendix to M. Black, *An Aramaic Approach to the Gospels and Acts*. 3d ed. Oxford: Oxford University Press, 1967.

Wilken, Robert L. *The Myth of Christian Beginnings*. Garden City, N.Y.: Doubleday, 1971.

INDEX OF SCRIPTURE
AND RELATED TEXTS

OLD TESTAMENT
(Septuagint, unless otherwise noted)

Genesis
1–3	109
1–10	107
1–11	107–8, 118
1:1–2:4a (RSV)	108
1:25 (RSV)	115
1:26 (RSV)	116
2–3	108–9, 111, 113, 115
2–11	108
2:16–17 (RSV)	116
2:17 (RSV)	115
3:1 (RSV)	115
3:4–6 (RSV)	115
3:22 (RSV)	110, 116
10:5 (RSV)	108–9
10:10 (RSV)	108
10:20 (RSV)	108
10:31 (RSV)	108
11:1	109–10, 114
11:1–9	64, 107
11:2	108
11:4	118–19, 122
11:5	109, 155
11:6	110
11:7	110, 119
11:8	119, 123
11:9	108, 110, 123
12:1 (RSV)	108
17:4–5 (RSV)	139
17:10–11 (RSV)	139
21:23	201
32:29 (RSV)	202
32:30	201
48:16	201–2

Exodus
2:22 (RSV)	140
3:13–15	201
3:15	201
4:22–23	140
4:24–26	140–43, 148
6:3	201

6:12 (RSV)	138
9:16	201, 203
18:21 (RSV)	188
20:7 (RSV)	201
20:10 (RSV)	187
20:24	201
23:21	201
33:19	201

Leviticus
19:12	201
24:5–9 (RSV)	187

Numbers
6:23	201
6:27 (RSV)	202
14:21	201

Deuteronomy
4:2 (RSV)	25
4:25–31 (RSV)	42
5:14 (RSV)	187
18:19–20	201
25:4 (RSV)	95

Judges
13:18	201–2

1 Samuel
21:1–6 (RSV)	173, 186
21:2	186
24:22	201
25:5	201–2
26:19	155

2 Samuel
6:12–19 (RSV)	174
7:13	201
7:14	155
12:28	201

1 Kings
5:19	201
8:16	201–2
8:18–19	201

1 Kings (continued)
8:29	*201*
8:39	*155*
9:3	*201*
9:7	*201*
11:36	*201*

2 Kings
21:4	*201*
21:7	*201*
22:8 (RSV)	*41*
22:11 (RSV)	*41*
22:13 (RSV)	*42*
22:15 (RSV)	*41*
22:16 (RSV)	*42*
23:3 (RSV)	*41*
23:27	*201*

1 Chronicles
22:8	*201*
22:10	*201*
28:3	*201*

2 Chronicles
6:5–6	*201*
6:8–9	*201*
6:30	*155*
7:14	*201*
7:16	*201*
7:20	*201*
33:4	*201*
33:7	*201*
35:19	*201*

1 Esdras
4:37	*155*
8:85	*201*

2 Esdras
11:9	*201*
14:3–6 (RSV)	*42*
14:21–22 (RSV)	*42*
14:40–42 (RSV)	*42*

Esther
8:8	*201–2*

Job
16:21	*155*
19:14	*201–2*
25:6	*155*
35:8	*155*

Psalms
4:3	*155*
8:5	*155, 157, 170*
10:4	*154*
11:2	*155*

11:9	*155*
13:2	*155*
20:11	*155*
30:20	*155*
32:13	*155*
35:8	*155*
44:3	*155*
48:3	*155*
52:3	*155*
56:5	*155*
57:2	*155*
61:10	*155*
65:5	*155*
79:16	*155*
79:18	*155, 170–71*
88:25	*201*
88:48	*155*
89:3	*155*
89:24 (RSV)	*202*
90:14	*201*
102:1	*201*
106:8	*155*
106:15	*155*
106:21	*155*
106:31	*155*
113:24	*155*
118:22–23 (RSV)	*171, 174*
118:26 (RSV)	*174*
143:3	*155*
144:12	*155*
145:3	*155*

Proverbs
8:4	*155*
8:31	*155*

Ecclesiastes
1:13	*155*
2:3	*155*
2:8	*155*
3:10	*155*
3:18	*155*
3:19	*155*
3:21	*155*
8:11	*155*
9:3	*155*
9:12	*155*

Isaiah
6:9–10 (RSV)	*213, 216*
9:7 (RSV)	*174*
22:22 (RSV)	*176*
29:23	*201*
41:25	*201*
42:8	*201*
43:7	*201*
48:9	*201*
48:11	*201*

49:1	*201–2*
51:12	*154, 155*
51:15	*201*
52:5–6	*201*
53:3	*158*
55:3 (RSV)	*174, 181*
65:1	*201*
66:19	*201*

Jeremiah

2:6	*155*
4:4 (RSV)	*138*
7:10–12	*201*
7:14	*201*
7:30	*201*
12:16	*201*
14:14–15	*201*
16:21	*201*
23:5 (RSV)	*174*
23:25	*201*
23:27	*201*
27:40	*155*
28:43	*155*
30:12	*155*
30:28	*155*
31:31–33 (RSV)	*135*
32:29	*201*
34:15	*201*
36:9	*201*
36:23	*201*
36:25	*201*
39:19	*155*
39:34	*201*
41:15–16	*201*
51:16	*201*
51:26	*201*

Ezekiel

2:1	*155*
2:3	*155*
2:6	*155*
2:8	*155*
3:1	*155*
3:3–4	*155*
3:10	*155*
3:17	*155*
3:25	*155*
4:1	*155*
4:16	*155*
5:1	*155*
6:2	*155*
7:2	*155*
8:5–6	*155*
8:8	*155*
8:12	*155*
8:15	*155*
8:17	*155*

11:2	*155*
11:4	*155*
11:15	*155*
12:2–3	*155*
12:9	*155*
12:18	*155*
12:22	*155*
12:27	*155*
13:2	*155*
13:17	*155*
14:3	*155*
14:13	*155*
15:2	*155*
16:2	*155*
17:2	*155*
17:12	*155*
18:2	*155*
20:3–4	*155*
20:9	*201–2*
20:14	*201*
20:22	*201*
20:27	*155*
20:39	*201*
20:44	*201*
21:2	*155*
21:7	*155*
21:11	*155*
21:14	*155*
21:17	*155*
21:19	*155*
21:24	*155*
21:33	*155*
22:2	*155*
22:18	*155*
22:24	*155*
23:2	*155*
23:36	*155*
24:2	*155*
24:16	*155*
24:25	*155*
25:2	*155*
26:2	*155*
27:2	*155*
28:2	*155*
28:12	*155*
28:21	*155*
29:2	*155*
29:18	*155*
30:2	*155*
30:21	*155*
31:2	*155*
31:14	*155*
31:18 (RSV)	*135*
32:2	*155*
32:18	*155*
33:2	*155*
33:7	*155*

Ezekiel (continued)
33:10	*155*
33:24	*155*
33:30	*155*
34:2	*155*
35:2	*155*
36:1	*155*
36:17	*155*
36:20–23	*201*
36:26 (RSV)	*135*
37:3	*155*
37:9	*155*
37:11	*155*
37:16	*155*
37:24 (RSV)	*174*
38:2	*155*
38:14	*155*
39:1	*155*
39:7	*201*
39:17	*155*
40:4	*155*
43:7	*155, 201*
43:10	*155*
43:18	*155*
44:5	*155*
47:6	*155*

Daniel
2:38	*155*
3:82	*155*
7:13	*151, 155–57, 161, 166–67, 170, 203*
7:14	*156*
7:27	*151*
8:17	*155*
10:16	*156–57*
12:4 (RSV)	*vii*

Joel
1:12	*155*

Amos
9:11 (RSV)	*174*
9:12	*201–3*

Jonah
1:17 (RSV)	*211*
2:10 (RSV)	*211*
3:3–9 (RSV)	*211*

Micah
5:6	*155*
7:4	*26*

Zechariah
5:4	*201*
13:9	*201*

Malachi
1:6	*201*
1:11	*201–2*
1:14	*201*
2:2	*201*
2:5	*201*
3:5	*201*
3:20	*201*
4:5–6 (RSV)	*158*

Judith
8:12	*155*
8:16	*155*
13:6	*26*

Tobit
3:15	*201–2*

4 Maccabees
7:21	*26*

Odes
8:82	*155*

Ecclesiasticus
17:30	*155*
36:23	*155*

Psalms of Solomon
9:4	*155*

Wisdom of Solomon
2:4	*201*
9:6	*155*

Baruch
2:32	*201–2*

NEW TESTAMENT

Matthew
1:1	*175, 178*
1:6	*175*
1:17	*175, 178*
1:20	*175–76*
1:20–25	*184*
1:21	*204, 206*
1:23	*204*
1:25	*204, 206*
3:16	*184*
4:3–10	*180*
5:11	*200*
6:9	*204*
8:20	*163*
8:28–34	*188*
9:6	*162*
9:22	*210*

9:27	*175*	21:1–7	*189*
10:2	*204*	21:5	*183*
10:10	*95*	21:9	*174–75, 183, 204*
10:18	*200*	21:13	*188*
10:22	*202*	21:15	*174–75*
10:23	*163*	21:15–16	*183*
10:39	*200*	21:33–46	*171, 174, 188*
10:41–42	*204*	21:42	*171*
10:42	*205*	21:45–46	*189*
11:2–6	*210, 212*	22:35	*183*
11:19	*166*	22:41–42	*178*
11:21	*210–11*	22:41–46	*182*
11:27	*163*	22:42–43	*175*
12:3	*175*	22:45	*175*
12:3–4	*186*	23:37–39	*191*
12:8	*162, 186*	23:39	*204*
12:21	*204*	24:3	*209*
12:23	*175, 190*	24:5	*202*
12:24–32	*165*	24:9	*202*
12:29	*188*	24:23–24	*207*
12:31–32	*165*	24:24	*209*
12:32	*163*	24:27	*163*
12:38	*210*	24:30	*163, 209*
12:38–39	*209*	24:37–39	*163*
12:39–41	*210–11*	24:44	*163*
12:40	*163*	25:29	*217*
12:42	*212*	25:31	*163*
12:46–50	*165*	26:2	*162*
13:2	*213*	26:3–4	*189*
13:10–17	*216*	26:8	*189*
13:12	*217*	26:17–19	*189*
13:13	*213*	26:24	*162*
13:37	*163*	26:45	*162*
13:41	*163*	26:48	*212*
13:44	*188*	26:51	*189*
13:53–58	*210*	26:55	*189*
15:22	*175*	26:64	*162*
15:28	*210*	27:16–17	*188*
16:1	*209–10*	27:37	*188*
16:1–4	*214*	28:19	*204*
16:3	*212*		
16:4	*209*	**Mark**	
16:13	*163*	1:4–15	*158*
16:25	*200*	1:10–11	*184*
16:27–28	*163*	2:10	*159, 161*
17:9	*162–63*	2:25	*175*
17:11–12	*163*	2:25–26	*185–87, 189*
17:12	*162*	2:27–28	*159, 161, 163, 186*
17:22	*162*	3:19–35	*165, 168*
18:5	*202–3*	3:27	*188*
18:20	*202*	3:28	*154, 157, 159, 165–72*
19:28	*163*	3:28–29	*164*
19:29	*202*	3:30	*168*
20:18	*162*	3:34–35	*171*
20:28	*162*	4:10–13	*216*
20:29–34	*178*	4:11	*213*
20:30–31	*175*	4:25	*217*
20:34	*179*	5:1–20	*188*

Mark (continued) _____
5:9	*202–3*
5:34	*170, 179, 210*
6:1–6	*210*
6:3	*178*
6:14	*204*
6:14–29	*158*
6:40	*188*
7:29	*170, 179, 210*
8:1–10	*216*
8:11	*210*
8:11–12	*209, 215–16*
8:22–25	*179*
8:27–33	*158, 206*
8:31	*159*
8:35	*200*
8:36–37	*160*
8:38	*159, 215*
9:7	*184*
9:9	*159, 163*
9:12–13	*158–59, 163*
9:24–25	*210*
9:31	*159*
9:37	*202*
9:38	*204*
9:38–41	*205–7*
9:39	*202*
9:41	*204*
10:29	*200*
10:33–34	*159–60*
10:45	*160, 163*
10:46–52	*178*
10:47–48	*175–76*
10:51–52	*179*
10:52	*210*
11:1–7	*189*
11:9	*204*
11:9–10	*175, 177*
11:10	*174–76*
11:13	*188*
11:17	*188*
11:23–24	*170, 179*
12:1–12	*171, 174, 188*
12:6	*160*
12:10	*171*
12:12	*189*
12:13	*183*
12:34	*183*
12:35	*176, 178–80, 182*
12:35–37	*175, 182–84, 186*
12:40–41	*189*
12:43–44	*189*
13:3–4	*209*
13:4	*212*
13:6	*202–4, 207*
13:9	*200*
13:13	*202*
13:14	*171*

13:21–22	*207*
13:22	*209*
13:26–27	*160, 190*
13:32	*160*
14:1–2	*189*
14:4	*189*
14:12–16	*189*
14:21	*160*
14:35–41	*184*
14:36	*114*
14:41	*160, 163*
14:47–48	*189*
14:48–49	*1, 10*
14:61–62	*206*
14:62	*160*
15:7	*188*
15:26	*188*
15:34	*184*
15:34–35	*158*
16:8	*162*
16:17	*202–3, 209*
16:20	*209*

Luke _____
1:1–4	*197*
1:5	*204*
1:13	*204*
1:27	*174–76, 204*
1:31	*204, 206*
1:32	*175, 178*
1:49	*204*
1:59	*138, 204*
1:63	*204*
1:69	*175, 178*
2:4	*174–76*
2:11	*174–75*
2:12	*212*
2:21	*138, 204, 206*
2:34	*212*
3:22–23	*184*
3:31	*175*
4:3–12	*180*
5:24	*162*
6:3	*175*
6:3–4	*186*
6:5	*162, 186*
6:22	*163, 204*
7:18–23	*210*
7:24–35	*166*
7:34	*166*
8:4	*213*
8:10	*216*
8:18	*217*
8:19–21	*165*
8:26–39	*188*
8:48	*210*
9:14	*188*
9:22	*162*

9:24	200
9:26	162
9:44	162
9:48	202
9:49	204–5
9:50	205
9:58	163
10:7	95
10:13	210–11
10:17	204–5
10:20	204
10:22	163
10:25	183
11:2	204
11:15–23	165
11:16	209–10, 212
11:21–22	188
11:29	209
11:29–30	212
11:30	163, 212
11:31–32	212
12:8	163
12:10	163, 165
12:40	163
12:54–56	214
13:33–35	191
13:35	204
16:1–9	188
16:8	163
17:22	163
17:24–30	163
18:2–5	188
18:8	163
18:31	163
18:35–43	178
18:38–39	175
18:42	179, 210
19:10	163
19:26	217
19:29–35	189
19:38	174, 204
19:46	188
20:9–19	171, 174, 188
20:17	171
20:19	189
20:34	163
20:41	178
20:41–42	175
20:41–44	182
20:42	181
20:44	175
20:47	189
21:1	189
21:3–4	189
21:7	209, 212
21:8	202
21:11	209
21:12	202

21:17	202–3
21:25	212
21:27	162
21:36	163
22:2	189
22:7–12	189
22:22	162
22:27	163
22:48	163
22:49–50	189
22:52	189
22:69	162
23:8	209–10
23:38	188
24:7	162
24:47	204

John

1:1–14	192
1:1–18	158
1:12	204
1:51	157
2:11	209
2:18	209–10
2:23	204, 209
3:2	209
3:13–14	157
3:18	204
4:48	209
4:54	209
5:27	157
5:43	204
6:2	209
6:14	209
6:26	209
6:27	157
6:30	209
6:53–54	157
6:57	200
6:62	157
7:22	181
7:22–23	138
7:31	209
7:42	174–76, 185
8:28	157–58
9:16	209
9:35	157
10:9	200
10:25	204
10:41	209
11:47	209
12:13	204
12:18	209
12:23	157
12:30	200
12:34	157–58
12:37	209

John (continued)
13:31	*157*
14:6	*200*
14:13–14	*202*
14:26	*202*
15:16	*202*
15:21	*202*
16:23–24	*202*
16:24	*204, 207*
16:26	*202*
17:11–12	*204*
17:26	*204*
18:36	*190*
20:30	*209*
20:31	*204*

Acts
1:16	*175*
1:16–20	*181*
2:1	*124*
2:1–42	*110*
2:2–3	*121*
2:4	*121, 124*
2:4–6	*110*
2:4–11	*128*
2:5–6	*127*
2:6	*111*
2:7–8	*111*
2:8	*121, 126, 129*
2:12	*124, 224*
2:13	*128*
2:14–43	*124, 127*
2:17–18	*111*
2:19	*209*
2:21	*204*
2:22	*209*
2:25	*175*
2:29	*175*
2:29–30	*185*
2:29–36	*181*
2:32	*125*
2:34	*175*
2:37–43	*125*
2:38	*204*
2:41	*125*
2:43	*209*
2:44–47	*125, 128*
2:45	*119*
3:6	*204*
3:16	*204*
4:10	*204*
4:16	*209*
4:18	*204*
4:22	*209*
4:24–30	*181*
4:25–27	*177*
4:25	*175, 182*
4:30	*204, 209*

5:12	*209*
5:40	*204*
6:8	*209*
7:8	*138*
7:36	*209*
7:45	*175, 185*
7:51	*138*
7:55–56	*157*
8:6	*209*
8:12	*204*
8:13	*209*
8:16	*204*
9:14	*204*
9:15–16	*202–3*
9:27–28	*204*
10:43	*204*
10:45	*138*
10:48	*204*
11:2–3	*138*
11:29	*119*
13:6	*204*
13:8	*204*
13:22	*175*
13:22–23	*176*
13:33–36	*174*
13:34	*175*
13:34–39	*181*
13:36	*175*
13:36–37	*185*
14:3	*209*
15:1	*138*
15:5	*138*
15:12	*209*
15:14	*204*
15:16	*174–75*
15:17	*202*
15:26	*204*
16:3	*138*
16:18	*204*
18:7	*204*
19:5	*204*
19:13	*204*
19:17	*204*
21:13	*204*
21:21	*138*
22:16	*204*
26:9	*204*

Romans
1:3	*175–76*
1:5	*204*
2:24	*204*
2:25–29	*135*
2:25–3:1	*138*
3:30	*138*
4:4–8	*181*
4:6	*175*

4:9–12	*138*
4:9–13	*139*
4:11	*212*
7:6	*136*
9:17	*202–3*
10:13	*204*
11:5–10	*181*
11:9	*175*
14:17	*190*
15:8	*138*
15:9	*204*
15:19	*209*

1 Corinthians

1:2	*204*
1:10	*204*
1:13	*204*
1:15	*202–3*
1:17	*203*
1:22	*212*
5:4	*204*
5:11	*204*
6:11	*204*
7:18–19	*134, 138*
14:22	*209*
15:49–50	*190*

2 Corinthians

3:1–6	*135*
3:2	*139*
3:3	*42*
3:6	*42*
3:7–4:6	*139*
3:15	*139*
3:17	*138*
3:18	*139*
10:13	*26*
10:15–16	*26*
12:12	*209*

Galatians

2:3	*138*
2:7–9	*138*
2:12	*138*
3:6	*139*
3:16	*139*
4:23–24	*139*
4:29	*139, 177*
5:2–3	*138–39*
5:2–4	*134*
5:5–6	*134*
5:6	*139*
5:11	*139*
5:12	*134*
6:12–13	*139*
6:15	*139*
6:16	*26*

Ephesians

1:21	*204*
2:11	*139*
2:19–20	*94*
3:5	*156, 167*
5:20	*204*

Philippians

2:1–11	*192*
2:10	*204*
3:3	*139*
3:5	*139*
3:23	*134*

Colossians

2:11	*139*
2:13	*139*
3:11	*139*
3:17	*204*
4:11	*139*

2 Thessalonians

1:12	*204*
2:9	*209*
3:6	*204*
3:17	*212*

1 Timothy

5:8	*95*
6:1	*204*

2 Timothy

2:8	*175–76*
2:19	*204*
3:16–17	*25*

Titus

1:10	*139*

Hebrews

2:4	*209*
2:6	*157*
2:12	*204*
4:7	*175, 181*
6:10	*204*
11:32	*175*
11:32–33	*185*
13:15	*204*

James

5:10	*204*
5:14	*204*

1 Peter

4:14	*204*

1 John	
2:12	*204*
3:23	*204*
5:13	*204*

Revelation	
1:13	*157, 203*
1:18	*203*
2:3	*202–3*
2:13	*202–3*
3:1	*204*
3:5	*204*
3:7	*175–76*
3:8	*202–3*
3:12	*202–4*
5:5	*175–76*
8:11	*204*
11:13	*204*
11:18	*204*
12:1	*209*
12:3	*209*
13:1	*204*
13:6	*204*
13:8	*204*
13:13–14	*209*
13:17	*204*
14:1	*204*
14:11	*204*
14:14	*157*
15:1	*209*
15:2	*204*
15:4	*204*
16:4	*209*

16:9	*204*
17:3	*204*
17:5	*204*
19:13	*204*
19:20	*209*
21:12	*204*
21:14	*204*
22:4	*204*
22:6–7	*vii*
22:16	*175–76*
22:18–19	*26*

NONCANONICAL TEXTS

1 Enoch	
60:10	*155*
69:6	*155*

Gospel of Thomas	
1–2	*214*
28	*169*
50	*214*
53	*135*
91	*214*
98	*188*
106	*153, 169–70*
114	*141*

"Secret Mark"	*197–98*

Talmud	*47–49, 64–65*

INDEX OF NAMES

Adam, A. K. M., 213
Adams, D., 127
Aichele, G.
  on the identity of Jesus, 168, 180,
    187
  on intertextuality, 10, 18–19, 22–23
  on semiotics in general, 15–16, 112,
    136
  on theology, 12, 81
Aland, B., 3, 28, 43, 67, 197
Aland, K. See B. Aland
Altieri, C., 8–9, 12
Altizer, T. J. J., 12
"Aristeas (letter of)," 64, 67
Assmann, A., 120
Auerbach, E., 94

Bailey, R., 81
Barnstone, W., 31, 118, 123
Barr, J., 6, 12, 20, 22, 24, 26, 28–29,
    37, 68, 190
Barthes, R.
  on connotation and denotation,
    76–78, 131–33, 177
  on readerly and writerly, 74, 123,
    192, 199
  on semiotics in general, 1, 4, 48,
    97, 109, 140, 148, 159, 194,
    233–35
  on work and text, 15–16, 70, 73
Barton, J.
  on canon in general, 16, 21, 25,
    170, 194, 207
  on the Jewish canon, 2–3, 6, 26, 28,
    32–33, 36, 45–47, 94, 181
Bauer, W., 32–34, 81–82, 95, 98–100,
    102
Beckwith, R., 4, 30

Benjamin, W.
  on Kafka, 143, 145–46
  on print culture, 223, 230
  on the Tower of Babel, 110, 118,
    120, 128
  on translation, 35, 71–75, 78, 80,
    123
Berg, T., 216
Berquist, J., 28, 96
Black, C., 196
Boer, R., 70, 142
Borges, J. L., 31–32, 34–37, 73, 147,
    224
Boyarin, D., 82, 129, 134, 137,
    141–42, 149
Brumberg-Kraus, J., 29
Budick, S., 65
Bultmann, R., 165
Burnett, F., 119
Burns, R., 140
Burroughs, W., 218

Calvino, I., 62, 130, 157, 173
Carroll, L., 207–8, 224
Carroll, R., 81
Castelli, E., 136–37, 149
Celsus, 32, 94
Cervantes, M. de, 31–32
Constantine, 27, 89, 96, 98, 100
Coote, M., 28, 99
Coote, R. See M. Coote

Dan, J., 29, 66
Davies, P., 6, 8, 27–28, 40, 67, 151,
    153–56, 171, 230
Debray, R., 4, 15, 39, 53, 150
Deist, F., 28
Deleuze, G., 97, 101, 119, 123–25,
    189, 215, 228

de Man, P., 73, 132
Derrida, J.
  on logocentrism, 8, 29–30, 93, 132, 233
  on translation, 62, 70, 107
  on writing, 40–41, 66, 130, 146–47
Detweiler, R., 30, 94, 103
Dilthey, W., 91
Dodgson, C. *See* L. Carroll
Ducrot, O., 112
Dunn, J., 5, 7, 31, 98–100, 165–66

Eagleton, T., 8
Eco, U., 1, 109, 111–18, 120, 122, 128–29, 132
Ehrman, B., 20, 29, 33, 93, 98–99, 102
Eisenstein, E., 51–53, 54, 221–22, 224
Eissfeldt, O., 141
Eliot, T. S., 34–35, 87–90, 92, 96, 100–101, 103, 231
Epicurus, 120, 225
Epiphanius, 197–99
Eusebius, 27, 95, 98, 196

Faur, J., 24, 35–36, 65–66, 73, 83, 139
Fenton, J. C., 212, 214
Fernhout, R., 5
Fishbane, M., 11, 35–36, 140–42
Flew, A. 5, 7
Foucault, M., 17, 100, 153
Fowler, R., 5, 157, 167, 187, 200, 218
Frege, G., 70–71, 75–76, 78–79, 132–33, 233
Funk, R., 5, 7, 35, 43, 54, 86–87, 93, 98

Gadamer, H.-G., 92
Gamble, H.
  on canon, 6–8, 19, 21, 30, 33, 84–86, 94, 96, 98, 164, 195
  on manuscript culture and the codex, 38, 43, 46–47, 49–50
Graham, W., 26
Green, W., 66
Greenspoon, L., 155

Guattari, F. *See* G. Deleuze
Gutenberg, J., 52

Hall, C. *See* T. Oden
Halpern, B., 45
Haraway, D., 153
Hare, R. M., 5–7, 233
Hartman, G., 8, 65
Hayles, K., 60, 118, 153, 226–27, 229–30
Hays, R., 11, 136, 138, 147, 149
Hjelmslev, L., 113
Homer, 89, 152, 224
Hurtado, L., 46
Husserl, E., 4, 224, 233

Ingarden, R., 23
Ingraffia, B., 12

Jabès, E., 130
Jaffee, M., 38, 41, 45, 47, 49
Jakobson, R.
  on denotation, 77
  on linguistic functions, 20, 79, 90, 111–12, 137, 147, 199
  on translation, 61, 63,
Jameson, F., 8, 16, 53, 97, 100–102, 220
Jobling, D., 125
Johnson, S., 167, 178, 187
Joyce, J., 224
Kafka, F., 34–35, 86, 107, 120–21, 123, 133, 142–50, 224

Kant, I., 91
Kermode, F.
  on the classic, 87–89, 91–93, 95–98, 100–101, 103, 195, 220–21
  on codex and scroll, 48
  on Jewish vs. Christian reading, 29, 31, 129, 170
  on secrecy, 216
Kmiecik, U., 167
Koester, H., 99
Kristeva, J., 1, 4, 15–16, 18, 118, 144, 147, 224, 233–34
Kuhn, T., 222

Lattimore, R., 1, 206
Lévi-Strauss, C., 39–41, 53, 96, 122
Lieberman, S., 36
Lohmeyer, E., 169, 171
Lucretius, 120
Luther, M., 52, 92
Lyotard, J.-F., 1, 78, 100–101, 122–23, 142, 219–21, 234

Mack, B., 98
Magritte, R., 211
Marcion, 32–33, 82, 87, 100, 138, 147, 184
Marcus, J., 11, 158, 178
Marks, H., 138, 147
Marx, K., 128, 223
McIntyre, A., 5, 7
Metzger, B., 27, 196
Mitchell, W. J. T., 8
Morris, W., 119, 128
Moule, C. F. D., 5, 93, 98, 156, 159, 197

Neirynck, F., 175
Nickelsburg, G., 166–67
Nida, E., 68–71, 77, 80
Nietzsche, F., 142
Nineham, D. E., 167, 184, 187, 189, 206

Oden, T., 196
Ong, W., 38, 51, 56, 136, 193
Origen, 26–27

Papias, 94–95, 196, 199
Peirce, C. S.
   on icon, index, and symbol, 130–34, 140, 143, 146, 149, 207, 215
   on representamen, interpretant and object, 20, 138, 208, 233–34
   on semiotics in general, 1
Petersen, W., 33, 99
Phillips, G., 19
Philo, 64

Pippin, T., 81
Plato, 40–42, 44, 59, 63–4, 122, 135–36, 224–26

Quine, W. V. O., 62, 69, 71, 74

Rabkin, E., 19
Resnick, I., 33, 36–37, 47–48
Ricoeur, P., 8, 102
Roberts, C., 45–47, 49
Robinson, J., 30, 34, 99, 187

Sanders, J., 5, 18, 23, 58, 147, 190
Saussure, F. de, 1, 114
Schleiermacher, F., 91
Schneidau, H., 86
Scholem, G., 73
Schüssler-Fiorenza, E., 86
Serres, M., 121–22, 124–25, 128, 142
Shakespeare, W., 152
Skeat, T. C. *See* C. Roberts
Smith, J., 24
Socrates. *See* Plato
Spina, F., 108, 119
Steiner, G., 62, 70, 72, 74, 111, 120–22, 128
Stendahl, K., 86
Stephenson, N., 108, 114, 118, 227–31
Sterne, L., 224
Sundberg, A., 32–33, 67

Taber, C., 68–71, 77, 80
Tatian, 33, 82
Taylor, V., 158, 165, 184, 206
Todorov, T., 112, 161
Tödt, H. E., 161, 165–67, 169
Tracy, D., 85–86, 88–89, 93, 96, 98, 102–3

Vermes, G., 156–57
Vico, G., 120

Wilken, R., 31, 89, 94, 98, 124–25